Women and Poverty
in the Third World

THE JOHNS HOPKINS STUDIES IN DEVELOPMENT
Vernon W. Ruttan and Anne O. Krueger, Consulting Editors

Women and Poverty in the Third World

Edited by

Mayra Buvinić, Margaret A. Lycette,
and William Paul McGreevey

The Johns Hopkins University Press/*Baltimore and London*

The Johns Hopkins University Press, Baltimore, Maryland 21218
The Johns Hopkins Press Ltd., London

Library of Congress Cataloging in Publication Data
Main entry under title:

Women and poverty in the Third World.

(The Johns Hopkins studies in development)
Includes rev. papers prepared for a workshop held in May, 1978 and
discussed at a policy round table held in June, 1978; both sponsored by
International Center for Research on Women.
Includes bibliographical references and index.
1. Underdeveloped areas—Women—Congresses.
2. Underdeveloped areas—Poor—Congresses.
3. Underdeveloped areas—Women's employment—Congresses.
I. Buvinić, Mayra.   II. Lycette,
Margaret A.   III. McGreevey, William Paul.
IV. International Center for Research on Women.
V. Series.
HQ1870.9.W64   1983   305.4'09172'4   82–8992
ISBN 0–8018–2681–0   AACR2

Contents

Preface

As development assistance in the 1970s increasingly turned to the creation of programs that would directly affect the poor, policymakers and project implementers were faced with the need to learn about those who would receive their aid. Aware that knowledge about poor women's economic roles is largely unavailable, and believing that such knowledge would contribute to the design of better development programs, the International Center for Research on Women (ICRW) organized, in the spring of 1978, a research workshop and a follow-up policy round table on the economic condition of poor women in developing countries.* This volume includes a selection of articles that were prepared for the workshop and discussed at the policy round table and that have since been updated.

The essays presented herein explore in particular two areas in which available information about poor women has been most deficient: women's contribution to the economy of poor households, and the extent of women's poverty. Assessing women's productivity within the home implies looking at the relationship between this productivity and women's work outside the home. It also calls for establishing a link between their work, both inside and outside the home, and their welfare.

Thus, the essays in the first section of this volume, "Women and Work," address the dual nature of poor women's roles—poor women are not only responsible for home tasks and the nurturing of children but also must contribute to the economic support of their households. These women appear to meet the heavy demands upon their time and labor in ways that maximize the well-being of their households but, at the same time, impose heavy costs on the women themselves—in terms of leisure forgone and, perhaps, limited productivity.

The essays in the second section, "Women and Welfare," explore the relationship between women's roles and their welfare, as well as the welfare of their children and society as a whole. Contrary to a once-popular belief, women who

*Workshop: "Women in Poverty: What Do We Know?," May 1978, Belmont Conference Center, Maryland. Policy round table: "Poverty as a Women's Issue," June 1978, Carnegie Conference Center, Washington, D.C.

devote substantial time to work outside the home do not significantly reduce the time they spend in child care. The welfare of the women themselves does suffer, however, as does that of the society that limits the potential contribution of its female members by restricting their social environment and preventing them from participating equally in the educational system.

The essays in the third section, "Women and Alternative Household Structures," focus on the particularly difficult situation of poor women who are heads of household. Households headed by women, de jure or de facto, are disproportionately represented among the population of poor households.

Exploring the extent of women's contributions to poor households and the magnitude of women's poverty raises the issue of how women's work and poverty can be measured. Many of the essays in this volume, reporting the results of time-allocation analyses, in-depth interviews, and small-sample case studies, implicitly suggest particular approaches to the measurement of women's work and poverty. The essays in the fourth section, "Measurement of Women's Work and Welfare," however, specifically address the measurement issue, focusing on the shortcomings of present data collection methods and suggesting possible alternatives.

The four sections are preceded by an introduction that provides an overview of some of the main findings of the research presented and an analysis of the policy implications of these findings.

Many questions about women's work and welfare remain unanswered; these should be a challenge to researchers who wish to undertake truly significant work. The essays in this volume, however, do provide information sufficient to promote the inclusion of women in development programs. The outcome will be an improvement in the welfare of poor women and their families, increased economic equality for women, and economic growth for developing countries.

Acknowledgments

The International Center for Research on Women (ICRW) workshop and policy round table were two of the first major activities undertaken by the center. They were made possible thanks to the vision of the women and men who founded, supported, and believed in the center. Irene Tinker, Coralie Turbitt, Elinor Barber, Arvonne Fraser, and James Brown deserve special mention. Nancy Birdsall and Thomas Merrick brought substantial knowledge, effort, and enthusiasm to the organization of the meetings. Mayra Buvinić and Margaret Lycette, ICRW, edited the essays in this volume. William Paul McGreevey, World Bank, played a major role in organizing the meetings from which this volume was developed.

The publication of this volume was made possible, however, by the work and support of the staff at ICRW—in particular, by the intellectual and moral support of Nadia Youssef, ICRW Research Director. We thank Judith Johnson for editing the earliest versions of the essays and especially acknowledge the excellent editorial and production assistance, and good humor, of Karen White and Mary Lee Schneiders.

Part I

INTRODUCTION: OVERVIEW AND POLICY ANALYSIS

1. Women, Poverty, and Development

Nancy Birdsall and William Paul McGreevey

The essays in this volume substantiate women's double role in poor economies. Women do not only work for cash income; they are also the providers of services in the home—child care, food preparation, the gathering of wood and water. The special contribution of the essays in this volume is to document the nature and magnitude of the difficult trade-offs women in poor economies face because of their double roles at home and in the job market. The authors use analytic techniques to examine systematically women's household and nonhousehold activities, and the way these activities intersect with and are affected by the presence and activities of other household members. Further, the essays in this volume show that women are indeed the second sex in the poor countries of the world: They are less educated than men, have fewer occupational options, and earn less when they work. Married women with young children work more hours per day than married men; unmarried women are much more likely than men (married or unmarried) to be poor, and their burdens are usually greater, for they must care for children and the household and also contribute to the family income. In fact, the research presented in this volume makes clear that poverty is very much a women's issue, at least in part because of women's double roles. Poor women have needs and make contributions that are different from those of poor men; thus, their problems command qualitatively different solutions. Particularly in the short run, improvements in the productivity and lives of poor men will not necessarily redound to the benefit of poor women or their children—who become the next generation of mothers and fathers.

In discussing women, poverty, and development, one point deserves special emphasis: Women both affect and are affected by development processes. The essays compiled here show that benefits to, and contributions by, women cannot be dealt with separately. In fact, the "woman issue," once thought of as no more than a welfare issue, affects the prospects for efficiency, growth, and development in the economy as a whole.

Note: The views presented in this essay are those of the authors and do not necessarily reflect those of the World Bank.

WOMEN AND WORK: WOMEN'S CONTRIBUTION TO THE HOUSEHOLD ECONOMY

The System of National Accounts (SNA), used with some degree of consistency in most countries, includes in household income an estimated value for some of the goods and services that are produced and consumed within the household. These goods include farm products such as grains, animal products, and fruit. The system, however, excludes "imputed values for time spent preparing food, watching children, cleaning, etc." (United Nations, 1981*b*, pt. 2, p. 28). There is, of course, no logic in a system that values the work of growing wheat and processing grain but not the act of using that grain to bake bread, even if the two steps are accomplished in the same household by the same person. The experiences of industrial countries, where there is typically a division of labor between agricultural and industrial enterprises that produce wheat and process flour, and households that bake bread, are the basis of this system. Nonetheless, the system results in a serious misrepresentation of the structure of work and the contribution of women to total output. Wheat and flour are not final products; flour must be combined with time and effort and other ingredients to yield a product for final consumption. It is that time and effort that have been unaccounted for in estimates of women's contribution to production.

The labor required for gathering firewood, obtaining water, preparing food for consumption, and supervising the household members who perform these tasks is excluded from the approved SNA approach to the estimation of household income. For women in poor countries, this so-called housework can include hard physical labor—sowing and weeding, fetching water, grinding wheat and corn. For poor women, who tend to have large families, the bearing and nurturing of children can add considerably to physical chores and physical stress over a lifetime. In Nigeria, for example, 60 percent of a sample of urban Yoruba women in the 25–34 age-group were found to have spent more than half of their adult lives either pregnant or breast-feeding (Chap. 7, Tables 7.3 and 7.4).

In Chapter 14 Boulding shows that in censuses and employment surveys, in most of which work had been defined as an activity that produces cash income, women have been treated inconsistently or overlooked altogether. For example, 49 percent of the women in North Africa/Middle East and 38 percent of the women in Latin America fall into neither of the two census categories of "labor force participant" and "economically inactive homemaker." Only a small percentage of women could, in fact, be in the residual category of students, retired persons, and those institutionalized and totally dependent. Most women, including teenage daughters, widowed aunts, and grandmothers, contribute to family well-being by producing home services, yet these women are unaccounted for in international compilations of data. The unpaid family worker in a small shop or on a farm is often a woman and is similarly included in the misleading statistical categories "employed" or "unemployed."

An alternative to the distinction between "economically active" and "economically inactive" is the time-use survey, which provides direct information on how household members use their time (Birdsall 1980). Time is certainly the most important (in the poorest households, perhaps the only) resource that the poor have available to them. The poorer the country, the more hours women work. Women in the United States work at home and outside the home an average of 6 hours per day; women in the Philippines work 10 hours a day (see Chap. 3). Within societies, of course, not all women work the same number of hours, and poor women probably work longer hours than do more well-to-do women. In Malaysia, "rural women in general and rural female heads of household in particular, work much longer hours, i.e., forgo much more leisure, than their urban counterparts" (Kusnic and DaVanzo 1980, p. 58).

Moreover, evidence is accumulating that poor women work longer hours than poor men. In parts of East Africa, women work 16 hours a day—doing housework, caring for children, preparing food, and raising between 60 and 80 percent of the food for the family (Fagley 1976). In Upper Volta, Mossi women have only a little more than 1 hour a day of free time in which to perform personal care, become involved in community affairs, and socialize (McSweeney 1979). Rural Javanese women work an average of 11 hours a day; the men work almost 2½ hours less per day (Nag, White, and Peet 1978). Women in rural Botswana work about 7 hours a day, whereas men work about 5 hours per day (Mueller 1979).

How and why does this pattern of long working hours for women emerge? Several essays in this volume contribute to an understanding of the problem. Popkin (Chap. 8), King and Evenson (Chap. 3), and DaVanzo and Lee (Chap. 4) report on analyses of household surveys of time use in the Philippines and in Malaysia. A simple but striking picture of use of household members' time over the household life cycle emerges from these studies. Men devote almost all their work time to work that produces market income, in the form of wages or agricultural produce for sale or for direct consumption. Men's work time at home varies only slightly with the numbers, ages, or activities of other household members. In contrast, women devote their work time to a combination of market work (work that generates cash income or income in kind—this can include work on a family farm or home garden) and home maintenance, food preparation, and child care. Children share the household work from about their fifth year onward. Children also do a considerable amount of market work after about their tenth year.

Men's use of time does not vary much during their adult working lives. In contrast, time allocation by women and children is flexible, changing with the number and ages of children in the household and the annual cycle of agriculture and schooling (when children go to school at all). As the demand for child-rearing time and for cash income increases over the household's life cycle, the burden of meeting this demand falls primarily on the wife and, as they grow older, on children. King and Evenson find, for example, that in the rural Philippines the father's time spent in child care, food preparation, marketing, and other chores is 1 to 2 hours daily, whether there is one child or seven. The nonfarming man spends more time in household work than the farmer, but this time is still less than 1½ hours. Filipino women spend about 3 hours per day in market production (wage employment, farming, fishing, and income-earning work at home)—more if they are farmers—and 7 to 8 hours in home production—slightly less if they are farmers. Women with infants spend about 2 hours in market production and about 9 hours in home production. Women with seven or more children spend less time in child care and home production than those with fewer children, but they increase proportionately their time spent in market production. In large families, the older children take on some of the mother's home chores, including child care.

As Popkin puts it, "there is close to a one-to-one correspondence between an increase in maternal work time and the decrease in maternal leisure time." Rural Filipino women working for cash income give up nearly 4 hours per day of leisure. When women work, older children substitute for the mother in home chores and care of siblings. When there are seven or more children, men actually reduce their child care time (to about 10 minutes a day) and increase their leisure time; thus children reduce the work load of the father but not of the mother. In rural Peru as well, as Deere (Chap. 6) shows, it is mothers and children who substitute for each other in cooking, hauling water, and animal care.

It is likely, of course, that women's work intensity is not as great as men's. Many activities within the household can be performed at varying levels of intensity. Cooking a meal may take 4 hours instead of 2, with a good deal of pride and satisfaction gained from the extra time used. Waiting in line at the village well takes time, but some of that time is spent in social exchanges that are more like leisure than work. In short, there is a conceptual problem with the measurement of time use: By necessity, it deals with the inputs (time) into home production and not the outputs.

Moreover, there is usually not a market for the work that is done by women; typically, a woman cannot sell her cooking labor at a wage equivalent to that of a professional cook. Because the major services that women and children provide within the household are never evaluated and priced by the market, there is no one way, satisfactory to all analysts, to place a value on those services. Market-cost and opportunity-cost approaches to the estimation of the value of household work produce strikingly different estimates of the value of such work in the United States (Murphy 1981). That said, however, it hardly seems appropriate to value those services at zero wage rates, which is the current practice in the System of National Accounts.

In Chapter 3, King and Evenson measure Filipino households' full income, that is, income measured by adding to market income payments family members would receive if their child care, food preparation, fetching water, chopping wood, and other home production activities were valued and paid for explicitly. Using a method based on measurement of time inputs to specific activities in households in Laguna, a province of the Philippines, they have obtained results that offer a new perspective on the relative contributions of family members to family well-being, even if, given differences in work intensity, they represent upper-bound estimates of the relative contribution of household work to household welfare. In rural households in the Philippines, women and children together bring in about 40 percent of household market income. The father garners the largest proportion of market income, but if home production time is valued and added to market income so that full income is considered, the mother and children together contribute twice as much as the father.

In evaluating the contribution of housework to total income in Malaysia, Kusnic and DaVanzo (1980) made comparisons between their findings and those of studies conducted in the United States, Canada, and the Philippines (the Laguna study just discussed). Nine studies made in the United States and Canada showed the value of housework as a share of personal income to be between 41 and 53 percent. In Malaysia the share was 38.5 percent, and in the Philippine study, the share was 104.0 percent (Kusnic and DaVanzo 1980, p. 108). Part of the reason that the Philippine study showed a larger percentage than the other studies is that it included the contribution to housework of minor children and the value of time the children spent in school. A good deal of empirical and theoretical work remains to be done before the value of home production can be estimated in a way that will be satisfactory to all interested parties. The efforts to evaluate such time described in this volume do make clear, however, that failure to value work in the home at all grossly understates the contribution of women.

TRADE-OFFS AMONG MARKET WORK, CHILD CARE, AND LEISURE

Why do women work for market income, particularly when the costs are high, in terms of their own leisure time or the time of older children spent at home instead of in school? Popkin (Chap. 8) and King and Evenson (Chap. 3) indicate that they do so to increase total family welfare. For example, estimated full income is higher, by 11 percent, in the Filipino households when women are employed outside the home. They do so, in short, when the benefits outweigh the costs.

Analyses by DaVanzo and Lee (Chap. 4), Deere (Chap. 6), and Bunster (Chap. 5) indicate that the principal way in which women minimize the costs of undertaking market work, in terms of child care, is by choosing particular occupations. The costs of trading off mothers' market work against children's well-being are minimized when mothers choose occupations that allow flexible hours or permit them to bring children along. DaVanzo and Lee (Chap. 4) report that most Malaysian women are employed in the low-paying fields of agriculture, cottage crafts, and small-scale marketing. Less than 5 percent of all women reported working in the professions or in management, or as clerical workers. In nearly one-third of the jobs in sales and production occupations (weaving, dressmaking, food processing) filled by women who have young children, women have their children with them while they are working. This is true in only 16 percent of the agricultural jobs filled by mothers of young children (indicating that agricultural occupations may be less compatible with child care than those in sales or production), but women in agriculture work fewer hours on average than those in marketing, minimizing in a different way the time away from young children.

Work in agriculture is, of course, physically difficult, whereas work in small-scale marketing has a largely social, somewhat leisurely component. Yet there is some trade-off even between marketing and child care; in Malaysia women in marketing with children under age 5 reduce their hours proportionately more than women in agriculture with such young children.

Moreover, the cross-sectional data analyzed by DaVanzo and Lee suggest that although poor women adjust the hours they work in a given occupation as their child care responsibilities change over their lifetimes, they are not likely to change their occupations over their lifetimes. It is apparent that the expectation of child care responsibility, or the fact of having once had such responsibility, governs the occupation of even those women who do not currently have young children. Between Malaysian women with young children and those without, there are virtually no differences in the proportions who work in agriculture, marketing, cottage crafts, the professions, or management. Only for clerical workers did a statistically significant difference exist between proportions of women with and without young children (Table 4.1).

In Chapter 5, Bunster describes the work and home life of market women in urban Lima, Peru, based on in-depth interviews with a small sample. Her description indicates that these women, like market women in Malaysia and the Philippines, choose their occupation for the specific reason that it is compatible with child care and home responsibilities. In contrast with the situation in more formal jobs, they are able to have their children not only accompany them, but also assist them in important ways, such as transporting goods from the wholesale market, working in the stall, and bringing lunch from home to their mothers. Bunster reports that children aged 8 to 12 years are able to sell, handle money, and market food like adults, temporarily replacing mothers who must be home with sick babies. Nevertheless, a statement by one woman illustrates the trade-off urban market mothers face between income-generating activities and the welfare of their children: "Sometimes everything is so hard! Shortages of certain products make it so tough for us! It is then my children practically don't go to school; they are exhausted and go to sleep in class, under the teacher's nose. The school year ends and my children are behind. I blame myself because I've had my children stay awake all night helping me out at the wholesale market. When I see them so tired, it breaks my heart and I feel so guilty and so powerless!''

In Chapter 12, Merrick and Schmink report on a study of female heads of households employed in the labor market in Belo Horizonte, Brazil—a study that takes into account the household duties of those women. Their analysis of income differentials between male and female heads suggests that the lower income of female heads is only partly explained by their somewhat lower level of education; more important is the fact that these women are much more likely to have jobs in the informal sector with flexible hours. In Belo Horizonte, male and female heads of households do not differ markedly in age or education, but more than 50 percent of the women work in the informal sector, compared with 12 percent of the men. Working in the informal sector has a significant negative effect on male earnings, but the negative effect for women is twice as great.

Of course, the reason for the higher earnings of male heads may be that they work more hours per week at their jobs. But if female heads of household work fewer hours outside the home because of their household responsibilities, their lower monetary income may be a reasonable reflection of their lower level of welfare, even if market hours are not controlled for.

Furthermore, males earn more in the *informal* sector than females do in the *formal* sector (Table 12.8), and they earn a higher return from whatever education they have. As a result, households headed by women are much more likely to be poor than are households headed by men; 45 percent of all households headed by women in the Belo Horizonte sample had a total income too low to satisfy the most fundamental needs, even according to the government-established minimal standard. Only 27 percent of male-headed households were so classified.

The data available from time-use studies demonstrate that poor women make a large contribution to their families' well-being through their work inside the home as well as through their income-producing work outside the home. There is no question that their contribution is important to their communities. The data also show the trade-offs these women face in balancing market work with the demands of housework and child care—especially the latter. The conflict between the need to care for children and the need to bring in income affects these women's decisions about what kind of work to do and for how many hours. The fact that they work in the informal sector, to obtain the flexibility they need, means that they cannot earn very much. In order to work at all, they must have the help of their children (who in turn may need to give up school) to help provide subsistence for their families. Women and their children are thus caught in a cycle of poverty.

WOMEN AND WANT: WHY ARE WOMEN WORSE OFF?

At what age do women start down the road toward working-age poverty? Section 2 presents a number of studies that differentiate between treatment of young boys and young girls. Studies made in the Philippines and Guatemala show that parents favor boys up to about age 10 only slightly with their time and goods but that boys and girls are treated very differently from a social point of view. After the age of 10, girls are less likely than boys to continue in school and more likely to spend time with younger siblings as mother-substitutes, a role consistent with the earlier differences in social treatment.

Engle (Chap. 10) reports on measures of the mental and physical development of all children in several Guatemalan villages that were taken over a 7-year period as part of a study of the effects of a nutritional supplementation program. No differences were found in the physical environment of boys and girls; reported home diets, prevalence of diarrhea, and length of lactation were similar for children of both sexes. Despite the apparent similarity for boys and girls with regard to diet, lactation, and morbidity, the mental development scores of girls improved much more than the scores of boys in the course of the program. The effect of the nutritional supplements themselves did not explain the differential in improvement between boys and girls, however. Even the scores of girls not receiving the supplements improved. Since the scores of girls improved more the later they entered the program, Engle suggests that the nutritional supplementation program may have affected the mental development of girls more than that of boys by creating a new social environment for girls. The program personnel were mostly females who were well dressed and well educated. About six of them were present in the villages each day; all homes were visited at least once every two weeks. A girl of about age 15 from each village was hired as an assistant. As the study progressed, children in the villages were observed "playing INCAP" (the acronym for the organization conducting the program) and pretending to be program personnel.

The chance to observe the female nurses, nutritionists, and program assistants may well have changed girls' expectations of their own futures and appears to have done so more in later years, as program inputs expanded, than in earlier years. Prior to the program, girls had only their mothers to imitate. Of those women in the villages who earned any cash income, most worked at home in crafts. Interestingly, 64 percent of the village women said they would like to do additional work for money, and most preferred marketing or work that could be done at home (ironing, mending, washing). Seventy-four percent of the women's husbands, however, were opposed to having their wives work. These limited options for adult village women were mirrored by the sex typing of child play and chores. Boys were much more likely to play far away from home than girls, and for young children there was a considerable difference in chores by sex.

A similar picture has emerged in the Philippines (Navera 1978). Families in one area were found to spend somewhat more on food for boys than for girls, especially in the age-group, 1–6 years, but this may reflect differential needs rather than any discrimination against girls. A more important difference was found in the amount spent on schooling for teenage girls and boys. Parents spent 281 pesos annually for education of boys, but only 152 pesos annually for education of girls. Time inputs of parents also differed somewhat between girls and boys; mothers and fathers both spent somewhat more time with boys than with girls.

Throughout the Third World, there are many more boys than girls enrolled in school. In almost all African countries, the ratio of females to males enrolled in secondary education is less than 35 percent; the ratio is less than 20 percent at the higher educational level. In Latin America, the ratios are about 50 and 40 percent, and in Asia they are about 30 and 25 percent (World Bank 1980, pp. 46–47). In Chapter 9, Selowsky makes the assumption that ability is distributed similarly between males and females and then estimates the social loss attributable to the fact that able girls are less likely to attend school than able boys. An economy's return to education is maximized when the most able people attend schools at all levels; thus the value added of the educational system is reduced when some women are excluded. Selowsky's calculations depend on the overall rate of interest in the society, the rate of return to additional years of schooling, and the costs of providing that schooling. Making reasonable assumptions about these variables, he shows that there would be significant social gains from increasing female participation in education.

Low enrollment rates for girls probably reflect parental expectations with respect to their daughters' choices and chances in life. Few families foresee major income-earning responsibility for their daughters. Yet many women may actually have to take on such responsibility—especially those who, because of divorce, dissolution of an informal union, or the death of a husband, become heads of households.

For most countries, we have no information on such households. Youssef and Hetler (Chap. 11) point out that the lack of data and the poor quality of available data on woman-headed households make it difficult to determine their incidence. Available data from Brazil, however, show that the number of households headed by women in that country nearly doubled between 1960 and 1970 (Chap. 12). Households headed by women in Morocco increased by 33 percent between 1960 and 1971 (the number of those headed by men increased minimally), as Moroccan men migrated to Western Europe (Buvinić and Youssef 1978). In one district of Kenya, 40 percent of the households sampled in 1975 were headed by female farm managers. Of the taxpaying households in Lesotho, 25 percent were headed by females in 1970, reflecting male migration to the mines of South Africa. In Latin America, more women than men migrate to cities. Households in Santiago,

Chile, headed by migrant women had a median monthly income of 49 escudos in 1961; for native women the figure was 84 escudos. For migrant and native men the figures were 93 and 109 escudos, respectively (Buvinić and Youssef 1978).

Only a few countries provide census tabulations indicating the ratio of children to women within categories of married, divorced, and single. In the few that do, the child-to-woman ratio for divorced and widowed women who are mothers ranges from 3.4 (Peru—divorcees only) to 5.1 (Botswana) to 6.6 (Honduras). These women do not necessarily have adult children to support them. In Guatemala, widowed and divorced women have, on average, five children by the age of 35, when support from adult children is still unlikely (Buvinić and Youssef 1978).

In Chapter 13, Mueller has brought together data for six countries showing the percentage of women in their fifties who were widowed, divorced, or separated, that is, who could not depend on the nuclear family and a male partner for economic support. Nearly half of all Indonesian women aged 50–54 in 1977 were in that category. The percentages were lower for other countries, but even for the two Latin American countries, in which women have much longer life expectancies than those typical of women in South Asia and Africa, about one woman in five in her early fifties was widowed, divorced, or separated. As death rates for males decline, this problem may be somewhat ameliorated. At the same time, however, intergenerational obligations—the expectation that children will care for their aged mothers—are being blurred by migration and by the resulting physical separation between parents and children. As the traditional support systems deteriorate, problems for older women will become more severe.

Single mothers, too, must rely on some support system—for child care, credit, and other forms of financial assistance—as they attempt to support their families through market work. With economic development, private support systems are waning, but there has not been sufficient concomitant growth in public support systems. Female household heads are only the most obvious examples of potential victims; many other women, because of social restrictions on their labor force participation, low wages, childbearing responsibilities, and greater longevity, are more dependent for survival on some support system beyond the nuclear family than are men.

Women, Poverty, and Development

In drawing a rich and fascinating picture of women's lives in poor countries, the essays that follow go well beyond the themes we have discussed in this introduction, and a summary cannot do them justice. We have, however, emphasized three themes that we hope will help to show the relationships among women, poverty, and development.

First, the time-use studies indicate that the typical woman spends most of her day working, not only in the labor market, as do men, but also in home production. The home production activities of women are not included in conventional household and labor force surveys in poor countries, yet they are a critical part of the poor household's total production and are important to any understanding of the dynamics of poverty.

The combination of work at home and work outside the home shifts over a woman's lifetime, in response to the changing demands of her household. The combination is one that maximizes family full income, but of course it entails costs. The most obvious cost is leisure for the women themselves; when women work outside the home they enjoy less leisure. They manage not to reduce child care time—both by sacrificing leisure and by working relatively less outside the home when they have young children.

Our second major theme is another, less obvious cost. It is apparent that women in poor countries, and particularly poor women, end up—by choice or by custom—in the particular occupations that enable them to adjust hours between home and market work as the size and structure of the household change. Occupations that allow this flexibility, however, are not usually found in the modern sector; they tend to be labor intensive, poorly remunerated, and low in productivity.

This leads us to our third theme. The expectation that the typical woman's occupational choice will be limited (due perhaps to household responsibilities) and that she will spend less time in work for cash income than the typical man, probably helps explain the pattern of less education for women in many countries and the minimal emphasis in development programs on raising productivity in typically female jobs. Less education, however, entails costs to society, not only because of the loss of women's potential for higher productivity in market work, but also because women as mothers make the first investments in the nutrition, health, and education of children—investments that are critical to future economic growth. Worse, many women will not at every stage of their lives be "typical" in the sense of sharing economic needs and work with husbands. Some will become heads of households—their numbers may be growing because of higher rates of differential migration by sex and a general weakening of the fabric of traditional societies. Others will be widowed or divorced or will never marry. Their poverty is only the most obvious symptom of how development can bypass women. To escape that poverty, women must become more productive, and societies must seek ways to make that possible—because of, and in the context of, women's double roles.

2. Women's Issues in Third World Poverty: A Policy Analysis

Mayra Buvinić

This chapter examines the progress made between 1975 and 1981 in translating research findings on women's economic roles into participation by women in economic development programs.[1] Three phases of progress are identified: the acknowledgment that findings regarding women's economic participation have policy implications, the translation of these policy implications into development strategies, and the implementation of these strategies in development programs.

The basic argument presented is that women's problems have now been recognized by the development community and are being incorporated into development plans but that the plans have yet to produce significant results. This argument is developed by exploring in the first (content-of-policy) section changes in conceptual and analytical approaches to research on women's economic participation that have affected both the nature of policies toward women and the acceptance of the research findings as having development policy implications. Equity-oriented approaches are contrasted with those that are poverty-oriented, and two main themes of the latter type of approach, women's poverty and women's work, along with their methodological tools, are discussed.

The second (context-of-policy) section analyzes those factors in the environment that affect the translation of research findings into action. Changes in the priorities of development policy are identified as contributing to interest in the role of women in development; the prevalence of welfare-oriented strategies over production-oriented ones is attributed to the nature and the political implications of such strategies; and the gap between plans and action is linked to institutional, political, technical, and economic obstacles. Selected policy suggestions are presented at the end of the chapter.

THE CONTENT OF POLICY

Two distinct approaches to policy-oriented research on women have affected the acceptance of women's issues as being important for development policy. Both approaches start from the basic premise that women are economic actors,

14

but they emphasize different aspects of women's economic performance and use different analytical languages. The first, "equity"-oriented approach, developed in the early stages of interest in women's issues, has focused on the effect of economic development programs on the economic status of women, suggesting that women lose ground relative to men as development proceeds (Tinker and Bo Bramsen 1976). The main premises of this argument are: (1) women have productive as well as reproductive roles in society, and the less monetized the economic system, the more important is their productive role; (2) conventional (i.e., Western) measures of economic activity underestimate the magnitude of women's productive roles by failing to acknowledge the value of unpaid work and by undercounting women's paid work outside the modern sector; (3) this underestimation and the glorification of motherhood in industrialized societies have helped to define a development policy for the Third World that erects barriers to paid work for women; and (4) as a result of this development policy, women are relegated to the economy's traditional sector, and the income gap between the sexes is widened.

On the one hand, these premises have been supported by retrospective case studies of the adverse impact of particular interventions, such as the introduction of animal-drawn plows, modern harvest tools, and road construction, on the status of women in small communities (Elmendorf 1976; Remy 1975). On the other hand, functional and conflict (Marxist) sociologists and political scientists have analyzed at the macro level changes that accompany capitalist development, such as urbanization, industrialization, and class stratification (Blumberg 1978; Giele and Smock 1977a), and have developed quantifiable indicators of the effect of these changes on women's status. Because they lack an adequate data base, however, these studies cannot empirically test the hypothesis of the negative impact of development on sexual equality.

The fact that only qualitative evidence of the negative impact argument and few quantitative results have been obtained from both types of analysis has contributed to the lack of communication between those doing research on economic development and those doing research on women's issues in development. To convince economic development theorists of its validity, the argument should be stated in quantitative terms; scientific evaluations of the impact of current development interventions on women could provide the data base to develop this quantitative language.

Preintervention baseline data could be obtained and compared with postintervention data, thus solving the major problem—lack of a quantitative standard by which to assess women's situation after intervention—faced by researchers who would like to verify the adverse impact argument. These impact evaluations have not yet found support in the development community, ostensibly because of presumed high financial costs, but more likely because of potentially high political costs for those who have developed and financed the programs that would be evaluated.

In the face of economic theorists' and policymakers' lack of interest, the equity approach to research on women has evolved into an alternative approach that links women's issues to poverty and tries to quantify the positive effects that may result from incorporating women's concerns into economic development programs (Safilios-Rothschild 1980; Staudt 1979). Focusing on women as participants in, rather than as beneficiaries of, development programs and restricting those being studied to women in economic need, this approach is based on the following premises: (1) the ratio of women to men is greater in the poorest income groups than in the population as a whole; (2) the economic performance of households in the lowest income brackets is directly related to the economic activity of women in these households; (3) the importance of women's productive role increases with poverty but the extent of their reproductive functions does not diminish, resulting in a dual burden for poor women; and (4) to promote balanced economic growth, a major goal of development policy should be to increase the productivity and income of women in the lowest income households.

This shift in emphasis from an equity-oriented to a poverty-oriented approach substantially changes research questions and methods, as well as the issues raised for the consideration of policymakers—that is, the content of policy. There is a shift from description to analysis of women's condition, from the definition of women's economic problems to the quantitative documentation of their existence, and from anthropological to sociological and economic methodologies. Measurement of the economic contribution of women to the household and in the marketplace is undertaken, rather than retrospective assessment of the impact of programs on Women's economic condition.

Phrasing women's issues in terms of poverty and economic growth facilitates the translation of women's issues into development policy issues and hence their incorporation into development strategies. Women's issues are presented in a quantitative language that breaks down communication barriers between economic development theorists and practitioners. This language, however, has its drawbacks. Both these drawbacks and the main issues that the poverty approach has raised regarding women's participation in economic development are examined in the section that follows.

Two Policy Issues

Conceptualizing women's issues in economic development in terms of poverty and economic growth brings into the foreground two issues relevant to the formulation of development policy: first, the magnitude of women's poverty; second, the measurement and valuation of their productive work in the home and in the marketplace. The use of the household rather than the individual as a unit of analysis and the measurement of women's home production by time-use surveys are two important means employed to assess these issues quantitatively.

Women's Share of Poverty

The increasing incidence and poverty of households headed by women emerged as an issue with significant policy implications for both industrialized and developing nations in the mid-1970s (Ross and Sawhill 1975; Buvinić and Youssef 1978). Subsequent research in the Third World has provided data on women's share of poverty and has made an impact largely because it has focused on the household rather than the individual and therefore has yielded results that can be incorporated into more recent frameworks of research on poverty in the Third World.

This research examines the incidence of poor woman-headed households and the factors that affect this incidence, measures household income levels, and analyzes the socioeconomic characteristics of woman-headed households and how they influence the households' economic performance (see Kossoudji and Mueller, forthcoming; and Chaps. 11 and 12 in this volume). The evidence to date is far from conclusive, but it is sufficient to suggest that woman-headed households tend to have the lowest incomes and that this is due in large part to a lack of productive resources. These households most often generate their income in the traditional sector of the economy; have less access to land, capital, and technology; and include more dependents and fewer secondary earners than male-headed households. These studies have also postulated a close association between the emergence of these households and changes resulting from economic development, such as male labor migration, urbanization, and the provision of services and job opportunities for women. The predicted permanence of the woman-headed household in developing economies, its significance as an economic rather than a cultural phenomenon, and the use by researchers of the household as the unit of analysis have made woman-headed households in the Third World an accepted focus of policymakers and a target of development policy.

Although poverty in the Third World is not restricted to woman heads of household, concerns about the poverty of these women have tended to overshadow concern about other categories of women in policy statements and in policy-oriented research. Research is needed to uncover other categories of women who also bear the burden of poverty but are not as visible as woman heads of poor households.

The Language of the Household. Research on women from the perspective of the household has helped carry women's issues into the policymaking arena. There are, however, potentially serious conceptual problems and policy risks associated with using the household as the preferred unit of analysis in an attempt to understand women's situation and poverty. This is because the household emphasis ignores economic and social behavior that occurs both within and without the household, and because the concept of household "behavior" precludes exploration of the individual needs and preferences of household members and their different roles in decision making. Household models have assigned a reality that disguises the behavior of individual members with subordinate preferences or low status—that is, women (Galbraith 1973).

Three main problems can be identified by using household models and the household as a unit of analysis. The first problem derives from assuming that the physical boundaries of the household define units of social and economic organization. People living together are assumed to constitute a family (nuclear or extended), and domestic functions are assumed to take place within the physical boundaries of the household (Bender 1967). Individuals sharing a roof often do not constitute families, however, and this seems to be particularly true among poor woman-headed households in the Third World (Nieves 1979). Similarly, domestic functions often include interhousehold social and economic exchanges, and these seem to be an especially important source of support for poor women (see Chap. 13).

The second problem arises from the economic principle that defines the household as a basic decision-making unit behaving according to the rule of maximization of household utility. This assumption does not allow for recognition of the different preference schedules of individual members and masks any sex or age discrimination in the intrahousehold allocation of production and consumption. As many of the essays in this volume show, however, discrimination by sex in the distribution of work and benefits (food, leisure, social stimulation) is pervasive within poor households in the Third World. The corollary emphasis on decision-making outcomes rather than decision-making processes ignores the possibility of conflict between family members in decision making and the use of power as a means of conflict resolution (Leibenstein 1981). The household model cannot pick up the divergent interests of those women who are less powerful than men. Recent evidence on the socioeconomic determinants of fertility shows that husband and wife can exhibit different and sometimes opposite interests regarding family reproductive behavior (Anker, Buvinić, and Youssef 1982). There is reason to believe that differences also occur in other important areas of family decision making, such as household expenditures, employment, and education.

The third problem derives from the implicit assumption, based on the model of the industrialized world, that only nonmarket production and consumption take place within the household (and are in women's hands). Therefore, when market production/consumption is investigated, farms and firms rather than households are chosen as the units of analysis and the household's (women's) contribution to market (farm) production is ignored. Few studies recognize the interdependence of production and consumption activities in most farms/households (David and Meyer 1979), and thus women's contribution to farms/households is ignored. The failure to see this interdependence can confound analysis of the effects of development programs that are dependent on farm/household behavior and decison making—for instance, analysis of the effects of credit that is formally granted for agricultural purposes but diverted to nonfarm or household uses. More important, such an approach is a major deterrent to the recognition of women's productive roles and thus has affected the delivery of productive resources that would help to modernize women's farm/household production (Schultz 1980).

Women's Work

The acceptance of the results of poverty-oriented research is enhanced because the research coincides with the recognition in the economic development literature of the weakness of conventional measures of labor force participation in Third World economies. Poverty-oriented research utilizes two techniques to avoid the tendency to undervalue women's work by measuring their economic participation, particularly their work in traditional sectors of the economy.

First, poverty-oriented research on women's work uses individual and household surveys to measure women's contribution to market production. It investigates the extent of the undercounting of women's work by conventional measures (Recchini de Lattes and Wainerman 1979; Lewin, Pitanguy, and Romani 1977), the sexual division of labor within the home and in the marketplace, the reasons for and conditions of women's participation in agriculture and in the informal sector (see Chap. 6; also León de Leal 1980), and determinants of their participation (Standing and Sheehan 1978; Papola 1982).

The evidence shows an increasingly large "invisible" female contingent working in low-paying seasonal or part-time occupations on farms and plantations and in some of the lowest paid and lowest status jobs in the service and informal sectors of urban economy. This pattern is replicated in different countries and situations: the poorer the household, the more time women tend to devote to working in low-paying occupations.

Although economic (rather than cultural) variables appear to be the main determinants of the extent and nature of women's participation in the marketplace, there are instances where cultural variables can influence their participation. Although poverty, for example, breaks down traditional divisions of labor between the sexes in some countries, such as Peru (see Chap. 6), it fails to do so in others, such as Bangladesh (Cain, Khanam, and Nahar 1979). More and more, however, research is showing that sex segregation patterns in the labor market that are cultural in origin break down easily in the face of changes in labor market demand (Youssef, Nieves, and Sebstad 1980).

Past research focused on variables affecting the supply of female labor in order to explain the lack of participation of women in the modern sectors of the economy, but recent evidence shows that these variables—high fertility and lack of education—do not have great explanatory power. Increasingly, women with many children are participating in the labor force, and this participation peaks at the lowest and highest educational levels. Therefore, research has begun to focus on the demand for, rather than the supply of, female workers and the variables that may restrict this demand.

Second, poverty-oriented research on women's work employs time-use surveys to measure women's contribution to home production. The research defines, measures, and assigns economic value to home production activities and investigates the determinants of women's allocation of time between production (home or market) and leisure (McSweeney 1977; Acharya 1981). Because many time-allocation studies were originally formulated to elicit answers to questions about the socioeconomic determinants of fertility, a main line of inquiry has focused on the trade-offs women make between child care and labor force participation (Ho 1979; Anker, Buvinić, and Youssef 1982).

Evidence on the unpaid work of poor women in home production obtained through time-use surveys indicates the following: (1) Poor women tend to work longer hours and have less leisure time than poor men (McSweeney 1977; Kossoudji and Mueller, forthcoming). (2) When these working hours are assigned an economic value and added to the household's cash income, the contribution of poor women and children to household income can be greater than that of poor men (see Chap. 3). (3) Unlike the evidence from industrialized societies, which shows a trade-off between market work and child care, evidence from the Third World indicates that poor women tend not to make trade-offs between child care and market work. When these women enter the labor market, it is leisure time rather than home production time that is reduced (see Chap. 8). The need for more income makes it necessary for poor women to work in the marketplace, and there is no surplus income with which to purchase child care or other household services (Mueller 1982; Alauddin 1980). (4) As in industrialized countries (Hawrylyshin 1976), women and children in the Third World must adapt to the differing demands of household and market, whereas men's roles remain resistant to change. Increasing household burdens, such as additional children, tend to change women's and children's but not men's allocation of time among market work, work at home, and leisure (Mueller 1982).

In summary, the evidence shows that poor women in developing countries have both home and market production roles and that the poorer the household, the more burdensome both roles become. The division of labor between the sexes within the household assigns women to labor-intensive production, and the division of labor within the market restricts women to work characterized by low technology, inefficient production, and marginal wages.

This evidence supports the view that women's issues are also development policy issues. Women are producers and thus participants in the process of economic growth, but their production occurs within a dualistic economy in which women are relegated to sex-specific, traditional work or to occupations with neither access to productive resources nor large economic returns. The corollary to this view is that women's poverty requires different solutions from men's poverty. Policies specifically designed to increase women's productivity and income will reduce income differentials between men and women, *and* economic dualism, by modernizing production that is in the hands of women. Conventional antipoverty policies that place no specific emphasis on women will tend to ignore the large subgroup of women among the poor who work in home production and in sex-segregated occupations.

Time as a Measure of Work. The translation of women's work within the home into quantitative terms by using time-use surveys both adds to and detracts from an understanding of women's issues. The advantages and disadvantages of time-use surveys for policy formulation are briefly explored here.

Imputing economic value to time spent in home production and adding this value to market income to estimate the household's full income allows a more reliable assessment of productivity, of productivity change, and of women's share in this productivity than conventional market measures. Including the value of home production in income gives a better indication of total output than measures derived from the gross domestic product (GDP), particularly in rural economies where a sizable fraction of output is generated by the home production process.[2] Such inclusion also allows more accurate measurement of the increasing industrialization that results from the transfer of production over time from the home to the marketplace.

Hence, measuring home production would enable policymakers to assess more accurately an economy's growth and would highlight shifts in production from the home to the market sector. Since the evidence shows that a majority of home production participants are women, the valuation of home production through measures of full income would be a significant step in acknowledging the economic contributions of women in developing economies. More important, however, information on home production is particularly relevant to designing programs that seek to increase household income by (1) reducing the time required for household production; (2) increasing the efficiency, output, and returns of economic activities in which women currently engage; (3) transforming subsistence activities into income-generating activities; and (4) creating new employment opportunities for women.

Time-use surveys, however, also have shortcomings that can affect the content of policy. The first problem is conceptual and pertains to the question of which household activities are productive and which can be considered leisure. Some investigators consider home production to include only activities that are very close to or that actually contribute to market work, whereas others extend the concept of home production to include activities such as child care. Definitions of home production should be dictated by the socioeconomic characteristics of the population under consideration and its specific stage of development. If child care services, for example, are traded in the marketplace, it would then be useful to include them in the definition of home production. Otherwise, including them would be a theoretically appropriate, but impractical, alternative. This variable situation thus makes it difficult to assign a definition to home production that is applicable in all situations.

A second problem is that the methodology of time-use surveys assumes that all time units have equal value, are interchangeable, and have equivalent outcomes. Time-use studies therefore tend to ignore or misrepresent those situations where quantity of time is not a good measure of the quality of output, where time units have varying intensiveness or are not interchangeable, and where social variables change the value of particular time units. Is there, for instance, a one-to-one correspondence between the quantity and the quality of child care, or between the productivity of time spent in child care and that spent processing foodstuffs? Is there interchangeability between the time units spent on particular tasks by individuals with very different productivity levels? Development policy that is based on results valued only in terms of time units may be misguided.

A related problem is the assignment of economic value to home production. Home production can be valued according to the outputs of the home production process or the time spent in home production. When the outputs from home production are valued at market prices, the value given to the output is more reliable the closer the economy is to a level of modernization where similar outputs are traded in the marketplace. On the other hand, if home production activities are valued by approximating the wage individuals would obtain for similar activities in the marketplace, minimal educational attainments and labor market demand for workers enhance the reliability of the values assigned. To the extent that sex discrimination exists in the marketplace and in access to education, with the result that women have very low educational and labor force participation scores, home production values based on market wages will reflect these market imperfections and underrate the value of home work. Policy based on these values may result in women's devoting more time to home production than is economically efficient.

This discussion raises the following questions that should be considered by policy-oriented researchers: Which definitions of home production and consumption, or of work and leisure, are useful for policy formulation? Which techniques are most appropriate for setting a value on home production activities? How can time valuation measures be designed to take account of market imperfections, such as discrimination?

THE CONTEXT OF POLICY

On the road from ideas to action, from identifying the problems facing poor women in the Third World to implementing programs to improve their lives, where do we stand today? Unfortunately, significant action in response to women's issues has yet to occur. A sign of progress, however, is the integration of women's concerns into economic development plans (Papanek 1978), which some nations have already achieved. For instance, India's Six-Year (1978) Development Plan includes policies directed toward women, as does Honduras's Five-Year (1978) Development Plan. Women have also become a focus of concern (at least nominally) for many international, bilateral, and private development agencies. The integration of women's issues into development plans provides no guarantee, however, that there will be successful implementation of woman-oriented development programs. The gap between plans and action does not seem to be one that merely time will close. Obstacles related to the context of policy will also have to be overcome before successful implementation occurs.

Acceptance of Women's Issues as a Development Policy Issue

The establishment of a conceptual link between women's issues and economic development theories was a major step toward achieving acceptance of the fact that women's issues have development policy implications. The change in emphasis from equity- to poverty-centered analyses translated women's questions into the language used by economic development theorists and practitioners. But the right message had to find a receptive audience, and in the mid-1970s, the development community was ready to listen, thanks to two major events that helped awaken their interest: changes in the theory and policies of economic development that eventually were translated into new directions in development assistance, and the new emphasis placed on the condition of women as a result of the International Women's Year (IWY), 1975.

Three new ideas or priorities in economic development theory and policy in the 1970s promoted receptivity to women's questions. First came the growing awareness of a world population problem, along with the realization that women are the main actors in determining population trends. Concern with population growth led to the targeting of Third World women as the primary beneficiaries of family planning programs and as important subjects of development-oriented research.

The second priority grew out of the acknowledgment that the "trickle down" approach to development had failed. Realizing that the capital and technology transferred from the industrialized countries had not filtered down to the poor in developing societies, development agencies changed priorities and established a new strategy designed to improve directly the levels of living of the poor. In his address to the World Bank's Board ofGovernors in 1973, Robert McNamara made explicit the need for a target group approach to development interventions. This approach made it necessary to ask questions such as: Who are the poor? Where do they live? What do they do? How do they survive in the face of poverty? What problems do they encounter in their attempts to overcome poverty? The earlier concentration of development agencies on macroeconomic development had left them ill-equipped to provide reliable answers, and the target group approach made theorists more receptive to research that would yield insights into these questions. Research on the economic roles of Third World women met the new information needs of the development agencies.

The third idea was the development of a "basic needs strategy" against poverty. The basic needs strategy calls for assurance to all individuals of the basic requirements for life (food, shelter, and clothing) and of access to essential community services, such as safe drinking water, sanitation facilities, public transportation, and health and education facilities. Interest in women then burgeoned because of their traditional importance in satisfying many of these basic needs (Palmer 1976).[3]

These three changes in economic development more or less coincided with IWY. A main theme of the IWY conference in Mexico City in 1975 was international economic development. The development-related activities undertaken for and during the conference provided political support for researchers and practitioners working in the field and lent legitimacy to the work on women's issues done by international and national development agencies. In turn, this support led to small but nonetheless significant budgetary allocations for research and action projects intended to improve the situation of poor women in developing countries.

Translation of Policy Issues into Development Strategies

Once women's concerns were accepted as having development policy implications, the question became one of determining how much importance should be given to strategies with a welfare orientation relative to strategies with a production orientation. Poor women in the Third World had become the main beneficiaries of welfare programs begun by national and international relief agencies soon after the end of World War II. These welfare programs were designed to relieve poor women's needs exclusively in terms of their roles as mothers and housewives. In the early 1970s, in response to the world population problem, development agencies reinforced this view of women's roles by making women the primary targets of family planning, maternal and child health care, and nutrition programs. (The basic human needs approach is also based on the view that women are main actors in economic development primarily because of their functions as housewives and mothers.)

The objectives and the modus operandi of relief, population control, and basic needs programs may be quite diverse, but they share a common perception of women's functions in poor socieites and a common way of dealing with women in action programs. Programs for women are directed mainly toward improving family (particularly children's) welfare. They provide food, information, or education; training and services (such as food, contraceptives, and information) are nearly always free handouts to women. Such programs invariably give women training in the skills that are appropriate for nonworking homemakers and mothers. They seldom entail significant disbursements for components (such as intermediate credit institutions) designed to improve the economic opportunities and productive capabilities of women (see Rogers 1979). With the exception of family planning programs, they are also politically safe—they do not run counter to socially sanctioned views of women's work and do not have the potential of causing conflicts between classes of women or between women and men.

Welfare-oriented strategies for women prevail throughout the developing world, even in programs ostensibly designed to improve the productive capabilities of women. Classic examples are income-generating programs for women in areas such as handicrafts, where the intention is to capitalize on women's assumed "traditional" skills in sewing, knitting, and cooking by giving them training and donations of cash, sewing machines, or materials. These programs continue to operate despite the fact that they are very time-consuming, bring little or no income to woman participants, and cannot be easily upgraded to yield higher earnings (see Dhamija 1981 for an incisive analysis of handicraft programs).

The continued survival of welfare-oriented programs for women can be traced to the fact that they are technically simple and politically safe to implement. The only problem that could make these programs difficult to implement would be ambiguity with regard to the true beneficiaries—mothers or their children. Potential conflicts between women's and children's welfare are customarily resolved in these programs by emphasizing women's motherhood roles, thereby making children's welfare the ultimate objective (see Cleaves 1980 for an analysis of program characteristics affecting successful implementation).

Women in developing countries, particularly those who are living in poverty, have been doubly affected by welfare-oriented programs. Welfare-oriented policies cannot and do not address the issues of women's poverty and their lack of access to economic opportunities and resources. Additionally, welfare-oriented policies lead to the exclusion of women from development programs operated by the mainstream development agencies that provide a significant proportion of development funds and human resources (see Germaine 1977).

The alternative is an antipoverty strategy that justifies assistance to poor women in terms of economic growth rather than welfare and that is embodied in projects to raise women's economic productivity and income. Such a strategy, however, has at least three major obstacles to conquer on the path to implementation. First, productivity programs (for men or for women) are inherently more difficult to implement than welfare-oriented programs because of the very nature of the task. Such programs are necessarily more expensive and staff intensive, are of longer duration, and have greater need of technical expertise (Buvinić 1980). They also often include innovative or untried approaches. Furthermore, such programs have inherent monopolizable aspects that can significantly affect their successful implementation as far as women are concerned. Productivity programs in general tend to be easily monopolized by the more powerful people in the community, and the likelihood that this may happen to programs for poor women increases because virtually all other groups in the community are powerful relative to poor women.

Second, programs intended to improve the economic opportunities of women imply changes in the political and social relations between men and women beneficiaries. Productivity programs for women usually require some restructuring of the cultural fabric of society, and development agencies do not like to tamper with unknown or unfamiliar social variables. As a rule of thumb, they tend to believe in upholding social traditions and thus are reluctant to implement these programs.

Third, these programs often have a redistributionist connotation for both beneficiaries and implementers, and redistributionist strategies have high political and economic costs that affect program implementation (see Grindle 1980; Uphoff 1980). The implication of economic redistribution is stronger when women's issues are approached from an equity perspective rather than from a poverty perspective, however, which makes poverty-oriented programs somewhat more popular than equity-oriented ones.

The redistributionist connotations of equity-based programs (such as programs in response to the adverse impact argument) arise from the emphasis of these programs on women as beneficiaries of, rather than as participants in, development, and from their concentration on women in all socioeconomic groups.[4] If women beneficiaries have lost ground relative to men, the implication is that men have to begin sharing a fixed amount of benefits; that is, this approach implies gains to women and losses to men. Focusing on all women, rather than on poor women only, calls for equality at all levels, both among program beneficiaries and among program implementers. In other words, this approach calls for equality between the sexes in the staffing of development agencies, which helps to explain the reluctance of predominantly male-staffed development agencies to respond to the questions of equity that are part of women's concerns. For example, the response to the adverse impact thesis by international development agencies was to implement weak affirmative action programs in which woman professionals were hired to fill mostly low-level positions (Rogers 1979; Davidson and Croke 1977), and to require or suggest the use of impact statements in development project reports. More often than not, such requirements were satisfied merely by making a theoretical argument that interventions would have no known adverse impact on women.

Although policies that focus on relieving poverty can have redistributionist implications, the deemphasis on women as beneficiaries and the concentration on poor women rather than on all women tone down the implication that development programs are zero-sum games (i.e., a gain to women implies a loss to men).

Programs with a welfare orientation most assuredly do not have redistributionist tendencies. This helps to explain their popularity. Welfare programs are implemented in a sex-segregated environment where providing aid to poor women does not imply commensurate losses to male beneficiaries or male implementers. The frequent support of welfare programs by special funds from international agencies adds assurance that assistance to poor women does not mean the sharing of regular funds and consequent potential losses for other programs or segments of the population. Welfare strategies are therefore essentially positive-sum situations, and the perception of those involved is that nobody will lose as a result of their implementation.

The relative task simplicity, the congruence with accepted social norms, and the positive-sum nature of welfare programs substantially reduce the social, financial, and political costs of implementing those programs. The costs of programs that focus on poverty, on the other hand, are relatively high, and the costs of programs that center on equity can become prohibitive. In short, productivity strategies for women compete badly with traditional, low-cost welfare strategies.

From Issues and Plans to Action

The acceptance of women's issues as development policy issues, and their translation into development plans, is not sufficient to ensure better lives for poor women in the Third World. Aside from finding ways to compensate for the costs of a poverty-oriented strategy, four other prerequisites appear critical for assuring successful implementation of the appropriate programs for these women: appropriate institutional mechanisms and sufficient economic, technical, and political resources. The lack of any one of these will block successful implementation. Each is briefly discussed in the following paragraphs.

Institutional Mechanisms

National and international agencies have yet to identify effective institutional mechanisms by which to translate woman-oriented plans into action programs and to monitor their implementation. Women's questions have been dealt with by the creation of women-only institutions, on the one hand, and by the integration of women's issues into existing institutional mechanisms, on the other. At the national level, typical examples of women-only institutions are the women's bureaus usually created within the social welfare ministry or some similar cabinet-level agency (Papanek 1978). In only a few countries, such as Bangladesh, have these women's bureaus been elevated to the status of cabinet ministries.

Women's bureaus have seldom been effective or efficient institutional mechanisms. Operating without a rational plan of action including the coordinated efforts of public- and private-sector institutions, women's bureaus (at least in Latin America) conduct the same kinds of programs again and again, benefiting only a small proportion of the total female population. These programs are almost always conceived independently of national strategies and do not give women access to the benefits of mainstream economic development programs.

In addition, women's bureaus often have severe financial and technical constraints that hamper their effectiveness as well as their flexibility in undertaking innovative action. Women's bureaus have adhered to welfare strategies even when their stated objectives have been to increase women's productivity and incomes; it is apparent that because of their institutional weakness and lack of resources, they have almost no choice but to implement what are, in fact, welfare-oriented programs. On the positive side, women's bureaus have created pressure groups and provided women with at least a potential framework for political organization.

The alternative approach, which has been adopted by many bilateral and international development institutions, has been to integrate women's issues into the existing institutional framework by adding an office to act as an advocacy, technical, and evaluation-monitoring unit on behalf of women's interests. Most of these offices were created in the late 1970s as a result of IWY. Like women's bureaus, however, these offices have had few financial and technical resources. Like women's bureaus at the national level, they have functioned well as advocates, but in the transition from an emphasis on equity to an emphasis on poverty, they have had neither the funds nor the technical expertise necessary to bring about the integration of women into mainstream poverty programs. This has often created a disjunction between policy and action, between "what to do" and "how to do it," which has affected these offices' technical credibility.

Technical and Economic Resources

An economic growth strategy for women requires a supply of technical resources, expertise, and services at the action level. Although there is a clear demand from women for access to economic and technical resources that will help them increase their economic productivity and incomes (see Dixon 1980), the supply of these resources is generally low or nonexistent. Furthermore, the resources that are available often do not reach women because of various constraints, such as ineffective channels of communication about the availability of assistance, and because of the high costs to potential woman users of the resources.

Political Resources

Two political resources are crucial for the successful implementation of women's programs oriented toward economic growth. First, the policy in question must have political legitimacy; second, the political power of program beneficiaries must be recognized (Uphoff 1980). The political legitimacy of women's issues has been fostered by discussion at the United Nations and strengthened by an emphasis on distributive rather than redistributive policies.

The political power of poor women is another question. Historically, women have had little political power in either capitalist or socialist systems (Newland 1975). Elite women have relatively more political power than their poor counterparts, but their power is usually the result of family ties to men with political power. This kind of power often limits their access to institutional, financial, and technical resources when they have to compete with powerful men. Heads of women's bureaus in Latin America usually have no legitimate power vis-à-vis heads of competing bureaus in the fight for scarce government resources.

The absence of political pressure groups composed of women is the last and biggest hurdle to overcome on the road from policy to action, and the incorporation of women's issues into mainstream development plans does not guarantee the existence of a political power base that will ensure action (Grindle 1980). Vina Mazumdar's analysis (1979) of India's Six-Year Plan supports this argument. According to Mazumdar, India's plan illustrates the effectiveness of an emphasis on poverty/economic growth in attempts to incorporate women's concerns into a development framework, as well as the importance of political support for action. She attributes the acknowledgment of women's questions by policymakers to research on the links among mass poverty, unemployment, rural inequality, and the condition of women, and to India's constitutional commitment to equality of opportunity. But she goes on to mention the obstacles that will be faced in trying to implement the plan and concludes that successful implementation will be largely a function of organized pressure from women's groups.

SELECTED POLICY SUGGESTIONS

The following list of suggestions, which is based on the analysis made in this chapter, includes only those that seem critical, are controversial, or are often overlooked in the translation of research findings into policy recommendations and in the actual implementation of policies.

1.   For policy and planning, socioeconomic indicators should be devised to measure women's absolute and relative poverty. Access to resources (capital and credit, land, home technology, transfer payments) seems to be a sensitive measure of absolute poverty, whereas time spent on leisure activities appears to be a discriminating measure of women's poverty as compared with that of men.

2.   The household can be a unit of economic analysis of women's situation (Watts and Skidmore 1978), but it should not be the only one used. Rather, the household should be used as one of the standards for comparison, or reference points, for understanding the behavior of women, and its use should be complemented with an analysis of the behavior of women as individuals in the marketplace. (Otherwise, any increase in well-being among individual household members that is attributable to development programs might be assessed inaccurately.)

3.   Time-use surveys should be used to single out inefficient home production activities that could be improved through access to credit and/or technology.

The information on time use (*how much* men and women work), however, should be complemented with methods that yield information on how output varies according to *who* does *what* and under what constraints.

4. Given the methodological limitations of time-use studies and the economic valuation of home production, the following recommendations can be made:

• Policies based on comparisons among time units should be based on the real versus the assumed equivalence of these time units and should ensure that the sex of the actor or the nature of the activity does not change the value assigned to time.

• Policymakers should be aware that attributing economic value to home production activities does not in any way imply that these activities are equivalent in real terms to similar market activities. Women who are theoretically earning more through home production are not better off than women earning less in the marketplace, and households with a high full income but a low market income are not necessarily richer than other households. Market income can be used to purchase home-produced goods; it can be stored or exchanged. Time spent in home production, however, cannot be used to borrow, buy, or invest, nor can it be easily transferred.

5. The probability of successful implementation of productive programs for poor women will depend, first, on devising technically uncomplicated, clearly defined, short-term projects with no more than one objective (Cleaves 1980). Examples of such projects include providing women with access to credit, establishing an agricultural extension service, and teaching women modern technologies to increase their productivity at home or on the farm. This policy suggestion challenges the approach of a majority of the existing productivity projects for women, which have many purposes and varied components.

Second, the monopolizable aspects of productivity projects should be reduced by designing women-only interventions. This does not imply women-only projects but women-only components within larger projects. One example of this would be the establishment of a credit line for women only, thus avoiding the problem of unfair competition from potential male borrowers, who have easier access to collateral (among other things) than women (Schumacher, Sebstad, and Buvinić 1980).

Third, social science research should be carried out to establish the constraints women face in attempting to increase their productivity and incomes, including exploration of the traditional division of labor between the sexes and how much innovation in this area can be tolerated by the community.

Fourth, the innovative aspects of productivity projects should always be carefully evaluated. Information on the factors responsible for project success should be collected and published.

6. Although a strong policy mandate to implement women's programs is essential, development institutions should also provide incentives to their personnel to implement economic growth projects for women. These incentives are

needed because such projects may have high perceived costs for implementers; to an objectively difficult task—increasing the productivity and income of poor women—are added institutional and financial constraints and perceived high political costs.

7. Successful implementation of an economic growth strategy that affects women would be facilitated by creation of technical and monitoring units within existing institutions. In the short run, it is critical and feasible to establish these units within the international development agencies. To be effective, they must be allocated sufficient financial resources.

8. International and bilateral development agencies should make significant allocations of funds to support national-level programs for women that have an explicit orientation toward economic growth. Such programs have a greater chance of being implemented when foreign assistance is available, since this can alleviate competition for funds from other national programs.

The financial backing of international funding agencies would minimize the redistributionist implications of the programs and encourage national governments to proceed with such programs, because they would have few direct economic costs in the short run.

9. External support, however, is no substitute for support within the nation in the long run. Over the long term, national political leadership and national resources will be essential for assuring the continuation of programs that affect women. Therefore, the organization of women into groups with political influence should be promoted. As soon as men and women perceive that their interests and goals are shared, they can unite and exert more effective political influence. The task ahead is to convince implementers and beneficiaries that the shared, long-term objective for both men and women is economic growth with equity.

Notes

1. Some of the main ideas in this chapter are based on the author's observations in Central and South American countries. The sparsity of literature on the subject makes it difficult, however, to demonstrate that these ideas are valid in other regions of the world.

2. In the United States, the value added generated by the home sector seems to account for over one-third of the output produced for the market (Hawrylyshin 1976). In Pakistan, home production in a sample of urban households was almost one-third of the households' contribution to gross national product (GNP) and GDP (Alauddin 1980).

3. The basic needs strategy includes as essential components the expansion of employment opportunities and the utilization of currently underemployed and unemployed labor resources by facilitating access to productive resources. As it is commonly interpreted, however, the employment side of the basic needs strategy is made secondary to the provision of basic services.

4. The beneficiary/equity emphasis is reflected in the World Plan of Action adopted at the IWY conference, which calls for "equality between men and women" (paragraph 16) and for "giving women their fair share of the benefits of development" (paragraph 22).

Part II

WOMEN IN POVERTY: WHAT DO WE KNOW?

SECTION 1 Women and Work

3. Time Allocation and Home Production in Philippine Rural Households

Elizabeth King and Robert E. Evenson

Until the late 1960s, home production, home management, and home technology were the concern of home economists only, even though the concepts included in the study of such subjects are not alien to general economics. (Agricultural economists, for instance, focus extensively on farm production, farm management, and farm technology.) The neglect of home production was primarily the consequence of the development of the conventional theory of consumption and the emphasis on market activity by economists in general. Economists have rediscovered home production, however, and a modern body of theoretical and empirical work on households is being developed. Related efforts, of which this essay is one, are being made to adapt the general body of modern household economic theory to the low-income rural household setting.

The basic household economics model used in this study (described fully in Appendix A) assumes that the household maximizes a utility function that has as its arguments commodities called "consumables," produced by combining market goods and time via a household production function. Because time is an input into nonmarket production and leisure as well as into market production, it becomes a constraint to the maximization of household welfare. Besides allocating time among alternative uses, households allocate their time resources among members, resulting in activity roles within the household. Changes in the price of time, reflected in changes in market wages, thus induce not only a substitution between goods and time inputs in the production process, but also a substitution between husband's time and wife's time in different activities. The amount of time supplied to the market and to the home become interrelated household decisions, simultaneously made, and dependent on market wages as well as on productivity of time, tastes, and other characteristics of the household.

This essay analyzes the determinants of time allocation in rural households in Laguna, a province of the Philippines, using this basic framework. The analysis is the basis for a discussion of the value of home production and of the need to include that value in any estimates of the full income of rural households. If the value of household production is added to market income in determining full income, the importance of the nonmarket production of women in rural households becomes clear.

The data used in this study were gathered in a multipurpose survey and resurvey of rural households in Laguna. Two sets of time data were generated by the first survey in 1975. The "recall" data (376 households) were collected in the initial phase of the project. Respondents were asked to recall how much time was spent on particular activities—in the past week, for nonseasonal activities, and over a longer period, for seasonal activities. Leisure time was calculated as a residual. The "observation" data were collected by direct observation of the households in three separate 24-hour visits over an 8-month period (97 households, 291 observations). Time allocation was recorded in great detail; more than 40 activities were specified. Leisure time was measured directly, and joint activities, such as food preparation and child care, were recorded as separate activities; therefore, the observation data may actually total more than 24 hours per day.[1] The resurvey conducted in 1977 covered 245 of the original 376 households. Time-allocation data were gathered, again using both the "recall" and "direct observation" methods (for a comparison of observation and recall data, see Appendix B).

The first section of this essay describes patterns of time allocation in the households surveyed. The remainder of the essay is devoted to a presentation of empirical results and a discussion of the value of home production and policy implications.

PATTERNS OF TIME ALLOCATION

There are a great number of different activities in a day. The Laguna survey divided daily activities into several classifications, which for this study have been aggregated into three broad categories: market production, home production, and leisure (see Table 3.1).

Market production includes various types of income-earning work, such as wage employment, practice of profession, management of business, and farming. On the average, fathers in the Laguna sample households spent about 7 hours a day in market production, and mothers spent about 2½ hours.

The activities that constitute work at home or home production are difficult to identify. One problem is that the product of income-earning home production time may not be entirely offered in the market, making it difficult to separate the home production time component from the market work time component. A second difficulty, which stems from the fact that time itself is a direct source of utility in leisure as well as a productive resource, is that certain home activities, such as child care, can be considered either work or leisure. For our purposes, home production is simply defined as those activities which are carried on, by and for the members, which activities might be replaced by market goods, or paid services, if circumstances such as income, market conditions, and personal inclinations permit the service being delegated to someone outside the household group (Reid 1934).

In the Laguna rural households, the average mother allocates approximately 7½ hours a day to home production, whereas the average father devotes less than 1½ hours daily to the home. Child care and food preparation are the two most important home activities of the mother.

The third major activity group is leisure, which includes time for personal care (sleeping and eating), active and passive recreation, church activities, and festivals. According to the data, the leisure hours of father and mother consist chiefly of time spent for personal care—approximately 8½ hours for fathers and over 9 hours for mothers. Passive recreation (leisure activities that do not require much physical effort) occupies 3 to slightly more than 4 hours of each parent's day. Very little or no time is devoted to any form of active sports. The data show that men spend more time on festival activities, such as weddings and town fiestas, than women. Women, on the other hand, allocate more time than men to church activities.

On the whole, the average household allocates about 15 hours a day to market production and 12 hours a day to home production (excluding school time). Approximately 3 hours daily are spent on child care (including bottle-feeding, breast-feeding, and storytelling). Slightly more time is spent on food preparation, and about 6 hours are spent daily on other home production tasks (excluding school time). The father's market production time alone accounts for 46 percent of the family's total market production time, indicating that he is the primary breadwinner. The mother contributes about 60 percent of total home production time (excluding school time).

Children do participate in both market and home production. It is interesting to note the importance of children in crop cultivation, livestock raising, and fishing. The market production time of children, which is, on the average, 37 percent of the total for the family, exceeds the mother's; their home production time, 29 percent of the family total (excluding school time), is greater than the father's. Children in these rural households play a significant role as producers, both in the market and in the home.

Determinants of Time Allocation

Every household is unique, and each therefore is expected to exhibit its own pattern of time allocation. Comparisons of time use between farmers and nonfarmers, between big and small households, and between employed and unemployed individuals can, however, reveal some underlying determinants of time allocation behavior.

Occupation. Occupation affects time allocation, as is shown in Table 3. In the total sample, more than 40 percent of the fathers and about 5 percent of

TABLE 3.1   TIME BUDGETS IN LAGUNA RURAL HOUSEHOLDS
(AVERAGE HOURS PER DAY)

Activity	Father	Mother	Children[a]
Market Production			
Wage employment	1.91	.56	1.17
Profession	.35	.14	.11
Business	.45	.44	.50
Preharvest	1.32	.28	1.10
Postharvest	.58	.27	.54
Coconut production	.54	.16	.62
Sugar cane production	.02	0	.02
Vegetable production	.15	.11	.24
Home gardening	.07	.03	.05
Livestock raising	.70	.28	.57
Handicraft	.02	.13	.05
Marketing	.08	.05	.05
Fishing	.25	.01	.22
Repair	.16	.03	.02
Travel	.25	.08	.18
Hunting	0	0	.12
Other	0	0	0
Total	6.85	2.57	5.56
Home Production			
Cooking	.41	2.06	.84
Breast-feeding	—	.36	—
Bottle-feeding	.01	.01	.01
Caring for children	.38	1.69	.44
Marketing and travel	.10	.39	.3?
Fetching or chopping	.13	.07	.?
Household chores	.22	2.76	1.?
Storytelling	.01	.003	
Care of aged and sick	.004	.04	
School or class	.04	.04	
Total	1.30	7.42	
Leisure			
Sleeping	7.89	8.64	
Eating	.59	.67	
Playing with children	.02	.04	
Passive recreation	4.22	3.77	
Active recreation	.01	0	
Being sick or immobile	.08	.10	
Church activities	.02	.09	
Festival activities	.77	.60	
Social service utilization	.07	.08	
Other	0	0	
Total	13.67	13.9	

NOTE: Sample size = 99.
[a]The average number of children in the sam

TABLE 3.2 TIME ALLOCATION OF FATHERS AND MOTHERS
IN LAGUNA RURAL HOUSEHOLDS, BY OCCUPATION GROUP
(AVERAGE HOURS PER DAY)

Activity	Father		Mother	
	Farmer	Nonfarmer	Farmer	Nonfarmer
Market Production				
Wage employment	1.06	5.02**	1.10	2.19**
Farming	5.17	.97**	3.36	.01**
Livestock raising	.59	.44	.02	.32
Other	.69	1.21*	.13	.34
Total	7.51	7.64	4.61	2.86
Home Production				
Child care	.26	.37	.79	1.64**
Food preparation	.34	.32	1.74	1.76
Other	.41	.45	1.80	2.66
Total	1.01	1.14	4.33	6.06*
Leisure				
Personal care	9.75	9.20	11.58	10.37
Recreation	4.21	3.64	2.93	2.98
Other	.64	.58	.44	.67
Total	14.60	13.42**	14.95	14.02

NOTE: Sample size = 99.
**Difference between means is significant at the .01 level.
*Difference between means is significant at the .05 level.

mothers are farmers—that is, they report farming (including fishing and/or livestock raising) as their primary occupation. More than 50 percent of the fathers and about 30 percent of the mothers are nonfarmers—hired farm laborers, factory workers, government or private-enterprise employees, entrepreneurs, and others. Most nonfarmers do not have second jobs, whereas many farmers do report second occupations. This is not surprising, since individuals who have jobs with less rigid working hours or with more seasonal variation would be able to, and perhaps would be compelled to, supplement their incomes. Many women do not claim an occupation.

The total market production time of both farmer fathers and nonfarmer fathers is about 7½ hours a day; there is no significant difference between them. Total market production time of farmer mothers, however, is greater than that of nonfarmer mothers. As expected, nonfarmer fathers devote more time to wage employment than do farmer fathers, who spend more hours on farming activities. Some degree of diversification in the economic activities of all fathers is evident: Nonfarmers do spend a few hours on farming and livestock raising, and farmers also earn income from wage employment and other market production. Farmer mothers, as would be expected, spend more time on farming than nonfarmer mothers, who, in turn, spend more time in wage employment.

Farmer fathers allocate less time to home production than do nonfarmer fathers. Farmer mothers spend about 2 hours less on home production than do nonfarmer mothers, particularly child care and other home chores; however, both groups spend about the same amount of time on food preparation. Farmer fathers have about 15 hours of leisure in a day, compared with about 13 hours for nonfarmer fathers. The difference in the mean time spent for leisure by farmer mothers and by nonfarmer mothers is not significant.

2. Time spent on market work. The time budgets of employed fathers and mothers are grouped in Table 3.3 according to their hours of employment. Fathers who allocate fewer hours to work in the market devote significantly more time to child care, food preparation, and other home chores (although the time they spend on work at home—approximately 2½ hours—is still significantly less than the time spent by women with the same degree of market participation—approximately 7½ hours). They also enjoy more leisure hours—more time for such things as personal care and recreation. The general pattern observed is that, in contrast with unemployed fathers, fathers who do less than 4 hours of market

TABLE 3.3 TIME ALLOCATION OF EMPLOYED FATHERS AND MOTHERS IN LAGUNA RURAL HOUSEHOLDS, BY HOURS OF WORK PER DAY

Activity	Father				Mother			
	0	−4	4–6	6+	0	−4	4–6	6+
Market Production								
Wage employment	0	.26	.69	5.06**	0	.34	1.77	4.90**
Farming	0	.68	2.62	3.84**	0	.32	1.46	2.48**
Livestock raising	0	.35	1.08	.47*	0	.27	.94	.22*
Other	0	.51	.60	1.25**	0	.37	1.04	1.32*
Total	0	1.80	4.99	10.62**	0	1.30	5.21	8.92**
Home Production								
Child care	.13	.63	.72	.19**	2.72	2.02	.84	.68**
Food preparation	.31	.88	.47	.16	2.00	2.10	2.17	1.30**
Other	1.46	.90	.78	.29**	3.65	3.51	2.15	1.32**
Total	1.90	2.41	1.97	.64**	8.37	7.63	5.16	3.30**
Leisure								
Personal care	13.24	11.43	10.39	9.38**	11.15	10.35	10.16	9.76*
Recreation	5.85	6.34	5.68	3.02**	3.71	4.02	3.09	1.80**
Other	2.41	1.38	.44	.32*	.78	.84	.12	.26
Total	21.50	19.15	16.51	12.72**	15.64	15.21	13.37	11.82**

NOTE: Sample size = 99.
**Difference between means is significant at the .01 level.
*Difference between means is significant at the .05 level.

work have more home production time. Those who do 4 to 6 hours of market work have more home time and leisure time than fathers who work more than 6 hours. It may be noted, in particular, that only when market production time averages more than 10 hours a day do fathers greatly reduce their time for children and for other household tasks. Moreover, their time for personal care and recreation is also drastically reduced.

The time allocation of mothers is similar to that of fathers. In general, women who are active in the market for only a few hours a day still devote time to home production and to leisure, but time for both activities is reduced as market production time increases. Only when market time exceeds 6 hours a day do mothers reduce their food preparation time. This implies that labor force participation of women per se need not result in a decrease in time spent for essential home production activities. Rather, such time is determined by the degree of market participation or the quantity of labor supplied to the market. When the labor market structure allows flexibility in the number of working hours, as may be true in the informal business sector and in agriculture, labor force participation does not necessarily imply a decline in the role of these women at home. The findings here also suggest that, since active market participation can cut deeply into home production time, full income rather than cash income would be a better measure of household welfare.

3. Children. One factor that is known to affect greatly the time allocation of married persons is the presence and number of children in the household (Gronau 1976*a*; Boulier 1976). The sample households in this study have an average of four children. Table 3.4 compares time budgets for households according to the number of children born to the family.

Apparently, the number of children does not materially affect the fathers' total market production time. On the other hand, the total market production time of mothers in larger households is greater than in smaller households. Furthermore, fathers and mothers with many children spend less time caring for their children than parents with fewer children, and fathers with many children enjoy more leisure time. This result is not surprising, as larger households will probably have older children who can substitute for the parents in caring for younger children.

More important, perhaps, than the size of the family are the ages of the children, because infants and preschoolers need more parental attention and care than older children. Table 3.4 shows that having an infant significantly decreases the mother's market and leisure time and increases her home production time.

ECONOMETRIC ANALYSES OF TIME ALLOCATION

In this section, several predictions of the household production model with regard to time allocation are compared with the empirical results, thus testing the rigor of the model. It is important to note that the model used in this study (see

TABLE 3.4 TIME ALLOCATION OF FATHERS AND MOTHERS IN LAGUNA RURAL HOUSEHOLDS, BY NUMBER OF CHILDREN AT HOME (HOURS PER DAY)

	Father			Mother				
Activity	1–3 Children	4–6 Children	7+ Children	1–3 Children	4–6 Children	7+ Children	Without Infants	With Infants
Market Production								
Wage employment	2.33	2.52	2.68	1.08	.91	1.78	1.35	1.06
Farming	2.78	2.54	1.91	.53	.64	.83	.79	.59
Livestock raising	.33	.41	.42	.22	.16	.34	.28	.10
Other	1.22	.65	.98	.46	.45	.60	.54	.35
Total	6.66	6.12	5.99	2.29	2.16	3.45*	2.96	2.10*
Home Production								
Child care	.88	.27	.16*	2.10	2.04	1.26*	1.04	3.96**
Food preparation	.55	.38	.26	1.95	1.71	1.71	1.92	1.89
Other	.45	.61	.71	3.39	2.54	2.66	2.97	3.12
Total	1.88	1.26	1.13	7.44	6.29	5.63*	5.93	8.97**
Leisure								
Personal care	8.97	11.50	12.06*	9.73	12.46	10.74*	10.38	10.70
Recreation	5.23	3.10	4.32	4.10	2.64	3.52	3.83	2.30**
Other	.13	.36	.72	.43	.41	.67	.11	0*
Total	14.33	14.96	17.10*	14.26	15.51	14.93	14.32	13.00**

NOTE: Sample size = 99.
**Difference between means is significant at the .01 level.
*Difference between means is significant at the .05 level.

42

Appendix A) is subject to certain implicit and explicit restrictions. For example, we have assumed that the wife can simply substitute for the husband's home time in a two-person household and that the wife can substitute her farm time for the husband's farm time. We have also assumed simple fixed job costs that do not depend on the hours worked.

A number of testable implications are directly related to these restrictive assumptions and this should be clearly recognized. A change in these assumptions would yield different implications. It seems most reasonable, however, given the current state of the art, to start with a relatively simple and restricted model and submit it to the evidence. In future modeling development we can be guided by whether or not the evidence rejects the present model.

The Husband's Market Wage

Theoretically, when the husband's wage increases, the price of leisure rises, inducing a substitution of market time for leisure. The wage increase also produces an income effect that runs in the opposite direction. More leisure is desired when income rises. The increase in wage rate has no effect, of course, unless the husband is working in the market (or is induced by the increase to enter the market). We generally expect the substitution effect to dominate the income effect; thus an increase in the husband's wage will induce him to work more hours in the market. He will also work less in the home, unless he is already fully specialized in the market. If he has the option of farm work, he will work fewer hours on the farm (and in the home), and this displacement of time will result in a larger market time effect.

An increase in the husband's wage rate will also affect the wife's time allocation primarily through an income effect for her. She will increase her leisure time unless there is agreement on leisure sharing. With equitable leisure sharing, the wife will reduce her leisure, even though the value of her time has not changed per se. If she is in the market, this decrease in leisure should not affect her home time at all—rather, her market time will increase.

Table 3.5 reports the results of a regression analysis that estimates the effects of such variables as market wages, home and farm capital, and children on time allocation. The estimated coefficients of the husband's wage rate have the expected signs. The effect of an increase in the husband's wage rate on the wife's allocation of time to market production is positive, suggesting that leisure is "shared" in households with wives working in the market. For those women who are not working in the market, an increase in the husband's wage rate results in reduced home production time due to the standard income effect. The regressions reported in Table 3.6 also support the expectations regarding an increase in market time of the husband and a decrease in his farm time. The evidence in Table 3.6 again suggests the sharing of leisure in households with wives working in the market.

TABLE 3.5 REGRESSION ANALYSIS OF LAGUNA DIRECT OBSERVATION
TIME-ALLOCATION DATA FROM 1975 SURVEY

	Wife		Husband	
Independent Variable	Home Time	Market Time	Home Time	Market Time
Constant	363.20	196.63	88.06	266.06
Wife's market wage	−3.53	6.16*	−.28	4.76
Husband's market wage	−27.22**	13.01	−5.10**	26.69**
Home capital	29.35**	—	−9.18*	—
House	−2.90*	—	1.56*	—
Farm capital	—	2.39	—	7.31**
Children aged 0–1 yr.	186.77**	−37.43	27.35*	−7.16
Children aged 1–6 yrs.	37.18**	−3.68	−1.05	12.47
Children aged 7–15 yrs.	−5.47	9.03	−6.96	18.97
Children aged 16+ yrs.	12.60	−8.90	5.85	−14.78
Education of wife	−4.19**	16.82*	7.51*	4.76
Education of husband	−6.46	2.50	5.56	−14.29
Wife's age	10.78	−13.42*	—	—
Wife's age^2	−.24**	.26**	—	—
Husband's age	—	—	3.32	.82
Husband's age^2	—	—	−.07	−.03
Wet season	−8.13	20.78	−30.67**	14.60
Cool season	−5.03	−5.17	−19.84	16.34
R^2	.320	.118	.113	.108
Number of cases	(291)	(291)	(291)	(291)

**Significant at .01 level.
*Significant at .05 level.

The Wife's Market Wage

A change in the wife's market wage should have no effect unless she is actually working in the market (or would be induced to enter the market because of the wage change). If she is working, there will be income and substitution effects, with the substitution effect probably dominating. It is expected that she, like her husband, will *displace* home and farm time, so that there will almost certainly be a positive effect on market time and a negative effect on home and farm time. The effect on the husband will depend on whether and how leisure is shared.

The results reported in Table 3.5 are generally not significant. Table 3.6 shows strong positive effects on the wife's market time and negative but much less significant effects on her home and farm time. In nonfarm households, the husband's home and market times appear to be reduced, implying a standard income effect and no leisure sharing. In farm households, an increase in the wife's market wage appears to affect positively, though not significantly, the husband's farm and market times, suggesting the possibility of leisure sharing.

TABLE 3.6 REGRESSION ANALYSIS OF LAGUNA RECALL TIME-ALLOCATION DATA FROM 1977 RESURVEY

| Independent Variable | Nonfarming Households (101) | | | | Farming Households (124) | | | | | |
| | Wife | | Husband | | Wife | | | Husband | | |
	Home Time	Market Time	Home Time	Market Time	Home Time	Farm Time	Market Time	Home Time	Farm Time	Market Time
Nonwage income	-.00004	.00006	.00084	-.00004**	.098*	.014	.045*	-.002	-.009	.012
Wife's market wage	-1.085*	.983**	-.474*	-.796*	-.32	-.76	.708**	-.014	.155	.035
Husband's market wage	.091	.015	.007	.336**	.275	-.56	.069	-.014	-.336**	1.01**
Home capital	.0018	.0018	.0004	-.0003*	.00025	.0005	.00005	-.00005	.0005**	-.0001
Farm capital	—	—	—	—	.0005	.0003*	-.0003*	-.0005**	-.0004	-.58*
Farm replacement wage—wife	—	—	—	—	.0276**	.0063**	-.060*	.002	.002	.0046
Farm replacement wage—husband	—	—	—	—	.020	-.0002	-.0098*	-.0004	.084	-.002
Cost of market job	—	.208	—	3.17**	—	—	.049	—	—	.009
Children aged 0–3 yrs.	-2.99	-4.53	3.19	-2.61	6.16	-1.48	-3.55*	.98	.30	-4.22
Children aged 3–6 yrs.	1.67	-2.05	.009	1.37	7.19*	1.98	-1.36	-.28	2.55	.34
Children aged 6–9 yrs.	-2.65	4.16*	-.25	5.36*	-4.04	-.10	4.82**	.13	-1.31	.31
Children aged 9+ yrs.	-5.40**	1.43	-1.14	-.61	-.55	-.08	.27	-.22	-.94	.78
Education of wife	-.25	.16	-.67**	.27	.42	-.46	.085	.27*	-.30	.21
Education of husband	-.66	-.20	.54**	.56**	-1.53**	.52	.031	-.093	.23	.61**
Year married	.61**	.15	-.016	.29*	.51*	.80	.05	.13	.36	.21
Days sick	.339	-.03	-.011	-.033	-.607	-.282	-.20	.38**	.067	-.07
R^2	.331	.226	.237	.550	.297	.157	.508	.452	.291	.459

**Significant at .01 level.
*Significant at .05 level.

Farm Replacement Wages

Farm replacement wages, defined as the wage a farmer would have to pay another worker to do the farmer's job, reflect the productivity of farm time and would be expected to predict time allocation in farm households. These wages should be negatively associated with market time, because high farm productivity will lead to a displacement against market time. Table 3.6 shows that in farm households, the wife's replacement wage does allow more farm and home time and less market time for her. The husband's replacement wage coefficient is also negative for his market time, although not significant.

Cost of Market Jobs

The household production model predicts that when job costs are fixed (do not vary with the number of hours worked), they will have a negative income effect. As job costs rise, market workers, in an attempt to maximize average net returns to their labor, will work more in the market and allocate less time to leisure. In Table 3.6 the effect of the cost of a market job is positive on market time for husbands and wives in farm and nonfarm households but is significant only for husbands in nonfarm households.

Farm and Home Capital

An increase in home capital should increase the productivity of home time and thus increase home work and decrease farm and market work for the wife. If the husband earns a market wage that is higher than that of his wife, the effect on the husband should be to induce market work. The results reported in Table 3.5 tend to support this expectation: An increase in home capital appears to have a positive effect on the wife's home time and a negative effect on the husband's home time, which could mean that he is allocating more time to market work. In Table 3.6, however, the only significant coefficients for home capital imply a decrease in the market time of husbands in nonfarm households and an increase in the farm time of husbands in farm households.

Similarly, an increase in farm capital should lead to an increase in farm work and a decrease in market work and home time for both husband and wife. In Table 3.5, the effect of increased farm capital on the market time of both husband and wife is positive, presumably because in these regressions market time includes farm time. In Table 3.6, which reports regressions that distinguish between farm time and market time, the effect on the market time of both the husband and the wife is negative. The effect on the home time of the husband is also negative and significant. Finally, the effect on the farm time of the wife is positive, as expected, but the effect on the farm time of the husband is negative (although not significant).

Nonwage Income

The effect of an increase in nonwage income depends on whether the husband and wife work in the market. Increased income expands the goods-for-leisure trade-off opportunities available to the household (see Appendix A, Figure A3-2, panels C and D). If both husband and wife work in the market, both will reduce market time because of a pure income effect—that is, since leisure is a normal good, both will opt for more. If the wife is not in the market but the husband is, the wife will reduce home production time. The effect on home production time will be smaller than it is when both husband and wife are in the market, however, because the wife's marginal product of home time will increase as her home time decreases. The effect on the wife's farm time will be similar. When neither husband nor wife works in the market, negative effects on both home and farm time for each are predicted.

We did not explore this effect in the first survey, but Table 3.6 reports some results. The expectation of a negative effect is borne out rather poorly. The effect is statistically significant for only the husband's market time in nonfarming households and has the wrong sign in some of the regressions.

Effect of Education

The effect of education when wages are held constant is difficult to predict, since wages presumably reflect the effects of skills to some extent. We might expect education to induce more market work because of taste factors. This seems to hold for the husband in Table 3.6 and for the wife in Table 3.5, but our results are not very informative in this regard.

Effect of Children

The effect of children in the household can be thought of as having three components:

1. A household life-cycle effect
2. A goods effect (Children's services are relatively home-time-intensive goods.)
3. A work effect (Children's time can be employed in home and market production.)

The life-cycle effect is determined by the timing of the other two effects. Consider the early life cycle, during which children are present but contribute little to home production. The home production curve is raised because children are home-time-intensive, and because they are intensive users of the mother's time, the addition of children at this stage increases the productivity of the mother's home time in the same way as an increase in home capital (see previous discussion).

Now consider a middle life cycle, where the household has both younger children and older children. Here we have two effects. One is the increased home production just discussed. The other is the addition to the model of children as workers. Without developing a further formal analysis, it can readily be seen that the addition of children as workers is roughly equivalent to the addition of a second person. Just as the wife displaced her husband's home production time to make possible gains from specialization, older children will replace the home production time of the wife, at least in certain tasks. At a later stage in the life cycle, when only older children are present, the work effect of those children will dominate. The results reported in Table 3.5 indicate that younger children (aged 6 years or under) do have a significant and positive effect on the home time of the wife. Table 3.6 indicates that older children have a negative effect on the home time of the wife and a positive effect on her market time.

The analysis made here is quite modest in terms of the statistical properties of the regression results. Nonetheless, it supports the model.

THE VALUE OF HOME PRODUCTION AND FULL INCOME

Conventional household income can be measured in two equivalent ways. It can be measured as the payment to nonlabor assets held by a household plus the payments to household members for work performed. It can also be measured in terms of expenditures on consumption and investment goods. The modern household concept of full income may be similarly measured. It differs from the conventional concept in its definition of productive resources and of goods, however. Full income, measured in terms of payments to productive resources, includes payments to nonlabor earning assets, payments for work required for the production of market goods (which includes farm production work and wage employment), *plus* the value of time devoted to home production as well as the value contributed to home production by home capital. Full income, measured by expenditures, is the sum of expenditures on household or home goods and expenditures on investment goods.

Little has been done actually to estimate the value of home production, which presents several problems. First, classifying most home activities as work-oriented or consumer-oriented presents a problem because of the pervasiveness of joint production, time itself being a source of utility as well as a productive resource. Perhaps the more serious problem is that of assigning a monetary value to the items produced, however. On the one hand, they can be valued at the prices for which similar items can be bought from the market. On the other hand, their value can be based on the production costs of home goods and services to the household. The weakness of the first approach is that household goods that are not generally traded in markets do not have market prices. The second approach takes into a consideration that household goods have "shadow prices," which can be imputed and which can be defined as the costs of production of household goods. The implicit assumption of a constant marginal product of home time when using shadow prices and the difficulty of assigning prices to other inputs of home production are the limitations of the second approach.

Another problem, associated with attempting to use the wage rate as a substitute for the marginal product of home time, can be illustrated by examining the situation in which fixed job costs exist. In this case, if an individual is working in the market, the marginal product of home time must be less than the observed wage rate. If the individual is not working in the market, however, the marginal product of home time is not necessarily greater than the individual's potential market wage rate. For example, when the amount of home goods produced affects the ability to work (i.e., there is a nutrition effect), the individual may choose not to work in the market even though the marginal product of home time is less than the market wage rate (see Appendix A for a fuller explanation).

Gronau (1976a) has developed a method for using home production time-allocation regressions similar to those reported in Table 3.5 to estimate the marginal product of home time.[2] Use of this method with the Laguna data affords an opportunity to estimate the value of home production and thus full income. The estimates of the value of home production are summarized in Table 3.7.

TABLE 3.7   VALUE OF HOME PRODUCTION
IN LAGUNA RURAL HOUSEHOLDS, BY TYPE OF HOUSEHOLD,
BASED ON REGRESSION ESTIMATES (PESOS PER YEAR)

Type of Household	Father	Mother	Children[a]	Total
Farm	631	3,342	2,820	6,793
Nonfarm	710	3,280	1,757	5,747
Mother employed	396	3,067	2,275	5,738
0–3 children	460	3,274	1,009	4,743
4–6 children	354	2,833	3,057	6,244
7+ children	288	2,967	4,869	8,124
Mother not employed	661	3,954	1,217	5,832
0–3 children	788	3,874	541	5,203
4–6 children	511	3,862	1,481	5,854
7+ children	783	4,169	1,658	9,610
Mother employed	396	3,067	2,275	5,738
With infant	630	4,864	845	6,339
Without infant	331	2,554	2,038	4,923
Mother not employed	661	3,954	1,217	5,832
With infant	884	5,368	1,381	7,633
Without infant	578	3,359	1,162	5,099
Mother's education				
0–6 yrs.	463	3,338	2,212	6,013
7+ yrs.	507	2,955	1,062	4,524

[a]Excluding school time.

These estimates are based on home-time-allocation regression estimates for *employed* fathers, mothers, and children, which are not reported here but were quite comparable to the results shown in Table 3.5. It might also be noted that the estimates in Table 3.7 are quite close to those obtained simply by multiplying home time by wage rates.

Table 3.7 is of considerable interest, for it shows that (1) home production is indeed quite important, (2) the value of home production is somewhat higher in farming households than in nonfarming households, and (3) the value of home production is higher in households where the mother is not employed and in households with a greater number of children. It might be noted from Table 3.8, however, that when the market income of the mother is added to the value of home production, full income (excluding school time) in households where mothers are employed is about 11 percent higher than in households where mothers are not employed. Table 3.8 also shows the impact of children on the value of home production, which reflects the value of children both as consumers and producers. Indeed, estimation of the full income for these households shows the role of mothers and of children to be dramatically different from that indi-

TABLE 3.8 VALUE OF MARKET INCOME,
HOME PRODUCTION, AND FULL INCOME,
BASED ON REGRESSION ESTIMATES
FROM LAGUNA DIRECT OBSERVATION DATA,
1975 SURVEY (PESOS PER YEAR)

	Value
Market Income	
Father	3,334
Mother	1,148
Children	1,301
Total	5,783
Home Production	
Father	668
Mother	3,287
Children (excluding school time)	2,061
Total	6,016
Children (including school time)	3,599
Total (including school time)	7,554
Full Income	
Father	4,002
Mother	4,435
Children (excluding school time)	3,362
Total	11,799
Children (including school time)	4,900
Total	13,337

NOTE: Sample size = 99.

cated by conventional market income measures. The mother contributes only 20 percent of market income, but her contribution to full income (excluding school time) is about 38 percent. Children in these households contribute 22 percent of market income and 28 percent of full income, if school time is not regarded as productive. If the more reasonable definition of school time as a form of home production is used, the contribution of children to full income increases to 37 percent. The father contributes about 58 percent of market income but only about 34 percent of full income.

The Role of Women

The focus on full income as a modern household measure of income has shown that home production should not be disregarded in the study of economic activities. In poor households, for which time represents the dominant household resource, time will be allocated to several activities in such a way as to minimize the cost of producing household goods. Time-budget studies show that the non-market time of women can hardly be described as "leisure." The employment of women outside the home means reducing not only their leisure time but also home production. On the one hand, the importance of nonmarket production to household income and welfare cannot be overemphasized. On the other hand, the opportunity to increase market income could encourage the introduction of technical change in home production and provide the means for acquiring labor-saving home capital.

Table 3.9 compares the time budgets of men and women in five countries. Briefly, it shows that in terms of number of hours spent on income-earning and home activities, Asian women appear to be more "hardworking." Not only do rural Filipino and Javanese women spend more time per day working at home, they also spend more hours in market production. The Bangladesh women report more than 9 hours of home production. That Asian women devote more hours to home production may be explained partly by the greater number of children in Asian households, and partly by the absence of labor-saving home capital in their homes. That they spend more time on market work may be attributed to the availability of low-paying part-time and seasonal jobs on the farm and in their own home lots.

POLICY IMPLICATIONS

Rural development policies have stressed improvements in farm technology and the dissemination of more efficient farm practices. Inasmuch as home production constitutes about half of full income in Philippine rural households, it makes sense for rural development policies also to support improvements in home technology and the wider use of more effective home management practices. A new nutrition and health technology, for instance, includes more effi-

TABLE 3.9   CROSS-COUNTRY COMPARISON OF TIME BUDGETS (HOURS PER DAY)

Country	Market Production Time	Home Production Time	Leisure	Number of Observations
		Women		
Laguna, Philippines (1975)				
Employed	3.54	6.86	17.01	(211)
Not employed	0	8.95	15.09	(80)
Total	2.55	7.44	13.99	(291)
United States (1974)				
Employed	3.44	3.52	17.05	(1,022)
Not employed	—	5.14	18.86	(968)
Total	1.76	4.31	17.93	(1,990)
Israel (1968)				
Employed	4.30	4.40	14.87	(281)
Not employed	.11	7.18	16.06	(510)
Total	1.60	6.19	15.64	(791)

SOURCES: The time data of United States and Israeli married women were taken from Gronau (1976a and b)—specifically, a survey of Israelis conducted by the Institute of Social Research, and the Michigan Study on Income Dynamics (1968–74). In the former, the interviewees were asked how they had spent each hour of the preceding day; 48 different activities were identified. In the latter, the head of the household was asked the number of weeks he and his wife had worked in the market in the preceding year and the number of hours worked per week. Also, he was asked the number of hours he and his wife had spent on housework in an average week. The reported annual hours devoted to home work may underestimate the real extent of home production because it is not clear whether the respondents included activities like shopping and child care in their replies about home time. Leisure was calculated as a residual. To make the United States annual data comparable with the Israeli and Philippine data, the number of hours in each of the three activity divisions was divided by 365 days.

The Bangladesh survey (Farouk and Ali 1975) was conducted in seven unions (states) throughout the country, representing modern and traditional urban and rural situations. The time data collected refer to the respondent's use of time on the day before the interview. To allow comparison with other time data, the Bangladesh activity groups were aggregated as follows. Amounts of time spent on wage-earning work and self-employed income-earning

(continued)

cient ways of obtaining the nutritive components of food and more effective means of disease control. The impact of such technological changes on the welfare of household members is clear and direct. Such changes also have an indirect effect on time-allocation decisions of the household (such as those concerning labor force participation), as home production time becomes more efficient.[3]

TABLE 3.9 *Continued*

Country	Market Production Time	Home Production Time	Leisure	Number of Observations
Bangladesh (1974)				
Total	1.68	9.22	13.14	(700)
Java (1972–73)				
Employed	5.83	5.42	—	(28)
Men				
Laguna, Philippines (1975)				
Employed	7.70	1.41	14.54	(257)
Not employed	0	1.15	21.41	(34)
Total	6.86	1.29	13.67	(291)
Bangladesh (1974)				
Total	9.02	1.14	13.83	(700)
Java (1972–73)				
Employed	7.99	.85	—	(25)

work were added and labeled as "market production"; expenditure-saving home production time (such as going to market, washing clothes, cooking, cleaning the house, teaching one's children), time spent for study and training, and time spent on unpaid but necessary work were summed and classified as home production time; time for personal care (such as time used for toilet, eating, and bathing) and sleeping time (defined as a residual item) made up personal care (or Gronau's "physiological needs") time; and time for recreation and religious work and unused time (which, in the Bangladesh survey, included "sitting idle" or "moving about aimlessly") constituted the recreation category.

White's (1976) data on Java, collected in 1972–73 from the village of Kali Loro (in south-central Java), were based on a sample of 20 households that included a total of 104 individuals. Each household was visited for 60 days per year and annual time data for 50 females and 54 males aged 6 to 50+ years were obtained. No clear distinction regarding civil status was made. For the purpose of the comparison, the daily average time budgets of men and women aged 20 to 50+ years were estimated from the average annual time. Market production time was the sum of hours spent for handicrafts, preparation of food for sale, animal care or feeding, trading, agricultural wage labor, and nonagricultural wage labor. The components of home production time were number of hours spent for child care, housework, food preparation, firewood collection, and shopping.

We have seen from the empirical analysis in this chapter that the home time of the wife is the single most important component of total household production and that the wife contributes as much as approximately 38 percent of full income. It is clear, then, that the target of home management extension programs should be the wife, whose managerial skills are the key to the adoption of technological changes in home production. Yet, even as we stress the wife's home production, we must point out that women do play a major role in income-earning market production too. We have noted that the full income of households with employed mothers is significantly higher than that of households in which the mother is not employed. Greater labor force participation of women, then, enhances the welfare of the household.

The role of women in rural households is clearly twofold, as the Laguna data have shown. The woman is the *maybahay*, or "keeper of the house," and as such, her main concerns are the nutritional and health needs of the family. But her traditional role is being extended by the need to engage in an occupation in order to help the family financially. As a result of the rediscovery of home production by economists, the wife, in fact, is being recognized as a producer in both capacities (as are other household members). This is a big step toward a better understanding of household decisions regarding the allocation of time among market, farm, and home production, and among household members.

Appendix A

MODELS OF TIME ALLOCATION IN RURAL HOUSEHOLDS

The household goods model employed in the analysis of fertility and related investment behavior also provides a framework for the analysis of time allocation (Becker 1965; Gronau 1973). In its full development, it is capable of analyzing the household's choice of household goods and the minimum cost allocation of the household resources utilized in the production of those goods. The time of household members will be allocated to home production of each good, to market work, and to leisure in such a way as to minimize the total cost of producing any set of household goods (including leisure) chosen by the household. In these models, changes in wage rates, prices of market goods, nonlabor income, or home production factors will lead to changes in the household goods consumed and in the allocation of time.[4]

The multiple household goods analysis is critical to the analysis of choice of household goods but is less important for the analysis of time allocation. In this essay, we concentrate only on the allocation of time among home production activities, market or farm production activities, and leisure. The specialization in time allocation within a household among husband, wife, and children adds complexities that are not easily handled in the more general household goods model; therefore, we follow Gronau (1976a) in utilizing a model with only two goods—a composite consumption good (Z) and leisure. This allows us to utilize a geometric approach and to focus more directly on the questions of interest.

The Single-Person Household

Even though in this essay we are primarily interested in the behavior of multiple-person households, the single-person household makes possible a simpler exposition of the basic features of the model. Figure A3-1 shows several cases of interest, of which panel A is the

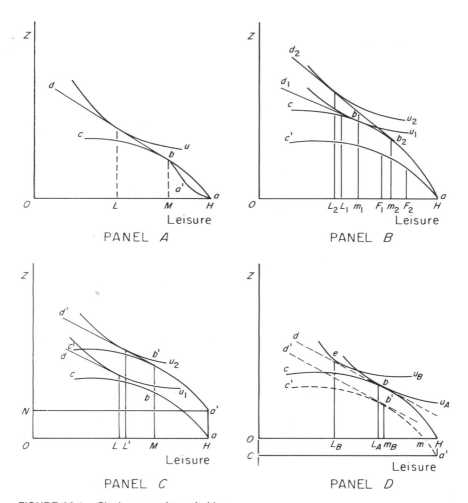

FIGURE A3-1. Single-person household cases.

simplest. The household is presumed to have a minimal amount of household resources in the form of shelter, cooking utensils, and a small home garden in addition to household time resources. We will also presume that the composite good Z can be either produced in the home or purchased in the market.[5]

The composite good is measured on the vertical axis. Leisure is measured on the horizontal axis. Point H is maximum possible leisure. Curve abc might be termed a home production curve. Its actual shape depends on other sources of income. If sufficient nonlabor income is available to ensure adequate nutrition with no home production, the curve will take the shape of abc. If this is not the situation, a relationship between production and consumption will exist. Curve $aa'bc$ shows a nutrition-work effect in which productivity is low at low levels of home production. The home production curve is based on rational work organization in which the most productive tasks are undertaken first. Because of fixed home capital resources, a diminishing marginal product will be a characteristic of the curve after some point.

Segment bd in panel A shows the goods-leisure locus offered by the labor market. The slope of the line is the wage rate divided by the goods price. The line is tangent to the home production function, reflecting the fact that at points to the left of the point of tangency, b, the marginal productivity of time in the market exceeds the marginal productivity of time in the home.[6] In equilibrium in this simple case, this household will devote OL units of time to leisure, LM units to work in the market,[7] and MH units to home production.

Panel B shows the case where the household has access to land resources and engages in agricultural production. Curve ac' is a home production curve as in panel A. Curve ab_2b_1c reflects the *combined* product from both home production and farm production.[8] Farm production is net of payments to landlords and to variable factors of production, so this curve may represent the case of a small tenant farmer. Segment b_1d_1 again reflects the opportunities afforded by a labor market.

In the initial equilibrium with indifference curve u_1, with market opportunities b_1d_1, this household will have OL_1 units of leisure, L_1m_1 units of market time, m_1F_1 units of farm time, and F_1H units of home time. Note that the marginal products of home, farm, and market time will be equated, so point F_1 is located where the slope of curve ac' is equal to the slope of segment b_1d_1.

Panel B also shows the simple analytics of the consequences of a rise in the market wage. Segment b_2d_2 reflects the higher wage rate. Note that the point of tangency with the combined home and farm production curve shifts to the right from b_1 to b_2.

The effect of the rise in wages has two parts. The first is the conventional income and substitution effect on leisure, which in this sample results in a decrease in leisure from OL_1 to OL_2. The substitution effect is shown as outweighing the income effect. This is for convenience of exposition and is not dictated by the theory. The second part of the effect is the displacement effect against both farm time and home time. In panel B, farm time is reduced from m_1F_1 units to m_2F_2 units, and home time is reduced from F_1H units to F_2H units.

Thus, even if the income effect of a rise in the wage rate outweighed the substitution effect (and total leisure increased), the displacement effect could still produce a positive labor supply response to a change in the wage rate. A backward-bending supply curve of labor is highly unlikely for a single-person household.

Panel C shows the effects of an increase in nonlabor income. Suppose that nonlabor income is increased by an amount sufficient to purchase ON units of goods. The total opportunity curve shifts upward in a parallel fashion to $a'b'd'$. Point b' is directly above point b, so the increase in nonlabor income has no effect on the amount of home time (or of combined home and farm time if farm activities are engaged in). It will increase leisure (from OL units to OL' units), however, as long as leisure is a normal good. Consequently, it will reduce market time (from LM units to $L'M$ units).

Panel D shows the effects of fixed job costs. Suppose that job search costs and maintenance costs equivalent to OC units of goods must be incurred. The relevant opportunity locus if market work is undertaken becomes $a'b'd'$. Note that if there are job costs, a certain minimum number of time units (mH) will be devoted to market work if market work is undertaken. Note also that small differences in the shape of the indifference curve can yield large differences in time allocation. With indifference curve u_A, the equilibrium at point b indicates OL_A units of leisure, no market work, and L_AH units of home (or farm and home) time. With indifference curve u_B, the equilibrium at point e produces only OL_B units of leisure, $L_B m_B$ units of market work, and only $m_B H$ units in the home, read off $a'b'c'$. (A slight rise in the market wage with indifference curve u_A would have produced a similar time allocation.)

The Two-Person Household

Figure A3-2 represents an extension of the previous analytic framework to the two-person household. Here we are concerned with the economics of specialization within the household.

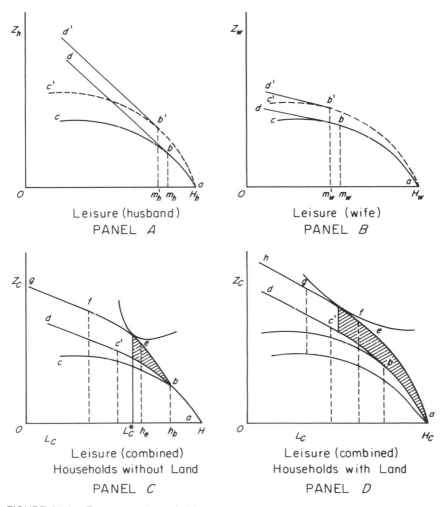

FIGURE A3-2. Two-person household cases.

Panel A and panel B show the single-person cases for a husband (panel A) and a wife (panel B) acting independently. The opportunity curves abd are for households without land. The opportunity curves $ab'd'$ are for households with land. The home production curve for the husband is equivalent to that for the wife. Note, however, that the husband commands a higher wage in the market and is more productive on the farm in this example. This specification is consistent with most empirical evidence.

Panel C shows the combined case for landless households. The axes measure goods per member and leisure per member. Curve $abc'd$ represents the nonspecialization combination and is a simple average of the single-person household goods cases. In segment ab, both husband and wife work in the home. In segment bc', the husband is working in the market and the wife is working at home. In segment $c'd$, both work in the market.

Curve $abefg$ represents specialization according to comparative advantage within the household. We suppose here that the wife's time is a perfect substitute for the husband's time in home production. If so, the following sequence takes place. Along segment ab, both will work in the home as this maximizes their combined product. Along segment be, the husband will be working in the market at his higher wage rate. It will now be optimal for the wife to replace her husband's home time. Each additional hour that she replaces allows the husband to work one more hour in the market without changing the leisure of either. Segment be in panel C will have the slope of the husband's wage rate, and Hh_b will be the same length as $h_b h_e$ because the husband's home time will have been entirely replaced.

Along segment ef, the husband will continue to work in the market and the wife will work on both her own and her husband's home production curves. She will not enter the market until her marginal product on both home production curves has fallen to equal her wage rate. Both husband and wife will be in the market after this point, along segment fg.

In the equilibrium (given a household utility function) shown in panel C, the wife does not work in the market. The "gains" from specialization are shown as the shaded area. These gains can be measured by segment be, which will be longer the higher the husband's wage rate and the more productive the wife's home time. The segment to the left of e will be longer the more productive the wife is in the home and the more easily substitutable her home time is for her husband's home time. It can also be seen from panel C that as the wife's wage is increased, point f moves to the right. As the wife's wage rises to equal her husband's level, the gains from specialization are reduced.

Panel D shows the combined case for households with land. Curve $abc'd$ is the simple combination of the single-person household cases. Curve $aefgh$ is based on specialization. Here the specialization begins immediately because of the presumption that the husband is more productive on the farm. In segment ae, the husband works on the farm only and the wife is replacing her husband's home time up to the point where the marginal productivity of her home time equals the marginal productivity of her farm time and the marginal productivity of her husband's home time. She may not fully replace his home time at point e. In segment ef, the husband enters the market and the wife replaces both his farm time and his home time. Again, because she is less productive on the farm this is a partial replacement. Along segment fg, the wife continues to work on the farm and in the home and to replace some of her husband's farm time. At point g, where the marginal productivity of her home and farm time has fallen to equal her wage rate, she will enter the market but will not have fully replaced the husband's farm time. Gains from specialization are indicated by the shaded area.

Appendix B

COMPARISON OF "RECALL" AND "OBSERVATION" DATA

Comparing the two sets of data presents problems, because the "recall" data were recorded in hours per week and the "observation" data were recorded in minutes per day. Transforming the recall data into minutes per day may be reasonable for home production time, but similar treatment of market production time could be misleading, since there are not necessarily 7 workdays per week in the various market occupations. In addition, since the recall data were collected from the wife of the household, who might have seen her husband leaving for work in the morning and returning at night but who did not actually observe how much he worked during the day, the market production of fathers is likely to be overstated in the recall data, whereas that of the mothers is likely to be more consistent for both data sets. Table B3-1 appears to bear this out to some extent, as use of the recall method resulted in reporting of a substantially higher level of market production time for fathers. The clear consensus of both the field staff and the researchers associated with the Laguna project is that the observation data are highly accurate and not subject to significant bias. Accordingly, we may interpret differences between the two data sets as reflecting biases in the recall collection method.

The recall method may also overstate the home production time of mothers. The major discrepancy between the two methods, however, is the drastic understatement of the market production time of children. The observation method measured more than three

TABLE B3-1 COMPARISON OF RECALL AND OBSERVATION DATA
ON TIME BUDGETS OF LAGUNA RURAL HOUSEHOLD MEMBERS (HOURS PER DAY)

Activity	Recall			Observation		
	Father	Mother	Children	Father	Mother	Children
1975 Survey						
Market Production						
Wage employment	4.40	1.40	1.40	2.71	1.14	.78
Farming	1.80	.10	.10	2.60	.82	2.52
Livestock raising	1.40	.60	.20	.70	.28	.57
Fishing	.20	.00	.00	.25	.01	.22
Income-earning home production	.40	.40	.20	.09	.16	.10
Other	—	—	—	.51	.14	.37
Total	8.20	2.50	1.90	6.86	2.55	4.56
Home Production						
Child care	.20	1.70	.60	.41	2.11	.97
Food preparation	.20	3.60	.70	.41	2.06	.84
Other	.20	3.00	1.30	.47	2.27	11.55
Total	.60	8.30	2.60	1.29	7.44	13.36[a]

(continued)

TABLE B3-1 *Continued*

	Recall			Observation		
Activity	Father	Mother	Children	Father	Mother	Children
Leisure						
Personal care	—	—	—	8.48	9.31	37.48
Recreation	—	—	—	4.23	3.77	14.16
Other	—	—	—	.89	.96	3.11
Total	15.20	12.90	91.60	13.60	14.04	54.75
	1977 Resurvey					
Market Production						
Wage employment	2.33	.49		3.31	1.92	
Farming	1.10	.50		2.49	.62	
Livestock raising	—	—		.12	.15	
Other	—	—		.84	.71	
Total	3.44	1.06		6.76	3.40	
Home Production						
Child care	.42	1.62		.17	1.60	
Food preparation	.21	2.90		.24	1.70	
Other	.59	1.80		.77	2.66	
Total	1.22	6.32		1.18	5.96	

NOTE: Only a few market production activities were identified in the 1977 resurvey. Leisure time was computed only as a residual in the recall data.

[a]This figure includes time spent by children in school or doing schoolwork (9.77 hours per day). The corresponding figure using recall data does not include this because class or school time was classified as leisure.

times as much market production time for all children as reported under the recall method. Parents apparently have a tendency to view children's work on the farm as leisure or as a training activity.

The Laguna resurvey, which included many of the original respondent households of the direct observation phase plus some new households, also generated time data using both methods. The recall questions in the resurvey were revised to improve the accuracy of reporting. Leisure was still calculated as a residual. The bottom part of Table B3-1 shows that in the resurvey, the home production time of both husband and wife collected by the recall method does not differ significantly from the home production time generated by the direct observation method. This implies a gain in accuracy with the revision of the interview questions. The market production time obtained by using the recall method, however, was understated for both fathers and mothers.

Notes

1. The total recorded time may also be less than 24 hours per day, depending on whether time spent outside the home was fully reported. No time component was calculated as a residual in the observation data.

2. Gronau estimated the marginal productivity function of employed and nonemployed women. Integrating the function yields the value of home production:

$$x_H = f(H) \int_0^H f'(y)dy = (a_0 - a_{1y} + a_zZ) \, dy$$

3. It is useful to clarify the distinction between technology and home capital. Some technology is embodied in home capital, but much is not. There are many types of home technology improvement that do not require the purchase of new home capital items.

4. These models postulate that household-produced goods are arguments in household utility functions. Production of these goods utilizes market goods and the home production time of household members. Maximizing utility subject to the full-income constraint implies that the household acts as a cost-minimizing firm in the production of household goods.

5. This is a critical assumption as it implies that the mix of home-produced and market-produced goods does not affect the productivity of home production time. When households have land and farm production occurs, this is not as critical.

6. We are presuming here that home time is not sold.

7. This labor market may be for work on other farms.

8. The relative shapes of the home and combined curves will determine the relative displacement effects on home time and farm time.

4. The Compatibility of Child Care with Market and Nonmarket Activities: Preliminary Evidence from Malaysia

Julie DaVanzo and Donald Lye Poh Lee

Gary S. Becker's (1965) seminal paper on time allocation[1] formalized the treatment of time costs as a component of the "full price" of all commodities produced by individuals. This generalization of the traditional labor-leisure choice model recognized that the alternatives open to an individual were those of market work, home production, and leisure. This approach offers new insights for the analysis of the female labor supply because in most societies many women are heavily committed to household production. The division of a woman's time between market work and home production depends on her (potential) market wage rate, her productivity in the home, and the price of available substitutes for her time in the home. Thus, an understanding of the variables affecting women's home production should contribute to improved analyses of the female labor supply.

Many analyses of the female labor supply are based on the assumption that market work is incompatible with household production—particularly child care—but that the degree of incompatibility is not so great in developing countries as it is in the more developed ones. This assumption, however, is rarely explicitly investigated.

In this essay, time budget data from the Malaysian Family Life Survey[2] are used to investigate household demand for time to be devoted to housework, intrahousehold allocation of time to these activities, and the compatibility of these activities and various market activities with child care. These data afford a unique opportunity to examine this last topic, for they indicate whether children of various ages accompany the mother when she performs market and out-of-

Note: The authors wish to thank Terry Fain for his very capable programming assistance and Bill Butz, John Cogan, and Arleen Leibowitz for their helpful comments.

The research on which this essay is based was performed by its authors during a collaborative visit to the Rand Corporation in Santa Monica, California, by Donald L. P. Lee, a member of the Faculty of Economics and Administration, University of Malaya, between November 1977 and January 1978. That visit was funded by the Office of Population of the Agency for International Development, under Contract No. AID/PHA-1057 with the Rand Corporation.

home nonmarket tasks. Among the questions addressed in this chapter are the following:

- How do family size and composition and the presence of modern labor-saving devices affect the amount of housework done?
- How do the wages of household members affect their allocation of time to various household tasks?
- With what activities and in what settings are husbands and children most likely to help?
- Which home activities lose most of the mother's attention when she enters the labor force?
- Which types of market and nonmarket activities are most compatible with child care? How does this compatibility vary with the age of the children?
- How does the presence of small children affect the efficiency with which a mother performs a particular task?
- All other things being equal, is the amount of time that a woman devotes to housework or child care positively or negatively related to her education?

The analyses presented here must be regarded as preliminary. They are primarily descriptive, use relatively simple statistical techniques (cross-tabulations and ordinary least squares regressions), and do not address some important questions (e.g., what types of women take their children with them when they perform various market and nonmarket activities?). The essay begins with a discussion of the underlying conceptual framework. This is followed by a description of the data used in the study, an analysis of the empirical results, and a summary with suggestions for further research.

CONCEPTUAL FRAMEWORK

In this section, we briefly sketch the Becker model of time allocation within the household that is the basis for this research.

The household is viewed as consuming "commodities," such as meals or clean clothes, that its members produce by combining their time inputs with market goods. Household members can either devote their time to this type of nonmarket production, or they can sell their time on the labor market and earn a wage. The household members will allocate their time and their expenditures on market goods in a way that will produce that combination of commodities that results in maximum utility.

An important determinant of a household's "demand" for a given commodity, say, clean clothes, is the number of persons in the household.[3] Age composition of the household is another important influence, as persons of different ages have different preferences or requirements (e.g., the household's demand for child care will be greater the more children there are in the family, and probably the younger they are).

In equilibrium, the household devotes to the production of each commodity the number of hours necessary to produce the amount of the commodity it demands. Each person will devote more hours to the production of those commodities in which he or she has a comparative advantage relative to production of other commodities and to other household members. Persons who are relatively more productive (i.e., can command higher wages) in the labor market should devote more time to labor market activities and less time to nonmarket activities, compared with persons who are relatively more productive in nonmarket activities.

A number of factors might affect an individual's productivity in performing an activity. For example, more highly educated persons may have higher productivity in all types of activities; this increased efficiency may be neutral across activities, or it may be greater in certain pursuits. (A more highly educated woman may be able to type more letters and wash more clothes per hour than a less well educated woman, but the relative difference may be greater for letters than for clothes, in which case we would expect to see her spend more time in market activities than her less well educated counterpart.)

One factor that may affect a woman's efficiency in performing certain tasks is whether her children accompany her while she performs these tasks. Other things being equal, we would expect women who have children along to be less efficient in an absolute sense (i.e., produce less) compared with women who do not have them along, although the presence of children might affect relative efficiencies in various activities differently.

It seems reasonable to assume that mothers are most likely to have their children accompany them when they are performing activities in which the child's presence impairs the mother's efficiency least, and that they are least likely to take them along when the opposite is true.[4] In the former situation, the efficiency loss is likely to be less than the cost of making alternative child care arrangements; in the latter situation, the cost of child care is likely to be less than the efficiency loss.

DATA USED IN THE STUDY

The empirical analyses presented here use data from the Round I Female Time Budget of the Malaysian Family Life Survey (although a few explanatory variables derive from other Round I instruments). This time-budget questionnaire was administered to ever-married women less than 50 years old and elicited information on their time use in the 4-month period preceding the interview.[5] For all market activities and for nonmarket activities of interest, including all jobs, unpaid family work, schooling, training, cottage industry, housework, and child care (but excluding recreational activities and sleep), the questionnaire documents the number of hours spent at the activity in the last 7 days during which it was performed, the number of weeks the activity was performed in the 4 months preceding the survey (a 17-week period), the rate of pay (if any) in cash and/or in kind for the activity, the distance from home to the place of the activity, the amounts of help received and from whom, and the presence of children aged 10 years or under while the activity was being performed. The Female Time Budget documents the time use of female respondents and of their children living with them.[6]

EMPIRICAL RESULTS

Two types of empirical analyses are presented in this section. The first is concerned with the compatibility of market and nonmarket activities with child care. It includes tabular information concerning the likelihood that women with children of particular ages will have these children along when they perform these activities, by type of activity and age of the children. We also consider how the presence of children affects the number of hours that the woman spends performing the activity.

In the second type of analysis, we estimate ordinary least squares regression equations that will explain variations in the amount of time the household as a whole devotes to five household activities (washing and ironing clothes, shopping, preparing meals, cleaning, and caring for children), as a function of the size and age structure of the household, the presence of modern labor-saving devices (such as washing machines), the area of residence, and husband's and wife's education. These equations specify the determinants of the total time spent in providing to household members clean clothes, prepared meals, a clean house, and child care, all of which households want and can provide for themselves with varying degrees of quality, completeness, and intensity depending on household income and tastes. These equations may thus be interpreted as equations of derived demand for the labor services devoted to each activity.[7]

We also estimate equations that will explain the numbers (and, in some instances, shares) of hours that the wife, husband, and children devote to these activities. These time inputs are a function of the explanatory variables just discussed, as well as of some variables measuring the relative opportunity costs of the time of various household members, since we have hypothesized that these costs should be a major influence on *intrahousehold* allocations of time.[8]

Compatibility of Market Activities with Child Care

The percentage distribution of jobs held by women with children aged 10 years or younger who have them along when they perform various market activities is shown in Table 4.1, column 3. In nearly one-third of the sales and production jobs (mostly weaving, food and beverage processing, and dressmaking) filled by women who have children aged 10 years or younger, the women have (some of) their children with them when they work. On the basis of this crude measure, sales and production occupations appear to be the most compatible with child care—perhaps because these activities can often be performed at home—whereas other occupations (including agricultural jobs) are less compatible. The lesser compatibility of agricultural activities with child care is a bit surprising. It is often presumed that child care and market work are more compatible in developing countries than in developed countries precisely because more women in developing countries engage in agricultural activities, which are assumed to be very compatible with child care.

Future analyses of the situation in which children accompany the mother when she performs various market activities should seek to explain (1) which women "choose" to take their children with them and whether their decision is affected by the distance of the place of work from home; and (2) how these considerations may affect occupational choice. The percentages in columns 1 and 2 of Table 4.1 do suggest that women with young children are less likely to have occupations, such as clerical or professional positions, that are relatively incompatible with child care (although the difference between the percentages in columns 1 and 2 is statistically significant only for clerical positions).

TABLE 4.1 COMPATABILITY OF VARIOUS OCCUPATIONS WITH CHILD CARE: PERCENTAGE DISTRIBUTION OF JOBS HELD BY WOMEN WITH AND WITHOUT CHILDREN

Occupation	(1) Percentage of Jobs Filled by Women with No Children Aged ≤ 10 Yrs.[a]	(2) Percentage of Jobs Filled by Women with Children Aged ≤ 10 Yrs.[b]	(3) Percentage of Column 2 Jobs Filled by Women Who Are Accompanied by Their Children
Professionals	3.0	2.0	5.9
Managers	.3	.1	0
Clerical	2.3*	.5	0
Sales	8.4	7.4	31.8
Service	2.4	2.5	14.3
Agriculture	69.0	72.6	15.8
Production	14.5	14.8	32.0

[a]Since many women report more than one market activity, the number of job observations exceeds the number of women. Percentages reported in this column are based on 297 job observations. Number of women = 189.

[b]Percentages based on 1,657 job observations. Number of women = 1,073.

*Significantly greater (at the .05 level) than the corresponding percentage for women with children aged ≤ 10. No other differences are significant at or above .05 level.

Table 4.2 presents a more detailed breakdown of the three broad occupational groups (agriculture, production, and sales) to which Malaysian women with children aged 10 years or under (and, indeed, Malaysian women in general) are most likely to belong. (Sample sizes are too small to permit similar comparisons for other occupational groups.) We consider how the likelihood that the child will accompany the mother when she performs the activity in question varies with the age of the child, and how the child's accompanying the mother and the child's age are related to the number of hours the mother devotes to the activity over the 4-month reference period. (Full-time work would be approximately 680 hours, that is, 40 hours/week × 17 weeks.)

If we consider the proportions of women accompanied by children who are under 11 years old, we see that for all three occupations, women with children aged 2 to 5 years are the most likely to have children accompany them when they perform these market activities. For example, 31 percent of women who perform agricultural activities and have children 2 to 5 years old (and no other children younger than 10) bring these children with them to work. The corresponding figures for women with children under 2 or 6 to 10 years old are 17 percent and 15 percent, respectively. Similar differences exist for women who have production and sales occupations. Even when women have children in two different age-groups, they are more likely to be accompanied by one or more of their children when they have a child aged 2 to 5 years. Mothers of children aged 6 to 10 years are typically least likely to be accompanied by their children, presumably because the children are better able to take care of themselves, or because they are in school.

Next we consider the number of hours that women devote to these three market activities and how these hours vary by type of activity and the ages of a woman's children, and by whether these children are with her when she works. The presence of children may affect the number of hours a woman devotes to an activity because it affects her efficiency in performing that activity. If a mother is less efficient (i.e., produces less output) during the hours when a child accompanies her than she is during the same number of hours spent without the child, her marginal productivity and hence her wage rate will be reduced. Whether she works more or fewer hours as a result of reduced wages will depend on whether the income or substitution effect predominates.

First, we note from Table 4.2, column 2, that for each child age category for which adequate data are available, women spend more than twice as many hours in sales occupations as they spend in agricultural or production activities. Second, we consider how the ages of children affect the number of hours that a woman works in these three activities when none of those children accompany her (see Table 4.2, column 4). In agricultural occupations, even when the children do not accompany their mother, women with infants generally work fewer hours than other women engaged in the same occupation. The sample sizes for the other occupations are too small to permit valid comparisons, but they do

TABLE 4.2 AVERAGE TIME WOMEN SPEND IN PARTICULAR MARKET ACTIVITIES, BY TYPE OF FAMILY

Type of Family	Market Activity	All Women		Women Not Accompanied by Children		Women Accompanied by Children	
		(1) Number of Women	(2) Average Hours	(3) Percentage of Row Total	(4) Average Hours	(5) Percentage of Row Total	(6) Average Hours
No children aged ≤ 10	Agriculture	205	224.5				
	Production	43	156.1				
	Sales	25	636.5				
Children aged < 2 yrs. only	Agriculture	52	190.8	83	209.4	17	101.9
	Production	14	273.3	57	—	43	—
	Sales	8	—	75	—	25	—
Children aged 2–5 yrs. only	Agriculture	144	239.3	69	278.6	31	152.8
	Production	28	169.9	36	—	64	173.2
	Sales	8	—	63	—	37	—

Children aged 6–10 yrs. only	Agriculture	302	231.4	85	229.1	15	244.5
	Production	50	242.2	82	273.8	18	—
	Sales	31	556.7	77	474.6	23	—
Children aged < 2 and 2–5 yrs.	Agriculture	79	204.2	68	230.6	32	147.2
	Production	32	144.6	41	213.5	59	96.7
	Sales	10	340.3	50	—	50	—
Children aged < 2 and 6–10 yrs.	Agriculture	36	177.1	86	156.3	14	—
	Production	12	181.3	50	—	50	—
	Sales	12	614.8	42	—	58	—
Children aged 2–5 and 6–10 yrs.	Agriculture	391	237.7	72	278.0	28	133.4
	Production	63	148.8	52	182.2	48	112.6
	Sales	39	494.0	36	339.5	64	580.5
Children aged < 2, 2–5, and 6–10 yrs.	Agriculture	199	185.9	73	209.5	27	122.5
	Production	47	156.0	30	58.1	70	197.5
	Sales	15	297.2	27	—	73	—

NOTE: Hours data are for a 4-month reference period (17 weeks). Dash (—) indicates sample size < 10.

suggest that even when the children do not accompany the mother, women with children aged 10 or under spend less time in sales activities, but often spend more time in production activities, compared with women in those occupations who have no children aged 10 or under. Having three (or more) children aged 10 or under, all in different age-groups, does appear to cause a substantial reduction (to approximately 3½ hours a week) in the amount of time devoted to production activities.

Third, we consider how the presence of children affects mothers' hours of work (see Table 4.2, column 6). In most instances, women whose children accompany them when they perform agricultural and production activities work fewer hours on the average than those with similarly aged children who do not accompany the mother while she performs these tasks. The presence of younger children appears to reduce the number of hours worked more than does the presence of older children; in fact, women working in agriculture who have children aged 6 to 10 years often work *more* hours when those children go along. Sample sizes are too small to permit similar comparisons for other occupational groups, although the data suggest that women with sales occupations who take children along work more hours than those who do not.

Compatibility of Nonmarket Activities with Child Care

Table 4.3 presents figures for two housework activities (shopping and washing) usually performed outside the home in Malaysia. Here, the number and ages of children may affect the household's demand for the commodities (clean clothes and groceries) produced by time inputs to washing and shopping—more children mean more clothes to be washed. In addition, the presence of children while the activity is being performed may increase the amount of time it takes the mother to produce a given amount of a commodity and hence may affect the quantity she decides to produce. We cannot predict a priori whether women whose children accompany them will spend more or less time in accomplishing these tasks than otherwise similar women whose children do not accompany them.

With regard to the likelihood that the mother will be accompanied by children (see Table 4.3, column 5), only mothers of children in the age-group 6 to 10 years are more likely to take along children when they go shopping than when they do washing, perhaps because the former activity is more likely to be away from home than the latter. In both of these activities, mothers of children aged 2 to 5 years only are most likely and mothers of children aged 6 to 10 years are least likely to be accompanied by their children. Women with children in all three age-groups considered here are the most likely to take children along when they do their washing.

Surprisingly, women with no children under age 11 spend more hours washing clothes than women with young children (regardless of whether those children

TABLE 4.3 AVERAGE TIME WOMEN SPEND IN PARTICULAR HOUSEHOLD ACTIVITIES, BY TYPE OF FAMILY

Type of Family	Household Activity	All Women		Women Not Accompanied by Children		Women Accompanied by Children	
		(1) Number of Women	(2) Average Hours	(3) Percentage of Row Total	(4) Average Hours	(5) Percentage of Row Total	(6) Average Hours
No children aged ≤ 10 yrs.	Washing	189	213.8				
	Shopping	189	58.9				
Children aged < 2 yrs. only	Washing	86	123.0	56	115.8	44	132.0
	Shopping	86	54.9	66	45.2	34	74.0
Children aged 2–5 yrs. only	Washing	126	130.2	53	106.9	47	156.6
	Shopping	126	63.5	60	48.3	40	86.6
Children aged 6–10 yrs. only	Washing	242	133.5	88	133.0	12	137.2
	Shopping	242	69.5	84	66.5	16	85.0
Children aged < 2 and 2–5 yrs.	Washing	102	130.3	62	128.5	38	133.2
	Shopping	102	63.0	64	50.9	36	84.3
Children aged < 2 and 6–10 yrs.	Washing	43	120.3	75	106.5	25	160.4
	Shopping	43	55.2	88	52.8	12	73.4
Children aged 2–5 and 6–10 yrs.	Washing	296	142.0	55	132.0	45	154.3
	Shopping	296	75.3	61	59.3	39	100.5
Children aged < 2, 2–5, and 6–10 yrs.	Washing	178	159.6	50	146.2	50	173.0
	Shopping	178	53.7	65	46.3	35	67.5

NOTE: Hours data are for a 4-month reference period (17 weeks).

accompany the mother), although the former may have older children (a fact that we control for later in this chapter in our regression analyses). Among women with children under age 11, women with children aged 6 to 10 typically spend relatively more time washing and shopping (see Table 4.3, column 2).

Of the women with young children, those whose children accompany them spend more time performing these activities than women whose children do not accompany them. The relative differences are nearly always greater for shopping than for washing. For both activities, the efficiency of mothers of children aged 2 to 5 years, the group most likely to be accompanied by their children, is most impaired (i.e., hours of work are increased most), whereas the efficiency of mothers of children aged 6 to 10 only, the group least likely to be accompanied, is least affected.

These results on compatibility of nonmarket activities with child care are generally consistent with those in the preceding section on market activities: (1) Mothers are less likely to be accompanied by children as the average distance from the home to the place where the activity is conducted increases, assuming that washing takes place closer to home than shopping and that agricultural and production activities take place closer to home than sales activities. (2) Mothers of children aged 2 to 5 years are the most likely, and mothers of children aged 6 to 10 years are the least likely, to be accompanied by their children. Women tend to devote less time to market activities when their children go along, but they tend to spend more time in nonmarket activities when accompanied by children.

Variations in Time Inputs to Nonmarket Production

Next we turn to regressions explaining the number of hours the wife devotes to the nonmarket activities just discussed (washing clothes and shopping). We also estimate equations that will explain variations in the number of hours the household as a whole spends on these activities (household "demand") and equations that will explain the number of hours that husbands and children devote to helping women with these tasks. We then estimate similar equations that will explain variations in the numbers of hours that the household as a whole, the wife, the husband, and the (older) children spend preparing and cooking meals, cleaning house, and caring for children.

Before analyzing the regressions, let us consider the mean number of hours that households and their members devote to the five nonmarket activities considered in the regressions (see Table 4.4). Child care is the activity to which the household and its various members devote the most time (approximately 48 hours per week for the household), followed by cooking and preparing meals (approximately 28 hours per week). Washing, cleaning, and shopping each take from approximately 9 to approximately 13 hours a week.

Wives contribute about two-thirds of all hours that the households devote to these nonmarket activities; children devote nearly 20 percent and husbands de-

TABLE 4.4   MEAN NUMBER OF HOURS HOUSEHOLDS SPEND IN NONMARKET ACTIVITIES

Activity	Entire Household[a]		Wife		Husband		Children	
Washing and ironing	216	(12)	151	(13)	1.76	(1.1)	54.4	(15)
			(70)		(.8)		(25)	
Shopping	151	(8)	80.1	(6.7)	55.8	(35.0)	20.6	(5.7)
			(53)		(37.0)		(14)	
Cooking and preparing meals	480	(26)	313	(26)	7.43	(4.7)	100.0	(28)
			(65)		(1.5)		(21)	
Cleaning house	202	(11)	132	(11)	4.09	(2.6)	71.3	(20)
			(65)		(2.0)		(35)	
Child care	817	(44)	522	(44)	89.9	(57.0)	116.0	(32)
			(64)		(11.0)		(14)	
Total	1,866		1,198		159		362	
			(64)		(8.5)		(19)	

NOTE: Numbers in parentheses below hours figures are percentages of the row total. Numbers in parentheses to the right of the hours figures are column percentages. The mean number of hours for the entire household will be less than the sum of the wife's, husband's and children's hours if other household or nonhousehold members help with the activity. For shopping and housecleaning, the sum of the average wife's, husband's and children's hours slightly exceeds the number of hours for the entire household because of round-off error. Hours data are for a 4-month reference period (17 weeks).
[a]Includes nonhousehold help.

vote less than 10 percent. Both in absolute terms and relative to total household hours, husbands' contributions are greatest in child care (about 5 hours a week) and in shopping (3½ hours a week). Malaysian husbands contribute about three-eighths of the family's total shopping hours but give little help with washing, cooking, and cleaning.

About 21 hours of nonmarket activity are performed each week by the children of average households. Children help at least 1 hour per week with each of the five listed activities. Sixty percent of their time is spent caring for siblings and helping with cooking. Another 20 percent is spent helping to clean the house; they contribute approximately one-third of all household hours to this task. They also contribute one-fourth of all household hours spent washing and ironing.

Nonhousehold members (including paid helpers) and household members other than the wife, husband, and children frequently help with child care and cooking. The total number of hours spent by the wife, husband, and children for each of these two activities is less than 90 percent of the total number of hours that each activity is performed for the household.

Total Number of Hours Devoted to Nonmarket Activities ("Demand")

Household size and composition appear to be the most important determinants of the total number of hours that the household as a whole devotes to nonmarket activities (see Tables 4.5–4.9), with the exception of shopping (where race and location of residence are the main correlates). For example, we see in Table 4.8 that it is the number of persons in the household, rather than the number of rooms per se, that affects the number of hours that household members spend in cleaning.

It is interesting that wives spend significantly more time cleaning when their houses are provided by their employers. Household capital also affects time allocation. For example, households with washing machines (1.8 percent of the sample) spend nearly 25 percent less time washing clothes, although the difference is not statistically significant (see Table 4.5). No other house characteristic (e.g., type of water supply) appears to affect the number of hours that household members devote to household chores,[9] although husbands do more of the family shopping in households with an automobile (see Table 4.6).

The number of additional hours devoted to a chore due to the presence of an additional household member is positively related to that member's age with regard to cooking (Table 4.7), and negatively related to that member's age with regard to child care time (Table 4.9). An (additional) infant increases the total number of household hours devoted to child care by about 31 hours per week. The same infant increases washing hours (Table 4.5) by just over half an hour per week and meal preparation hours (Table 4.7) by approximately 2 hours a week. Children aged 2 to 5 years appear to require 12½ additional hours of child care (Table 4.9) each week when other variables are held constant; children aged 6 to 10 appear to require about half that amount.[10] Households that include nonrelative adults other than servants (typically boarders) devote considerably more time to child care (Table 4.9) and meal preparation (Table 4.7) than households without such persons. Households with children in school spend less time on child care (Table 4.9) than households with similarly aged children not in school, presumably because schools are a type of child care.

An additional servant will increase a household's washing time (Table 4.5) considerably, but not the time devoted to the other activities considered, suggesting that servants' main contribution is washing clothes and that, for a given family size and composition, households that hire servants may be those with relatively greater demands for clean clothes.[11]

Husbands' and wives' education has little effect on the amount of time allocated to most household activities, although we do find that households significantly increase the amount of time devoted to washing clothes (Table 4.5) the more highly educated the husband is, and they significantly increase cooking (Table 4.7) and cleaning (Table 4.8) time the more highly educated the wife is. The reason for the former finding may be that more highly educated husbands are likely to have jobs for which clean and pressed "white collars" are required. When family composition is held constant, households headed by highly educated husbands and wives spend no more (and no less) time caring for their children than households in which the parents have less education.[12]

TABLE 4.5 DETERMINANTS OF TIME SPENT WASHING AND IRONING

Explanatory Variables	Household Hours (Coefficient)	Wife's Hours (Coefficient)	Children's Hours (Coefficient)	Wife's Proportion of Total Hours (Coefficient)
Household Composition				
Children aged < 2 yrs.	10.34	-5.19	-1.22	-.053***
Children aged 2–5 yrs.	-1.10	-10.63	9.40*	-.012
Children aged 6–10 yrs.	16.19**	5.57	7.15	.001
Children aged 10–14 yrs.	25.82***	17.40	25.96***	-.065***
Children aged 15+ yrs.	37.58***	8.23	51.00***	-.110***
Relatives aged 15–49[a]	30.44***	14.80*	-6.90	-.049***
Relatives aged 50+[a]	27.25***	30.48**	7.98	-.033**
Other adults[b]	-34.26	-25.56	8.64	-.125*
Servants[b]	128.69**	-12.48	-27.24	-.205**
Dummy = 1 if woman has husband,[b,c]	31.19	65.79	-16.25	.185**
Children in school[d]	-7.99	-6.70	-11.78	.015
Area of Household Residence				
Metropolitan[e]	1.34	38.59*	-12.97	.001
Other town[f]	-30.03**	10.54	-15.09	.006
East coast	6.75	-2.18	.90	.023
Education (years of schooling)				
Wife	.73	-.93	-.28	-.011***
Husband	5.51***	-1.42	.77	-.006**
Race				
Chinese	-56.45***	-74.51***	-24.14**	-.003
Indian	-5.85	-32.02	25.48*	-.013
Other than Chinese, Indian, or Malaysian	48.72	-27.74	48.06	-.109*

(continued)

TABLE 4.5 *Continued*

Explanatory Variables	Household Hours (Coefficient)	Wife's Hours (Coefficient)	Children's Hours (Coefficient)	Wife's Proportion of Total Hours (Coefficient)
Month of Interview				
August	15.53	90.54*	37.11*	.061*
September	3.65	54.97	−28.21	.106***
October	−28.47	2.00	−7.14	.065**
November	−37.68**	18.95	−22.56	.101***
Wife's Age	.72	−3.33**	.01	−.004***
Children Accompanying Mother Washing				
Aged < 2 yrs.	18.77	37.59	—	.041*
Aged 2–5 yrs.	14.07*	−2.93	—	.038***
Aged 6–10 yrs.	−8.15	54.62**	—	.043**
Water Supply and Washing Machine				
Dummy = 1 if household has washing machine	−50.87	−19.72	−11.60	.045
Water supply scale[g]	−1.18	1.09	5.64*	.005
Wife's Work outside Home				
Distance from home to work[h]	—	−3.50	8.70**	−.023***
No. hours[i]	—	−.03	.02**	−.001***
Wage Rates of Family Members[j]				
Wife	—	−3.96	−2.71	−.003
Children (average)	—	−14.70	−4.06	.029***
Husband	—	−3.07	1.53	−.015***

Constant	158.51	248.98	−6.82	1.154
R^2	.147	.036	.160	.345
$\bar{R}^2$	.127	.009	.138	.326
Mean of dependent variable	216.1	151.0	54.4	.734

[a]Does not include husband, wife, or their children.

[b]Category includes all adults other than relatives and children of the husband and wife; hence it includes the husband and wife as well as servants and a few boarders and lodgers. Therefore, the total effect for husband and servants is the coefficient of those variables plus the coefficient of "other adults."

[c]This dummy equals 1 if a husband is listed as a household member in the household roster.

[d]To compare the effect of having children in school with that of having no children at all, add this coefficient to that of the appropriate "children" variable.

[e]A dummy that equals 1 if the household is located in one of the three largest cities in Malaysia—Kuala Lumpur, Ipoh, and Penang.

[f]A dummy that equals 1 if the household is located in a town or village (other than the three largest cities in Malaysia) whose population was more than 10,000 in 1967 or in an area of less than 10,000 where it is estimated that at least 50 percent of the worker force is engaged in nonagricultural occupations.

[g]A scale that = 0 if household (HH) has no piped water; 1 if HH has piped water outside the home and not exclusive to it; 2 if HH has piped water outside the home exclusive to the HH; 3 if HH has indoor piped water, not exclusive to this HH; and 4 if HH has indoor piped water exclusively for its use.

[h]A scale that = 0 if wife does not work or works at home; 1 if her place of work is less than 1 mile from home; 2 if distance to work is 1 to 3 miles; and 3 if distance to work is 3 miles or more.

[i]Number of hours wife worked for pay (in cash or in kind) in the 4-month reference period.

[j]Hourly wage rate (includes payments in kind, as well as in cash).

***Significant at .01 level (two-tailed test).

**Significant at .05 level (two-tailed test).

*Significant at .10 level (two-tailed test).

TABLE 4.6 DETERMINANTS OF TIME SPENT SHOPPING

Explanatory Variables	Total Household Hours (Coefficient)	Wife's Hours (Coefficient)	Husband's Hours (Coefficient)	Wife's Proportion (Coefficient)	Husband's Proportion (Coefficient)
Household Composition					
Children aged < 2 yrs.	-4.52	24.60	12.70	-.049	.039**
Children aged 2–5 yrs.	-2.47	-14.51	-5.33	-.009	-.004
Children aged 6–10 yrs.	6.44	4.11	7.02	-.001	.003
Children aged 10–14 yrs.	11.36*	2.01	-6.78	-.010	-.020**
Children aged 15+ yrs.	6.74	11.45	3.79	-.009	-.038
Relatives aged 15–49[a]	11.80**	-1.29	-7.05	-.025	-.038***
Relatives aged 50+[a]	9.48	-8.19	5.39	-.099	-.029**
Other adults[b]	18.40	26.67	-6.48	-.022	-.012
Servants[b]	-22.69	61.96	129.70	.001	-.043
Dummy = 1 if woman has husband[b,c]	-11.01	-14.26	56.75	-.163	.288***
Area of Household Residence					
Metropolitan[d]	.08	74.45	4.18	.174	-.103***
Other town[e]	-2.39	30.06	6.18	.043	-.035*
East coast	62.82***	18.20	-3.80	.055	-.039
Education (years of schooling)					
Wife	-.088	.97	-.64	-.001	.0010
Husband	.470	-2.29	.33	-.004	.0003
Race					
Chinese	-34.41**	-19.05	-52.50	.166	-.153***
Indian	-34.35*	2.48	14.34	-.096	.128***
Other than Chinese, Indian, or Malaysian	-91.46*	-29.41	-59.50	.045	-.159**
Month of Interview					
August	7.62	106.32	24.35	.055	-.038
September	22.55	30.72	26.95	-.034	.064*
October	-28.37	-13.16	8.46	-.050	.080*
November	12.71	-8.93	27.80	-.102	.089**
Wife's age	.25	-2.07	-.39	-.004	-.001
Children Accompanying Mother Shopping					
Aged < 2 yrs.	14.30	-25.10	—	.140	—
Aged 2–5 yrs.	31.08**	17.27	—	.081	—

Aged 6–10 yrs.	-.64	-4.97	—	.088	—
Other					
Cars owned by household	23.31	33.11	28.04	-.082	.055**
Dummy = 1 if household eats homegrown crops	33.91**	-13.24	15.48	.049	-.081***
Dummy = 1 if household eats homegrown animals	-20.49	-10.18	-6.04	.034	-.006
Dummy = 1 if household runs a food store or business	38.18	-8.36	18.27	-.128	.114
House quality scale[f]	-3.28	—	—	—	—
Wife's Work outside Home					
Distance from home to work[g]	—	-.33	-.07	.0040	.0130*
No. of hours[h]	—	.02	.02	-.0001	.0001***
Wage Rates of Family Members[i]					
Wife	—	-5.79	-3.62	.0001	.007
Children (average)	—	-6.53	-4.18	-.0060	-.007
Husband	—	-1.35	-.34	.0080	-.003
Constant	80.74	62.86	-3.38	.756	.049
R^2	.050	.026	.071	.234	.255
$\bar{R}^2$	.026	0	.047	.212	.235
Mean of dependent variable	151.1	80.1	55.8	.532	.281

[a]Does not include husband, wife, or their children.

[b]Category includes all adults other than relatives and children of the husband and wife; hence it includes the husband and wife as well as servants and a few boarders and lodgers. Therefore, the total effect for husband and servants is the coefficient of those variables plus the coefficient of "Other adults."

[c]This dummy equals 1 if a husband is listed as a household member in the household roster.

[d]A dummy that equals 1 if the household is located in one of the three largest cities in Malaysia—Kuala Lumpur, Ipoh, and Penang.

[e]A dummy that equals 1 if the household resides in a town or village (other than the three largest cities in Malaysia) whose population was more than 10,000 in 1967 or in an area of less than 10,000 where it is estimated that at least 50 percent of the work force is engaged in nonagricultural occupations.

[f]A scale ranging from 0 to 12, with a mean of 3.7, where higher values indicate better housing quality (that is, house has indoor piped water exclusively for its use, has walls of brick or concrete, has a shower or a bath, has an indoor flush toilet exclusively for this household's use, and has a high rooms-per-person ratio).

[g]A scale that = 0 if wife does not work or works at home; 1 if her place of work is less an 1 mile from home; 2 if distance to work is 1 to 3 miles; and 3 if distance to work is 3 miles or more.

[h]Number of hours wife worked for pay (in cash or in kind) in the 4-month reference period.

[i]Hourly wage rate (incluces payments in kind, as well as in cash).

***Significant at .01 leve.

**Significant at .05 level.

*Significant at .10 level.

TABLE 4.7 DETERMINANTS OF TIME SPENT PREPARING MEALS

Explanatory Variables	Total Household Hours (Coefficients)	Wife's Hours (Coefficients)	Children's Hours (Coefficients)	Wife's Proportion of Total Hours (Coefficients)
Household Composition				
Children aged < 2 yrs.	33.31**	41.29**	-2.40	-.015
Children aged 2-5 yrs.	35.09***	-6.66	14.08**	-.005
Children aged 6-10 yrs.	4.23	21.17**	7.94	-.012*
Children aged 10-14 yrs.	32.81**	10.61	36.40***	-.033***
Children aged 15+ yrs.	78.19***	-8.91	73.94***	-.085***
Relatives aged 15-49[a]	70.95***	-7.83	-6.23	-.076***
Relatives aged 50+[a]	88.79***	8.83	-3.28	-.093***
Other adults[b]	174.41**	110.16	-13.74	.081
Servants[b]	-58.42	-173.31*	-35.45	-.385***
Dummy = 1 if woman has husband[b,c]	-103.11	-73.87	40.04	-.091
Children in school[d]	22.22	—	—	—
Area of Household Residence				
Metropolitan[e]	-74.95***	50.56**	-28.70*	.016
Other town[f]	4.91	25.05	-18.22	.014
East coast	25.24	40.37	3.33	.026
Education (years of schooling)				
Wife	7.56**	-2.96	1.25	-.010***
Husband	1.22	1.41	2.38	-.0002
Race				
Chinese	-40.49*	-25.10	-9.45	-.002
Indian	85.33***	36.00	16.15	.012
Other than Chinese, Indian, Malaysian	-7.41	-61.41	123.58**	-.071
Month of Interview				
August	-146.85***	-9.54	-118.86***	.090***
September	-131.67***	6.05	-107.57***	.091***
October	-102.50***	-21.77	-66.22***	.040*
November	-76.93**	33.38	-62.41**	.066**

Wife's Age	2.42*	.68	1.61*	−.004***
Wife's Work outside Home				
Distance from home to work[g]	—	−10.07	.17	−.00001**
No. of hours[h]	—	−.095***	.042**	−.00010***
Wage Rates of Family Members[i]				
Wife	—	−7.07**	1.60	−.00001
Children (average)	—	−11.32	−4.42	.03900
Husband	—	−3.40	−2.23	.00200
Household Runs a Food-related Business (dummy)	−189.89	—	—	—
Constant	15.95	145.97	−11.75	.968
R^2	.188	.043	.228	.354
$\bar{R}^2$	.172	.021	.211	.340
Mean of dependent variable	480.0	313.0	100.0	.730

[a] Does not include husband, wife, or their children.

[b] Category includes all adults other than relatives and children of the husband and wife; hence it includes the husband and wife as well as servants and a few boarders and lodgers. Therefore, the total effect for husband and servants is the coefficient of those variables plus the coefficient of "Other adults."

[c] This dummy equals 1 if a husband is listed as a household member in the household roster.

[d] To compare the effect of having children in school with that of having no children at all, add this coefficient to that of the appropriate "children" variable.

[e] A dummy that equals 1 if the household is located in one of the three largest cities in Malaysia—Kuala Lumpur, Ipoh, and Penang.

[f] A dummy that equals 1 if the household is located in a town or village (other than the three largest cities in Malaysia) whose population was more than 10,000 in 1967 or in an area of less than 10,000 where it is estimated that at least 50 percent of the work force is engaged in nonagricultural occupations.

[g] A scale that = 0 if wife does not work or works at home; 1 if her place of work is less than 1 mile from home; 2 if distance to work is 1 to 3 miles; and 3 if distance to work is 3 miles or more.

[h] Number of hours wife worked for pay (in cash or in kind) in the 4-month reference period.

[i] Hourly wage rate (includes payments in kind, as well as in cash).

*** Significant at .01 level.
** Significant at .05 level.
* Significant at .10 level.

TABLE 4.8 DETERMINANTS OF TIME SPENT CLEANING

Explanatory Variables	Total Household Hours (Coefficients)	Wife's Hours (Coefficients)	Children's Hours (Coefficients)	Wife's Proportion of Total Hours (Coefficients)
Household Composition				
Children aged < 2 yrs.	16.76*	55.26***	15.66	-.022*
Children aged 2–5 yrs.	19.00***	11.64	23.31**	.0011
Children aged 6–10 yrs.	3.98	2.16	6.10	-.009
Children aged 10–14 yrs.	24.85***	4.36	26.81***	-.050***
Children aged 15+ yrs.	25.29***	-10.15	39.57***	-.091***
Relatives aged 15–49[a]	25.63***	-7.59	-9.23	-.066***
Relatives aged 50+[a]	24.03***	-7.55	-6.40	-.071***
Other adults[b]	57.24	-13.23	-2.43	-.039
Servants	-46.41	-38.39	-42.06	-.201**
Dummy = 1 if woman has husband[c]	-60.57	45.19	43.67	.014
Area of Household Residence				
Metropolitan[d]	6.12	28.34	16.36	.033*
Other town[e]	-5.41	-4.70	-14.31	.016
East coast	9.31	18.12	6.10	.039*
Education (years of schooling)				
Wife	4.36**	6.20**	6.23**	-.011***
Husband	2.08	-2.12	-1.61	.002
Race				
Chinese	-58.26***	-67.98***	-16.96	-.090***
Indian	2.58	-36.08	57.69*	-.021
Other than Chinese, Indian, or Malaysian	82.95**	-14.21	45.65	-.184***
Month of Interview				
August	-10.83	-18.02	13.68	.085**
September	-52.44**	-8.89	-78.98**	.125***
October	-53.94**	-58.29*	-52.14	.053*
November	-61.20***	-78.35**	-78.18**	.095***

Wife's Age	2.08**	2.19*	2.86**	-.003***
Characteristics of House				
House provided by employer	24.26*	69.17**	50.87*	-.010
No. of rooms	0.33	-2.47	-.94	.006
Wife's Work outside Home				
Distance from home to work[f]	—	-10.98	1.390	-.018**
No. of hours[g]	—	.014	.078***	-.0001***
Wage Rates of Family Members[h]				
Wife	—	-7.10	-6.56	-.003
Children (average)	—	-.33	3.84	.003
Husband	—	-1.60	-1.97	-.012***
Constant	29.46	84.43	-113.50	8.50
R^2	.113	.038	.075	.333
$\bar{R}^2$	.095	.014	.053	.317
Mean of dependent variable	202.0	132.0	71.0	.680

[a] Does not include husband, wife, or their children.

[b] Category includes all adults other than relatives and children of the husband and wife; hence it includes the husband and wife as well as servants and a few boarders and lodgers. Therefore, the total effect for husband and servants is the coefficient of those variables plus the coefficient of "Other adults."

[c] This dummy equals 1 if a husband is listed as a household member in the household roster.

[d] A dummy that equals 1 if the household resides in one of the three largest cities in Malaysia—Kuala Lumpur, Ipoh, and Penang.

[e] A dummy that equals 1 if the household is located in a town or village (other than the three largest cities in Malaysia) whose population was more than 10,000 in 1967 or in an area of less than 10,000 where it is estimated that at least 50 percent of the work force is engaged in nonagricultural occupations.

[f] A scale that = 0 if wife does not work or works at home; 1 if her place of work is less than 1 mile from home; 2 if distance to work is 1 to 3 miles; and 3 if distance to work is 3 miles or more.

[g] Number of hours wife worked for pay (in cash or in kind) in the 4-month reference period.

[h] Hourly wage rate (includes payments in kind, as well as in cash).

***Significant at .01 level.
**Significant at .05 level.
*Significant at .10 level.

TABLE 4.9 DETERMINANTS OF TIME SPENT ON CHILD CARE

Explanatory Variable	(1) Total Household Hours (Coefficient)	(2) Total Household Hours (Coefficient)	(3) Wife's Hours (Coefficient)	(4) Husband's Hours (Coefficient)	(5) Children's Hours (Coefficient)	(6) Total Hours by All Except Husband and Wife (Coefficient)	(7) Wife's Proportion of Total Hours (Coefficient)	(8) Husband's Proportion of Total Hours (Coefficient)
Household Composition								
Children aged < 2 yrs.	528.49***	526.16***	293.22**	63.23***	60.65***	.51	.076***	.024***
Children aged 2–5 yrs.	212.52***	209.83***	148.60***	14.74*	66.62***	.48	.106***	.009**
Children aged 6–10 yrs.	117.81***	118.74***	21.90	−6.61	37.79**	.70	.044**	−.005
Children aged 10–14 yrs.	47.02	44.60	29.99	−12.71	85.45***	1.26	−.040**	−.016***
Children aged 15+ yrs.	−80.49***	−76.45***	−65.98***	−16.09**	17.49*	.18	−.038***	−.008**
Relatives aged 15–49[a]	11.07	30.82	−30.96*	−12.95*	−19.97*	−1.25**	−.021**	−.008*
Relatives aged 50+ [a]	−28.60	−32.82	−36.96	−40.78***	−14.05	−1.35*	−.079***	−.024***
Other adults[b]	318.37*	325.31*	62.23	−49.76	35.12	−2.43	−.049	−.040
Servants[b]	−55.44	−43.29	−147.86	104.08	−65.88	10.62*	−.109	.053
Dummy = 1 if woman has husband[b,c]	−347.98*	−363.13*	−20.76	134.40*	−32.58	−1.35	.089	.095***
Children in school[d]	−85.09**	−86.54**	−17.91	−8.71	−29.30	−1.55*	.021	.002
Area of Household Residence								
Metropolitan[e]	−56.12	−54.89	33.58	−16.56	16.34	.23	−.074	−.003
Other town[f]	54.42	61.08	20.05	−3.89	79.18***	−.80	−.015	.002
East coast	−71.24	−71.80	121.99**	31.89	−51.45	−.034	−.005	−.019*
Education (years of schooling)								
Wife	−9.97	−8.83	−5.30	1.22	−.80**	−.079	−.019	−.0004
Husband	3.96	4.73	.22	−2.66	−1.28	.042	.001	−.0004
Race								
Chinese	219.98***	220.90***	86.39**	−19.65	−40.40	2.01*	−.098***	−.048***
Indian	377.17***	370.92***	116.30**	39.93*	24.71	2.45	−.074**	.002
Other than Chinese, Indian, or Malaysian	250.08	225.46	132.77	22.03	13.06	−2.30	−.019	−.016
Month of Interview								
August	416.42***	428.82***	195.07**	28.10	106.06*	.92	.059	−.009
September	272.04***	270.07***	193.70***	10.23	28.80	.90	.089**	−.012
October	353.75***	345.21***	177.29**	21.86	102.07**	2.54	.084**	−.003
November	249.99***	243.54***	191.73***	19.29	86.62**	1.91	.041	.001
Wife's Age	−6.44**	−5.75*	−7.29**	−1.39	.48	.23***	−.003**	−.0008
Type of Other Child Care (Dummy = 1 for each type used)								
Own children	273.61***	280.58***	4.82	24.88	299.01***	27.45***	−.079***	.0002
Wife's or husband's parents	261.33***	267.30***	52.91	−6.68	66.60**	32.80***	.019	.003
Other relatives	226.37***	208.84**	−26.62	18.02	−33.59	29.02***	−.055*	.010
Neighbors	215.16	216.07	−45.61	164.45***	−80.60	36.25***	−.189***	.071***
Servants	444.96***	499.35***	235.36**	−71.70	54.76	44.13***	.016	−.035*

	(1)	(2)	(3)	(4)	(5)	(6)	(7)	(8)
Institutional help	251.21**	254.65**	191.47***	142.67***	357.94***	49.18***	−.056	.025
Other	−51.87	−44.79	−15.56	−35.38	11.97	72.76***	.036	−.020
Wife's Work outside Home								
Distance from home to work[g]	—	—	−17.63	−5.35	−9.45	−.74	−.019**	−.001
No. of hours[h]	—	—	−.17***	.037*	.29	.0056***	−.0002	.00002**
Wage Rates of Family Members[i]								
Wife	—	—	−7.58	−.30	−4.62	.61**	.002	.003
Children (average)	—	—	−10.50	6.31	3.53	−1.59**	.012	.003
Husband	—	—	1.14	−1.10	6.72	.013	.003	.002
Television								
(Dummy = 1 if household has TV)	23.70	21.71	19.02	34.19*	7.86	−1.71	.013	.016**
Income								
Wife	—	−.059	—	—	—	—	—	—
Children	—	−.034*	—	—	—	—	—	—
Husband	—	−.0046	—	—	—	—	—	—
Value of property	—	.0008*	—	—	—	—	—	—
Constant	−105.31	−118.79	304.02	104.54	−225.74	−1.97	.581	.173
R^2	.304	.308	.194	.089	.169	.589	.277	.157
$\bar{R}^2$	.286	.287	.169	.062	.143	.577	.255	.132
Mean of dependent variable	816.0	816.0	522.0	89.9	116.0	16.4	.506	.065

NOTE: The dependent variable in column 6 is hours per week.

[a]Does not include husband, wife, or their children.

[b]Category includes all adults other than relatives and children of the husband and wife; hence it includes the husband and wife as well as servants and a few boarders and lodgers. Therefore, the total effect for husband and servants is the coefficient of those variables plus the coefficient of "Other adults."

[c]This dummy equals 1 if a husband is listed as a household member in the household roster.

[d]To compare the effect of having children in school with that of having no children at all, add this coefficient to that of the appropriate "children" variable.

[e]A dummy that equals 1 if the household is located in one of the three largest cities in Malaysia—Kuala Lumpur, Ipoh, and Penang.

[f]A dummy that equals 1 if the household is located in a town or village (other than the three largest cities of Malaysia) whose population was more than 10,000 in 1967 or in an area of less than 10,000 where it is estimated that at least 50 percent of the work force is engaged in nonagricultural occupations.

[g]A scale that = 0 if wife does not work or works at home; 1 if her place of work is less than 1 mile from home; 2 if distance to work is 1 to 3 miles; and 3 if distance to work is 3 miles or more.

[h]Number of hours wife worked for pay (in cash or in kind) in the 4-month reference period.

[i]Hourly wage rate (includes payments in kind, as well as in cash).

***Significant at .01 level.

**Significant at .05 level.

*Significant at .10 level.

Chinese households spend significantly less time than Malaysian households in all nonmarket activities except child care, in which they spend significantly more time, other things being equal. Indians spend the most time with their children and also spend significantly more time preparing meals than either the Malaysians or the Chinese, *ceteris paribus*.

The significant coefficients for the month of interview suggest seasonal variation and/or regional variation, since different areas were interviewed in different months. Households interviewed in December (many of which were purposely selected from fishing communities) spent significantly more time cooking and cleaning and significantly less time caring for children. Families living on the east coast of Malaysia spent over 3½ hours more per week shopping than families in other parts of the country, whereas those in metropolitan areas spent significantly less time preparing meals.[13]

Intrahousehold Allocation of Time to Nonmarket Activities

In Tables 4.5 through 4.9 we present regression results explaining the number of hours that wives, husbands, and children devote to the five nonmarket activities considered here.[14] We also present regression results on the husbands' and wives' *shares* of total household hours spent on these activities.

We see in Tables 4.5 and 4.6 that wives spend significantly larger shares of total household hours washing and shopping when their children accompany them. The effects are stronger on wives' shares than on their absolute numbers of hours, suggesting that women who take their children along receive less help from other members of their households than women whose children do not accompany them. It may be that the woman who takes her children with her has fewer substitutes available for her in performing these activities or for watching her children while she performs these activities away from home.

Another finding to be noted in the regressions explaining the contributions of wives, husbands, and children to nonmarket production is the strong evidence that wives find substitutes among household members and also substitute market for nonmarket activities. The wife devotes less time, and especially a smaller proportion of total household time, to most nonmarket activities the greater are the number of hours she works outside her home for pay (in cash and/or in kind). Her wage rate and the distance to her place of employment are also usually negatively related to her hours of nonmarket work, although the coefficients are typically not significant (perhaps because much of their effect is picked up through the variable measuring the wife's hours of market work).

In absolute terms, child care is the activity that suffers the greatest reduction in the mother's time input as she increases the number of hours worked outside the home, although the effect is small. For every additional hour she works, a mother reduces her child care time by approximately 10 minutes. Women also reduce the amount of time they devote to preparing meals the more they work outside the home[15]—by about 5 minutes for every additional hour worked.

Since the amount of time devoted to other housework activities is not greatly diminished by the mother's work outside the home, her leisure time must be substantially reduced (see Chapter 8 for further evidence that mothers reduce leisure time, rather than child care or home production time, when they work outside the home).

Estimates of the effect of the number of hours the wife is employed outside the home on the amount of time husbands and children spend in household activities are positive, although they are small and associated with low significance levels. This indicates a possible substitution of time inputs among household members. Further evidence of substitution among household members is the positive child wage coefficient in Table 4.5 explaining wives' share of washing hours, suggesting that, for a given household composition, wives perform a greater share of certain activities when their children are gainfully employed outside the home.[16]

Husbands are most likely to help with shopping and child care and also with other activities (regressions not shown in this essay) when there are infants in the family. Husbands help less in families with older children, presumably because these children help instead.[17] Indeed, children's hours of nonmarket work are generally greatest in families with children 10 years of age or older. Chinese children typically spend less time on household chores than Malaysian children, whereas Indian children and those of other races help around the house more than Malaysian children.

Children in towns are more likely to help care for siblings than those who live in metropolitan and rural areas. Also, the less educated the children's mother, the more likely she is to entrust child care to other children in the family. Older children and institutional care appear to be used complementarily in caring for younger children (i.e., children frequently spend more time caring for siblings in households that also use institutional care).

Child Care by Others

In addition to equations explaining the number of hours (in the 4-month reference period) that the entire household, wife, husband, and older children spent caring for children, we also include in Table 4.9 an equation (column 6) explaining the number of hours spent (in a typical week) for child care by persons other than the husband and wife—by their children, parents, other relatives, neighbors, servants, and institutional help.[18] We include dummies in all regressions in Table 4.9 to indicate the types of alternative care used. (Several types may be used simultaneously.)

Coefficients of dummies for types of child care used show the additional number of hours spent in child care by households that use one of these types of care, compared with the number of hours spent by households in which the husband and wife are the only ones who care for children, when all other independent variables are held constant. Child care provided by siblings, grandparents, neighbors, and institutional help increases the total number of child care hours by 12 to 16 hours per week. Households with servants spend an extra 26 hours per week with children; the number of servants appears to have no effect.

The number of hours that persons other than the husband and wife spend in child care is positively related to the wife's wage and the number of hours she works away from home; the higher the cost of her own time spent on child care, the more likely she is to use alternative means of care. If some of her children work or are in school, she is less likely to use them or other children to care for younger children.[19] Alternative child care is also used more frequently by older mothers and by Chinese and Indians.[20]

SUMMARY AND SUGGESTIONS FOR FURTHER RESEARCH

The most interesting findings of this research can be summarized as follows.

• Agricultural activities appear to be less compatible with child care than sales or production occupations. In nearly one-third of the sales and production jobs filled by women who have children aged 10 years or under, the women have (some of) these children with them when they work. In comparison, this is true• of 16 percent of the jobs in agriculture filled by such women and 14 percent of the service positions. Other market occupations are not often filled by women who have their children with them when they work.

• Mothers of children aged 2 to 5 years are more likely to be accompanied by (some of) their children when performing market and out-of-home nonmarket activities than are mothers of older or younger children.

• Women who take their children with them generally spend less time in market activities and more time in nonmarket activities compared with women with similarly aged children who do not bring their children. Women who have their children along when they perform nonmarket activities may do so because fewer substitutes are available for the mother in the activity in question or because child care is not available.

• Women work slightly less in the home, and husbands, children, and others (including nonhousehold members) help more with household chores, the more hours the wife works outside the home. Husbands help more in families that include infants and less in families with older children.

• In absolute terms, child care is the activity that loses most of the mother's time when she increases the number of hours that she works outside her home. The effect is small, however, and since the amount of time devoted to other household activities is only slightly reduced, it appears that when they work, mothers primarily reduce their leisure time rather than the time they spend for child care or home production. In relative terms, child care and cooking have the greatest reductions.

• Household size and age composition are the most important determinants of the number of hours that the household as a whole spends in nonmarket production. Although other family members help in large families, and the wife's share of total hours is less in such instances, the *number* of hours that she devotes to nonmarket production is generally positively related to family size. This suggests that having a large family increases her obligations at home and reduces the number of hours she can participate in the labor force.[21]

There seem to be a number of potentially interesting directions in which the very preliminary analyses presented here could be extended.

1.   Market labor supply decisions should be integrated into the model and explored as a dependent variable. The Malaysian Family Life Survey includes information on women's previous work experience and local labor market characteristics. Such an analysis could yield estimated values of time for nonworkers that could be used as explanatory variables in the equations explaining time spent in nonmarket activities.

2.   Type of child care chosen (including the decision to have children accompany the mother when she performs various activities) could be treated as a dependent variable to explore what types of women choose various types of child care. Included here should be further analyses of the characteristics and types of jobs that are most compatible with child care (e.g., distance from home, self-employment, family business).

3.   Whether the sex of children affects their inputs to household activities when they are older or the number of hours they are cared for when young is another interesting topic that could be explored with these data. This aspect of nonmarket activity has potential implications about the "quality" and economic value of children. Also, interaction variables could be used to investigate whether particular age or sex combinations of children have especially detrimental or beneficial effects on family members' productivity. Such an analysis may yield information concerning the optimal spacing of children.

Notes

1.   Gary S. Becker, "A Theory of the Allocation of Time," *Economic Journal* 75 (1965): 493–517.

2.   This survey was designed by William P. Butz and Julie DaVanzo of the Rand Corporation in collaboration with, initially, persons at the Department of Statistics of the government of Malaysia, and subsequently, the staff of Survey Research Malaysia, who did the fieldwork. The survey consisted of 3 rounds, each 4 months apart. Of the 1,262 households that completed Round I, 1,207 were also interviewed in Rounds II and III. The sample households are located in 52 areas (called Primary Sampling Units, or PSUs) of Penisula Malaysia. Forty-nine of these areas were selected by area probability sampling methods. Three areas were purposely selected to give additional representation to Indian families and to families living in fishing communities. For more information about the survey, see William P. Butz and Julie DaVanzo, *The Malaysian Family Life Survey: Summary Report*, R-2351-AID, the Rand Corporation, March 1978.

3. This is analogous to the market demand for any good. An important determinant of the position of the market demand curve is the number of demanders, or the size of the market.

4. Accordingly, women who are relatively more efficient when their children accompany them may be more likely to take their children along. Consideration of this possible "selectivity bias" is beyond the scope of this essay.

5. Round I lasted 4 months, from August to December 1976; hence the 4-month reference period varies from April through August 1976 to August through December 1976, depending on when a household was interviewed for Round I.

6. Another questionnaire, which was not used for this analysis, elicited information on husbands' time use. We do use here, however, information from the Female Time Budget questionnaire regarding the help that the husband gave his wife with activities she performed.

7. In adding the hours spent by household members in various activities and using that total input as a substitute for the amount of output for those activities, we implicitly assume that the hours various household members spend on household tasks are equally productive.

8. Time and money constraints precluded us from attempting any joint estimation of the demand and supply equations for a given activity or across activities for a given individual. Although such procedures should improve the efficiency of the resulting estimates, the single-equation approach used here should produce unbiased estimates as long as all independent variables are uncorrelated with the equation's error. (The validity of this assumption is questionable for several of our explanatory variables, however.) Several other shortcomings of the particular empirical specifications used in the preliminary analyses presented should be noted.

a. The samples for equations explaining husbands' and children's hours of help with various household activities include all households in the survey sample, even households without husbands or children (of helping ages). In all regressions, we include explanatory variables that tell whether the household includes a husband or children (of helping ages); these variables provide a crude way of correcting for the fact that some households have a dependent variable whose value is zero simply because they do not include the members whose contribution is being explained.

b. Wage rates (of wives, husbands, or children) are set equal to zero for persons who did not work for pay (in cash or in kind) in the 4-month reference period, and hence do not measure the value of market opportunities for nonworkers.

c. The number of hours the wife works outside the home for pay, in cash or in kind, is treated as exogenous in the equations explaining the number of hours she and other household members devote to nonmarket production, despite the fact that decisions regarding the number of hours the woman works outside her home are likely to be made jointly with the decisions about the amount of time to be spent in nonmarket production.

d. Equations explaining proportions of the total activity done by the wife or husband are estimated by ordinary least squares, so some predicted values may fall outside the possible 0–1 range.

9. Data are also supplied on types of stoves, cookers, and irons, and whether the household has electricity, all of which could be investigated in further research.

10. The specification of the equation does not allow for economies of scale in child care because it does not explicitly consider combinations of children through interaction variables or allow for nonlinearities within age-groups.

11. The number of households with servants is small. The 1,262 households in the sample have 20 servants altogether.

12. Time-budget data for the United States show that more educated women devote *more* time, both overall and per child, to child care than their less educated counterparts. See Arleen Leibowitz, "Education and the Allocation of Women's Time," *American Economic Review* 64 (1974): 244.

13. It is puzzling that families that consume homegrown crops spend significantly more time shopping; perhaps they live farther from markets.

14.   We do not present equations for the hours spent by husbands in washing, cooking, or cleaning, or the hours spent by children in shopping, since the average levels are very low (see Table 4.4).

15.   The wife's distance elasticity is largest in absolute magnitude for cleaning, whereas the wife's wage elasticities are largest for shopping and cleaning.

16.   The significantly negative coefficient of the husband's wage in explaining the number of hours that the wife spends on washing is probably the result of an income effect (whereby higher income families can afford servants and laundry services).

17.   Also, husbands are more likely to help with shopping in families with servants and in families that own cars. Chinese husbands are significantly less likely to help with shopping than husbands of other ethnicities. Husbands spend more time with their children in households that have television sets (which we thought might provide a substitute for human child care). Watching children and watching television may be complementary activities for fathers. Alternatively, this might be a measurement of an income effect; that is, wealthier fathers (as indexed by the presence of a television set) may choose to spend more time with their children. We do see in column 2 of Table 4.9 that wealthier families, as measured by the value of their property, spend more time in child care, but we have not investigated whether all family members, or only certain family members, increase their child care time.

18.   This information derives from the Female Retrospective questionnaire, which reports the *total* number of hours spent in child care in a typical week by persons other than the husband and wife.

19.   It is puzzling that the child wage coefficient is negative and significant in the equation explaining the total number of hours of alternative child care, which includes help from children, but is insignificant in the equation explaining the number of hours children help with child care.

20.   Chinese and Indian households, and those of races other than Malaysian, appear to spend more time caring for their children than Malaysian households. Non-Malaysian mothers and fathers both spend more hours in child care than do Malaysian parents. In addition, Chinese and Indian households supplement this care with that provided by nonhousehold members to such an extent that, despite the mother's larger number of hours devoted to child care, her share is smaller, especially in Chinese families.

21.   Of course, it is possible that the causation runs the other way: Women who are relatively more productive in the home than in the market may choose to have larger families.

5. Market Sellers in Lima, Peru: Talking about Work

Ximena Bunster B.

Fortunately, I am a market worker and I learned my trade at the age of 12 when I was hired as a domestic servant after both my parents had died. The woman for whom I worked was a market seller and she taught me. I became very good at running a business. I have spent my life doing it. But I have also been a factory worker and a domestic servant. This was when I had no children. After my girls were born I became independent as an *ambulante*. I did not want to work in factories or in private homes because then the mother has to lock the child up in order to go to work. And I said to myself, "My little daughter is not going to suffer. I won't let that happen." I've continued working in the market business all these years. One has to be awfully patient, for there are times when one earns a bit and there are times when one loses money instead. It's uneven—you earn, you lose.

Tomasa, a 44-year-old market seller in Lima, Peru

Many poor women in developing countries find that trading allows them the flexibility necessary to integrate daily maintenance of a household with income-generating pursuits. Of the scant occupational options available to them, proletarian mothers often value marketing most highly because it allows them to reduce, in part at least, the conflict stemming from their dual responsibility as workers and mothers.

Using a "talking pictures" approach—a combination of still photography and open-ended interviewing—a group of social scientists, including the author of this essay, conducted a study of market sellers with fixed stalls in Lima as part of a larger study of women in marginal occupations in the Peruvian captial.[1] Twenty-one women in the market Ciudad de Dios were interviewed in depth for 2 to 3 hours. Questions were structured around photographs relevant to their work[2] in an attempt to facilitate communication and to allow the interviewers to fully

Note: Funding for this study was provided by the National Institutes of Health (Grant No. 1 ROL MD 08353-01), the Social Science Research Council, the Smithsonian Institution's Interdisciplinary Communications Program, and the local office of the Ford Foundation in Lima. The research team included four social scientists: Ximena Bunster B., Elsa M. Chaney, Hilda Mercado, and Gabriela Villalobos.

understand these women's feelings about the value and significance of their work and their perceptions of their role in the marketplace.

This essay reports the results of these interviews, which shed light on the nature of the lives of market women in urban Lima and the strategies they use to balance the need both to care for their families and to earn an income. As we shall see, these women have structured a very rational and present-oriented economic role in order to keep from crossing the borderline between poverty and starvation. They have integrated activities within the household and marketing activities outside their homes in such a way as to be able to mobilize overlapping resources when critical economic or family crises arise. This essay first presents background information on the context within which market sellers operate—the market system in Lima and the market Ciudad de Dios. That section is followed by an analysis of central aspects of the working lives of the market sellers interviewed, such as their daily routine, their working conditions, and the specific problems they face. For each aspect analyzed, the women's own perceptions, as expressed by them during the interviews, are reported. The essay concludes with some suggestions for policy reforms.

BACKGROUND OF MARKET SELLING

The Market System in Lima

The market system in Lima is complex, almost chaotic, and unevenly organized. There are approximately 47,000 small traders who do their business in 290 selling areas distributed among the different districts of the Peruvian capital; 65 percent of these sellers work in fixed installations, and the rest are street vendors in and around markets. Of the 290 commercial areas, 41 percent are permanent markets, 32 percent are temporary markets set up in open lots (*mercadillos*), and 27 percent are stalls set up in streets (*paraditas*) (Oballe de Espada 1971).

The individual municipalities in Lima have been responsible for building municipal markets and renting the stalls and shops to market sellers. These municipal markets usually have facilities that other markets do not have, such as storage space and refrigeration rooms. Sometimes, however, these facilities are in need of repair or do not operate regularly. Therefore, the services rendered to market workers are very inefficient. The municipality assumes the responsibility of administering and cleaning the markets and also supplies guards.

Private markets, constructed by private companies or individuals, have stalls and shops for sale or rent and boast refrigerated rooms, ample storage space, and other services. Ironically, most of these markets are empty, because the sale or rental prices of the shops and stalls are too high for the average market seller.

Most of the cooperative markets have been built by cooperative organizations of market sellers and are found in the poorer districts of Lima. Stalls and services within the market are the sole property of the cooperative, which also manages the market and supervises its cleaning.

The cooperative markets have many more problems than the municipal and private markets. They have difficulty obtaining financing for land purchase or building construction, and frequently the land on which they stand has been seized by the sellers rather than purchased.[3] In addition, it appears that the cooperatives may be harassed by municipal authorities who believe that all markets should be run by the municipalities.

The municipal councils also harass and try to block the proliferation of street vendors. In an attempt to resist the pressure brought to bear on them by the authorities, the vendors often join together in *paraditas* in different districts of the city and sell their products from carts, tables, and the floor. Street vendors may work in their street stalls the year round or do business there temporarily. The vendors have access to no services of any kind, and the stalls are usually very unhygienic. *Paraditas* represent the first step toward the development of *mercadillos,* which consist of ramshackle stalls, built out of whatever materials are available.

The Market Ciudad de Dios

The market Ciudad de Dios is a cooperative market that, along with the Paradita del Niño Jesús and the municipal *mercadillos,* forms an important nucleus of trade in the district of San Juan de Miraflores, a low-income district with a high rate of unemployment. The unemployment rate in this district is evidenced by the large numbers of vendors who have invaded the streets and the cooperative markets. Most of these vendors are jobless men and women who have no other means of income. Through them, supplies are channeled to a large percentage of the population of metropolitan Lima. There are more market sellers, both street vendors and market workers with fixed stalls, than can be supported by the area's demand, however; therefore, competition for customers is fierce. Market sellers frequently have to close their shops when business is slack during weekdays and go with their merchandise into the neighboring *mercadillos* and *paraditas* or to other established Lima markets.

The market Ciudad de Dios offers a variety of products and services: vegetables, meat, poultry, fish, fruit, spices, prepared foods, baskets, notions, cloth, ready-made clothes and shoes, radio and television repair, cheap jewelry, tailoring and sewing, and hairdressing.

When we did our fieldwork, the market was functioning in provisionary wooden buildings but the members of the market cooperative had decided to build a permanent market site.

THE MARKET WOMEN

The ages of the market sellers interviewed at the time of the study ranged from 21 to 53 years. Sixteen of the women were living with a husband and one was living in a consensual union; four others resided with their children only and were heads of their families and the main providers.

These market women sold vegetables, poultry, fish, spices, baskets, prepared juices and foods, and notions such as thread and other sewing materials and yarn. Only a few women had small grocery shops; none owned meat stalls, operated the larger grocery shops, or sold ready-made clothes. In other words, they did not operate in areas requiring large capital investment.

Daily Routine

Market women start their working day at 3:00 or 4:00 in the morning, when they cook the midday meal for those of their children who go to school. Three or four times a week, and sometimes every day, they leave at 5:00 A.M. for the wholesale market, La Parada,[4] to buy their merchandise. Working mothers take along their youngest offspring, usually babies and toddlers, as well as one or two of the older children to help carry the merchandise. Some of the children—often the middle ones who cannot be carried, do not go to school, and have not yet started working alongside their mothers—are left behind under the care of an older sibling or an adult relative.

These market women finally arrive at their market at 6:30 A.M. They open their stands, distribute the freshly bought merchandise, and have breakfast with their older children before sending them off to school. Market activities start very early. The busiest selling hours are from 7:00 to 10:00 A.M., and business drops off around 1:00 P.M. Lunch is eaten on the premises. The more prosperous market women buy a hot lunch from one of the many restaurants inside the market. Most market women, however, have their lunch brought from home by one of the children on their way to the afternoon school shift.

At 5:00 P.M. the market closes and the mothers go home to their families. More work awaits them there: cooking the whole family's evening meal, sewing, washing and ironing clothes, and putting the children to bed.

Women's Perceptions

Most of the women in our study agreed that they preferred work *outside* the home, where they had a window to the world, to the drudgery of the household routine. All of them complained, however, about the difficulty of getting enough sleep because of the pressures exerted upon them by their double roles as homemakers and market sellers.

The women all agreed that market selling was more appropriate for a working mother than employment as a domestic or in a factory. Approximately half of them had done agricultural work before coming to the city; another half had been domestic servants. Many of them had progressed from agricultural activities to being a domestic, to street vending, and ultimately to market selling.

The decision to engage in street peddling and market activities had been reached by each woman independently of her husband or male partner (*compañero*), often after more than two children had been born or when the wage earnings of the father were found to be less than adequate. These women seemed to feel that, as market sellers, they could best minimize the conflict arising from their dual roles as workers and mothers.

Children of Market Women

The children of a market woman are organized and directed by their working mother. She decides who stays home to look after younger brothers and sisters and who cooks, runs errands, and brings lunch to the market. Children are constantly shuffled between home maintenance activities and market activities. At the age of 10 years, children start working alongside their mothers. It is very common to see children behind the counters while the mother is home looking after a sick baby or taking time off from her selling.

Children of 8 to 12 years rapidly learn the business and are able to sell, handle money, and market food as adults do. Sometimes they even make more than their mothers. Therefore, almost all women who have worked for long periods are aided by their offspring.

Women's Perceptions

With very few exceptions, market women look upon child labor as necessary for the survival of the family as a whole. Almost all the women interviewed in our study had been born in rural areas and had migrated to the city. It is easy to hypothesize that they had carried to the urban world the traditional attitudes toward child rearing of the rural areas, where the learning of income-generating skills by peasant children is a major part of their socialization. Carmen Diana Deere, an economist who has studied children's contribution to production within the peasant family economic unit on the Peruvian minifundia (small farms), has found that the more children, the more hands are available to relieve the mother of many small tasks, enabling her to devote more time to complementary activities for the family's subsistence. Also, a larger family increases the possibilities of generating income from the sale of handicrafts or processed products, which take a larger input. The more children, the greater the possibility of increasing the number of farm animals (generally under children's care), which improves the family's liquidity. A large family also increases the possibility of farming more land—first, because of the increased economic possibilities for saving, to rent or purchase more land; second, because of the possibility of having sufficient family labor power on hand to undertake the expansion of the land base.[5]

The proletarian urban market mother, like her rural counterpart working in the fields alongside her children, seems to attempt to maximize the utilization of her family's labor power in order to earn more cash. The average market seller cannot afford to hire an adult assistant to help her in the market trade; therefore, unless she is assisted by her children, she must work alone.

Health of the Family

If a market woman gets very sick, she will close up her stand and go home; if a child or relative becomes ill, she will stay home to care for him or her and send an older son or daughter to take over the business. Thus, whatever happens in her family affects her work, and vice versa. Crises are resolved with the collaboration of family members—children, the market worker's mother or sisters, and, in rare instances, the husband or mate.

It is likely that the conditions in the markets in which they work have a direct bearing on the frequent sicknesses of market women and their children. Markets like Ciudad de Dios have been constructed without taking into consideration the needs of the women selling there or the basic space requirements for cleaning the markets and disposing of waste products. There are no day-care centers, emergency clinics, or sanitary toilets in markets. If somebody gets sick, he or she has to be taken to a private doctor because no form of socialized medicine is available. Market women often go into debt to pay high doctors' fees.

Women's Perceptions

The market women interviewed attributed bronchitis, colds, varicose veins, gynecological problems, and kidney trouble to their unhealthful working conditions. They complained that because garbage was not removed daily from the market, infections were triggered that affected their children quite severely.

They claimed that if these conditions were improved, their work loads would be eased and they could greatly decrease their absenteeism from work; also, their earnings would increase if they did not have to close their stores for days and sometimes weeks to attend to the welfare of family members.

Lack of Storage Space and Refrigeration

Storage space and refrigeration are simply not available in most markets; Ciudad de Dios is no exception. Working mothers apply the same present-oriented criteria to the purchase of their groceries for home consumption as to the purchase of merchandise they resell in their business. Perishable goods that begin to spoil are taken home for the evening meal.

Fishmongers go practically every afternoon or evening to the fisherman's wharf in Chorrillos. They buy fresh fish that is stored in large baskets between layers of ice, the only way of keeping the fish fresh. Together, the fishmongers from Ciudad de Dios hire a van to take these baskets of fish back to the market for sale the next day. Despite these precautions, the fish spoil very rapidly.

Because there is no way to store or refrigerate poultry, live chickens are kept in cages in the market stalls and are slaughtered, plucked, cleaned, and cut up by the poultry vendors themselves. This procedure is expensive because money has to be invested in kerosene stoves, kitchen utensils, and wooden crates. Since stalls are small, they can hold only one crate at a time that can temporarily shelter 12 chickens.

Women's Perceptions

Market women who sell fish say that they are willing to assume the high risks involved because earnings are sometimes good. On days when sales are slack, however, they are forced to lower substantially the price of fish—otherwise, the fish will spoil due to lack of refrigerated storage facilities. The women do have an alternative to lowering prices. As one of the informants explained, "Anything that starts to rot, or that I was not able to sell and will not be fresh enough for customers the following day, I take home and fix for all of us in the family to have—usually a stew or a soup."

Women who sell poultry complain that when sales decrease, live hens must be kept for days in crowded conditions, and they lose weight rapidly in spite of efforts to keep them well fed.

Inefficient Buying Mechanisms

Cooperative markets like Ciudad de Dios do not buy in bulk directly from the producers; therefore, market sellers have to supply themselves individually. Wholesale dealers who buy vegetables, fruit, flowers, and chickens from the producers in the rural areas sell their wares from trucks parked in vacant lots adjacent to the markets and *paraditas*. They are the middlemen in the market supply chain. Small retail dealers, like the women of our study, either buy from them or go to La Parada. In either case, the products are more expensive because they have been through the hands of intermediaries.

If a woman decides to go to La Parada, she must set out at the crack or dawn, take her children along with her, spend money on bus fares, and pay carriers to load her purchases on a bus or truck or in a taxi.

The more prosperous market sellers, usually men, become major capitalists in their own right within Ciudad de Dios and other such markets because they can invest large sums of money in the purchase of goods. When a product is scarce, they rapidly buy it up and store it until the shortage becomes really severe. Sometimes market women have to turn to them and pay exorbitant prices for staples that they need to have in stock in their small shops and stalls. If women do not carry staples like rice, a basic ingredient in most native Peruvian dishes, they will lose their regular customers to other sellers.

Women's Perceptions

The amount of time, energy, and cash spent in supplying their stalls is a constant physical and financial strain on market sellers. For example, Marcela, 36 years old and mother of three, has a vegetable stall where she sells mainly potatoes and onions. Her plight is common to all market women. Marcela has to start worrying about the next day's purchase before she has finished selling for the day. She described at length what happened when she had to buy a sack of onions at a time when there was an acute shortage of this product.

Would you like to know what I do in order to make sure that I'm going to have access to a sack of onions? After I close my stall at 3:00 P.M., I go to the wholesale market and go into the onion and potato section as if I were a regular hoodlum! By this I mean that I have to lie to the guards to let me in after convincing them that I'm a wholesale dealer myself and that I'm going in to talk to my sister who's already inside. I go better dressed to impress them. At 5:00 P.M. one of the wholesale dealers arrives in his own truck. "Will you sell me a sack of onions, señor?" I beg of him. He answers, "Yes." But there I have to wait for about three hours till he finally gets around to selling me one. By this time it's already 8:00 P.M. I mark it with my name and go back home to eat supper. Then I return to the wholesale market where I sleep keeping an eye on my own sack.

Sometimes everything is so hard! Shortages of certain products make it so tough for us! It is then my children practically don't go to school; they are exhausted and go to sleep in class, under the teacher's nose. The school year ends and my children are behind. I blame myself because I've had my children stay awake all night helping me out at the wholesale market. When I see them so tired, it breaks my heart and I feel so guilty and so powerless!

The market women, who usually do business with scant capital, are perfectly aware that they are exploited by wholesalers even inside their own markets. As Juanaticilla, mother of seven children and the owner of a small grocery stand, put it, "These big sharks, the rich wholesalers, are the ones responsible for soaring prices. By hoarding products and exerting control by monopolizing them, they make the product more expensive to us and to consumers. The wholesalers are the ones who get enormous profits but we poor, common market sellers, suffer very much."

Lack of Cooperative Mechanisms

Cooperative markets are cooperative in name only, for they offer no credit assistance or other help to their members. Two-thirds of the women in our study have a stall in the market merely because they were part of the group that seized the plot of land on which the market is built. Many of them built their stalls themselves. They have to pay a high monthly fee for necessary services, such as guards to police the stocked stalls at night.

Women's Perceptions

In theory, the market belongs to the group, not to individual stallholders. The market sellers note that in practice, however, a great deal of speculation in stalls occurs and rents and transfer payments are demanded. Such demands are difficult to meet. In the group we interviewed there were two women who, because they needed extra cash to pay the transfer fee for a stall, had to hire themselves out as domestic servants for a period, leaving a relative to look after the market stall.

Business Capital

Most of the women in our study were illiterate or had received an average of 3 years of primary schooling (although a few exceptional women had had some high school education). As a rule, market women have not had the opportunity to learn the arithmetic and perhaps basic accounting that would help them to keep a record of the capital invested in their business and of their daily, weekly, and monthly earnings.

Thus, at no point in the process of buying and selling do these women have an exact idea of the amount of their capital. There are no fixed boundary lines between what percentage of their cash is spent on investment in merchandise and what percentage is allotted to fixed family spending or to emergencies.

Most women's earnings from a day's sale in the market are not high enough to compensate for the use of foodstuffs and other products from their stalls to fill family needs, so in the long run, women are forced to cope with a drain on their capital. This contributes to a gradual home and market impoverishment in periods when the market business is slow. At best, their capital remains stationary and they can never expand it enough to stock their stalls adequately and obtain higher earnings.

Women's Perceptions

Most market women are not familiar with accounting concepts and cannot, therefore, fully appreciate their usefulness. Although the habit of taking perishable stall merchandise home for family consumption or of drawing upon their nonperishable goods (infant's clothing, cloth, yarn) to meet private family needs contributes to their lack of capital, the women feel that they must draw from their capital quite regularly—especially to attend to urgent family needs and to cope with emergencies.

Harassment by Municipal Inspectors

The municipal council of each Lima district tries to regulate the market business in order to protect consumers. Uniformed municipal inspectors are sent out to see that the official prices (set by the government) are maintained.

Women's Perceptions

The market women report that many inspectors use their authority arbitrarily, intimidating the powerless market sellers in order to make them pay bribes—in cash or in scarce foodstuffs—to avoid fines or jail terms. Even though the sellers have not broken the law, they are powerless to fight back.

One day my son was helping me sell tripe. I was running an errand when a municipal inspector reprimanded my boy and confiscated our scales. Without scales we cannot do business. He also fined him for being outspoken. I went to talk to him and he insisted on the fine because, so he said, my son had insulted him. I couldn't believe him. I told him, "My son is going to school and he is learning lots of things, among others, respect for adults, so he couldn't have been offensive in his language toward you." The inspector said that he would only return the scales if my son begged his forgiveness. "Of course he won't do that, if he hasn't offended you! I would rather pay you this fine than have him come crawling to you." So I paid him 10 *libras* but he wouldn't return the scales until I had given him a kilogram of tripe free! He took the tripe forcibly away from me, a large quantity that I needed to sell!

Alina, mother of five

Many times these municipal inspectors will squeeze you like a sponge to get money out of you. I have cried so many times when I have been the easy prey to their injustice! One day I did not have any poultry to do business with so I brought a duck that I had at home. An inspector came along and he fined me because I did not have the invoice to show where I had bought the bird and how much it cost. I explained to him that it was my own, and that I needed to make a little money out of its sale. Instead of helping me, he *fined* me for not having the invoice! I appealed to the *Concejo Municipal*. I was so desperate that I wept in front of the authorities and I told them, "Please let me work in peace. I have a right to this life and so do my children. You oppress me with unfair fines and treatment. You oppress me to the point that you make me feel you don't want me to live. Look, I had to bring this duck from home out of need; otherwise I wouldn't have anything to sell!"

Maria, poultry seller

When a market woman is abused by a municipal inspector, her fellow workers do not come to her defense. In answer to the question "What do you do when a co-worker, a mother like yourself, is unduly fined?" all of the women interviewed said, "She has to deal with it herself, it's her problem."

SUMMARY AND POLICY IMPLICATIONS

The women market sellers of Lima seem to have adopted a survival strategy that combines home and market production. The women interviewed in this study agree that given the alternatives available to them, the market-selling activities they undertake best suit their need to perform dual roles. Their lives, however, are not easy. To some extent, they are forced to view their children merely as additional, necessary laborers. They must operate in an unhealthful environment with market facilities that tend to foster inefficiency. They are exploited by middlemen and harassed by public officials, and they lack access to both credit and technical expertise in capital management. The fact that market women are burdened by both household and income-generating activities contributes to their powerlessness as a group. Market women tend to work in isolation, with minimal ties to neighbors at home and co-workers in the marketplace. Therefore, they do not participate actively in community agencies, which would help them become aware of their common needs as working mothers, or in labor unions, which would foster their sense of solidarity.

Unfortunately, the problems of the market sellers of Lima are not atypical of those that poor women face in the cities of other developing countries. Policymakers have begun to recognize the dual roles that women, especially poor women, perform. Now, however, they must go beyond this recognition to the realization that, as a result of the need to balance responsibilities in both market production and home production, poor women are often forced to undertake such income-generating activities as trading and marketing, which yield highly variable returns and require exposure to poor working conditions. The difficulties that these women face are often exacerbated by a lack of offical willingness to recognize the legitimacy of their work. Street vendors and marketers are often harassed by officials who see the use of ramshackle stalls and makeshift carts as an affront to modernization efforts but who do not realize the significance of these activities for family survival.

Development policies that are not based on the recognition and acceptance of the survival strategies of poor women serve only to undermine further the tenuous economic position of these women. Policymakers must now begin to formulate policies and implement programs that address the need of poor women to balance dual working and family roles. Such policies must be based on an acceptance of the legitimacy of poor women's economic activities. Programs of economic assistance must provide market vendors access to working and investment capital and training in marketing skills, thus allowing them to circumvent the middleman system, establish appropriate infrastructure, and obtain crucial child care and health services.

Notes

1. See Ximena Bunster B. and Elsa M. Chaney, *Servants and Sellers: Women Working in Peru*, Praeger, forthcoming.

2. The photographs were taken with the cooperation of "key informants" selected from the group of vendors being studied. These key informants allowed the researchers to follow them around during their daily, weekly, and monthly work cycles in the market as well as during their routine at home. The most relevant aspects of their market and home activities were recorded on film, and the photographs were taken back to the group of key informants, who helped choose the pictures to be included in the final photo-interview kit by indicating which they thought were most representative of their daily routines.

The photo-interview kit included 120 photographs chosen from the 3,000 that were taken. These photos were pasted in a large album that could be placed on piles of vegetables and crates in markets. The photos were combined with a structured, open-ended questionnaire.

The photo-interview was divided into three sections: (1) the labor section, which dealt with work in the market—the daily work routine, availability of services, union participation, interpersonal relationships, socialization of children in the work environment, perceptions of different occupations, and women's aspirations for their daughters' future work; (2) The family section, which elicited information on the mother's present family life and her interpretation of the significance and meaning of family relations; and (3) The participation section, which focused on whether the women had been exposed to political institutions and processes at the national and union levels and elicited their reactions to political participation. For a more detailed discussion of the photo-interview method, see Ximena Bunster B., "Talking Pictures: Field Method and Visual Mode," in *Women and National Development: The Complexities of Change*, Wellesley Editorial Committee (Chicago: University of Chicago Press, 1977).

3. According to the 1971 study made by Ing. Aida Oballe de Espada, only 29 percent of the 290 marketing centers in Lima have finished buildings; 19 percent operate in half-finished buildings, and 52 percent are functioning in temporary installations. De Espada also discovered that in 41 percent of the marketing centers, ownership of the land was unclear (the land had been seized by the market workers themselves); in 26 percent of the marketing centers the land was owned by the municipalities; in 20 percent the land was owned by market sellers themselves; and in 13 percent the land was rented.

4. The best report on La Parada has been written by Richard W. Patch, *La Parada, Estudio de un Mundo Alucinante* (Lima: Mosco Azul Editores, 1973).

5. Carmen Diana Deere, "The Development of Capitalism in Agriculture and the Division of Labor by Sex: A Study of the Northern Peruvian Sierra," Ph.D. dissertation, University of California at Berkeley, 1978, chap. 5.

6. The Allocation of Familial Labor and the Formation of Peasant House- hold Income in the Peruvian Sierra

Carmen Diana Deere

This essay addresses the subject of rural women's contribution to peasant household income. The central propostion is that the allocation of labor within the peasant household is determined by a complex interaction of class and family structure variables, as well as by the social valuation of male and female activities. Peasant women's contribution to household income is affected by the household's access to the means of production and by its age and sex composition, as well as by the degree to which the household is integrated into the wider economy—the labor market or the commodity market.

In contrast to the firm or household in advanced capitalist economies, the peasant household is a unit of production of both use and exchange values. The production of use values is defined in terms of activities that are carried out in the household to meet the family's subsistence consumption requirements. Included are those activities that reproduce the capacity for work on a daily basis (cooking, cleaning, washing clothes, gathering wood, and hauling water), activities required to reproduce labor power (child care and nurturing), and direct production (agriculture, animal raising) for the family's consumption. The production of exchange values is defined in terms of the production of commodities: goods and services, embodying familial labor time, that are valued in the market and yield a monetary income to the producer.

The concepts of "use-value production" and "exchange-value production" are used rather than the standard concepts of "home production" and "market production" because the former allow us to emphasize the degree of integration of the household into the commodity market and hence into the broader capitalist economy. The concept of home production as used by most economists does not distinguish between production for subsistence consumption and production for market exchange.

Since a key proposition of this discussion is that the degree to which the peasant household interacts with the wider economy is crucial to determining the division of labor by sex, as well as women's contribution to household income, such a distinction is critical. A distinct feature of the labor process within the peasant household is that many familial activities both yield use values to the peasant household and are a source of exchange value. Agricultural activities, animal care, and artisan work are examples of petty commodity production that, depending on the degree of specialization in production, may also provide use values for the peasant family.

Conceptually, the peasant household may be viewed as starting with a given stock of resources and a given composition, by sex and age, of the familial labor force. Familial labor is allocated to a range of activities that are required to maintain the peasant household's level of subsistence consumption and, possibly, to generate a surplus. The surplus, depending on the form of integration of the household into the wider economy (the social relations of production), may be either appropriated by a nonproducing class or captured within the peasant household, thus permitting an increased level of consumption or accumulation of means of production. This dynamic process of the appropriation and distribution of the surplus forms the basis for the social differentiation of the peasantry over time.[1]

Degree of access to the means of production (principally land) is a key determinant of social differentiation, as well as of the range of activities in which peasant households participate. Rather than being viewed as a homogeneous population, the peasantry can be divided into different class groupings based on access to the means of production. Lack of access to the means of production requires the poorer strata of the the peasantry to depend on nonagricultural activities, principally the sale of labor power for a wage, to earn their livelihood. With the integration of the peasantry into the labor market, the household becomes less a unit of direct production and more a unit of production (and reproduction) of labor power. The end result of this process of specialization is the working-class family unit in advanced capitalist societies.

Access to sufficient resources allows the richer strata of the peasantry to engage in petty commodity production; such access may also allow these peasants to purchase wage labor to carry out their productive activities, thereby providing the means for increased capital accumulation. The end result of this process is the capitalist agricultural enterprise or the small factory. Here, too, the unit of production is divorced from the household.

A second key propostion is that the integration of the peasant household into the labor market or into the commodity market has singularly important implications for the economic and social roles of rural women. The class position of the peasant household may influence attitudes about which activities are proper for women. Economic necessity may lead to an expansion of women's economic roles—poor peasant women may pursue activities not deemed appropriate for rich peasant women. On the other hand, the possibility of capital accumulation in the rich peasant stratum may open up a new set of activities (commerce, for example) to women of this class—activities that cannot be pursued by the majority of poor women. Finally, opportunity costs of participating in the labor market that differ by sex may influence the sexual division of household labor in a manner that varies by class.

In sum, neither the peasant household nor the intrafamilial deployment of labor can be analyzed in isolation from the process of integration of the household into the dominant capitalist mode of production. The familial division of labor by sex is at once conditioned by the degree of integration of the peasant household into the labor market or the product market and by the labor market value of men's and women's work.

Comprehensive analysis of labor deployment in peasant families is necessarily complex, and the objectives of this essay are more limited.[2] Women's contribution to household income is herein determined by analyzing the division of labor by sex within the household in activities that produce use value and exchange value. The first section of the essay is a brief summary of the historical background of the Cajamarcan peasantry, on which this study focuses. In the second section, the allocation of family labor among activities producing use value and exchange value is described. The third section, an analysis of women's contribution to household income, summarizes the data on household income sources, on the sexual division of labor, and on the differential returns to female and male labor. It is followed by some concluding remarks.

The data presented here were gathered in two regional sample surveys. The 1973 Cajamarca Income Survey provided data on income sources for 1,050 households in 9 districts of the Peruvian province of Cajamarca. The 1976 Peasant Family Survey of 105 households was a follow-up survey that focused on the division of labor by sex and age. It was complemented by family case-study data gathered by the author during 15 months of fieldwork in the area.[3]

SOCIOECONOMIC CHARACTERISTICS OF THE CAJAMARCAN PEASANTRY

The Cajamarcan peasantry is a mestizo, Spanish-speaking group living in the northernmost sierra department of Peru. In this area the traditional hacienda agricultural system characterized by a dependent labor force, was dominant until the mid-1950s. The expansion of the haciendas during the colonial period, and in the nineteenth century, had been accomplished at the cost of the decimation of the indigenous communities in the area. Throughout the first half of the twentieth century, the haciendas held a virtual monopoly over the cultivable lands, and the majority of peasants gained access to land only through rental arrangements that included the provision of labor services to the landlord and/or the payment of rent in kind and in cash.

The development of the Peruvian economy in the 1940s and 1950s, a result first of export-led growth and then of the process of import-substituting industrialization, led to the dissolution of the hacienda system and to the development of a market in land as well as in labor. Central to this development was the establishment in 1947 of a milk-processing plant in the Cajamarcan Valley by the multinational corporation, Nestlé. The growth of a local market for milk was essential to the conversion of this area from grain production to pasture production for the nascent dairy industry and to fostering the development of agrarian capitalism.

Within approximately 10 years, the haciendas were transformed into modern dairy enterprises, which used advanced techniques of production and a fully proletarianized (i.e., dependent on wage income), but reduced, labor force. The major part of the peasantry, formerly dependent on the hacienda system, was either completely displaced or relocated to the least productive lands of the hacienda. With the development of the land market, landlords attempted to capitalize the hacienda-turned-dairy enterprise, as well as to rid themselves of obligations, and many peasants were able to purchase their land parcels. The outcome of the process of capitalist development was the creation of a sector of modern agrarian firms, on the one hand, and a large sector of independent peasant producers, on the other.

This process of capitalist development also resulted in social differentiation within the peasantry. A class of fully proletarianized peasants developed among those who no longer had access to land for farming and who therefore either found employment on the dairy farms or migrated to the coast in search of work. A rich peasant class also emerged, the members of which controlled sufficient resources to capitalize the production process, enabling them to become dairy as well as agricultural commodity producers. The majority of the peasantry became semiproletarianized (dependent on both agricultural production and wage labor for a living).

By 1972, 71 percent of the peasant households in the province of Cajamarca were smallholders, owning less than 3.5 hectares of land (which is officially defined by the Perurian government as the minimum needed to maintain the average peasant household). Some 19 percent of peasant households formed a middle stratum, with access to between 3.5 and 11.0 hectares of land. The rich peasant stratum, representing 8 percent of the total number of households, held between 11 and 30 hectares of land; those owning over 30 hectares—2 percent of rural households—represented the rural petty bourgeoisie.[4]

This social differentiation is highlighted by the fact that some 60 percent of the smallholder households offer their labor in the market, whereas the majority of households of the rich peasant stratum and petty bourgeoisie hire wage labor for use in their productive activities. Table 6.1, which documents the peasantry's integration into the labor market or the product market, shows the composition of mean net household income by land-size strata. In order to illustrate the importance of access to land in determining labor market or product market participation, the smallholder stratum has been divided into two groups: those households with less than .25 hectares of land (denoted as ''near-landless households'') and

TABLE 6.1 COMPOSITION OF MEAN NET HOUSEHOLD INCOME, BY IMPORTANCE OF SOURCE AND LAND-SIZE STRATA (IN PERCENTAGES)

Land-Size Stratum	Income from Agricultural Production	Income from Agricultural Processing	Income from All Animal Activities	Rental Income	Subtotal: Income from All Farm Activities	Artisan Income	Wage Income	Commerce Income	Remittance Income	Total Net Income
Near-landless households (n = 140)	1.0	.1	18.8	.4	20.3	9.2	55.5	10.3	4.7	100.0
Smallholder households (n = 619)	10.2	.2	10.0	.4	24.0	7.1	48.6	12.5	7.5	100.0
Middle peasant households (n = 177)	19.6	.1	27.0	8.7	55.4	4.1	23.5	10.4	6.6	100.0
Rich peasant households (n = 81)	42.0	.2	24.4	15.4	82.0	2.1	11.4	3.6	.9	100.0
Petty bourgeois households (n = 33)	26.1	.1	62.1	1.3	89.6	.7	5.7	3.3	.7	100.0
Total (n = 1050)	17.6	.2	23.6	5.4	46.7	5.2	33.8	9.2	5.0	100.0

SOURCE: Derived from 1973 Cajamarca Income Survey.

those households with .26–3.50 hectares (referred to as "smallholder households").

The relationship between farm income, as a proportion of total net income, and land-size stratum is clear. Whereas over half of the mean net income of middle and rich peasant households is derived from farm production activities, less than a quarter of the total net income of near-landless and smallholder households is derived from such activities. The majority of the peasantry, because of limited access to the means of production (land), cannot live from farm activities alone; instead, the single most important source of income for near-landless and smallholder households is wage work. The peasant household's access to the means of production is the key in determining the range of activities in which the family participates, as well as in determining the importance of various activities in generating household income.

ALLOCATION OF FAMILY LABOR

Table 6.2 is a matrix of participation of family members in the principal activities of the peasant household, according to the family member charged with the primary responsibility for directing and carrying out the activity. Data on the principal and complementary persons responsible for carrying out the activity are presented in Table 6.3; data pertaining to familial differences in time use by the several land-size strata are presented in Table 6.4.

The Production of Use Values

The production of use values for the maintenance of familial labor power on a daily basis is typically a female activity, and it is the responsibility of the mother in the overwhelming majority of households. In one-half of the households, mothers take full responsibility for cooking and washing clothes, although in one-third of the households, mothers and daughters share the responsibility for these activities (Table 6.3). Up until the age of 9 or 10 years, daughters complement the mother's labor; after that, young girls begin substituting for their mothers in cooking, on a meal-by-meal basis, and in their mid-teenage years they may replace the mother in cooking activities, freeing her completely for other kinds of work.

Meal preparation and the washing of clothes are the most time-intensive maintenance activities, according to survey data not reported here. The average household of 5.5 members dedicates a total of 4.2 hours of labor time daily to cooking and to cleaning up after the meal.[5] Laundry is generally a weekly activity, consuming an average of 6.0 hours of labor time per week.

The two activities that are most generally shared among all family members are hauling water and collecting wood. Nevertheless, these tasks are the respon-

TABLE 6.2 FREQUENCY DISTRIBUTION OF FAMILIAL ACTIVITIES ACCORDING TO PRINCIPAL FAMILY MEMBER RESPONSIBLE FOR THE ACTIVITY (IN PERCENTAGES)

Activity	Mother's Principal Responsibility	Father's Principal Responsibility	Children's Principal Responsibility	All Family Members' Responsibility[a]	Total
Use-Value Production					
Cooking (n = 105)	93.4	—	2.8	3.8	100.0
Washing clothes (n = 105)	93.3	—	4.8	1.9	100.0
Hauling water (n = 105)	78.3	1.8	10.3	9.6	100.0
Collecting wood (n = 105)	58.1	16.2	9.5	16.2	100.0
Use- and Exchange-Value Production					
Agricultural processing (n = 105)	93.4	—	1.9	4.7	100.0
Animal care (n = 92)	61.9	4.4	22.9	10.8	100.0
Agricultural production (n = 102)	5.7	64.5	7.6	22.2	100.0
Artisan production (n = 101)	66.7	18.4	11.5	3.4	100.0
Commerce (n = 28)[b]	85.7	10.7	—	3.6	100.0
Part-time wage work (n = 51)	9.8	47.1	17.7	25.5	100.0
Full-time wage work (n = 23)	13.0	43.5	30.4	13.0	100.0

Source: 1976 Peasant Family Survey.

a The category "All Family Members' Responsibility" includes cases where mother and father share responsibility for the activity, where other family members carry out the activity, and where parents and children carry out the activity with equal responsibility.

b Commerce is restricted to trading as a profession and the operation of country stores.

TABLE 6.3 FREQUENCY DISTRIBUTION OF FAMILIAL ACTIVITIES ACCORDING TO PRINCIPAL AND COMPLEMENTARY PERSONS RESPONSIBLE FOR THE ACTIVITY (IN PERCENTAGES)

Activity	Mother's Principal Responsibility				Father's Principal Responsibility				Children's Principal Responsibility			All Family Members' Principal Responsibility			Total
	Mother	Mother and Daughters	Mother and Sons	Mother and Children	Father	Father and Daughters	Father and Sons	Father and Children	Daughters	Sons	All Children	All Family Members	Mother and Father	Other Family Members	Total
Cooking (n = 105)	57.5	34.0	1.9	—	—	—	—	—	2.8	—	—	—	1.9	1.9	100.0
Washing clothes (n = 105)	59.9	32.4	1.0	—	—	—	—	—	3.8	—	1.0	—	—	1.9	100.0
Hauling water (n = 105)	35.9	24.5	2.8	15.1	.9	—	.9	—	4.7	.9	4.7	3.8	3.8	1.9	100.0
Collecting wood (n = 105)	32.4	14.3	1.9	9.5	8.6	—	5.7	1.9	3.8	1.9	3.8	9.5	4.8	1.9	100.0
Agricultural processing (n = 105)	67.6	23.8	1.0	1.0	—	—	—	—	1.9	—	—	2.9	1.0	1.0	100.0
Animal care (n = 92)	25.0	14.1	5.4	17.4	3.3	1.1	—	—	10.9	2.2	9.8	8.7	1.1	1.1	100.0
Agricultural production (n = 102)	3.9	.9	.9	—	42.2	1.8	6.7	13.7	.9	4.9	1.8	7.7	11.8	2.7	100.0
Commerce (n = 77)	57.1	2.6	—	—	18.2	—	3.9	—	—	—	—	3.6	—	—	100.0
Artisan production (n = 101)	53.1	13.6	—	—	14.3	—	3.4	.7	7.5	2.0	2.0	.7	—	2.7	100.0
Part-time wage work (n = 51)	7.8	—	2.0	—	27.5	3.9	15.7	—	—	15.7	2.0	—	25.5	—	100.0
Full-time wage work (n = 23)	8.7	4.3	—	—	34.8	—	8.7	—	4.3	26.1	—	—	4.3	8.7	100.0

SOURCE: 1976 Peasant Family Survey.

TABLE 6.4   AVERAGE TIME DEVOTED TO FAMILIAL ACTIVITIES
BY ALL PEASANT FAMILY MEMBERS, BY LAND-SIZE STRATA

Activity	Near-landless Households	Smallholder Households	Middle Peasant Households	Rich Peasant Households	All Households
Household maintenance,[a] hrs./wk. ($n = 100$)	44.1	43.6	44.6	44.2	43.9 hours
Animal care, hrs./wk. ($n = 83$)	31.6	35.6	42.3	46.7	37.8 hours
Agricultural processing, days/yr. ($n = 87$)	17.2	13.6	21.2	20.2	16.0 days
Marketing own products, days/yr. ($n = 38$)	—	37.4	16.5	35.3	33.9 days
Artisan exchange values,[b] days/yr. ($n = 23$)	192.0	177.7	30.0	52.0	164.4 days
Commerce,[c] days/yr. ($n = 28$)	225.0	129.0	200.0	—	162.0 days
Wage work,[d] days/yr. ($n = 58$)	224.9	153.6	58.8	—	149.9 days
Agricultural production, mo./yr. ($n = 57$)	1.2	4.0	10.5	7.9	5.3 months

SOURCE: 1976 Peasant Family Survey.
NOTE: The time-use data are based on recall of average time devoted to the activity over the specified period.
[a]Household maintenance activities include cooking, washing clothes, hauling water, and collecting wood.
[b]Time-use data refer only to those households where artisan production was an income-generating activity. A total of 101 households participated in artisan production, and in 77 households artisan production was a use-value activity, principally consisting of women's spinning wool for household requirements. Since this activity is complementary to women's work in animal care, child care, and leisure, time use was not reported consistently.
[c]Commerce includes only petty commodity circulation, trading as a profession, and the operation of country stores.
[d]Wage work is both part time and full time.

sibility of the mother in the majority of households. The participation of children of all ages in carrying out these tasks is essential. Daughters, however, are much more likely to participate in these tasks on a regular basis than are sons (see Table 6.3).

The time-intensiveness of these tasks depends on the household's proximity to the primary resources. The variation is, of course, great, but on the average, household members spend approximately 30 minutes a day making four or five trips to the stream or spring.[6] Wood-gathering activities take an average of 5 hours weekly; branches, dried cactus leaves, and brush are generally collected on a daily basis. In approximately 16 percent of the households, wood collection is principally the father's responsibility; these households are generally located in densely populated areas, so that wood collection means a weekly trip to more distant areas to chop down a tree. Firewood is becoming increasingly scarce in the area, and 16 percent of the households purchase wood from traders to complement their own gathering activities; 10 percent of the households, primarily those located near the city of Cajamarca, rely exclusively on purchased wood or kerosene.

For the sample as a whole, household maintenance activities take up a total of 44 hours of familial labor time per week.[7] There is little variation by family size; in larger families, more children spend a shorter amount of time on each activity, freeing the mother for other work. In extended families, a grandmother may take charge of all daily maintenance activities, again freeing the mother for income-generating activities. The time devoted to household maintenance activities does not significantly vary among land-size strata (see Table 6.4); across all strata of the peasantry, such activities fall into the female domain. In most households, mothers carry the largest burden for household maintenance, although the participation of children, particularly daughters, is quite important.

The Production of Use and Exchange Values

Petty commodity production activities that also generate use values for the peasant household include agricultural production, agricultural processing and product transformation, animal care, and artisan production. The whole family takes part in these activities, although the direction of a specific activity falls in either the male or the female domain. Men are considered the agricultural producers and women are considered the agroprocessors and animal caretakers. As Table 6.2 indicates, fathers take the primary responsibility for agricultural activities in 64.5 percent of the households. Mothers direct agricultural activities only in the households where no grown male is present (5.7 percent); if a teenage son is living at home, he will generally direct the agricultural activities (7.6 percent). Since the households headed by women are concentrated in the near-landless and smallholder strata, it is only in these strata that women direct agricultural production (see Tables 6.8 and 6.9). The households in which all family members share responsibility for agricultural activities are also concentrated primarily among the near-landless (23 percent) and smallholder (29 percent) strata. There are important differences among the peasant strata in men's and women's participation in specific agricultural tasks. There are also important differences in who controls the marketing and the income from agriculture—differences that are closely related to the scale of the activity.

A detailed accounting of the division of labor by sex reveals the importance of women's participation in agricultural production. Overall, women provide 25 percent of the total number of family labor days devoted to agricultural production. There are, however, significant differences among land-size strata, not only in women's relative participation as compared with men's, but in the tasks in which women of different strata participate. Whereas women from the middle and rich peasantry provide only 21 percent of the total number of family labor days devoted to agricultural activities, women from the landless strata provide 35 percent of the total.[8] Women from the upper strata confine their participation to activities that are generally considered female (placing the seed in its furrow or sweeping up the threshed grain) or to those tasks that do not require the use of implements (harvesting or weeding by hand). Women from the lower strata tend to participate in all agricultural tasks, with the exception of plowing.

The differences in the actual tasks in which women from different strata participate, as well as the differences among strata in women's use of implements, suggests the important role of economic necessity in breaking down the traditional definitions of "appropriate" work for women. Moreover, women's greater relative participation in agricultural field work is correlated with women's greater participation in agricultural decision making.[9] In the majority of near-landless households, women take responsibility for the provision of agricultural inputs as well as for product disposition; the actual organization of work is the responsibility of both men and women. Among smallholder households, all facets of agricultural decision making tend to be shared by men and women. In contrast, among middle and rich peasant households, agricultural decision making falls in the male domain. The differences in agricultural participation and decision making among the different strata of the peasantry suggest that only where agriculture is an important source of livelihood is it a male occupation. For the majority of peasant households, the importance of agricultural production in the generation of household income is declining; as its importance diminishes, women's participation in and responsibility for the activity correspondingly increase. The small amount of time that is devoted to agricultural production by the poorer strata of the peasantry should also be noted. Landless households reported spending approximately 1 month a year, whereas smallholder households estimated spending a maximum of 4 months yearly, on agricultural activities.[10] Middle and rich peasant households reported agricultural activities as requiring from 7 to more than 10 months annually (see Table 6.4).

Only 10 percent of the households in the sample considered agricultural production to be an income-generating activity; the vast majority of these were middle and rich peasant households. Agricultural production represented only 10.2 percent of the farm-generated monetary income of smallholder households in 1973; in contrast, agricultural production represented 42.0 percent of the farm-generated monetary income of rich peasant households (see Table 6.1).

In the overwhelming majority of poor peasant households, women are responsible for the marketing of produce; this is usually done on an extremely small scale, with the women taking a small sack of grain or 25 pounds of potatoes to sell at the weekly market. The income generated is then used to purchase the weekly necessities. In contrast, among rich peasant families the bulk of the marketing is carried out at the wholesale level, and primarily by males. An average of almost 34 days a year is devoted to marketing activities across all strata (Table 6.4).

Since the bulk of agricultural production among poor peasant households is destined for home consumption, agricultural-processing and product transformation activities constitute the use-value production, which is most time intensive. In the majority of households, this again is the responsibility of the mother and is carried out by the female members of the household. Agricultural-processing tasks are carried out on a daily, weekly, monthly, and annual basis, depending on the scale of production and the form of storage of the crop. For example, grain processing first requires sorting and cleaning the grain, usually following the harvest. The grain may then be toasted weekly and ground between stones as required for daily consumption. Among more prosperous households, the grain is taken to a mill (usually on a monthly basis), which means that several days must be devoted to toasting prior to the trip to town. If the wheat or barley grain is processed into flour at home, the complete preparation of a 25-pound sack takes approximately 2 days. Other processing activities include making dried potatoes after the harvest and preparing *quinoa* (ground pigweed, used as cereal), both labor-intensive tasks.

Product transformation includes the preparation of bread, *chicha* (a corn liquor), and cheeses. In contrast to grain processing, in which all households engage, only 38 percent of the households engage in product transformation. Nine percent of the households reported engaging in product transformation as an income-generating activity, primarily the weekly making of *chicha*. For the sample as a whole, 16 days a year were devoted, on average, exclusively to agricultural product transformation or processing (Table 6.4), primarily by mothers or mothers aided by their daughters (Table 6.3). The amount of time given to these activities appears to be related to the scale of agricultural production and thus to land-size stratum (Table 6.4).

Animal care is the mother's responsibility in 62 percent of all households (Table 6.6). As shown in Table 6.3, the participation of children in this activity is vital; in 22.9 percent of the households children take full responsibility for animal care, and in another 36.9 percent, children actively participate in animal care. In contrast to agricultural production, where in 19.5 percent of the households women participate actively in tasks that are principally the men's responsibility, the participation of men in animal care is minimal. Fathers participate in animal care in only 9.8 percent of the households and are the principal adults responsible for the activity in only 4.4 percent of the households—all of which are dairy farms.

The care of the household animals alone takes an average of 30 minutes to an hour daily in most households. Grasses and weeds must be collected from the fields to feed the guinea pigs and rabbits; the chickens must be fed their grain husks or corn kernels, and the pigs, the slop. The larger farm animals are generally tied up near the house, and fodder and water are brought to them several times a day. A household with dairy cattle usually has an enclosed pasture in which the animals are kept.

In caring for animals, the most time-consuming activity is the pasturing of sheep and goats. Since pasture, particularly open grazing land, is scarce, caring for sheep requires that one family member be available practically full time for this activity. As many women put it, caring for sheep depends on having a child at home, either to pasture the animals or to replace the mother in daily maintenance activities. Many women lamented the impact of primary education. Sending children to school is an economic hardship, not only because of the cost of school supplies, but also because it decreases children's participation in income-generating activities in the household. It is usually the mother who bears the increased work load of having children in school. Although children of both sexes are now attending school, there is a notable tendency for girls to attend for fewer years than boys. Not surprisingly, in 10.9 percent of the households, a daughter cared for sheep full time, whereas sons did in only 2.2 percent (Table 6.3).

Animal care is the second most time-intensive activity after general household maintenance. An average of 37.8 hours a week is dedicated to all animal-care activities (Table 6.4). The time spent on this activity closely correlates with both the land-size stratum and the number of people in the household. Whereas landless households spend an average of 31.6 hours a week on animal care, middle peasant households spend 42.3 hours, and rich households spend 46.7 hours a week. Richer peasants have greater access to land and therefore have larger herds of sheep; they also tend to have larger households, based on the extended family, so that one family member is usually available for full-time animal care. Landless peasants, however, tend to confine their animal care to activities that do not require much land or much time.

The 1976 Peasant Family Survey shows that animal care, like agricultural production, is considered an income-generating activity by only 10 percent of the households, the majority of which are middle and rich peasants. Most households perceive their animals as an investment, that is, a form of stored wealth, or as a form of savings for emergencies. Nevertheless, in 1973, the sale of animals and animal by-products represented over half of the monetary income generated from farm activities for all strata of the peasantry. Again, the scale of the activity is important in determining which family member controls the outcome of the activity. Among the landless and smallholder households, women generally take charge of marketing the animals—selling a chicken or a guinea pig in the market in order to purchase the weekly necessities. The sale of sheep is a major occasion, in which both the father and the mother participate. Where sheep raising is important (among the rich peasant households), the men control the marketing. Men also tend to control the marketing of milk to the milk-processing plant, although women generally milk and share responsibility for caring for the cattle.

The final activity that yields both use and exchange value to the peasant household is artisan production, in which 96 percent of all households engage. Although overall responsibility for artisan production appears overwhelmingly to belong to women (Table 6.2), there is an important sexual division of labor based on whether this activity is geared to use-value or exchange-value production. Women are primarily charged (in 76 percent of all households) with those activities which generate use values for the family's consumption: spinning, weaving, and sewing. When men are engaged in artisan production, they generally devote full time to it as tailors, brickmakers, carpenters, potters, or basket weavers.

In one-quarter of the households, artisan production is geared to the production of commodities—that is, generated cash income. Fathers are the artisans in 42 percent of these households and mothers are in 33 percent of them (Table 6.6). Artisan production as an income-generating activity and particularly as a male occupation, is a characteristic primarily of landless and smallholder households. The differences in the time devoted to this activity correspond to land-size stratum; landless and smallholder households devote at least 175 days annually to artisan production, and middle and rich peasant households that earn artisan income devote 52 days a year to it (Table 6.4).

Commerce

Petty commodity trading or "jiggling" is a family member's occupation in 17 percent of the households. This is predominantly a female occupation, although men occasionally participate. (Men tend to dominate large-scale or wholesale trading activities.) Before the opening of roads in the 1950s, the bulk of commodity circulation in the rural areas was carried out by women who would travel from market to market during the week. Today, these petty commodity traders have been largely replaced by traders from the city who scour the countryside in trucks during the harvest, buying up the crops. Nevertheless, petty commodity trading is still an important income source for rural women. Most women who engage in trade spend one day or so a week buying goods from their neighbors; they then take the goods to the city of Cajamarca for sale to the middlemen from the coast.

Another commercial activity in rural areas is the operation of country stores. Ten percent of the households in the sample had stores in their homes. Operating a store is an important activity among middle and rich peasant women, who have sufficient capital to set up a well-stocked country store.

Twenty-eight households devote an average of 162 days a year to commercial activities (Table 6.4). This activity is carried out by women in 86 percent of those households (Table 6.2); only in the landless and smallholder households do men run stores.

Wage Work

The single most important source of monetary income for Cajamarcan peasants, particularly those in landless and smallholder households, is wage work. In 1976, 55 percent of the households had at least one labor market participant in the household. In over one-third of these households, one family member worked full time for a wage; in the remainder, various household members were part-time participants in the labor market. As Table 6.2 illustrates, in most households the father is the principal wage earner, although frequently sons are also wage earners (Table 6.3). Not surprisingly, 85 percent of the labor market participants in the total sample are men (fathers and sons) (see Table 6.5).

Although women make up a smaller proportion (15 percent) of total participants in the labor market, their participation is significant in those households where they are the primary wage workers (10 percent of the households with part-time wage workers, and 13 percent of those with full-time wage workers). All of the female labor market participants come from the smallholder stratum of the peasantry.

More mothers are full-time than part-time wage workers, which is a reflection of the kinds of occupations that are open to women. Female occupations are limited to two: milker on the dairy farms and domestic servant in the city of Cajamarca. Milking jobs are most sought after by married women, for they provide stable employment and only require 4 or 5 hours of work a day, making them most compatible with use-value production on the farm. A domestic servant, however, must usually live in and thus be away from home. The only kind of part-time employment available to women is washing clothes or ironing on a daily basis, the activity carried out by the female semiproletarians in the sample.

TABLE 6.5 LABOR MARKET PARTICIPATION
OF FAMILY MEMBERS (IN PERCENTAGES)

Family Member	Full Time	Part Time	All Households
Father	39	54	49
	(n = 11)	(n = 30)	(n = 41)
Son	39	34	36
	(n = 11)	(n = 19)	(n = 30)
Mother	14	7	9
	(n = 4)	(n = 4)	(n = 8)
Daughter	7	5	6
	(n = 2)	(n = 3)	(n = 5)
Total	100	100	100
	(n = 28)	(n = 56)	(n = 84)

SOURCE: 1976 Peasant Family Survey.

The majority of maids in the city of Cajamarca are young girls who live away from home. Since only labor market participants who live in the household full time have been included in Table 6.5, the labor market participation of daughters has been underestimated. Nevertheless, when sons or daughters live away from home, not all of their wages are returned to the household; therefore, it is reasonable to exclude these participants in the calculation of household income.

Sons have a greater possibility of obtaining wage work in the rural areas, which possibly explains why daughters tend to leave the household at a younger age than sons. The primary sources of permanent employment for men are manufacturing, artisan production, and construction near the city of Cajamarca. These sectors are also important sources of temporary work. The agricultural sector employs the majority of semiproletarians.[11]

In summary, women in this peasant society do the bulk of the time-intensive tasks of daily maintenance and participate actively in a variety of activities that generate use and exchange values for the family's subsistence. Men, in contrast, engage primarily in the production of exchange values. Differences in the activities in which the family may participate as well as the relative participation of men and women in those activities are related to the size of land holdings.

Participation in farm activities, whether measured in terms of the total time devoted to the activity, the number of households within the land-size stratum participating, or the income generated by the activity, correlates positively with the household's access to the means of production. The activities that are an alternative to farming (wage work, artisan production, and commerce) correlate negatively with access to land.

As exchange values from farm production increase and an activity becomes an important source of cash income, men increasingly dominate the commercialization of the commodities that women have aided in producing. Among the upper strata of the peasantry, this is particularly true in animal production. Among the lower strata of the peasantry, women appear to take a more active role in agricultural production and in product disposition; they often control the proceeds from the sale of agricultural products as well as of animal products.

Petty commodity circulation is the major activity in which a degree of autonomy is exercised by women of all strata. Women of the lower strata tend to engage in petty trade, however, whereas women of the upper strata tend to run country stores.

Women of all strata also participate in artisan activities as a form of use-value production, but it is the women of the poorer strata who are most likely to depend on artisan activities as a source of income as well. Among the poorer strata of the peasantry, if men participate in artisan production at all, they tend to specialize in a given craft to generate exchange values. Wage labor, as well, is the domain of the poorer strata; both men and women engage in it, although men far outnumber women in the labor market.

WOMEN'S CONTRIBUTION TO HOUSEHOLD INCOME

Data on household income and the division of labor by sex reveal the important contribution of women and children to the generation of household income. Table 6.6 presents data on the principal person responsible for a series of household income-generating activities and the relative importance of the activity as a source of household income (Data by land-size strata are presented in Tables 6.7–6.10). Across all strata of the peasantry, adult women are principally responsible for commerce and animal care, which generate approximately one-third of both the mean *net* income and the mean *monetary* income of the household. The importance of children in the generation of household income is apparent: In almost one-quarter of the households, children have the primary responsibility for animal care, the activity that makes up approximately one-quarter of household mean net and mean monetary income. Men are primarily responsible for the activity that contributes most to household income—wage labor. In the majority of households, fathers are primarily responsible for the activities that together generate approximately 50 percent of household mean net and mean monetary income—agricultural and artisan production, and wage work.

Here it is important to consider the differences among land-size strata. As Tables 6.7–6.10 show, the predominantly female activities, animal care and commerce, show the greatest relative importance in the composition of household income among the middle and rich strata of the peasantry. A majority of women in the middle and rich peasant strata are charged with the animal care and commerce, which constitute approximately 37 percent of the household's mean net income in the middle stratum and 28 percent of the mean net income in the rich stratum. These activities account for approximately 35 percent of mean monetary household income (in which only exchange values are counted) in the middle stratum and approximately 40 percent of mean monetary income in the rich stratum. In contrast, among the near-landless and smallholder households, these female activities account for only approximately 29 percent and 22 percent of mean net income and for approximately 20 percent and 22 percent of mean monetary income, respectively, reflecting the lesser importance of, primarily, animal care in the composition of lower-strata household income.

Women's lesser contribution to income formation among poorer households also reflects the greater integration of the household into the labor market and the increased dependency of the household on wage income. Further, it appears that the greater the degree of integration of the household into the labor market, the less women contribute to the generation of exchange values. Women's efforts to raise the family's standard of living are by no means negligible, however, as their greater contribution to the generation of household mean net income, as opposed to mean monetary income (in all except rich peasant households) demonstrates.

TABLE 6.6 RELATIVE CONTRIBUTION OF FAMILY MEMBERS TO HOUSEHOLD INCOME, BY IMPORTANCE OF INCOME SOURCE: ALL PEASANT HOUSEHOLDS (IN PERCENTAGES)

Activity	Composition of Mean Net Income	Composition of Mean Monetary Income	Frequency Distribution of Principal Family Members Responsible for Activity				
			Mothers	Fathers	Children	Whole Family	Total
Agricultural production	17.6	11.3	7	60	8	25	100 (n = 102)
Animal care	23.6	25.0	62	4	23	11	100 (n = 92)
Artisan production	5.2	5.8	33	42	12	14	100 (n = 43)
Commerce	9.2	9.9	86	11	—	3	100 (n = 28)
Wage work	33.8	36.5	8	89	1	2	100 (n = 65)
All other income	10.6	11.5					
Total (n = 1,050)	100.0	100.0					

SOURCES: Income data (columns 1 and 2) taken from 1973 Cajamarca Income Survey. Participation data (columns 3–7) based on 1976 Peasant Family Survey with exception of wage work, which is based on 1973 Cajamarca Income Survey, the income data source. Commerce participation is restricted to trading as a profession and the operation of country stores; artisan production here includes only participation in income-generating activity.

TABLE 6.7 RELATIVE CONTRIBUTION OF FAMILY MEMBERS TO HOUSEHOLD INCOME, BY IMPORTANCE OF INCOME SOURCE: NEAR-LANDLESS HOUSEHOLDS (IN PERCENTAGES)

Activity	Composition of Mean Net Income	Composition of Mean Monetary Income	Frequency Distribution of Principal Family Members Responsible for Activity				
			Mothers	Fathers	Children	Whole Family	Total
Agricultural production	1.0	.4	15	62	—	23	100 (n = 13)
Animal care	18.8	8.5	73	—	27	—	100 (n = 11)
Artisan production	9.2	12.5	10	70	10	10	100 (n = 10)
Commerce	10.3	11.4	67	33	—	—	100 (n = 6)
Wage work	55.5	61.4	18	73	9	—	100 (n = 11)
All other income	5.2	5.8					
Total (n = 140)	100.0	100.0					

SOURCES: Income data (columns 1 and 2) taken from 1973 Cajamarca Income Survey. Participation data (columns 3–7) based on 1976 Peasant Family Survey with exception of wage work, which is based on 1973 Cajamarca Income Survey, the income data source. Commerce participation is restricted to trading as a profession and the operation of country stores; artisan production here includes only participation in income-generating activity.

TABLE 6.8 RELATIVE CONTRIBUTION OF FAMILY MEMBERS TO HOUSEHOLD INCOME, BY IMPORTANCE OF INCOME SOURCE: SMALLHOLDER HOUSEHOLDS (IN PERCENTAGES)

Activity	Composition of Mean Net Income	Composition of Mean Monetary Income	Frequency Distribution of Principal Family Members Responsible for Activity				
			Mothers	Fathers	Children	Whole Family	Total
Agricultural production	⁻0.2	5.3	8	52	11	29	100 (n = 65)
Animal care	10.0	8.2	61	5	20	14	100 (n = 59)
Artisan production	7.1	7.6	36	40	12	12	100 (n = 25)
Commerce	12.5	13.7	88	6	—	6	100 (n = 17)
Wage work	48.6	53.1	4	94	—	2	100 (n = 45)
All other income	11.6	12.1					
Total (n = 619)	100.0	100.0					

SOURCES: Income data (columns 1 and 2) taken from 1973 Cajamarca Income Survey. Participation data (columns 3–7) based on 1976 Peasant Family Survey with exception of wage work, which is based on 1973 Cajamarca Income Survey, the income data source. Commerce participation is restricted to trading as a profession and the operation of country stores; artisan production here includes only participation in income-generating activity.

TABLE 6.9 RELATIVE CONTRIBUTION OF FAMILY MEMBERS TO HOUSEHOLD INCOME, BY IMPORTANCE OF INCOME SOURCE: MIDDLE PEASANT HOUSEHOLDS (IN PERCENTAGES)

Activity	Composition of Mean Net Income	Composition of Mean Monetary Income	Frequency Distribution of Principal Family Members Responsible for Activity				
			Mothers	Fathers	Children	Whole Family	Total
Agricultural production	19.6	13.2	—	84	5	11	100 (n = 15)
Animal care	27.0	22.4	59	6	24	12	100 (n = 17)
Artisan production	4.1	5.6	20	20	20	40	100 (n = 5)
Commerce	10.4	12.4	100	—	—	—	100 (n = 5)
Wage work	23.5	27.9	13	87	—	—	100 (n = 8)
All other income	15.4	18.5					
Total (n = 177)	100.0	100.0					

SOURCES: Income data (columns 1 and 2) taken from 1973 Cajamarca Income Survey. Participation data (columns 3–7) based on 1976 Peasant Family Survey with exception of wage work, which is based on 1973 Cajamarca Income Survey, the income data source. Commerce participation is restricted to trading as a profession and the operation of country stores; artisan production here includes only participation in income-generating activity.

TABLE 6.10 RELATIVE CONTRIBUTION OF FAMILY MEMBERS TO HOUSEHOLD INCOME, BY IMPORTANCE OF INCOME SOURCE: RICH PEASANT HOUSEHOLDS (IN PERCENTAGES)

Activity	Composition of Mean Net Income	Composition of Mean Monetary Income	Frequency Distribution of Principal Family Members Responsible for Activity				
			Mothers	Fathers	Children	Whole Family	Total
Agricultural production	42.0	32.2	—	60	—	40	100 (n = 5)
Animal care	24.4	36.9	60	—	40	—	100 (n = 5)
Artisan production	2.1	1.7	100	—	—	—	100 (n = 3)
Commerce	3.6	3.3	—	—	—	—	(n = 0)
Wage work	11.4	10.6	—	100	—	—	100 (n = 1)
All other income	16.5	16.3					
Total (n = 81)	100.0	100.0					

SOURCES: Income data (columns 1 and 2) taken from 1973 Cajamarca Income Survey. Participation data (columns 3–7) based on 1976 Peasant Family Survey with exception of wage work, which is based on 1973 Cajamarca Income Survey, the income data source. Commerce participation is restricted to trading as a profession and the operation of country stores; artisan production here includes only participation in income-generating activity.

125

Conversely, the greater the degree of integration of the household into commodity production, the greater women's contribution to exchange-value generation appears to be. This result suggests an interesting paradox for, as previously noted, it is primarily among middle and rich peasant households that men play the dominant role in selling agricultural as well as animal products. The importance of an activity as a source of household income is related to the household's access to the means of production, and we may conclude that women's relative contribution to household income is a function of the household's degree of access to resources. A high degree of access to resources is, however, by no means a sufficient condition to ensure female autonomy in an activity.

The Differential Returns to Male and Female Labor

Table 6.11 presents data on returns to labor per day worked in a series of activities in 1973, by sex. Agricultural production has been attributed to men and animal production to women, based on the data presented in Table 6.2. Strictly speaking, however, as the preceding discussion has illustrated, the return to family labor from agricultural production is undifferentiable by sex, being a family activity in the majority of cases.[12]

What is immediately apparent from Table 6.11 is that in the activities in which both men and women engage—artisan production and wage work—men's remuneration is twice that of women's. Within each activity, there is task specialization by sex. Women spin, weave, and sew, whereas men specialize in the production of pots or baskets or are engaged in artisan services (such as carpentry and logging). The female artisan activities represent an extension of women's work in the production of use values in the home; men's artisan activities are considered occupations and are apparently remunerated as such.

In the labor market, as already noted, the jobs that are available to men and women are quite different. Although the average female proletarian worked one-third more days in 1973 (principally as a domestic servant) than the average male proletarian wage worker, female mean income from labor market activities was not quite half that of males in that year.

The remuneration data suggest that women's contribution to household income from these activities is not commensurate with the time women devote to these activities. Furthermore, the poor peasant household is affected most prejudicially by the differential returns to male and female labor, for it is primarily the women of the near-landless and smallholder households who engage in wage labor or in artisan production as an income-generating activity.

Commerce is the activity that yields the highest return to female labor. It should be noted, however, that in the 1973 Cajamarca Income Survey, female traders were underrepresented relative to owners of country stores, so the high return to commercial activities shown in the data accrues primarily to women from the middle stratum of the peasantry.

TABLE 6.11   AVERAGE RETURN TO FEMALE AND MALE LABOR PER DAYS WORKED, 1973 (IN PERUVIAN SOLES)

	Female		Male	
Activity	Average Return	Number of Days Worked	Average Return	Number of Days Worked
Agricultural production	—	—	S/.33	28
				(n = 105)
Animal raising	S/.80	246	—	—
		(n = 87)		
Artisan production	S/.20	42	S/.43	169
		(n = 11)		(n = 20)
Commerce	S/.71	243	—	—
		(n = 12)		
Wage work	S/.16	225	S/.42	176
		(n = 6)		(n = 61)

SOURCES: Data on number of days worked and income earned taken from 1973 Cajamarca Income Survey. With the exception of wage work, the division of labor by sex was not specified in this survey, so the allocation of return to female and male labor is based on the 1976 Peasant Family Survey. Artisan production was attributed to female or male family members based on the specific activity (i.e., spinning was attributed to women, carpentry to men).
NOTE: In 1973, U.S.$1.00 = S.43.

The most poorly remunerated activity in terms of time appears to be animal raising. It should be noted, however, that the labor time devoted to animal raising by women and children also includes time for the production of other use values. Grazing, for example, is carried out in conjunction with a number of other tasks, such as wood gathering and spinning, as well as child care. Nonetheless, the data show the lowest remuneration to labor in an activity that is a crucial source of total household income. Given the significant wage differentials between men and women in the labor market, the forgone income from women's use-value and exchange-value production on the farm may far exceed the income they can earn in the labor market. This is perhaps one determinant of the division of labor by sex; in order to maximize income, households may allocate women's labor to the farm and men's labor to the market.

CONCLUSION

The importance of taking into account the form and degree of integration of the peasantry into the economy is evident from this analysis. The relation between familial labor deployment and the parameters of the labor market and the product market is clear. First, the activities in which the peasant family may engage are a function of their access to subsistence means of production. Second, the differential rewards to male and female labor, determined by capitalist conditions of employment, encourage greater male labor market participation and determine division of labor by sex on the farm for the majority of poor peasant households. Women take on greater responsibility than men for activities that produce use value, such as agricultural work, and they contribute to the household's total income formation primarily through the generation of use values in farm activities. Thus women's poverty is determined by the household's poverty, which is conditioned by the household's degree of access to the means of production, on the one hand, and by capitalist conditions of employment, on the other.

Notes

1. This methodology is developed in Carmen Diana Deere and Alain de Janvry, "A Conceptual Framework for the Empirical Analysis of Peasants," *American Journal of Agricultural Economics* 62 (1979):601–11.

2. A complete analysis of intrafamilial labor deployment would have to take into account family structure and composition over the family life cycle. Over the family life cycle, the age and sex composition of the household changes significantly, so that the division of labor by sex and age within the household would also be expected to vary. Family structure and composition also figure heavily in determining the range of activities in which a given household may participate at a given time.

3. The 1973 Cajamarca Income Survey was carried out under the direction of Ing. Efraín Franco of the Proyecto Cajamarca-La Libertad, Programa de Estudios Socio-Económicos. The 1976 Peasant Family Survey gathered data on the population defined by the 1973 sample and was carried out by the author from June to August 1976. Analysis of the data from both surveys can be found in Deere 1978a.

4. *Catastro Rural*, Ministerio de Agricultura, Zona Agraria II, Cajamarca, 1972.

5. Housecleaning was not considered a separate household task, for in the majority of households it is carried out in conjunction with meal preparation and cleanup. The meal is usually served on a tablecloth on the ground in the lean-to kitchen or on the front porch of the one-room house, so the floor is generally swept and belongings are picked up before the major meal of the day. Extensive food preparation is usually required for just one meal, served some time between 2:00 and 5:00 P.M., depending on the family's activities that day. This meal includes a soup or porridge, which is then reheated in the evening or early morning.

6. Only 7 percent of the households were located near a potable water source; all of these households were in the rural areas surrounding the city of Cajamarca, the capital of the department of the same name.

7. The time that might be devoted exclusively to child care has not been taken into account in this calculation. Most respondents considered child care an activity complementary to their work in the household or in the fields, not a separate activity. Nevertheless, this underestimates the total amount of time devoted to such activity, since children, particularly daughters, are charged with looking after younger brothers and sisters.

8. Carmen Diana Deere, "The Agricultural Division of Labor by Sex: Myths, Facts, and Contradictions in the Northern Peruvian Sierra," a paper presented to the panel on the subject,

Women: the New Marginals in the Development Process? at the joint meetings of the Latin American Studies Association and the African Studies Association, Houston, November 1977; forthcoming in *Economic Development and Cultural Change* (July 1982).

9. Ibid.

10. The actual accounting of days worked in agricultural production in the 1976 agricultural year revealed that near-landless households spent 20 labor-days a year in agricultural production, while smallholder households spent fewer than 60 labor-days. Ibid.

11. Part-time work is becoming increasingly difficult to find; from 1973 to 1976, the mean number of days worked by semiproletarians in the sample decreased significantly, from an average of 130 days a year in 1973 to 66 days a year in 1976. This is reflected in the decrease in the total number of days devoted to the labor market by all participants, from 193 days a year in 1973 to 150 days a year in 1976. In the same period, the number of semiproletarians in the sample increased by 27 percent, whereas the number of proletarians in the sample stayed constant.

12. The significant variation among land-size strata in the average return to labor in agricultural production should be noted. Whereas landless farmers earned S/.14 and smallholders earned S/.22, middle peasants earned S/.37 and rich peasants earned S/1.19. The difference in magnitude is partly explained by the fact that the values of capital stock and land were not consistently reported, so that depreciation was not taken into account in the computation of gross and net income.

SECTION 2 Women and Welfare

7. Nutritional Stress and Economic Responsibility: A Study of Nigerian Women

Judith A. Harrington

Although attention has been, and is being, paid to population-related aspects of female status, demographers have not done as much work as is needed on the measurement of women's condition. Many demographic studies include data that have important implications and consequences for women, but the focus of these analyses has not always facilitated a clear understanding of these implications. The search for demographic indicators of female status in existing data sets needs to be conducted on a large scale and in a systematic way. Such analyses should, at one level at least, be centered on categories of real-life experience, so that our "subjects" can recognize themselves and their real-life situations and so that we can recognize their needs. Too often in following current policy or funding interests—or simply the trends of "professional" discourse—we have failed to measure and analyze the world as it is.

The issue of breast-feeding is an important example of this neglect of the real world. Currently, the importance of breast-feeding in both child spacing and child survival is receiving a great deal of attention. Investigations have demonstrated that declining lengths of lactation have detrimental effects on both spacing and survival and have underlined the desirability of breast-feeding as opposed to bottle-feeding, particularly in tropical developing countries. What has been neglected, however, is a key part of the total picture: Very prolonged lactation, such as is common in West Africa, constitutes a heavy physical burden on the women who spend a good part of their lives giving birth to and breast-feeding their children.[1] Breast-feeding on demand during 1½ to 2 years for each of five to seven children adds up to a very large proportion of adult life spent under heavy nutritional and physical stress. At the same time West African women, like most Third World women, are working and are expected to contribute to the economic support of the household.

Women from three areas of Nigeria are the focus of this essay. The women have very different economic roles in adulthood. Yoruba women, in Ibadan, are expected to be economically active outside the home (predominantly in trade); women in Benin and Kano have more restricted access to nondomestic spheres—in fact, women in the Kano sample often carry on their economic activity (crafts

130

and petty trade) from within a secluded household through their young children.[2]

In Yorubaland (where our Ibadan sample was sited), the much-touted "independent and economically active" women are expected as part and parcel of their adult role to support themselves and their children on a day-to-day basis.

> Basically, it is accepted that the husband is the breadwinner and must always provide for the wife/wives, and the children. However, whenever a wife has an independent job of her own from which she could earn some money, she may be expected to maintain herself or contribute to the maintenance of the family.[3] . . . it is customary for the husband to advance money to each of his wives by way of a loan for the wife's personal trade.[4]
>
> A woman shall carry on her own private business (in trade or industry) to provide for her own sustenance as well as for the nourishment of her own children, *especially when in infancy*[5] (italics added).

Women in this group are expected to maintain themselves and their children during the very periods that they are under heavy stress from their childbearing role—when the children are in infancy and not yet weaned. Yoruba women's "status" may be enhanced, maintained, and even ensured by their economic independence, but this independent role is one that the women are *expected* to play in addition to their other roles. Their physiological reproductive role encompasses pregnancy, birth, and a prolonged lactation of upwards of 2 years.

For those of us who analyze data in searching for policy and program implications, maintenance of a high birthrate may be a national policy issue, and breast-feeding may be ideal from a number of points of view, but both entail hard physical work by the women concerned. This essay explores the burdens imposed on Nigerian women by their reproductive and economic roles in order to temper advocacy of prolonged breast-feeding by highlighting the costs to the mother who must breast-feed. The first section presents information about the physical stress and nutritional requirements of pregnancy and breast-feeding. In the second section, data from the Nigeria Migration Project (NMP) are used to develop indexes of the relative nutritional stress and economic burden that the subjects of the study must bear. In the third section, these indexes are related to several socioeconomic characteristics of the Nigerian women, such as age at first marriage, education, and occupation. The concluding section presents some ways in which these women's burdens might be alleviated.

PHYSICAL STRESS AND NUTRITIONAL REQUIREMENTS OF PREGNANCY AND LACTATION

The "labor" of childbirth is appropriately named, but unfortunately it implies that the work lasts for a short period, whereas in reality, the whole period of pregnancy and lactation is a time of increased physical and nutritional stress.

Table 7.1 shows the percentage increase in daily nutritional requirements associated with pregnancy and lactation at various ages.

It should be noted that lactation as well as pregnancy increases nutritional needs and, for most nutrients, the demands of lactation are greater than those of pregnancy. The Report of the 1973 Joint Food and Agriculture Organization/World Health Organization Ad Hoc Expert Committee states that

> in many countries there are women for whom the burden of pregnancy is added to the physical work of running a home and caring for several small children. Such women need additional food to meet *all* the energy requirements of pregnancy. . . .
>
> Previously an allowance of 40,000 kcal (170 MJ) per pregnancy was recommended for calculating the energy requirements of countries. However, a safe level of energy intake is a basic requirement to insure satisfactory nutrition for the fetus and breast-fed infant. The present committee, recognizing that this recommendation differs from other estimates for energy that are average requirements, recommends 80,000 kcal (335 MJ) for pregnancy. . . .
>
> During 6 months of lactation the energy requirement is about 135,000 kcal (565 MJ). If the pregnant woman has laid down fat according to the full allowance for pregnancy, she has a reserve of about 36,000 kcal (151 MJ) that will be available for lactation. The additional energy requirement for lactation would then be 100,000 kcal (415 MJ) or about 550 kcal (2.3 MJ) per day. Mothers with less stored fat need a correspondingly greater food intake during lactation, as do women who continue breast-feeding beyond 6 months.[6]

The authors of this report are not referring to the needs of women with "full-time" employment outside the home, nor are they considering the needs of Nigerian women who often breast-feed three to four times as long as this report mentions.

What are appropriate nutritional requirements for the women we will be discussing? What are the costs of pregnancy and prolonged lactation to women of multiple stress, who have many children, long lactations, and heavy financial responsibility—women who do heavy physical work, are sometimes very young and are living in a disease-ridden environment where good-quality protein is in short supply? The costs to Nigerian women must be higher than those shown in Table 7.1, which are based on the needs of sedentary and relatively privileged North American women.

In 1964 Michael Latham wrote of his concern for the maternal nutrition of African women whose lives were often an almost unbroken cycle of pregnancy and lactation:

> Pregnancy can be regarded as a physiological process, but it has very definite pathological potential. It could . . . be argued that menstruation itself is an abnormal condition. . . . Life would consist of pregnancy, birth and lactation from the menarche to the menopause. . . . Certainly in Africa, pregnancy and lactation occupy many years of a woman's life and therefore have a very marked effect upon her nutritional requirements and status. . . .

TABLE 7.1 ADULT AND ADOLESCENT FEMALE RECOMMENDED DAILY DIETARY ALLOWANCES (BASED ON NORTH AMERICAN WOMEN)

Nutrient	Recommended Nonpregnant Allowance (RNPA)	Percentage of RNPA Needed in Adult Pregnancy	Percentage of RNPA Needed in Adolescent Pregnancy	Percentage of RNPA Needed for Lactation at Ages			
				11–14	15–18	19–22	23–50
Energy (Kcal)	2,000	115	—[b]	145	130	130	125
Protein (g)	46	165	—[c]	139	148	144	144
Vitamin A (RE[a])	800	125	625	150	150	150	150
Vitamin A (IU)	4,000	125	—	150	150	150	150
Vitamin D (IU)	400	400	400	400	400	400	400
Vitamin E (IU)	12	125	117	125	125	125	125
Vitamin C (ascorbic acid) (mg)	45	133	133	178	178	178	178
Folic acid (mg)	400	200	300	150	150	150	150
Niacin (mg)	13	115	123	154	138	138	131
Riboflavin (mg)	1.2	125	142	150	158	158	142
Thiamine (mg)	1.0	140	140	150	140	140	130
Vitamin B_6 (mg)	2.0	125	125	125	125	125	125
Vitamin B_{12} (mg)	3.0	133	133	133	133	133	133
Calcium (mg)	800	150	150	150	150	150	150
Phosphorous (mg)	800	150	300	150	150	150	150
Iodine (mg)	100	125	140	150	150	150	150
Iron (mg)	18	100+	100+	100	100	100	100
Magnesium (mg)	300	150	150	150	150	150	150
Zinc (mg)	15	133	133	167	167	167	167

Sources: From Food and Nutrition Board, National Research Council, National Academy of Sciences, *Recommended Dietary Allowances*, 8th ed. (Washington, D.C.: Government Printing Office, 1974), table 7.3; and B. S. Worthington et al., *Nutrition in Lactation and Pregnancy* (St. Louis: C. V. Mosby, 1977), table 3.3.

[a]Retinal equivalent (replaces IU as the standard measure of Vitamin A activity).

[b]Figures given in terms of Kcal/kg. Adolescent daily allowance = 40. Adult pregnant daily increase per kg = 5. Adolescent pregnant daily increase = 45.

[c]Figures given in terms of Kcal/kg. Adolescent pregnant daily increase per kg = 1.3. Adult pregnant daily increase per kg. = .4.

Relatively little is known of the clinical or pathological features of protein deficiency of adults; yet the protein intake of pregnant and lactating mothers in Africa is often extremely low. . . . Physicians frequently see the "wreck of a woman" following frequent pregnancies on an unsatisfactory diet. She is usually thin, miserable, anemic and often apathetic, with a dry scaly skin, sometimes rather lusterless hair, often with an ulcer that is reluctant to heal, and some mouth lesions. She is labelled in the clinic as a case of "general malnutrition," "multiple deficiency." There is no universally adopted term for this syndrome, nor a sure guide to its diagnosis; is it not, in fact, caloric protein deficiency disease of adults?[7]

These same conditions were discussed in a 1975 article by Henri Vis and others: "Women suffer from general endemic malnutrition which is intensified because they assume the burdens of most agricultural work and because their childbearing years are one long uninterrupted pregnancy and nursing experience. . . . In the Central African interlakes region, protein-calorie deficiency typically appears at 3½ to 4 years of age or later. It is, however, not at all unusual to find adults and nursing mothers displaying clinical and biological signs of marasmus kwashiorkor [caloric protein deficiency disease]."[8] Unfortunately, no data on such cases were presented.

DATA AND INDEXES

The Nigeria Migration Project included four sample surveys—three undertaken in urban areas and one undertaken in a rural area. The data used here are drawn from the urban surveys carried out in 1973 and 1974 in Ibadan, Benin, and Kano. Although the project was originally designed as a migration survey, it was set up in such a way as to be useful as a general population sample. Sampling frames were developed from recent aerial photos and the resultant urban samples were multistage probability cluster samples of households. Within selected households *all* individuals, male and female, aged 15 years and older, were interviewed. (Details of sampling and responses are given in Appendix A.) Given the lack of reliable public census information for the three cities, it is not possible to estimate the representativeness of the three urban samples.

The NMP data set was structured around a short basic questionnaire that collected factual information from all respondents: background social and demographic characteristics, migration histories, employment/unemployment histories, and marital and pregnancy histories. A 20 percent subsample received an additional longer and more detailed questionnaire, which asked for information on family-size attitudes and practice, health care, household economics, and job search, and for more detailed migration and work histories. It is from this subsample that the information for the economic responsibility index described in this chapter is drawn. The pregnancy and lactation information for the nutritional stress index applies to the entire sample. Questionnaires were administered

TABLE 7.2 SAMPLE SIZE AND BASIC DETAILED QUESTIONNAIRE BREAKDOWN

Sample	Short Questionnaire	Long Questionnaire	Total	Long Questionnaire as Percentage of Total Responses
Ibadan	1,086	240	1,326	18.1
Benin	631	161	792	14.7
Kano	777	128	905	20.5

in local languages by trained secondary-school graduates and university students. Sample size and questionnaire breakdown are shown in Table 7.2.

The Indexes

The data gathered permitted an analysis of women's "burden" in areas of physical and nutritional stress associated with the total childbearing role and the economic contribution of the women in their familial/domestic role.

The Index of Physical and Nutritional Stress

The index of physical and nutritional stress measures the wear and tear and physical work of pregnancy and lactation in terms of time spent in these states— that is, the proportion of a woman's reproductive life to date spent either pregnant or breast-feeding. The basic unrefined index is defined, using available NMP data, as:

$$\frac{\text{Total Length of Physical and Nutritional Stress}}{\text{Length of Reproductive Life to Date}} \times 100.$$

It should be noted that there are some problems associated with this index.
1. Age distribution effects. The index does not take into account the declining fecundity and eventual infecundity at menopause of older women and therefore may understate their burden by including years that are less likely to include pregnancy or lactation. The health of women in these later years may be detrimentally affected by the steady reproductive activity of earlier years.
2. Distortions in the time and age data. These data were carefully checked in the interviewing and editing stages but memory problems inevitably detract from their accuracy. Unfortunately, many cases had to be excluded from the analysis due to lack of sufficient age data (see Table 7.3). These excluded cases are most likely women who have experienced a high degree of physical and nutritional stress—older, less educated women with high fertility. Thus, the exclusion of these cases may result in an index that understates the burdens of the sample population.

TABLE 7.3   PERCENTAGE OF "DON'T KNOW" (*DK*) RESPONSES
IN RELATIVE AGE–ADJUSTED PHYSICAL AND NUTRITIONAL STRESS INDEX,
BY SELECTED SOCIOECONOMIC STATUS–RELATED VARIABLES

	Ibadan		Benin		Kano	
Variable	DK	*n*	DK	*n*	DK	*n*
Age						
15–24	33.6	(434)	36.6	(306)	88.0	(469)
25–34	39.7	(383)	34.6	(217)	38.1	(270)
35+	49.1	(277)	43.5	(186)	24.8	(145)
Marital Arrangement						
Monogamous	51.5	(672)	44.9	(448)	40.4	(612)
Polygamous	55.9	(363)	58.2	(206)	28.6	(192)
Age at First Marriage						
10–14	27.3	(11)	40.0	(20)	37.2	(360)
15–19	40.6	(293)	38.2	(314)	32.7	(300)
20–24	39.0	(336)	35.9	(128)	22.9	(48)
25+	28.2	(71)	34.8	(23)	14.3	(7)
Number of Times Married						
0	5.6	(234)	4.9	(121)	4.1	(98)
1	53.2	(909)	48.2	(569)	37.9	(661)
2+	50.0	(124)	54.2	(94)	34.5	(91)
Education						
None	60.0	(625)	56.5	(322)	27.9	(129)
Primary-Koranic	33.7	(430)	38.0	(347)	36.0	(726)
Secondary+	18.3	(213)	14.8	(115)	11.9	(42)
Occupation Last 3 Mos.						
Housewife	35.1	(387)	44.7	(488)	38.0	(652)
Unskilled service	4.5	(22)	14.3	(14)	9.1	(66)
Traders	56.7	(582)	51.6	(155)	28.5	(123)
Large-scale commercial	48.6	(72)	33.3	(15)	33.3	(3)
Skilled modern sector	41.4	(70)	22.7	(44)	23.5	(34)
Clerical/low prof.	11.1	(45)	10.0	(20)	40.0	(5)
Medium-low prof.	25.7	(70)	25.7	(35)	10.0	(10)

3.   Overlap between pregnancy and lactation. Theoretically, at least, the women in some of our samples are not supposed to have had intercourse while breast-feeding. This is because of a myth that sperm will poison the mother's milk, which is no doubt a cultural expression of the awareness of the kwashiorkor–child displacement syndrome. A taboo on intercourse during lactation is common in most West African societies, and in Yorubaland it is reported to be strictly observed; the reason for weaning, however, is often reported to be subsequent pregnancy.

The Index of Economic Participation in Payment of Basic Household Necessities
   The economic responsibility index was constructed using women's responses to a series of questions about who paid for clothing for self, spouse, and children;

food; and housing. By scoring the responses to each question 100 if the woman paid, 0 if anyone else (such as husband) paid, and 50 if "both" paid, we were able to approximate the extent of the woman's participation in providing the basic necessities of the household as a percentage of a possible total of 500 points (see Table 7.4 for a comparison of male and female responses to these questions). When a category of expenditure was not applicable—that is, women were

TABLE 7.4   COMPARISON OF FEMALE AND MALE RESPONSES TO QUESTIONS ABOUT WHO PAYS FOR HOUSEHOLD EXPENSES

Question	Ibadan		Benin		Kano	
	F	M	F	M	F	M
Who pays rent?						
Respondent	7.8	82.4	16.9	74.2	14.0	89.0
Spouse	79.2	1.3	62.5	0	72.9	0
Both	1.3	2.6	.7	0	.9	2.0
Other	11.6	13.8	19.8	25.8	12.2	9.0
Total	99.9	100.1	99.9	100.0	100.0	100.0
n	(154)	(153)	(136)	(124)	(107)	(100)
Who pays for food?						
Respondent	12.2	78.8	16.1	76.1	15.1	91.2
Spouse	62.2	.5	60.4	.7	76.5	.9
Both	19.4	14.5	8.7	3.7	3.4	5.3
Other	6.1	6.3	14.8	19.4	5.0	2.6
Total	99.9	100.1	100.0	99.9	100.0	100.0
n	(196)	(193)	(149)	(134)	(119)	(114)
Who buys respondent's clothes?						
Respondent	48.2	91.8	30.6	84.8	16.8	93.2
Spouse	19.3	.5	38.8	.8	58.8	0
Both	26.4	4.1	18.4	1.5	19.3	3.4
Other	6.1	3.6	12.3	12.9	5.0	3.5
Total	100.0	100.0	100.1	100.0	99.9	100.1
n	(197)	(195)	(147)	(132)	(119)	(117)
Who buys spouse's clothes?						
Respondent	5.9	29.4	11.5	67.0	10.1	78.8
Spouse	87.2	35.9	82.0	14.3	86.2	1.9
Both	4.3	34.6	4.1	15.4	2.8	19.2
Other	2.6	0	2.4	3.3	.9	0
Total	100.0	99.9	100.0	100.0	100.0	99.9
n	(187)	(153)	(122)	(91)	(109)	(104)
Who buys children's clothes?						
Respondent	11.6	37.5	15.5	67.4	12.0	70.4
Spouse	26.0	6.3	46.6	7.0	54.0	0
Both	56.9	54.9	32.8	17.4	32.0	28.6
Other	5.5	1.4	5.2	8.2	2.0	1.0
Total	100.0	100.1	100.1	100.0	100.0	100.0
n	(181)	(144)	(116)	(86)	(100)	(98)

not married and/or had no children—the index was calculated as a percentage of a possible total of 300 or 400 points. Because of the scoring system, the index scores do not form a continuous variable.

Since accurate collection of detailed data on total expenditures was quite difficult and was beyond the scope of the NMP, this index represents the best approximation possible, given the data at hand, of the degree of women's economic responsibilities and burdens in the areas studied. The index is admittedly crude, however, and has several shortcomings.

1.   The index measures women's contributions to specific categories of expenditure only, rather than their contributions to the total household budget. Since the proportion of the budget devoted to each of the five categories considered here will vary, it is not appropriate to assume that two women with the same score on this index actually contribute to the total household budget to the same extent.

2.   If a woman contributes to a category of expenditure along with her husband or other household members, she is assigned a score of 50 for that category of expenditure. This fixed score may not reflect the proportion of expenditure in that category actually contributed by the woman and, thus, may either understate or overstate the degree of her economic burden.

3.   The categories of expenses to which women contribute may vary according to their socioeconomic status (SES). Women with a low SES may well contribute to basic household expenditures only, whereas women with a higher SES may contribute to nonbasic expenditures, leaving the basics to their husbands. If this is true, the index will understate the economic responsibility of higher SES women relative to lower SES women. The analysis presented here does examine variations in index scores across a number of SES-related variables, however, so that, to some extent, the degree of this bias can be determined.

4.   The index scores do not necessarily reflect the degree of effort required for a woman to make a given level of contribution to the basic expenditures of her household. Women engaged in well-remunerated work may be able to contribute a great deal to household expenditures, even though their work is not necessarily more taxing than that of lower paid women who may contribute less to household expenses. This analysis presents index scores by age-group, a proxy for cultural setting, in an attempt to deal, at least partially, with this problem. Ideally, scores should also be compared by education and occupation groupings, but the sample sizes were too small to permit this comparison.

5.   Finally, the degree of economic participation reported by the women may not reflect the actual situation. For this reason, the responses of both males and females to questions on expenditures are reported in Table 7.3 to aid the reader in evaluating the data and findings presented here.

It is to be hoped that the shortcomings just listed will encourage other social scientists to undertake the great effort required to gather the more detailed data necessary to determine definitively the economic responsibilities of Third World women.

Measurement of Relative Burdens

While controlling for both age and cultural setting, we divided the distribution of Ibadan, Benin, and Kano women in both indexes into three groups: the bottom 50 percent of the distributions, the economic participation groups who experienced "average" physical and nutritional stress; the middle 51–75 percent, who experienced medium-high physical and nutritional stress; and the top 25 percent, who experienced a high degree of stress. (Cut-off scores for each group are given in Tables 7.5 and 7.6.) These relative burden indexes were then cross-tabulated with each other and with variables related to socioeconomic characteristics (education, occupation) and life conditions/status in marriage (age at first marriage, monogamy or polygamy, and number of times married), in order to see how the life situations of these women have affected their chances of ending up in the various burden groups.

TABLE 7.5   PERCENTAGE SCORES ON PHYSICAL AND NUTRITIONAL STRESS INDEX USED TO RECLASSIFY WOMEN INTO RELATIVE AGE-ADJUSTED INDEX

Age-Group	Average (bottom 50%)	Med-High (51–75%)	High (76–100%)
Ibadan			
15–24	0	—	20–100
25–34	0–66	67–83	84–100
35+	0–46	47–61	62–100
DK	0	10–48	49–100
Benin			
15–24	0	—	40–100
25–34	0–66	67–84	85–100
35+	0–49	50–62	63–100
DK	0	—	40–100
Kano			
15–24	0	—	10–100
25–34	0–30	31–68	69–100
35+	0–25	26–44	45–100
DK	0	—	40–60

NOTE: DK = ages unknown.

TABLE 7.6 PERCENTAGE SCORES ON INDEX
OF PARTICIPATION IN PAYMENT OF BASIC NECESSITIES
USED TO RECLASSIFY WOMEN INTO RELATIVE
AGE-ADJUSTED INDEX

Age-Group	Average (bottom 50%)	Med-High (51–75%)	High (76–100%)
	Ibadan		
15–24	0–10	12–25	33–80
25–34	0–25	33–40	50–100
35+	0–25	33–40	50–100
DK	0–25	33–37	50–100
	Benin		
15–24	0	1–25	33–100
25–34	0–12	16–25	33–100
35+	0–25	33–50	60–100
DK	0	1–20	25–100
	Kano		
15–24	0	1–12	20–100
25–34	0	1–20	25–100
35+	0	1–25	33–100
DK	0	1–25	50

NOTE: Women falling in the bottom 50 percent of the distribution of scores in the age-group 15–24 in the Ibadan sample had scores of 0–10 percent participation in the payment of basic necessities.

ANALYSIS OF FINDINGS

Table 7.7 shows the distribution of all women aged 15 and over in the basic nutritional stress index by current age. The table includes women who have not yet had a pregnancy—they are at the 0 percentile and heavily influence the 15–24 age distributions. According to this table, it is women aged 25–34 who fall most often into the highest stress ranges, having spent more than 60 percent of their time either pregnant or lactating. The proportions of women over 35 in the heaviest stress groups are lower; these women are distributed all along the index. In the Kano sample there are lower proportions of women of all ages in the higher stress groups, and higher proportions of women at the 0 percentile. This reflects a situation of lower fertility in Kano, where there is evidence of infertility and subfecundity, possibly associated with gynecological problems stemming from early marriage and childbirth (often prolonged and unattended),[9] preferred cross-cousin marriages, and venereal and other diseases.[10]

Table 7.8 shows the distribution in the nutritional stress index of women who have had at least one pregnancy. It appears that the 15–24 age-group is under very heavy stress; 42.4 percent of the women in Ibadan, 56.5 percent of the women in Benin, and 34.7 percent of the women in Kano in this age-group have spent over *80 percent* of their adult lives to date pregnant or lactating. Of course, they are just beginning—they have not yet lived very long in their reproductive lives. The proportions of women aged 25–34 in this category are lower, but still approximately *one-third* of the women in Ibadan and Benin and *one-quarter* of the women in Kano have spent more than 80 percent of their adult reproductive lives to date actively engaged in reproduction. For women over age 35 with declining fecundity and eventual menopause, the situation improves, yet 28.0 percent, 30.0 percent, and 21.1 percent of the women over 35 in Ibadan, Benin, and Kano, respectively, have spent at least 60 percent of their adult lives physiologically committed to motherhood and therefore under nutritional and physical stress.

TABLE 7.7 PERCENTAGE DISTRIBUTION OF ALL WOMEN
IN INDEX OF NUTRITIONAL STRESS, BY CURRENT AGE

Current Age	Percentage of Adult Life Pregnant or Breast-Feeding						Total	n
	0	1–20	21–40	41–60	61–80	81–100		
				Ibadan				
15–24	81.9	—	.7	2.8	6.9	7.6	99.9	(288)
25–34	11.6	2.6	6.1	19.8	29.8	30.2	100.1	(232)
35+	6.4	8.5	25.5	33.3	19.2	7.1	100.0	(141)
DK	61.2	4.1	2.0	10.2	10.2	12.3	100.0	(49)
Total	42.6	2.8	7.5	14.9	17.0	15.1	99.9	(710)
				Benin				
15–24	76.3	—	—	4.2	6.2	13.4	100.1	(194)
25–34	4.2	6.3	12.7	19.8	27.5	29.6	100.1	(142)
35+	4.8	14.3	21.9	30.4	20.0	8.6	100.0	(105)
DK	75.0	—	—	8.3	16.7	—	100.0	(12)
Total	37.1	5.3	9.1	15.6	15.9	17.0	100.0	(453)
				Kano				
15–24	76.1	.6	2.6	4.5	7.9	8.2	99.9	(314)
25–34	33.5	5.4	15.3	13.2	16.8	17.4	100.1	(167)
35+	22.0	19.2	32.1	10.1	12.8	3.7	99.9	(109)
DK	80.0	—	—	20.0	—	—	100.0	(5)
Total	54.3	5.4	11.1	8.1	11.2	9.9	100.0	(595)

NOTE: DK = ages unknown.

Nigerian women are spending extremely long periods under the physical and nutritional stress associated with their total childbearing-mothering role. This is shown in Table 7.9, which reports actual numbers of years spent pregnant or breast-feeding by all women over age 15 in our three sample areas. Some women have not yet completed all the years of pregnancy and breast-feeding that await them. Even so, approximately 15 percent of the women in Kano, 21 percent of the women in Ibadan, and 30 percent of the women in Benin have spent more than 10 years pregnant or breast-feeding. These figures are probably underestimates since many women were dropped from the analysis because of insufficient data on ages and dates. As mentioned earlier, such women are likely to be older and/or less educated and may have higher fertility and longer periods of lactation.

TABLE 7.8 PERCENTAGE DISTRIBUTION OF WOMEN WITH AT LEAST ONE PREGNANCY IN INDEX OF NUTRITIONAL STRESS, BY CURRENT AGE

| Current Age | Percentage of Adult Life Pregnant or Breast-Feeding | | | | | Total | n |
	1–20	21–40	41–60	61–80	81–100		
			Ibadan				
15–24	—	3.8	15.3	38.5	42.4	100.0	(52)
25–34	2.9	6.8	22.4	33.6	34.1	99.8	(205)
35+	9.1	27.3	35.6	20.4	7.6	100.0	(132)
DK	10.5	5.3	26.3	26.3	31.5	99.9	(19)
Total	4.9	13.0	26.0	29.8	26.2	99.9	(407)
			Benin				
15–24	—	—	17.4	26.0	56.5	99.9	(46)
25–34	6.6	13.2	20.5	28.7	30.9	99.9	(136)
35+	15.0	23.0	32.0	21.0	9.0	100.0	(100)
DK	—	—	100.0	—	—	100.0	(3)
Total	8.4	14.4	24.9	25.3	27.0	100.0	(235)
			Kano				
15–24	2.6	10.7	18.7	33.3	34.7	100.0	(75)
25–34	8.1	20.7	19.8	25.2	26.1	99.9	(111)
35+	24.7	41.1	12.9	16.4	4.7	99.8	(85)
DK	—	—	100.0	—	—	100.0	(1)
Total	11.6	24.2	17.6	24.6	21.7	99.9	(272)

NOTE: DK = ages unknown.

TABLE 7.9 YEARS SPENT PREGNANT OR BREAST-FEEDING:
ALL WOMEN AGED 15 YEARS AND OLDER WITH AT LEAST ONE
PREGNANCY

Number of Years	Ibadan		Benin		Kano	
	n	Percent	*n*	Percent	*n*	Percent
1–3	(283)	28.9	(163)	26.8	(199)	34.6
4–5	(186)	19.5	(123)	20.2	(117)	20.3
6–7	(169)	17.8	(73)	12.0	(97)	16.8
8–9	(111)	11.7	(63)	10.3	(72)	12.5
10–14	(103)	16.1	(123)	20.2	(59)	10.3
15–20	(37)	3.9	(50)	8.2	(20)	3.5
21+	(11)	1.2	(14)	2.3	(11)	1.9
	(950)	100.0	(609)	100.0	(575)	99.9
1–5	(469)	48.4	(286)	47.0	(316)	54.9
6–9	(280)	29.5	(136)	22.3	(169)	29.3
10+	(201)	21.2	(187)	30.7	(90)	15.7
	(950)	100.0	(609)	100.0	(575)	99.9

Economic Responsibility Index

Table 7.10 shows the distribution of all women aged 15 and over for whom the information necessary to construct the economic participation index was available. The cultural differences among the samples are quite evident. Ibadan (Yoruba) women are most likely to participate in paying for basic necessities in the household. Only 23.1 percent of Ibadan women pay for none of the basics of their households, compared with 47.4 percent of the Benin women and 56.3 percent of the Kano women. Most of the women in Ibadan and Benin who do contribute to the basic expenditures included in the index scored from 25 to 40 percent on the index, whereas in Kano most women who contributed to these expenditures scored from 10 to 20 percent. In all three sample areas there are some women who scored over 80 percent; Kano has the highest proportion of women in this high-scoring group.

Participation in payment of basic expenditures varies by age, being least likely for women aged 15–24, probably because many women in this group are still in school and in a dependent status. Still, approximately 13 percent of the women in this age range in both Benin and Kano scored over 80 percent on the index. Women in the 25–34 age-group are more likely than the younger women to participate in paying basic expenditures but the majority still scored lower than 40 percent on the index.

The proportions of women over age 35 who score at least 50 percent on the index are higher than those of women in the younger age-groups. In Ibadan and

TABLE 7.10   INDEX OF PARTICIPATION IN PAYMENT OF BASIC HOUSEHOLD
NECESSITIES, BY CURRENT AGE (IN PERCENTAGES)

Current Age	0	10–20	25–40	50–60	62.5–80	83.3–100	n
			Ibadan				
15–24	47.8	21.7	21.7	6.5	2.2	—	(46)
25–34	16.7	15.3	48.6	12.5	2.8	4.2	(72)
35+	14.3	16.0	44.6	7.1	12.4	5.4	(56)
DK	16.0	20.0	52.0	—	4.0	8.0	(25)
Total	23.1%	17.6%	41.2%	8.5%	5.5%	4.0%	(199)
			Benin				
15–24	63.9	6.5	11.5	3.3	1.6	13.1	(61)
25–34	45.0	17.5	25.0	—	5.0	7.5	(40)
35+	23.1	15.4	30.8	10.2	12.8	7.7	(39)
DK	50.0	16.6	25.0	—	8.3	—	(12)
Total	47.4	12.5	21.0	3.9	5.9	9.2	(152)
			Kano				
15–24	60.3	20.7	3.4	—	1.7	13.8	(58)
25–34	48.7	30.7	5.1	—	5.2	10.2	(39)
35+	61.1	11.1	5.6	—	11.1	11.1	(18)
DK	50.0	—	50.0	—	—	—	(4)
Total	56.3	21.8	5.0	2.5	2.5	11.7	(119)

NOTE: Sample sizes (n's) are smaller here than in previous tables in this chapter because
these data are for the 20 percent subsamples. DK = ages unknown.

Benin the proportions of women not assuming any economic responsibility decline in the higher age-groups and women are more likely to score 50 percent and
higher. In Kano the proportion of women who do not contribute to basic expenditures increases to 61.1 percent for women over 35 years of age, although a
substantial proportion of women in this age-group (22 percent) scored over 60
percent on the index, and 11.1 percent of the women scored over 80 percent.

Relative Burden Indexes

As already described, the distributions of women in both indexes were divided
into three parts—the bottom 50 percent of women ("average"), the middle 25
percent (medium-high), and the top 25 percent (high)—after first stratifying by
age and sample area, in order to get an idea of where groups of women stood
relative to their peers in the same age-group and culture group. Age is an

TABLE 7.11 RELATIVE BURDEN INDEXES:
CORRELATION OF NUTRITIONAL STRESS WITH HOUSEHOLD
ECONOMIC PARTICIPATION (IN PERCENTAGES)

Nutritional Stress Group	Household Economic Participation Group			Total	n
	High	Med-High	Average		
Ibadan					
High	28.6	20.6	51.4	100.6	(35)
Medium-high	11.8	41.2	47.1	100.1	(17)
Average	18.6	27.9	53.5	100.0	(43)
Benin					
High	28.6	14.3	57.1	100.0	(21)
Medium-high	13.3	26.7	60.0	100.0	(15)
Average	35.8	5.7	58.5	100.0	(53)
Kano					
High	45.5	22.7	31.8	100.0	(22)
Medium-high	—	44.4	55.6	100.0	(9)
Average	18.8	10.4	70.8	100.0	(48)

important control here, given the life-cycle effects of both fertility and economic role. Position in the nutritional stress index was then cross-tabulated with position in the index of participation in payment of basic necessities. The results, shown in Table 7.11, indicate that considerable proportions of women are in the high-burden groups relative to other women of the same age in both these areas of their lives. Almost *one-third* of the Ibadan and Benin women and *one-half* of the Kano women in the highest nutritional stress groups are also in the highest economic participation score groups. Approximately 49 percent of the women in the highest nutritional stress group in Ibadan, 43 percent of that group in Benin, and 68 percent of that group in Kano have medium-high or high scores on participation in the payment of the basic necessities of their households.

Unfortunately, sample sizes were very small, and further comparative analysis of these two indexes would not yield reliable findings. It is possible to analyze each index separately, however, to see how socioeconomic and life condition/status in marriage influence the degree of nutritional or economic stress. Tables 7.12 and 7.13 present the results of cross-tabulating each of the relative burden indexes with several such variables: marital situation, education, and occupation.

TABLE 7.12   RELATIVE NUTRITIONAL STRESS BURDEN, BY SELECTED SOCIOECONOMIC STATUS–RELATED VARIABLES (IN PERCENTAGES)

Variable	Ibadan Nutritional Stress Group					Benin Nutritional Stress Group					Kano Nutritional Stress Group				
	High	Med-High	Avg.	Total	n	High	Med-High	Avg.	Total	n	High	Med-High	Avg.	Total	n
Age at First Marriage															
10–14	25.0	12.5	62.5	100.0	(8)	41.7	25.0	33.3	100.0	(12)	31.9	10.6	57.5	100.0	(226)
15–19	41.4	12.6	46.0	100.0	(174)	36.1	18.0	45.9	100.0	(194)	25.7	17.3	56.9	99.9	(202)
20–24	32.2	28.8	39.0	100.0	(205)	23.2	22.0	54.9	100.1	(82)	35.1	18.9	45.9	99.9	(37)
25+	15.7	21.6	62.7	100.0	(51)	20.0	26.7	53.3	100.0	(15)	16.7	33.3	50.0	100.0	(6)
Marital Arrangement															
Monogamous	33.4	22.7	43.9	100.0	(326)	32.4	17.8	49.8	100.0	(247)	30.1	14.8	55.1	100.0	(365)
Polygamous	28.8	14.4	56.9	100.1	(160)	31.4	18.6	50.0	100.0	(86)	22.6	11.4	65.7	100.0	(137)
Number of Times Married															
0	2.3	2.3	95.5	100.1	(221)	1.7	1.7	96.5	99.9	(115)	3.2	1.1	95.7	100.0	(94)
1	33.4	18.6	48.0	100.0	(425)	32.9	18.6	48.5	100.0	(295)	30.2	12.7	57.1	100.0	(410)
2+	21.0	24.2	54.8	100.0	(62)	23.3	16.3	60.5	100.1	(43)	18.7	20.9	60.4	100.0	(91)
Education															
None	27.6	15.2	57.2	100.0	(250)	25.7	19.3	55.0	100.0	(140)	28.0	10.8	61.3	100.1	(93)
Primary-Koranic	24.6	15.8	59.6	100.0	(285)	29.3	15.3	55.3	99.9	(215)	24.9	12.5	62.6	100.0	(465)
Secondary+	12.1	9.2	78.7	100.0	(174)	10.2	4.1	85.7	100.0	(98)	5.4	10.8	83.8	100.0	(37)
Occupation Last 3 Mos.															
Housewife	19.1	10.0	70.9	100.0	(251)	25.6	15.2	59.3	100.1	(270)	24.3	12.6	63.1	100.0	(404)
Traders	27.0	19.8	53.2	100.0	(252)	29.3	17.3	53.3	99.9	(75)	30.7	19.3	50.0	100.0	(88)
Unskilled/service	4.8	—	95.2	100.0	(21)	8.3	8.3	83.3	99.9	(12)	16.7	1.7	81.7	100.1	(60)
Large-scale commercial	35.1	10.8	54.1	100.0	(37)	30.0	10.0	60.0	100.0	(10)	—	—	100.0	100.0	(2)
Skilled modern sector	29.3	12.2	58.5	100.0	(41)	17.6	8.8	73.5	99.9	(34)	22.2	—	77.8	100.0	(26)
Clerk/low prof.	10.0	12.5	77.5	100.0	(40)	5.6	—	94.4	100.0	(18)	—	—	—	100.0	(3)
Medium-high prof.	17.3	19.2	63.5	100.0	(52)	15.4	11.5	73.1	100.0	(26)	22.2	—	77.8	100.0	(9)

TABLE 7.13 RELATIVE HOUSEHOLD ECONOMIC PARTICIPATION, BY SOCIOECONOMIC STATUS-RELATED VARIABLES

	Ibadan					Benin					Kano				
	Economic Participation Group					Economic Participation Group					Economic Participation Group				
Variable	High	Med-High	Avg.	Total	n	High	Med-High	Avg.	Total	n	High	Med-High	Avg.	Total	n
Age at First Marriage															
10–14	—	100.0	100.0	100.0	(1)	25.0	—	75.0	100.0	(4)	25.7	22.9	51.4	100.0	(35)
15–19	22.7	20.5	56.8	100.0	(44)	18.4	12.2	69.4	100.0	(49)	22.9	22.9	54.2	100.0	(48)
20–24	27.3	37.7	35.1	100.1	(77)	20.7	31.0	48.3	100.0	(29)	33.3	16.7	50.0	100.0	(12)
25+	—	30.8	69.2	100.0	(13)	20.0	40.0	40.0	100.0	(5)	—	—	100.0	100.0	(2)
Marital Arrangement															
Monogamous	22.5	27.1	50.4	100.0	(129)	20.2	19.0	60.7	99.9	(84)	24.2	18.9	56.8	99.9	(95)
Polygamous	25.0	33.9	41.1	100.0	(56)	27.5	25.0	47.5	100.0	(40)	27.8	22.2	50.0	100.0	(18)
Number of Times Married															
0	25.0	12.5	62.5	100.0	(8)	42.3	3.8	53.8	99.9	(27)	44.4	—	55.6	100.0	(9)
1	22.0	30.4	47.6	100.0	(168)	21.5	20.6	57.9	100.0	(107)	24.0	18.8	57.3	100.1	(96)
2+	36.4	18.2	45.5	100.0	(22)	26.3	21.1	52.6	100.0	(19)	21.4	28.6	50.0	100.0	(14)
Education															
None	26.5	20.6	52.9	100.0	(102)	24.1	24.1	51.7	99.9	(58)	27.8	22.2	50.0	100.0	(18)
Primary-Koranic	14.1	35.9	50.0	100.0	(64)	19.4	11.9	68.7	100.0	(67)	22.6	19.4	58.1	100.1	(93)
Secondary+	33.3	36.4	30.3	100.0	(33)	44.4	18.5	37.0	99.9	(27)	50.0	—	50.0	100.0	(8)
Occupation Last 3 Mos.															
Housewife	6.9	15.5	77.6	100.0	(58)	14.6	11.5	74.0	100.1	(96)	19.1	17.0	63.8	99.9	(94)
Unskilled/service	—	—	100.0	100.0	(3)	100.0	—	—	100.0	(3)	100.0	—	—	100.0	(2)
Traders	30.3	31.5	38.2	100.0	(89)	35.7	32.1	32.1	99.9	(28)	31.3	31.3	37.5	100.1	(16)
Large-scale commercial	25.0	37.5	37.5	100.0	(8)	—	—	—	—	—	—	—	—	—	—
Skilled modern sector	8.3	50.0	41.7	100.0	(12)	30.0	20.0	50.0	100.0	(10)	50.0	50.0	—	100.0	(2)
Clerical/low prof.	25.0	50.0	25.0	100.0	(4)	60.0	40.0	—	100.0	(5)	100.0	—	—	100.0	(1)
Medium-high prof.	47.8	30.4	21.7	99.9	(23)	55.6	33.3	11.1	100.0	(9)	66.7	—	33.3	100.0	(3)

Factors Affecting Nutritional Stress

The relationship shown between *age at first marriage* and relative nutritional stress in Table 7.12 is most interesting when the age-groups with adequate sample size (ages 15–19 and 20–24 in Ibadan and Benin and 10–14 and 15–19 in Kano) are compared. Women who have married at earlier ages are more likely to be found in the high nutritional burden groups. It is also interesting to note that higher proportions of women who were aged 15–19 at first marriage are in the high-burden groups in Ibadan (41.4 percent) than in Benin (36.1 percent) or Kano (25.7 percent). Although data from the Nigeria Migration Project show that Ibadan has a higher level of development, higher rates of female education, and higher female labor force participation than Benin and Kano,[11] there are indications that age at marriage has been decreasing over time (contrary to what might be expected). Thus, more young women who are pregnant and lactating may be found in this early-married group.

The data shown for the relationship between *marital arrangement* and nutritional stress are, like those for fertility-polygamy differentials generally, inconclusive. In these data there is little difference between monogamous and polygamous women. Still, in Ibadan and Kano, being monogamous gives a woman a slightly greater chance of being in a higher burden group. Even if monogamous women are likely to be better educated and younger than polygamously married women, they are spending more time than their polygamous peers in reproduction and lactation. This may be a reflection of the role of sterility and subfecundity in fostering polygamy; perhaps it is the presence of higher proportions of childless wives among the polygamously married women that accounts for their relatively low proportions in high nutritional burden groups.[12]

The *number of times married* variable shows an expected pattern: more marriages, lower nutritional stress. Not only may marital turnover depress overall fertility by reducing periods of exposure to intercourse, but the divorced woman is also more likely than the average woman to be infertile—hence her divorce. The presence of some unmarried women outside the average-burden group is a reflection of premarital fertility.

The *education* differentials confirm the earlier (Harrington 1978) NMP analysis: The difference between the reproductive activity (including lactation) of uneducated and primary-Koranic educated groups is minimal; it is the secondary-level education that lowers the nutritional burden.[13] Fertility differentials studied showed some decline with secondary education, but the inclusion of lactation in the nutritional stress index used here makes the differences clearer. Of course, the higher education category includes more younger women who have not yet begun their childbearing and thus have low nutritional burdens, than do other education categories.

The *occupation* differentials indicate that unskilled and service-sector women end up most often in the average nutritional burden categories. They are likely, in the areas of Nigeria studied, to be either domestic servants or prostitutes, and tend to be young with low fertility (a characteristic that may be either a cause or a consequence of their occupations).

Housewives have the next highest proportions in the average-burden groups with Ibadan being more "favorable" for housewives than other areas. "House-wife" is a deceptive category, however, and it would be unwise to rely heavily on these data. In an earlier analysis the housewife category was found to include both unemployed women and women still in school.[14] Data on economic participation presented here indicate that some women who claim no occupation other than that of housewife still contribute to basic household expenditures.

Traders tend to fall more frequently into high nutritional burden categories than do women in other occupations; approximately one-third of the women in large-scale commercial occupations in Ibadan and Benin are in the high-burden group. Women in these two occupations may be able to take their children to work with them during infancy and therefore may breast-feed for longer periods.

High proportions of women in the skilled modern sector and at both professional levels, are in the average-burden groups. Modern-sector employment has probably reduced lengths of lactation, if not fertility itself.

Factors Affecting Relative Household Economic Burden

Table 7.13 presents the relative household economic participation results. Unfortunately, these results are based on smaller sample sizes, so that they are not strictly comparable with the nutritional stress data. *Age at first marriage* seems to be positively correlated with economic participation scores. Of women who were older at first marriage, there were higher proportions in the medium-high and high ranges—perhaps because educated women, who tend to marry later, assume heavier economic roles than their less educated peers.

Polygamously married women, although they may be less likely to be in the high relative nutritional burden groups than the monogamously married, are more likely to be in the high and medium-high relative economic participation groups. Polygyny may mean higher status for men—indeed, polygynists have been found to be wealthier than monogamists in sociological studies. Interestingly, the higher scores of polygamously married women seen here may mean that it is the economic contributions of these women that allow their husbands to achieve such wealth.

The breakdown by *number of times married* shows that never-married women score high on the economic participation index in greater proportions than do women who married once. The proportions of never-married women in the high-score range are sizable. These are not women who fit the classic conception that women go from dependence on a father to dependence on a husband. The proportions of women married twice or more with high economic participation scores rise, particularly in Ibadan. In Kano, where divorce is more common and more culturally acceptable, the majority of the women in this marital category tend to be in the medium-high participation group. The higher scores of women married more than once may reflect greater economic participation due to a deterioration in their status and an increase in their vulnerability, or it may reflect increased economic activity with age and perhaps the exercise of more power in the marriage.

The *education* results are most interesting. Primary and Koranic-educated women are *less* likely than others to be found in the high range of the economic participation scores. Both the uneducated and the more educated women are the ones most likely to be found in the high and medium-high ranges. The women with a secondary-level education are *least* likely of the three groups to be found in the lowest range. Their education may keep them out of the high nutritional burden groups, but it places them securely under the burden of economic responsibilities.

The *occupation* results reflect the basic education findings. Traders, large-scale commercial dealers, and skilled modern-sector professionals are all more likely to be found in high and medium-high score ranges than in the average range. Generally the proportions of working women in the average group are low. Sample sizes are small, however, so the data must be interpreted with caution. Perhaps the most interesting finding is that in Kano, 19.1 percent of the women who are housewives score in the high range and another 17 percent score in the medium-high range. Obviously, some of the women reporting themselves as housewives need greater scrutiny.

POLICY IMPLICATIONS

The physical and health costs of many pregnancies have been widely discussed in the literature; what has not been fully recognized is that the lactation period is almost always longer and certainly more costly in terms of nutritional demand than the pregnancy itself. It would be appropriate, on the basis of the findings presented here, to redefine the reproductive role and the costs and benefits associated with it to include lactation. Certainly before advising women in the Third World to breast-feed for long periods in order to keep children alive or to space births, we need to evaluate more directly the maternal costs, keeping in mind the economic roles that those women also play. Some women, like the traders and women who work in large-scale commercial enterprises in the three sample areas analyzed here, must deal with high pregnancy and lactation burdens as well as substantial economic responsibilities. This is not to say that bottle-feeding is the solution. Breast-feeding for between 6 months and a year is not only desirable but is frequently necessary for child survival. If women breast-feed, however, they should be given ''room'' by the society to do so. Beyond the initial 6 months to 1 year of lactation, the larger community should recognize its responsibility for nurturing and feeding its children. Women should not have to shoulder this burden alone at the cost of their physical well-being.

Children over 1 year old do not need powdered milk in bottles; they need a varied, constantly available, protein-rich food supply. There are areas where this is not available or where food supplies are limited by seasonal variations and population pressures. Generally, however, Nigerian adult diets already include a variety of foods rich in iron, protein, and vitamins, such as groundnuts, beans, a wide variety of greens, smoked and dried fish, fruits, rice, millet, and sorghum—all available in local markets, although expensive. What is needed is a program to encourage the processing of these indigenous foods for toddlers and infants. Such an approach would be in line with policies and initiatives that focus on local foodstuffs and encourage agricultural production through investment concessions. Women already predominate in the agricultural areas of the type most needed—raising small animals and garden crops—as well as in food processing and marketing. That they have been spending so many years lactating to keep their children alive shows that they certainly have a high motivation for ensuring child welfare; their economic activity and motivation are legendary. Education of women in nutrition and other areas needed to make processing and marketing vigorous economic activities could help them control and develop a market that benefited them directly, as well as earning for them the income needed to buy nutritious foods, and it could help them to fulfill their economic responsibilities to their families.

There would be many problems to solve in such a venture—water shortages, parasites that drain off nutrients that are consumed, lack of organization, the necessity of working within the framework of the women's forms of economic activity that may be unfamiliar and not completely understood—but there is also much that is promising. Market women's associations and savings clubs could be used to disseminate information and to organize further economic activity. Problems of transport exist but have in the past been successfully solved, as in the case of the Hausa dealers in kola nuts who ship their perishable produce by truck on the basis of word-of-mouth reports of market shifts.[15] International agencies might help with credit and with technology related to storage, processing, and packaging, at a scale appropriate to the smaller village markets, and with investigations of the protein complementarity of indigenous foods.

There is a role here for family planning, too—the figures on nutritional stress certainly raise questions about the heavy physical cost of bearing and rearing many children. Since the greater physical burden in terms of time and intensity of nutritional stress is associated with lactation rather than with pregnancy itself, however, policies should focus specifically on the difficulties of feeding the children that are born and the fact that it is often the mother who must find the means to feed them. One thing is certain: Policies that seek to lower fertility by raising the costs of bearing and raising children are particularly inappropriate. In a situation such as this, they might even be termed sadistic, since they simply add to the burdens of already overburdened women. Reproduction is, after all, necessary for the maintenance of society. Women should not be made to bear the double brunt of both reproduction and "disincentives" for fertility. Since society ultimately needs new members, and women are the only ones to provide them, let us regulate the level of reproduction by some means other than those which squeeze these women between obligations. We should consciously plan to alleviate their stress by implementing more appropriately supportive policies that view children as future adults and citizens deserving of, and requiring, social and personal investments that will be returned to the society in terms of long-term human development.

The current conceptualizations of maternal labor force participation and adequate child care are unfortunate. Consider, for example, the tone of the following:

> Unlike the practice in other areas, the mother, who does most of the field work, only breast-feeds her child in the morning and evening. (Mothers say that the distance between the home and the fields is much too great.) During the day, the child is with the grandmother or older sister, who feeds him porridges of cassava, bananas and sorghum. . . .
>
> In other areas of the same tribe children accompany their mothers to the fields and are breast-fed on demand. The difference between infants in the two communities lies in the nutritional supply: in one group, 80–90 percent of energy needs are covered; in the other, only 60–70 percent of protein requirements are met. Where the children are left at home, their nutritional state is precarious, with periodic famine. And the woman on whom falls the responsibility of field work, meal preparation for the whole family, and care of the last-born child, must choose between these duties at any given moment. Because her own poorly nourished condition does not permit her to fulfill all the social functions imposed on her, she meets these demands by leaving her child at home. This problem, exceptional in rural Africa, is analogous to that which existed in the eighteenth and nineteenth centuries in Europe: because of overwhelming parental social responsibilities, undesired children were neglected.[16]

It is unfortunate that these authors interpret this situation as one of maternal neglect of unwanted children. One cannot assume that these children are unwanted. Whether the child is the first or the fifth, he or she will still be left at home simply because the realities of survival leave mothers and children little choice but to take from one another, at great cost to one another. Both mother and child are in need of, and deserve, supportive policies that do not pit them against each other.

Nigerian women live in a complex, changing, and tenuous economic environment, subject to the vagaries of weather conditions and natural disasters, government decree, and the incursion of new foreign-controlled businesses and modern-sector jobs. They must cope with the tail end of the worldwide repercussions of the changing international economic order. What is it like where they sit? The sociodemographic indexes discussed here are one reflection of their situation, but more information is needed. Perhaps, for example, the infant mortality rate— that telling index of economic development—should be supplemented with a measure of the length of lactation still required of mothers to maintain a given infant *survival* rate.

Appendix A

SAMPLING FRAME

That there is a lack of adequate sampling frames for most of West Africa is well known. Aerial photos and derived grid maps were used to select sample clusters, which were then located and delineated in the field, mapped, and fully enumerated. The Ibadan sample made use of 1:2,500 grid maps from 1966 aerial photos. A total of 6,096 grids was obtained, from which 36 were selected using a table of random numbers. On field inspection 32 of these 36 were found to have inhabitants and were retained for the enumeration stage. The Kano sample made use of 1:2,400 grid map series from 1967 aerial photos. A total of 527 grids was obtained, from which 23 were selected using random numbers. Nineteen of these 23 were found to be inhabited and were retained for the enumeration stage. Neither city had any reliable population figures or estimates on which to base a sampling fraction. Educated guesses were made in order to sample a sufficient number of clusters to arrive at the desired sample size. In Ibadan and Kano population size was underestimated, so fractions of the enumerated clusters were re-sampled. In Ibadan three-eighths of the households were selected for interviewing by dividing the list of enumerated households in each sample cluster into equal parts and selecting the desired proportion by coin toss. In Ibadan half the list was selected; then that half was broken down into quarters, and one of the remaining quarters was selected for *exclusion,* leaving three-eighths of the original list of enumerated households slated for interviewing.

The Benin sampling process was hampered by failure to locate available aerial photos of the city. The city is laid out quite regularly, however, with houses bordering well-defined streets, quite unlike the traditional areas of Ibadan and Kano. Finally, use was made of a 1:10,000 grid street map. Grids were enumerated from 1 to 100 and 20 were selected in the first stage of sampling by random numbers. Streets within each sampled grid were then numbered consecutively and two in each grid were selected for full enumeration using random numbers. At this point the sampling process became restrictive in the sense of representativeness. The streets selected were completely enumerated. If fewer than 120 persons were enumerated on a street, all were slated for interview. If more than 120 persons were enumerated on a street, a fraction of the households was selected, using the same listing, division, and random selection process prescribed for Ibadan and

TABLE A7-1   FRACTION OF HOUSEHOLDS
SAMPLED ON STREETS SELECTED FOR
INTERVIEWING: BENIN SAMPLE

Number of Streets	Sampling Fraction
10	0 (empty)
16	1 (fewer than 120 persons)
3	½
7	⅓
2	¼
1	⅕
1	2⁄15

Kano, to yield a total of approximately 120 persons per street. The decision to impose an upper cut-off point on the number interviewed per street means that the sample is under-representative of denser areas. It was decided that this restriction was preferable to the bias that would be introduced by sampling entire streets, however, given the fact that since some streets run diagonally across grids, they are of unequal lengths within selected clusters. The fractions actually sampled on the 40 streets are given in Table A7-1.

Nonresponse

Interviewers were required to account for interviews scheduled with all members of the enumerated population assigned to them. They were instructed to call back three times before recording a nonresponse. Interviewers were found to be quite zealous about track-

TABLE A7-2   NONRESPONSE RATES AND REASONS FOR NONRESPONSE
(IN PERCENTAGES)

Reason	Ibadan	Benin	Kano
Not available, never met	44.7	38.0	8.7
Refused to answer	30.7	23.0	3.3
Traveling (away visiting)	8.1	26.0	25.0
Head of household refused	2.6	1.7	0.9
Visitors who had been enumerated left region before interview	3.3	8.7	22.8
Woman returned to home region for childbirth	.5	—	—
Language difficulty	—	—	4.6
Not ascertained	7.4	1.3	32.6
Other	2.7	1.3	2.0
Total	100.0	100.0	100.0
Total nonresponses	(646)	(300)	(448)
Total interviewed	(2,327)	(1,612)	(1,723)
Nonresponse rate	21.7	15.7	20.6

ing down interviewees, returning many times beyond the three times required in an effort to establish closure in the area where they were working. Some populations, such as taxi drivers, were particularly difficult to track down. Interviewers reported difficulty in meeting such people at home because of the long working hours they keep. Nonresponse rates and reasons for nonresponse are given in Table A7-2. The enumerated population was found to differ from the interviewed population because of specifically determined nonresponse reasons reported in Table A7-2, incorrect information provided to original enumerators, and population movements into the area between the time of enumeration and interview. Out-migration occurring between the time of enumeration and interviewing is accounted for in the nonresponse reports. Figuring nonresponses as those cases identified as appropriate for interview but not interviewed, and the nonresponse rate as nonresponses divided by the total number of persons interviewed plus those appropriate but not interviewed, we arrive at the following nonresponse rates for the whole samples (male and female): Ibadan, 21.7 percent; Benin, 15.7 percent; and Kano, 20.6 percent.

Appendix B

CONSTRUCTION OF PHYSICAL AND NUTRITIONAL STRESS INDEX

The physical and nutritional stress index was constructed by using the following equation:

$$\frac{\text{Total Length of Physical and Nutritional Stress}}{\text{Length of Reproductive Life to Date}} \times 100.$$

Total length of physical and nutritional stress in months consists of total months pregnant plus total months spent breast-feeding. Total months pregnant were calculated from the pregnancy history of each case by assigning the following month values:

Live birth	= 9
Pregnancy lasted 1–3 months	= 2
Pregnancy lasted 4–6 months	= 5
Pregnancy lasted 7 months	= 7
Pregnancy lasted 8 months	= 8
Pregnancy lasted 9+ months but no live birth	= 9

The total months of lactation were then added, this figure being the sum of the length of lactation variables in each individual history. (A value of 6 months was assumed for those women currently breast-feeding.)

Length of reproductive life to date is the woman's current age minus her age at first birth expressed in months. If either age question had a ''don't know'' response, the birth interval variable (the length of time between one birth and the next in months) was used. In this case the month values were added across individual histories and the month value for the open-ended interval following the most recent birth was calculated by subtracting the woman's age at that most recent birth from the date of the survey.

Any case for which these calculations could not be performed because of "don't know" responses was deleted from the analysis. The proportions of cases for whom it was not possible to calculate the index are given in Table 7.3, cross-tabulated by the variables used in this analysis.

Notes

1. See, for example, Judith Harrington, "A Comparative Study of Infant and Childhood Mortality in West Africa: Ghana, Niger, and Upper Volta," Ph.D. dissertation, Cornell University, 1971; Arrudh K. Jain, Ronald Freeman, T. C. Howard, and M. D. Chong, "Demographic Aspects of Lactation and Amenorrhea," *Taiwan Population Studies* 1, Population Studies Center, University of Michigan, n.d.; John Knodel, "Demographic Aspects of Breastfeeding," *Science* 198 (December 1977): 1111–15; and Alan D. Berg, "The Crisis in Infant Feeding Practices," in Alan D. Berg, ed., *The Nutrition Factor: Its Role in National Development* (Washington, D.C.: Brookings Institution, 1975), pp. 39–61.

2. See Jean Trevor, "Family Change in Sokoto: A Traditional Moslem Hausa-Fulani City," chap. 10 in J. C. Caldwell, ed., *Population Growth and Socioeconomic Change in West Africa* (New York: Columbia University Press, 1975); Jerome H. Barkow, "The Institution of Courtesanship in the Northern States of Nigeria," *Genève-Afrique* 10 (1):58–71; Polly Hill, "Women's House Trade," chap. 9 in *Population, Prosperity, and Poverty: Rural Kano 1900 and 1970* (Cambridge: At the University Press, 1977); Mary Smith, *Baba of Karo* (London: Faber & Faber, 1954), with an introduction by M. G. Smith; and Naira Sudarkasa, *Where Women Work: A Study of Yoruba Women in the Market Place and in the Home* (Ann Arbor: Museum of Anthropology, University of Michigan, 1973).

3. R. O. Ekundare, *Marriage and Divorce under Yoruba Customary Law* (University of Ife Press, 1969), p. 47.

4. A. K. Ajisape, *The Laws and Customs of the Yoruba* (Rutledge and Sons, 1924), p. 62, as quoted in Ekundare, *Marriage and Divorce*, p. 25.

5. Ekundare, *Marriage and Divorce*, p. 67.

6. Joint FAO/WHO Ad Hoc Expert Committee, *Energy and Protein Requirements of Pregnancy* (WHO Technical Report Series, no. 522) 1973, pp. 35–36.

7. M. C. Latham, "Maternal Nutrition in East Africa," *Journal of Tropical Medicine and Hygiene* 67 (4):90–91.

8. Henri L. Vis, Michael Bossuyt, Philippe Hennart et al., "The Health of the Mother and Child in Rural Central Africa," *Studies in Family Planning* 6 (12):437–41.

9. Approximately half the Kano sample married before age 14.

10. See B. K. Adadevoh, ed., *Subfertility and Infertility in Africa* (Ibadan: Caxton Press, 1974); pp. 47–48, 66–67.

11. See Judith A. Harrington, "Education, Female Status, and Fertility in Nigeria," paper presented to Population Association of America meetings, Atlanta, Georgia, 1978.

12. Polygamy in Africa is often a response to the infertility of the first wife. For related discussion, see Harrington, "Education, Female Status, and Fertility," pp. 9–14.

13. Ibid.

14. Ibid., pp. 15–18.

15. See Cohen, *Custom and Politics in Africa,* for a most interesting analysis.

16. See Vis et al., "Health of Mother and Child."

8. Rural Women, Work, and Child Welfare in the Philippines

Barry M. Popkin

Most women who play active parts in household economic life commonly are expected to continue to perform major household duties. In some instances the mother's economic role may be compatible with her child care functions; in other instances there are likely to be some conflicts and compromises (i.e., trade-offs) between home-related needs and market activities. Some studies have shown that female labor force participation may have desirable results—reduced fertility, for example.[1] Other studies have shown that the deprivation of maternal inputs may adversely affect child welfare, especially those aspects that require large amounts of the mother's time.[2] Women who engage in market production may have a negative child orientation or may have less ability to nurture children, however, and these may be the factors that actually have a negative effect on child welfare.[3]

A mother's participation in market work is based, according to economic theory, on a perception that the benefits of market work outweigh its costs. Any negative effect on child welfare that may result from the mother's labor force participation is consistent with this theory, since the current and future costs of her labor force participation, in terms of child welfare, may not be fully perceived, or these costs may be outweighed by the perceived benefits of her work in the form of increased family welfare or income, personal satisfaction, and so on. In addition, the potential social costs, in terms of child welfare, of the mother's labor force participation may be unknown or may not be weighed as heavily as the perceived personal or social benefits of her work.

Note: This study utilizes data from the Laguna households study (see Chap. 3). The author thanks the Agricultural Development Council, the Philippine Population Center Foundation, the Interdisciplinary Communications Program of the Smithsonian Institution, the Rockefeller Foundation, and the University of the Philippines School of Economics for their support for that study. The author was associated with the University of the Philippines School of Economics and the Rockefeller Foundation during the period of this study. The author also thanks Bryan Boulier and Robert E. Evenson for their substantial help with regard to earlier versions of this essay; John Akin, T. Paul Schultz, and Finis Welch for later suggestions; Monica E. Yamamoto for her assistance in its preparation; and Jim Brown for his comments on the final version.

In this essay, data from 34 rural barrios in Laguna, a province of the Philippines, are used to analyze the effects of mothers' labor force participation on the amount of time they devote to preschool children, their children's diets, and the resultant impact on rural preschool children's nutritional status. In the first section a conceptual framework is developed for analyzing the impact of the mother's market work status on household time allocation, children's dietary intake, and children's nutritional status. Presentation of data from rural Filipino barrios, empirical analysis, and discussion follow.

CONCEPTUAL FRAMEWORK

A direct relationship between the nutritional status of children and participation of the mother in market production, as well as the influence of other socioeconomic variables such as income and education, is often hypothesized. Thus:

$$NS = f(LFPM, SES) \tag{1}$$

where

NS = child's nutritional status;

$LFPM$ = labor force participation of the mother; and

SES = vector of socioeconomic variables.

This is in fact a reduced-form relationship derived from a more complete structural model of household production, however. Direct estimation, by the ordinary least squares method, of equation 1 is frequently undertaken due to lack of data on the fuller structural model. The results of such estimation are statistically biased and inconsistent because of the correlation of the independent variables, *LFPM* and *SES,* with the disturbance terms of the equation.

In the underlying structural model, utility is assumed to be a positive function of the nutritional status of children and other complex goods or consumables (Becker 1965; M. Nerlove 1974). Children's nutritional status is assumed to depend on a multivariate production function that includes such variables as child care time, diet, genetic endowment, sanitation, household technology, and birth weight. This production function interacts with the income and preferences of parents, various prices, and the number of children to determine the level of nutrition of each child. The age and sex of children affect the cost of raising the average level of child nutrition. Thus:

$$T = g(LFPM, SES) \tag{2}$$

$$D = h(LFPM, SES) \tag{3}$$

$$NS = j(T,D,H) \tag{4}$$

where T = child care time, D = dietary intake of the child, and NS = child's average nutritional status.

Using an instrumental variables approach, this essay presents the results of estimation of the triangular structural system, relating the average level of child nutrition to average child dietary intake, child care time, and conditions contributing to health in each household.[4]

It is useful to begin by examining the determinants of the total time allocation of the mother, the father, and the older siblings. In the equation

$$T_{ki} = a_{0ki} + a_{1ki}LFPM + a_{2ki}SES, \tag{5}$$

T = time spent in activity k by person i;

k = market production time, child care time (cc), nonchild care home production time, or leisure;

i = mother (m), father (f), or older siblings (c);

$LFPM$ = market labor force participation of the mother; and

SES = a vector of household socioeconomic, age/sex composition, and household capital variables.

The ordinary least squares method is used to estimate this relationship.[5]

The determinants of the average dietary intake of these preschool children are analyzed in a similar manner. In the equation

$$D_j = b_{0j} + b_{1j}LFPM + b_{2j}SES, \tag{6}$$

D = average dietary intake of preschool children and j = intake of protein or calories.

To examine the effect of the intrahousehold substitution of time and "the market-purchased food for home-time trade-offs" on children's nutritional status, the following formulation is used:

$$NS = c_0 + c_i\hat{T}_{ccm} + c_2\hat{T}_{ccf} + c_3\hat{T}_{ccc} + c_4\hat{D}_{pro} + c_5\hat{D}_{cal} \tag{7}$$

$$+ c_6H. \tag{7}$$

NS = average nutritional status of children;

$\hat{T}_{cci}$ = predicted instrumental variable based on equation 5 regressions;

$\hat{D}_j$ = predicted (instrumental) variable based on equation 6 regressions;

H = health factors that directly affect NS.

Equation 7 is essentially a biological relationship that many may term a household production function.

In this study the use of data on average child care time, dietary intake, and preschool children's nutritional status is important. Intrahousehold allocation of food and of child care time will vary as household and community relationships change. Rather than examining the impact of the mother's market work status on each child and having to face these intrahousehold allocation issues, this study focuses on average child inputs (diet, child care time) and outputs (nutritional status).[6]

The purpose of these equations is to facilitate an understanding of the impact of the mother's market work status on time and dietary inputs to nutritional status. There are several key issues. One is the compatibility of the mother's job with child care. One of the more interesting differences between industrialized and low-income areas may be that in the latter there is a greater prevalence of jobs that allow the working mother to be more responsive to child-rearing needs. Hours may be less rigid, the job may be located in or near the home, and there may be greater possibilities for the child to accompany the mother to the work site.

Another issue is the effect of the mother's market work experience and the number of hours worked per week on child nutrition. Women who work fewer hours may be able to substitute both leisure and crucial home activities for market work, whereas those who work longer might be expected to reduce all home activities to some extent.[7] Mothers with more work experience should be more efficient in their use of scarce home production time than women who have engaged in market work a short time. On the other hand, the negative effects of maternal work on children's nutrition could be greater if they occurred over a longer period. No data on maternal work history are available, so this theory cannot be examined.

The availability and quality of the substitutes for the mother's time are crucial. Siblings or older persons who have less child care skill and/or interest in the child's welfare can have a significant impact on the child's nutrition. Fraiberg (1977) feels that there are only rare occasions when child care substitutes in the United States provide child care equivalent in quality to that of the mother. In low-income areas where child care substitutes may be more closely related to the family, it is possible that these substitutes provide higher quality child care.

The effects of intrahousehold time substitution on children's nutritional status can be examined by comparing the impact of mother's labor force participation on the child care time per child of the mother ($\hat{a}_i com$), and older siblings ($\hat{a}_i ccc$). (The symbol $\hat{}$ refers to estimated regression coefficients.) In turn, in equation 7 the net effect of these time changes on children's nutritional status can be determined ($\hat{c}_1 \hat{\text{Time}}_{ccm} + \hat{c}_2 \hat{\text{Time}}_{ccf} + \hat{c}_3 \hat{\text{Time}}_{ccc}$). It is hypothesized that the quality of the time provided by the father and older siblings does not match that of the mother and that the net effect of the mother's market work will be to reduce the child's nutritional status.

The market-purchased food substituted for home time may also affect the linkage between mother's labor force participation and children's nutritional status. (Other market-purchased goods, including child care services, are not considered in this study, as they are not important in the population studied.) The net effect of maternal market work on child care time is compared with the effect on diet ($\hat{c}_4\hat{\text{Diet}}_{pro} + \hat{c}_5\hat{\text{Diet}}_{cal}$) to determine this food-for-time trade-off. It is hypothesized that maternal market work status is associated with increased market food purchases and increased children's dietary intake of calories and proteins. The nutritional status effect cannot be predicted.

DATA USED IN THE STUDY

Data used are from a survey of 573 households in 34 rural barrios in the province of Laguna, Philippines (Boulier 1977; Evenson, Popkin, and Quizon [King] 1979). Detailed cross-sectional information was collected on economic, demographic, and nutritional status from May to July 1975. Some of the 34 barrios were representative of the major rural occupational groups (fishing, low-land rice farming, and diversified upland farming), and others were semiurban barrios close to industrial employment. Random samples of households were selected from each barrio. The child care time data for this sample were based on specific recall questions answered by the mother in each of these households. Pretesting of this recall technique, as well as comparison between observations of time use and the recall data, show a surprisingly high level of accuracy of the child care time data. (Evenson, Popkin, and Quizon [King] 1979).

Additional data were collected in revisits to 99 households in three separate cycles. The first cycle's data, which are used here, were collected about 4 months after the initial cross-sectional survey. Two-day observations of the time each member of the household spent in each activity were collected by an observer stationed in the household. The child care time variables for this smaller sample were computed from observational data on the caring for, playing with, reading to, and feeding of the preschool child. The dietary data, available for these 99 households only, were based on 2-day individual food weighings conducted by trained nutritionists. This method consists of weighing all items used in the food preparation process, foods consumed by each member, and food wastage. To eliminate observer bias, the first day's time and dietary data were excluded from analysis.

Editing of the data led to the deletion of several families and children because of incomplete dietary, time, or demographic data. In the following analysis, both the initial cross-sectional data set and the smaller intensive data set are used.

Within each, concurrent mother's market work status and household demographic, physical capital, and child nutritional status and household demographic, physical capital, and child nutritional status are analyzed. Family income and the father's value of time data were obtained from the initial survey. Equation 5 is estimated for 571 households, from the initial cross-sectional data. Equation 6 is estimated for 70 households, from the smaller intensive data set for households with preschool children. Equation 7 is estimated for 68 households with preschool children only. (Two households for which nutritional status data were incomplete were eliminated.)

The variables used in the analysis are presented in Table 8.1. The mother's market work status is represented by a (0–1) market work variable and one that divides her market work into a three-way, no work/work some/work much, category. The proximity of the mother's work to the home is the first job compatibility variable used. A second job compatibility variable is also examined: each rural job was ranked by the field interviewers as to its compatibility with child care. Occupations that usually allowed the mother to care for the child while she worked (such as laundry woman) are coded as good jobs.[8] Characteristics of the mother include her education level, which presumably affects her productivity in various activities; her age, which can affect her productivity in both home and market activities; and her nutritional status (as judged by her weight), which can affect her home productivity and directly affect the nutritional status of the infant. Household capital could include the value of various home- and market-production-related assets or the presence of specific assets. Electricity is used as a household capital variable because of its potentially significant effects on time allocation, especially the time available for home production (Popkin 1976; Herrin 1979).

The demographic factors include the age and sex of children residing in the household in the week prior to the collection of survey data and the number of other persons living in the household (grandparents, other relatives, unrelated residents, and servants). The specific child age and sex variables used are based on previous analyses that examined some of the intrahousehold time patterns (Boulier 1976; Popkin 1976, 1978). Boulier found that each additional preschool child increased the child care time of the mother and older siblings and increased the father's market time, and that older female children substituted for the father's child care and home production time. The impact of older children on the mother's time varied with the family's age and sex composition. In general, he found that older males substituted more for the mother's market time and older females substituted more for the mother's home production time.

In the following empirical analysis, historical data on goods and time inputs to children or maternal work experience are not considered because they are not available. It is not clear how this deficiency biases the result, because it is difficult to state whether there will be greater variation over time in child care time or dietary intake.

TABLE 8.1   VARIABLES USED IN REGRESSION

Dependent Variables

Hours of child care time given to preschool children over a 7-day period by mother, father, and all older siblings (aged 6 yrs. and over)

Child care time per preschool child in each household

Hours per week of nonchild care, nonincome-earning home production time

Hours per weeks of market production time, including income-earining home production (gardening, handicrafts, etc.)

Leisure time of mother, father, older siblings (168 hours minus the sum of child care, home production, and market production time in previous week)

Average protein intake (in grams) of all preschool children in each household 1–71 months

Average number of calories consumed by all preschool children

Preschool child's average weight as a percentage of the normal weight for each child's age and sex based on international standards (Jeliffe 1966). (The same nutritional status variables were calculated for anthropometric data collected at the time dietary and time observation data were obtained.)

Preschool child's average height as a percentage of the normal height for the age and sex of each child based on international standards. (The nutritional status variables were calculated from anthropometric data collected along with each cycle's dietary and time observation data.)

Independent Variables

Labor force participation of mother (= 1 if she works in market, = 0 otherwise)

Mother works up to 39 hours/week = 1, = 0 otherwise

Mother works $\geq$ 40 hours/week = 1, = 0 otherwise

Mother works > 99 minutes and < 333 minutes per day = 1, = 0 otherwise

Proximity of mother's work to home (= 1 if job is in or very close to home, = 0 otherwise)

Compatability of mother's work with child care (= 1 if occupation is rated as usually allowing mother to take child with her, = 0 otherwise)

Mother's job is not close to home but allows a break (= 1 if job is not near home and allows breaks for mother to go home)

Formal education level of mother

Age (in yrs.) of mother

Income per capita of household members excluding the mother (in hundreds of Philippine pesos) [peso 7.35 = U.S.$1.00 in 1975 and 1977]

Electricity (= 1 if household has electricity, = 0 otherwise)

Number of children aged 0–1 yr. in household during previous week

(continued)

TABLE 8.1 *Continued*

Independent Variables

Number of children aged 1–6 yrs.

Number of boys aged 7–15 yrs.

Number of girls aged 7–12 yrs.

Number of girls aged 13–15 yrs.

Number of children aged 16–24 yrs.

Number of children aged 16 yrs. and over

Number of grandparents, other relatives, unrelated residents, and servants living in the household

Percentage of mother's weight in relation to the normal weight for her height based on international standards (Jeliffe 1966)

Piped water supply into the home (16 percent of households in the study had this)

Predicted per capita child care time of the mother (father) (children) based on regressions for the total sample

Average predicted intake of protein or calories for all preschool children in household

---

EMPIRICAL ANALYSIS

Household Time Allocation

The the purpose of examining the effects of the mother's work status on household time allocation, the time of the mother, father, and older siblings (aged 6 years and older) has been divided into four categories: time devoted to the care of preschool children (child care time per week), time spent in nonincome-earning home production, time (in home or market) spent in income-earning work, and leisure (defined as the residual time in the week).

Table 8.2 presents means for the time allocation of the mother, father, and older siblings for households of working and nonworking mothers and for mothers whose work is varying distances from home. Note the approximate 4-hour difference in mean child care time for working and nonworking mothers. Working women have much less leisure time than nonworking women and their husbands. Also, working women who engage in jobs father away from home engage in significantly less child care on the average. These relationships are explored more systematically in the multivariate analysis presented later in this chapter.[9]

Table 8.3 presents regression results on several determinants of the total time allocation of mothers in all households. Part 1 of Table 8.4 presents regression coefficients for the effects of the mother's work only, in all households, on the weekly time allocation of the mother, father, and children—measured first by the labor force participation dummy variable (A) and then by dummy variables based on the number of hours worked (B and C).

Part 2 of Table 8.4 presents estimated coefficients for the effect of the mother's job proximity and compatibility of job with child care in households with mothers engaged in market work. Table 8.5 shows regression estimates of the effects on child care time of the mother's labor force participation in all households, and the effects of the mother's job proximity in households with mothers engaged in market work when child care time per preschool child is used as the dependent variable in place of total child care time.

We examine first the effect of the mother's work status on the mother's time allocation. In the total household sample, when the mother works her leisure time declines significantly, by almost 28 hours per week on the average (Table 8.4, part 1A). In this sample, women who work 0 to 39 hours average approx-

TABLE 8.2 AVERAGE HOUSEHOLD TIME ALLOCATION
AND MOTHER'S LABOR FORCE PARTICIPATION (HOURS PER WEEK)

Time Allocation	Mother's Participation in Market Production		Location of Mother's Job	
	None	≥ 1 Hour/Week	No Job or Job Near Home	Job Far from Home
Mother				
Child care	12.0	8.8[b]	10.7	7.8[b]
Nonchild care home production	40.4	42.1	42.0	39.9
Market production	0	31.1	13.7	38.8[b]
Leisure[a]	115.6	86.0[b]	103.7	85.9[b]
Father				
Child care	1.0	.4	.6	.7
Nonchild care home production	2.7	2.8	2.7	2.9
Market production	50.9	51.4	50.4	54.1
Leisure[a]	113.4	113.4	115.3	114.9
Older Siblings (total)				
Child care	2.5	4.5[b]	4.0	3.0
Nonchild care home production	12.1	16.0[b]	13.6	17.7[b]
Market production	11.0	15.8	13.6	15.2
Average % weight for age[c]	77.2	76.1	76.8	75.4
Average % height for age[c]	90.8	90.3	90.6	90.2
Number of children	(214)	(349)	(440)	(133)

[a]Leisure is a residual category.

[b]Paired *t* test for difference in means significant at .05 level.

[c]Percentage of child's weight or height in comparison with the weight or height of a U.S. child in the 50th percentile for the same age and sex.

TABLE 8.3   DETERMINANTS OF HOUSEHOLD TIME ALLOCATION OF TOTAL SAMPLE
OF RURAL MOTHERS (HOURS PER WEEK)

Independent Variable	Child Care	Home Production	Leisure	Market Production
Constant	9.8	52.3	108.36	8.80
Labor force participation	−1.2	2.7*	−27.7***	
Education	.2	−1.8***	1.2*	.7
Age	−.2***	−.2**	.3**	.3***
Per capita income of other household members	−.03	−.03	.1	−.2**
Electricity	.3	2.1	−2.9	−1.7
Number of children aged 0–1 yr.	10.7***	.04	−6.5**	−7.7**
Number of children aged 1–6 yrs.	5.3***	2.8***	−8.4***	1.2
Number of boys aged 7–15 yrs.	−.2	.4	.93	−2.0**
Number of girls aged 7–12 yrs.	−.3	−1.5	.7	3.2**
Number of girls aged 13–15 yrs.	.1	−1.6	.3	.3
Number of children aged 16–24 yrs.	−.4	−1.5**	1.7*	.3
Number of others living in household	1.1*	−2.1**	.9	−.9
R^2	.28	.07	.24	.05
Adjusted R^2	.27	.053	.22	.03
F	18.3	3.7	14.4	2.77
n	(571)	(571)	(571)	(571)

***Significant at .01 level.
**Significant at .05 level.
*Significant at .10 level.

imately 14 hours of work per week, and those who work more than 39 hours average approximately 60 hours of work per week. Thus, as may be seen in Table 8.4, part 1B, there is close to a one-to-one correspondence between an increase in maternal work time and the decrease in maternal leisure time.

The effect of the mother's work on her child care time is not statistically significant, and the estimated coefficient is very small, both in regression 1A and in regression 1B. In addition, when the mother works her home production time actually increases, although the increase is small with low significance. For households with working mothers (Table 8.4, part 2), job proximity is associated with increased home time (home production time and leisure time) and reduced market time. The impact on child care time of having a job close to home is not significant. A good job that allows the mother to be with her young children has, again, no significant impact on her child care time.

Changes in the mother's work status have no significant impact on the father's time allocation in the total household sample but do have a significant impact on the time older children spend on child care and, when the mother works more than 39 hours a week, on their home production time. What is surprising, however, is that children whose mothers work more than 39 hours per week provide no more child care than do those whose mothers work less. When the

TABLE 8.4 EFFECTS OF MOTHER'S LABOR FORCE PARTICIPATION ON TOTAL HOUSEHOLD TIME ALLOCATION (HOURS PER WEEK)

Independent Variable	Mother				Father				Older Siblings		
	Child Care Time	Home Production Time	Market Production Time	Leisure Time	Child Care Time	Home Production Time	Market Production Time	Leisure Time	Child Care Time	Home Production Time	Market Production Time
1. All Households											
A. Mother's labor force participation	-1.2	2.7*	—	-27.7***	-.6*	.3	1.4	-.2	2.3***	2.1	3.9*
B. Mother works up to 39 hours	-.8	3.0*	—	-14.4***	-.5	.3	.8	-.2	2.3***	.5	3.6*
C. Mother works 40 hours or more	-1.8	2.3	—	-61.6***	-.6	.2	4.6	-1.9	2.1**	4.1**	2.4
2. Families with Mothers Engaged in Market Work											
A. Proximity of work to home	1.0	3.1	-16.9***	12.0***	-.4	-.4	-7.9**	5.5*	1.3	-.6	.8
B. Compatibility of work with child care	.8	4.0*	-19.6***	14.2***	-.4	-.4	-6.2*	3.9	1.5*	-1.9	-.1

***Significant at .01 level.
**Significant at .05 level.
*Significant at .10 level.

TABLE 8.5   EFFECT OF CHANGE IN MOTHER'S WORK STATUS ON CHILD CARE TIME
PER PRESCHOOL CHILD

	Source of Child Care		
	Mother	Father	Older Siblings
All Households			
Mother's labor force participation	−1.4	−.3	1.3*
Families with Mothers Engaged in Market Work			
Proximity of work to home	.7	−.1	.9

*Significant at .05 level.

mothers work less than 40 hours per week, siblings' child care time increases by
2.3 hours per week, and when the mother works 40 or more hours in the week,
siblings increase their child care time by 2.1 hours. (Table 8.4, part 1, B and C).

In households with mothers engaged in market work (Table 8.4, part 2), the
compatibility of the mother's job with child care is associated with a very slight
decrease in the child care time of fathers and a small but nonsignificant increase
in the child care time of older children. It is possible that the presence of
mothers, as a result of job compatibility, forces older children to spend more
time with their siblings. The mother who is nearby may be better able to super-
vise the child care time of the older children. This effect could explain why a
separate study of breast-feeding behavior in this same sample found women with
compatible jobs breast-fed less than other working women (Popkin 1978). Another possibility is that women with compatible jobs are better able to recall the
child care time of the older siblings. In other words, measurement error might
explain this effect.

The results reported in Table 8.5, which shows the effect of mother's work
and job proximity on per capita child care time allocations, are similar to those
reported in Table 8.4. The effect of the mother's labor force participation on her
per capita child care time, as well as on the father's per capita child care time, is
negative but very small and not significant. In contrast, the effect is positive and
significant, although small, on older siblings' per capita child care time. The
proximity of the mother's job, for households with mothers engaged in market
work, has no significant effect on the child care time of the mother, father, or
siblings.

The use of per capita time exaggerates the positive increase in the child care
time of older siblings relative to the decrease in the child care time of parents. In
this sample, however, results are similar when either per capita or total time
variables are used.[10]

In summary, it would appear that when mothers work, their child care time
declines very slightly, if at all. The leisure time of mothers declines, however, in
close to a one-to-one correspondence, as their market production time increases.

In addition, the home production time of mothers who work seems to increase slightly, except for those mothers who engage in market work for more than 39 hours per week.[11]

Children's Dietary Intake

The determinants of the calorie and protein intake of preschool children are presented in Table 8.6 for all households and for those with working mothers. Once again, these are averages for preschool children (aged 1 month through 71 months) in the household. In general, children of women who work have an improved daily consumption of about 145 calories and 3 grams of protein. (Note, however, that the coefficient for the effect of *LFPM* on protein intake has a low significance level—below .10.) The mother's market work status is associated

TABLE 8.6 AVERAGE DAILY CALORIE AND PROTEIN INTAKE
OF ALL PRESCHOOL CHILDREN IN HOUSEHOLD

Independent Variable	All Households		Households with Working Mothers	
	Average Calorie Intake	Average Protein Intake (g)	Average Calorie Intake	Average Protein Intake (g)
Constant	35.16	23.2	718.7	26.9
Proximity of mother's work to home	—	—	−28.9	−1.6
Labor force participation of mother	145.4**	3.1	—	—
Mother's education	32.6*	−.02	40.4*	.3
Mother's age	21.5***	.3*	22.9***	.4
Per capita income of other household members	−6.0	−.02	−7.3	.05
Electricity in home	30.5	2.4	277.0***	5.3*
Number of children aged 0–1 yr.	−176.4**	−6.6**	−267.0**	−8.8**
Number of children aged 1–6 yrs.	−51.0	−1.8	−102.9**	−2.9*
Number of boys aged 7–15 yrs.	71.3**	2.1**	−61.1	−1.0
Number of girls aged 7–12 yrs.	60.0	2.7**	−3.7	2.0
Number of girls aged 13–15 yrs.	10.5	−.8	−6.6	.4
Number of children aged 16–24 yrs.	−1.1	−.9	−38.0	−1.8
Number of others living in household	−95.3**	−2.1*	62.8	2.2
R^2	.55	.37	.57	.35
Adjusted R^2	.48	.28	.46	.19
F	8.39	4.13	5.25	2.14
n	(70)	(70)	(37)	(37)

***Significant at .01 level.
**Significant at .05 level.
*Significant at .10 level.

with an increase of 7 percent in the household's consumption of calories and protein derived from food market purchases, other things being equal.[12] The average sample household buys about 39 percent of its calorie intake from food markets. Households with working mothers purchase about 42 percent of their calories from food markets, and those with nonworking mothers purchase about 35 percent of their calories from food markets. About 33 percent of the former's and 26 percent of the latter's protein consumption comes from food market purchases.

Among households with working mothers, the effect of proximity of the mother's job on preschool children's diet was not significant. In general, however, significant negative effects of job compatibility on their diet might be expected if jobs near the home were associated with lower levels of income than jobs far from the home. In this sample, among working women's households, the average annual per capita income of households that include women with jobs close to home is about $18 less than that of women with jobs far from home. If the preparation and feeding of calories and protein are time-intensive activities,[13] however, we would expect a positive effect of job compatibility on diet, if increased job compatibility were associated with increases in nonchild care home production time, which includes food preparation and food marketing. In this study, mother's labor force participation was found to be associated with an increase in home production time in the total household sample, as were both measures of job compatibility (a job close to home and a good job) in the subsample of households with working mothers (Table 8.4). Another study, in comparing mean time allocation, found that "mothers working at home spent an average of three hours more per week (on food preparation) than those who worked outside the home in the same barrio, and an average of five hours more than those who worked outside the barrio" (Jayme-Ho 1976, p. 51). A comparison of means does not, of course, control for other socioeconomic factors as does the regression analysis reported here.

Children's Nutritional Status

The previous sections of this chapter have shown that when mothers are engaged in market work, their per capita child care time is perhaps slightly less; there is an increase in the child care time of older siblings, and there are increases in calorie and protein consumption. The proximity of the mother's market work has no significant effect on child care time or dietary intake.

Table 8.7 shows estimates of the effect on nutritional status of predicted per capita child care time and predicted per capita dietary intake. The predicted (instrumental) variables are based on regressions of equations 5 (using per capita child care data) and 6. Very few of the coefficients are statistically significant. It does seem that increased per capita child care time of the mother is associated with a significant, although very small, increase in average child height and that

TABLE 8.7   EFFECT OF PREDICTED CHILD CARE TIME AND DIETARY INTAKE
ON NUTRITIONAL STATUS OF PRESCHOOL CHILDREN IN RURAL HOUSEHOLDS

Independent Variable	Average Child Weight as Percentage of Normal Weight for Age	Average Child Height as Percentage of Normal Height for Age
Constant	69.2	70.7
Predicted per capita child care time of father	−.01	−.1
Predicted per capita child care time of mother	.01	.04*
Predicted per capita child care time of siblings	−.1*	−.1*
Percentage of mother's weight in relation to height	.04	.05
Piped water in house	.47	1.0
Average predicted intake of calories for preschool children in household	.0004	−.0002
Average predicted intake of protein for preschool children in household	.04	.04
R^2	.07	.07
Adjusted R^2	.01	.01
F	.93	.90
n	(68)	(68)

*Significant at .05 level.

increased per capita child care time of siblings is associated with small but significant decreases in average child height and weight. Although the amount of variation explained by the regression (R^2) is low and the F-statistics are not significant, we are most interested in the size and level of significance of the individual coefficients.

Based on regressions reported in Table 8.5, we expect that when a mother joins the labor force, her per capita child care time will decrease very slightly and that the per capita child care time of older siblings will increase somewhat. Thus we expect, based on results from Table 8.7, that average child weight and height will decline by a very small amount (multiplying the changes in child care time associated with the market status of the mother, from Table 8.5, by the appropriate coefficients from Table 8.7). The net result of the diet-for-time trade-off cannot actually be predicted with any certainty, however, due to the low levels of significance associated with the coefficients reported in Table 8.7.

At this point it is interesting to refer to the results of direct estimation of the reduced form of nutritional status equation 1 (reported in Table 8.8). According to these estimates, there is a much more substantial and significant negative

TABLE 8.8 ESTIMATED DETERMINANTS OF THE NUTRITIONAL STATUS
OF PRESCHOOL CHILDREN IN RURAL HOUSEHOLDS

	All Households	
Independent Variable	Average Child Weight as Percentage of Normal Weight for Age	Average Child Height as Percentage of Normal Height for Age
Constant	79.6	84.8
Proximity of work to home	—	—
Mother's labor force participation	−3.9*	−1.0
Mother's education	1.1*	1.4**
Mother's age	.04	.06
Per capita income of other household members	.04	.008
Number of children aged 0–1 yr.	4.6*	1.3
Number of children aged 1–6 yrs.	−2.5**	−.5
Number of boys aged 7–16 yrs.	−.8	.12
Number of girls aged 7–12 yrs.	−1.04	−.70
Number of girls aged 13–15 yrs.	−1.3	1.5
Number of children aged 16–24 yrs.	1.9*	.5
Number of others in household	.3	.3
Electricity in household	1.8	2.7*
R^2	.11	.07
Adjusted R^2	.06	.03
F	2.55	1.71
n	(269)	(269)

**Significant at .01 level.
*Significant at .05 level.

effect of the mother's labor force participation on child nutritional status (average child weight as a percentage of normal weight for age). In the sample population, where average weight for age of preschool children is less than 69 percent in about 27 percent of households, indicating severe malnutrition, a reduction of 3.9 percent of weight for age would be quite detrimental. Thus reliance on these biased and inconsistent estimates could lead to the conclusion that child welfare does indeed suffer as a result of the mother's labor force participation—a conclusion that the more rigorous, instrumental variables analysis reported in Table 8.7 does not support.

DISCUSSION OF FINDINGS

These results must be interpreted cautiously because of the exploratory nature of this analysis. Inherent drawbacks should be mentioned. First, the effects of changes in the mother's work status on child welfare are best viewed within a broader household production model. A more complete analysis, which would include the effects of work status changes on the number and spacing of children and other dimensions of child welfare, is needed. Second, we must learn more about the mother's decision to work. We know very little about the determinants of her choices or about the constraints she faces. Third, it is possible that use of the mother's labor force participation variable, rather than her wage rate, biases the regression coefficients. (No significant effect of increases in the mother's wage rate on her child care time or on children's nutritional status could be ascertained in this sample, however.[14])

An additional need is to consider more carefully the health, nutrition, and socioeconomic factors that should be examined in order to understand more about the determinants of children's health and nutritional status and the way changes in the role of the mother can affect these relationships. Our understanding of these factors is presently at a relatively primitive level. Such issues include the impact of home management and child care skills of the mother and siblings and the impact of home assets that can indirectly affect child welfare through their effect on home productivity. Moreover, home assets can directly affect child welfare. For example, a large proportion of the households in low-income countries do not have access to potable water (note the effect of the piped water supply in Table 8.7) or sanitary kitchen facilities (see Briscoe 1978; Kawata 1978).

Finally, more careful attention should be given to the ways in which changes within the community, such as changes in labor market conditions to provide more compatible work (split work shifts, for example), affect child welfare. Not only can health and child care facilities and professionals directly affect the child's health, but they may also have more subtle effects on household attitudes and skills related to child welfare.

A significant proportion of the women in low-income nations engage in market work, and the potential conflict between women's market activities outside the household and some aspects of home production is now a focus of concern. This study reveals only minor negative effects, if any, of women's labor force participation on child welfare. In the future, however, the increased availability of public education, industrialization, and better access to agricultural technology may increase the demand for adolescents to be in school and have negative impacts on child care arrangements (Whiting 1977). The increase in the potential market productivity of better educated women may decrease their participation in time-intensive child-rearing activities and, since the rate of growth of urban areas will remain greater than that of rural ones, it may be more difficult to arrange high-quality child care in urban areas (e.g., Whiting 1977). Only through the use of careful research techniques can we hope to determine the relationships between maternal work and child welfare and thus formulate relevant and appropriate policy decisions. It is clear from the comparison of results using the instrumental variables approach versus direct reduced-form estimation that invalid conclusions, which are potentially harmful to women, can rather easily and unintentionally be drawn from the analysis of a very complex issue.

Notes

1. A decline in fertility associated with the mother's labor force participation, especially if the market work is incompatible with childbearing, has been reported (Birdsall 1976; Jaffe and Azumi 1969; Nibhon 1976; Rosenzweig 1976; Stycos and Weller 1967). Friedl (1978) has suggested that one adaptation to the requirements of women's work in many societies is lower fertility and wider spacing of children (also Quinn 1977), and that we should examine ways in which child care and other traditional maternal roles are accommodated to women's market work.

2. Fraiberg (1977) emphasizes the negative effects that the deprivation of maternal attachment can have on child behavior. Others have shown the significant effects of maternal deprivation on infant health and mental and psychomotor development (e.g., Barnes 1976; Chávez and Martínez 1975; Klaus and Kennell 1976; Monckeberg 1977; Torun et al. 1975). There is disagreement on some of these issues. Bronfenbrenner (1976) for example, does not feel that whether child care is given in a center or in a home with a mother or babysitter affects the child's emotional development. Time-intensive activities such as breast-feeding, the preparation of vegetables rich in vitamin A and the use of social services that require a significant amount of travel time have been shown to decline significantly when the mother works, especially if she has a market job that is incompatible with child care (Sharman 1970; S. Nerlove 1974; Popkin 1978).

3. Some fertility studies have shown that women with a higher commitment to market work have fewer children (Birdsall 1976). There is no evidence available as to how work preferences affect either child nutrition or the development of child nutrition. It has been shown, however, that women whose market work is compatible with child care may select such work because of their preference for having children (Brown 1970). Woolsey (1977) cites a study that concludes that "if the mother is satisfied with whatever she is doing—working at home or in the labor market—the children are likely to be better off emotionally" (p. 142).

4. There is a growing literature that shows that increased social stimulation and playtime may enhance the growth pattern of preschool children. Torun et al. (1975) have shown that in Guatemala, increased physical activity enhances nutrition rehabilitation. Similar results have been reported by Monckeberg (1977). These results point to one possible effect of child care time. We must note, however, that only Chávez and Martínez (1975) have looked at child care time specifically, but their study design did not allow them to determine its separate effect on growth and development. The time data in this essay measure only the quantitative dimension of child care.

5. When the total system of time allocation of a person is analyzed by using a method such as equation 1, the disturbance terms of the regressions of each of the k activities for person i can be correlated. When each of these seemingly unrelated regressions includes exactly the same variables for each of the k activities, then the use of ordinary least squares produces exactly the same explanatory variables as does a more complicated, generalized linear regression model, which is often used to develop efficient estimators for this case (Kmenta 1971). It is recognized that the labor force participation of the mother is determined simultaneously with the allocation of her time and most likely that of other household members. Attempts have been made to develop identifiable systems in which *LFPM*, or the hours worked by the mother, is estimated and then placed in equation 1. These attempts were unsuccessful.

6. The conservative assumption underlying the use of these per capita child care time variables is that there is no complementarity between the time inputs into each child (i.e., production is not shared). In reality, however, child care time given by the mother, father, and older siblings will

benefit more than one child. The exact time inputs into each child fall between the total time and per capita time variables.

7. It is not possible to examine the substitution between extra hours of market time of the mother and changes in the child care time of the mother, father, and older siblings because of the joint determination of these relationships and the resultant multicollinearity between the hours of market work of the mother and the *SES* factors. Thus mother's labor force participation is represented only by dichotomous (0–1) variables. This results in undertermined simultaneity biases. Unreported regressions eliminated this simultaneity bias by using the mother's wage rate (an exogenous factor) rather than her labor force participation.

8. In addition, the effect of having a distant job that allowed breaks adequate for the mother to go home is examined for an urban sample, based on a survey of 112 urban Manila families that the author conducted. This Manila subsample is composed of families with children under the age of 5 years who were selected from a random sample of 300 Manila households. Only market and child care time data were collected for this sample. Nutritional status data for all of the children were not collected. In this sample the effect of a distant job that allowed time for breaks is associated with a significant increase in the mother's child care time.

9. In Chapter 4, DaVanzo and Lee report that Malaysian mothers, fathers, and children spend about 31, 5, and 7 hours per week, respectively, in child care. Our Laguna recall findings are quite different. Moreover, a similar study I am conducting in rural Bolivian households reveals that child care time of the mothers, fathers, and older siblings is 11, 1, and 6 hours per week, respectively. The Laguna direct observation findings, which record as child care time all primary and secondary (joint) activities, are similar to the Laguna and Bolivia recall findings. Thus the difference is not related to the exclusion here of joint child care and other home activities. The greater time for the Malaysian fathers may reflect a tendency (also reported in time studies conducted in the United States) for the father in a household with a better educated or working mother to increase his child care time. The much higher amount (31 hours) of child care time by the Malaysian mother, however, cannot be easily explained. It may relate to differences in child-rearing patterns, although this would appear to be unlikely, as Filipino and Malaysian child-rearing patterns have been reported by some social scientists to be quite similar.

10. The predicted child care time variables, used in the final stage of the analysis (estimation of equation 7), are based on the per capita child care time regressions.

11. Unreported urban time-allocation results show that women in the urban sample who work reduce their child care time much more than working rural women. Moreover, this is not compensated by the child care of older children. Rather the fathers increase their child care time as, it appears, do other adult household members. An addition of other, nonnuclear family household members is associated with significant reductions of 5.0 and 3.3 hours in the mother's and father's child care time, respectively. A job close to home is also significant and is associated with a large increase in child care time by the mother. It is difficult to explain the greater effect on child care time in urban areas when the mother works and when she has a job close to home. Many more of the rural women have compatible jobs. Also, more rural market work would be expected to have a smaller effect on child care time. Even the rural, incompatible jobs (far from home) are probably less disruptive of desired child care patterns. In the urban areas, women with a job far from home who have a break that allows them to return home add 17.4 hours per week to their child time, *ceteris paribus*.

12. Percentage of calories purchased $= 39 + 7\dfrac{LFPM}{(2.5)} - 2\dfrac{EDUCM}{(2.4)} - .01\dfrac{MOAGE}{(.69)}$

$$+ .1\dfrac{YOTHCAPH}{(.72)} - 13\dfrac{DECLITE}{(4.6)}$$

$$+ 14 \text{ Household size.}$$
$$(2.59)$$

$$R^2 = .08 \text{ (t values in parentheses)} \qquad F = 8.1.$$

$LFPM$ = mother's labor force participation.

$EDUCM$ = mother's education.

$MOAGE$ = mother's age.

$YOTHCAPH$ = per capita income of other household members.

$DECLITE$ = presence of electricity in the household.

The results for percentage of protein purchased are similar.

13. The feeding of vegetables rich in vitamin A to children appears to be a more time-intensive activity. When women in the Laguna study work, household vitamin A consumption declines significantly (Gonzalo 1976). In Cebu, Philippines, children's vitamin A intake decreases as the mother's labor force participation increases and increases among children whose mothers have jobs compatible with child care (Popkin and Solon 1976).

14. Based on unreported regressions.

9. Women's Access to Schooling and the Value Added of the Educational System: An Application to Higher Education

Marcelo Selowsky

There are two widely accepted notions in the current literature on human capital. First, it is recognized that early traits or innate abilities of individuals do have an influence independent of education on future earnings and productivity. The measurement of these traits has become particularly important in attempts to isolate the net impact of education, given the assumption that the amount of education itself is influenced by the level of these abilities.[1] Second, the semilog functional form of the earnings function (relating earnings to human capital attributes, schooling, early abilities, experience, etc.) is the most plausible specification for this function from both a theoretical and an empirical point of view.[2]

In an earlier work (Piñera and Selowsky 1976), it was pointed out that the acceptance of these propositions has profound implications for what might be called "the optimal allocation of education across individuals." Since the semilog function implies complementarity between early ability and schooling (i.e., the effect of schooling on earnings will be greater the higher the level of early ability of the individual), an optimal allocation of educational resources across individuals would require a selection criterion (on which to base the decision of who receives how much schooling) based on these abilities only. Any system where the level of schooling is determined by factors other than ability (such as the level of family income or the sex of the student) induces a misallocation of existing educational resources. This misallocation is the difference between the value added of the present educational system and the value added resulting from a system where students at each level are selected according to their abilities only.

In the earlier work, the misallocation that results from a selection criterion based on family income was addressed. Here we compute the misallocation resulting from a selection criterion based on the sex of students. Higher educa-

Note: The views expressed are those of the author and do not necessarily reflect those of the World Bank.

tion will be used as the case study. The educational system under consideration is characterized as follows:

1.   The level of female participation in the educational system is lower than male participation, and the gap increases at higher levels of schooling.

2.   The female-to-male ratio among students applying for admission to higher education is lower than the female-to-male ratio among students graduating from secondary schools.

3.   In higher education, the excess of applicants over vacancies is rationed according to the level of abilities of the applicants; that is, ability is the selection criterion.

This essay derives the change in the discounted present value of (a given amount of) higher education for two types of increments in female participation: (1) a "marginal change," in which the ratio of females to males applying for higher education becomes equal to the female-to-male ratio among the students graduating from secondary schools; and (2) a more radical "full" change where, in addition, the participation of females in secondary schools becomes equal to male participation. In both cases, the increased participation of females leads to an increase in the mean level of ability of students accepted into the higher education system and, thereby, a positive percentage change in the net present value of an additional year of schooling.

The essay is composed of three sections. The first section, on the conceptual framework of the analysis, develops the link between the mean level of ability of students accepted into the higher education system and the value added of education, via the earnings function. It shows the effect of making the ratio of females to males applying for higher education equal to the ratio of females to males graduating from secondary schools, and it also shows the effect of making the number of females graduating from secondary schools equal to the number of males. The second section presents empirical results, that is, calculations of the percentage changes in the net present value of education that could be expected from increased female participation in higher education in various regions of the world. The final section is a brief discussion of the policy implications of the empirical results.

CONCEPTUAL FRAMEWORK

The Earnings Function and the Value Added of Education

Assume that the earnings function relating wages (W) with years of schooling (S) and early ability (A) can be written as:

$$LnW = a + bS + cA. \tag{1}$$

Let us assume for the moment that this function holds for males as well as females (i.e., the coefficients a, b, and c are independent of the sex of the individual). According to this specification, the marginal contribution of schooling becomes

$$\frac{\partial W}{\partial S} = be^{a + bS + cA} = bW(A). \tag{2}$$

Namely, the contribution depends on the level of early ability of the individual.

The net present discounted value of one additional year of schooling can be written as

$$NPV = \left\{\frac{b}{r} - (1 + k)\right\} W_0, \qquad k = \frac{K}{W_0}, \tag{3}$$

where W_0 represents the wage for an individual with $(S - 1)$ years of schooling, K represents the direct yearly cost of schooling (teachers plus capital costs), r represents the discount rate, and k represents the ratio of direct costs of education to forgone earnings (see Appendix A for derivations of equations 3–5).

The change in *NPV* when the level of ability of the student increases equals

$$\partial NPV = \left(\frac{b}{r} - 1\right) W_0 \, cdA. \tag{4}$$

Defining as Δ the percentage change in the net present value of additional education resulting from a change in A, we have

$$\Delta = \frac{\partial NPV}{NPV} = \frac{cdA}{1 - \left[k \dfrac{1}{\left(\dfrac{b}{r} - 1\right)}\right]}. \tag{5}$$

In order for equation 5 to be positive, the condition $b/r > (1 + k)$ must hold. This condition implies, as can be seen from equation 3, a positive initial net present value of education.

If $k = 0$ (forgone income is the only cost of schooling), the value of Δ becomes equal to cdA, and the percentage change in *NPV* is equal to the percentage change in wages resulting from a change in the level of ability.

If $k > 0$, the value of Δ will be larger than cdA. The reason is that the change in abilities affects only a fraction of the costs of schooling, namely, the forgone income component. The larger the value of k, the higher the value of Δ; a higher k tends to widen the gap between the percentage change in gross benefits and the change in cost, since a change in abilities, dA, does not affect the direct yearly cost component, K.

Marginal Increase in the Participation of Women in Higher Education

Effects on the Mean Level of Ability (A) of Graduating Students

In most developing countries there is a clear excess demand for higher education (i.e., the number of vacancies is substantially smaller than the number of students applying for admission). Several types of examinations and tests are usually used to select candidates.

Let us assume that in the absence of loans for education, a fraction of the students graduating from secondary schools could finance their higher education (basically their forgone income) if admitted. Denoting by M and F the number of males and females graduating from secondary schooling, we can define the potential candidates as

$$N_p = \gamma M + \gamma F. \tag{6}$$

Suppose, however, that only a fraction π of all the potential γF female candidates actually does apply for higher education. The present number of candidates becomes, therefore,

$$N = \gamma M + \pi \gamma F. \tag{7}$$

The value $(1 - \pi)$ is the "pure participation deficit" of females, net of the "lack of family income" effect—that is, income is not a constraint determining the value of $(1 - \pi)$.

There might be several explanations for this participation deficit, depending on the country and culture in which it occurs, which we will not discuss here. The only explanation we are explicitly excluding from our analysis is a differential earnings function for females. In other words, we exclude the possibility of $(1 - \pi)$ being the result of a rational choice based on a "pure" present value calculation if, for a given level of schooling and ability, females expect a lower economic return than males.

If ability (A) is a random variable, normally distributed, we can draw a distribution of the present number of candidates, N, according to ability, A, as shown in Figure 9.1.

Denote as $\bar{A}$ the mean expected level of ability of the N candidates. If there are only V vacancies $(V < N)$ and the selection tests do measure A, the last (or marginal) student selected will have a level of ability equal to A_{mg}. The mean expected level of ability of the accepted students is larger than A_{mg} and depends on (1) the shape (standard deviation) of the normal distribution of A, and (2) the existing ratio $v = V/N$. (The smaller this ratio, the higher the mean ability of the selected students.)

If males and females have the same distribution of ability, the ratio of females to males among the selected students will be equal to $(\pi F/M)$, that is, the ratio of

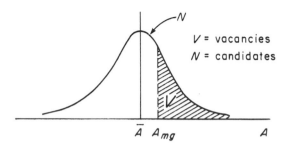

FIGURE 9.1

females to males among secondary school graduates corrected by the "participation" rate of females.

What will be the effect on the mean level of ability of the selected students if $\pi = 1$, that is, if all potential female candidates do apply for admission to higher education? The effect will depend on how the ratio of applicants to existing vacancies changes when the selection is now undertaken from the larger pool, N_p.

Denoting the new ratio of vacancies to potential candiates as $v' = V/N_p$, it can be shown that

$$v' = \left[\frac{1 + \pi f}{1 + f} \right] v \tag{8}$$

where $f = F/M$ (see Appendix A for derivation). Thus, since $\pi < 1$, v' is smaller than v and the mean level of ability of selected students has increased.

Figure 9.2 shows the effect of a larger base of students, N_p, applying to the given number of vacancies V; the marginal student accepted has a level of ability equal to $A'_{mg} > A_{mg}$.

The shaded area of Figure 9.2 shows those students who previously were admitted but now are excluded from the selection. Their sex composition is equal to πf (i.e., equal to the sex composition of the students who previously applied for admission). These students are now replaced by the new female applicants who are admitted, indicated by the dotted area in Figure 9.2.[1]

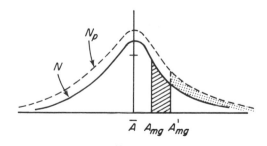

FIGURE 9.2

Thus, the effect of making $\pi = 1$ (taking as given the present share of females graduating from secondary schools) is to raise the mean level of ability of the accepted students. This implies, from equation 5, an increase in the net present value of additional education, $\Delta > 0$, since cdA is positive.

Full Increase in the Participation of Women in Higher Education

Now assume that we are interested in the effect of a long-run (more radical) educational reform that, in addition to making $\pi = 1$, would equalize the number of females and males in secondary schools—that is, $F = M$, or $f = 1$. Denote the new pool of potential candidates for higher education as N_p^*. Then

$$N_p^* = \gamma M + \gamma F = \gamma\ 2M. \tag{9}$$

Denote the new ratio of vacancies to potential candidates as $v^* = V/N_p^*$. It can be shown (see Appendix A) that

$$v^* = \left(\frac{1 + \pi f}{2}\right) v. \tag{10}$$

To the extent that $f < 1$ initially, v^* will be even smaller than v' and the mean ability of the selected students will be further increased. The marginal accepted student now has a level of ability of $A^*_{mg} > A'_{mg}$. This implies a further increase in the net present value of additional education ($\Delta > 0$) from equation 5, since cdA is (more) positive.

EMPIRICAL RESULTS

It is clear that marginal ($\pi = 1$) and full ($\pi = 1, f = 1$) increased participation of females in education will result in a positive percentage change in the net present value of additional education. The computation of the actual magnitude of the percentage change can be divided into three stages.

1. Computing the change in mean abilities resulting from the marginal and full increases in the participation of females, that is, dA. Results presented here are calculated from data on male and female graduates of secondary education, estimates of the ratio of vacancies to potential candidates (Piñera and Selowsky 1976), and basic assumptions about the distribution of ability (IQ) in the population.

2. Quantifying the effect of ability on earnings, that is, setting the value of c in the semilog earnings function, equation 1. A value of .01 is used here, consistent with findings reported in the current literature.

3. Adjusting for the fact that a fraction of the costs of schooling is not affected by a change in mean abilities, that is, computing the $[1 - k/(b/r - 1)]^{-1}$

factor. This coefficient can be calculated using data on internal rates of return to higher education, which are by now available for several developing countries, and assigned values for the discount rate (r) and k. The results reported here are based on a mid value for the internal rate of return ($\rho = .12$) and a value of k ranging between .5 and 3.0. The discount rate is assumed to be .10. This implies a value of (ρ/r) close to 1.0, which is the situation observed for higher education in most countries. (A detailed description of these computations is given in Appendix B.)

Tables 9.1 and 9.2 show values of Δ for the two types of increased participation of females in higher education considered here. It appears from Table 9.1 that the value of a marginal change in female participation in higher education

TABLE 9.1 PERCENTAGE CHANGE IN VALUE ADDED
OF EDUCATION (Δ) RESULTING FROM MARGINAL INCREASE
IN FEMALE PARTICIPATION
(FOR ALTERNATIVE VALUES OF v AND k)

Region		$k = .5$	$k = 1.0$	$k = 2.0$	$k = 3.0$
		Africa			
I	v_1	4.9	6.3	7.7	8.5
	v_2	4.6	5.9	7.3	8.0
II	v_1	4.9	6.3	7.7	8.5
	v_2	4.6	5.9	7.3	8.0
III	v_1	3.5	4.6	5.6	6.1
	v_2	3.0	3.9	4.7	5.2
IV	v_1	3.0	3.9	4.7	5.2
	v_2	2.4	3.2	3.9	4.2
		Latin America			
I	v_1	6.2	8.0	9.9	10.8
	v_2	7.6	9.8	12.0	13.0
II	v_1	4.0	5.3	6.5	7.0
	v_2	3.5	4.6	5.6	6.1
III	v_1	2.4	3.2	3.9	4.2
	v_2	1.9	2.4	3.0	3.3
		Asia			
I	v_1	3.0	3.9	4.7	5.2
	v_2	2.4	3.2	3.9	4.2
II	v_1	3.0	3.9	4.7	5.2
	v_2	2.4	3.2	3.9	4.2
III	v_1	8.9	11.6	14.2	15.5
	v_2	10.0	13.0	16.0	17.4

NOTE: $v_1 = .66$; $v_2 = .75$.

TABLE 9.2   PERCENTAGE CHANGE IN VALUE ADDED
OF EDUCATION (Δ) RESULTING FROM FULL INCREASE
IN FEMALE PARTICIPATION
(FOR ALTERNATIVE VALUES OF v AND k)

Region		$k = .5$	$k = 1.0$	$k = 2.0$	$k = 3.0$
			Africa		
I	v_1	21.0	27.3	33.5	36.6
	v_2	22.0	28.7	35.3	38.5
II	v_1	18.4	23.8	29.2	32.0
	v_2	20.5	26.6	32.7	35.7
III	v_1	16.2	21.0	25.3	28.2
	v_2	18.0	23.5	28.8	31.5
IV	v_1	13.0	16.8	20.6	22.6
	v_2	13.0	17.2	21.0	23.0
			Latin America		
I	v_1	16.2	21.0	25.8	28.2
	v_2	17.6	22.8	28.0	30.6
II	v_1	14.0	18.2	22.4	24.4
	v_2	15.7	20.3	25.0	27.3
III	v_1	10.3	13.3	16.3	17.9
	v_2	10.0	13.0	15.9	17.4
			Asia		
I	v_1	20.3	26.3	32.3	35.3
	v_2	22.0	28.0	34.4	36.6
II	v_1	16.2	21.0	25.8	28.2
	v_2	17.6	22.8	28.0	30.6
III	v_1	14.0	18.2	22.4	24.4
	v_2	15.7	20.3	25.0	27.3

NOTE: $v_1 = .66$; $v_2 = .75$.

(that is, when the ratio of female to male potential candidates for higher education who actually apply becomes equal to the ratio of female to male graduates of
secondary schools) is highest for the Asia III region (see Appendix C for a
breakdown of regions by countries). In 1976 this region had a high ratio of
female to male applicants (see Table 9.3, column 1), so we would not expect a
change in the ratio to have a substantial impact on the net present value of
additional education. The ratio of female to male graduates of secondary schools
(f) is also quite high for this region, however. Thus the marginal change considered here would affect a large number of women. In fact, the deviation of πf
from f is large enough (i.e., the "pure participation deficit" of females is high
enough) that this change in female participation in higher education would in-

crease the net present value of additional education by 8.9–15.5 percent when v = .66, or by 10.0–17.4 percent when v = .75, depending on the value of k (the ratio of direct costs of education to forgone earnings). The value of the marginal change in female participation is also quite large for the Latin America I region, for the same reason—both πf and f are relatively large. The Africa I region currently has the smallest ratio of female to male applicants to higher education, so we would expect an increase in that ratio to have a large effect. This region also has one of the smallest ratios of female to male graduates of secondary schools, however, so a change in female participation would affect only the relatively small number of women who have access to secondary education. The value of a marginal change in female participation for this region falls well below that of the Asia III region and somewhat below that of the Latin America I region, ranging from 4.9 to 8.5 percent when v = .66 and from 4.6 to 8.0 percent when v = .75.

The value of a full change in female participation in higher education (that is, when the participation of females in secondary education becomes equal to that of males) appears to be highest for the Asia I and Africa I regions. For Asia I, the value ranges from 20.3 to 35.3 percent when v = .66, and from 22.0 to 36.6 percent when v = .75. For Africa I, the range is 21.0 to 36.6 percent when v

TABLE 9.3   FEMALE PARTICIPATION IN SECONDARY AND HIGHER EDUCATION

Region	Female Applicants per 100 Male Applicants (πf)	Female Graduates per 100 Male Graduates (f)
Africa		
I	7.8	20.8
II	15.8	30.3
III	23.5	32.8
IV	41.0	49.0
Latin America		
I	25.0	48.0
II	33.2	47.2
III	45.2	51.8
Asia		
I	12.0	19.0
II	25.4	32.3
III	33.0	68.5

SOURCE: Appendix C.

= .66, and from 22.0 to 38.5 percent when v = .75. In this case of a more radical, long-run increase in female participation, the percentage change in net present value of an additional year of education will depend heavily on how far from 1 is the initial ratio of female to male graduates of secondary schools. Since Asia I and Africa I have the smallest current ratios (f), a reform making the number of females graduating from secondary schools equal to the number of males would have a strong effect on the mean level of ability of students accepted for higher education and, thereby, on the value added of the educational system.

It is important to note that the results presented in Tables 9.1 and 9.2 are not definitive. The only country-specific data used in the calculations were those on the number of female and male graduates of secondary schools, and these data were used to calculate average ratios of female to male graduates for the various regions. All other parameters, such as the discount rate reflecting the social cost of capital (r) and the ratio of vacancies to applicants in higher education (v), although based on estimates reported in the current literature, have been set at the same value for all regions. In reality, there are undoubtedly variations in these parameters, depending on the economic and demographic characteristics (among others) of each region and of the individual countries within the regions. In addition, the calculations are particularly sensitive to the (ρ/r) ratio. The value of Δ becomes large and extremely sensitive to (ρ/r) when this ratio is close to one, as it is assumed to be in the calculations just presented. Tables B9-4 and B9-5, which compare the values of Δ given alternative values for ρ, illustrate this sensitivity.

POLICY IMPLICATIONS

Although the results of this analysis must be interpreted with caution, they do suggest that the effects on the value added of higher education of both marginal and full changes in female participation in higher education may be substantial. In addition, these two types of increases in female participation, by inducing changes in the mean levels of ability of those students selected for higher education, may have a far-reaching impact on the educational structure of the labor force and labor's contribution to the economy.

In those regions with a currently high ratio of female to male graduates of secondary schools, such as Asia III and Latin America I, the effect of a marginal increase in female participation will be great, even though the ratio of female to male potential candidates who actually apply for higher education is already large, since the change will affect a relatively large number of women.

In those regions with a currently low ratio of female to male graduates of secondary schools, such as Africa I and Asia I, the potential impact of a marginal change in female participation is diminished due to the relatively small number of women who have access to secondary education and who, therefore, would be affected by the reform. A more radical, long-run (full) change in female participation could increase the value added of education in these regions by as much as 37 percent, however.

Appendix A

THE EARNINGS FUNCTION AND THE VALUE ADDED OF EDUCATION: MATHEMATICAL DERIVATION

Assume that the earnings function relating wages (W) to years of schooling (S) and early ability (A) can be written as

$$LnW = a + bS + cA. \qquad \text{A-(1)}$$

According to this specification, the marginal contribution of schooling becomes

$$\frac{\partial W}{\partial S} = be^{a + bS + cA} = bW(A). \qquad \text{A-(2)}$$

The net present discounted value of one additional year of schooling can be written as

$$NPV = \frac{(W_1 - W_0)}{r} - (W_0 + K), \qquad \text{A-(2a)}$$

where W_1 and W_0 are the wages for individuals with S and $(S - 1)$ years of schooling, K represents the direct yearly cost of schooling (teachers plus capital costs), and r represents the discount rate. Then

$$NPV = \left[\frac{(W_1/W_0) - 1}{r} - (1 + k) \right] W_0, \qquad k = \frac{K}{W_0}, \qquad \text{A-(2b)}$$

and

$$NPV = \left[\frac{b}{r} - (1 + k) \right] W_0, \qquad \text{A-(3)}$$

since, from equation A-2, for one year of schooling, $\partial W/\partial S = (W_1 - W_0) = bW_0$; $b = W_1/W_0 - 1$.

The change in NPV when the level of ability of the student increases can be obtained by differentiating equation A-3 with respect to A. Thus we have

$$\partial NPV = \left[\frac{\left(\dfrac{\partial W_1}{\partial A} - \dfrac{\partial W_0}{\partial A} \right)}{r} - \frac{\partial W_0}{\partial A} \right] dA \qquad \text{A-(3a)}$$

and

$$\partial NPV = \left[\frac{\left(\dfrac{\partial W_1}{\partial A} \cdot \dfrac{W_1}{W_1} \cdot \dfrac{1}{W_0} - \dfrac{\partial W_0}{\partial A} \cdot \dfrac{1}{W_0} \right)}{r} - \left(\dfrac{\partial W_0}{\partial A} \cdot \dfrac{1}{W_0} \right) \right] W_0 dA \qquad \text{A-(3b)}$$

The percentage change in wages resulting from an increase in the level of ability is equal to

$$\frac{\partial W}{\partial A} \cdot \frac{1}{W} = c,$$

A-(3c)

so we can write equation A-3b as

$$\partial NPV = \left(\frac{b}{r} - 1\right) W_0 \, cdA.$$

A-(4)

Defining as Δ the percentage change in the net present value of additional education resulting from a change in A, we have

$$\Delta = \frac{\partial NPV}{NPV} = \frac{\left(\frac{b}{r} - 1\right) W_0 cdA}{\left[\frac{b}{r} - (1 + k)\right] W_0} = \frac{cdA}{1 - \left[k \cdot \frac{1}{\left(\frac{b}{r} - 1\right)}\right]}.$$

A-(5)

Possible extensions of this analysis include one that allows the earnings function to differ for males and females. The technique that follows can be used to compute what might be called the "optimal" participation rate of females in education. This optimal participation rate can then be compared with their actual participation.

Assume that the earnings function differs in the intercept a and that a_f and a_m are the intercepts for females and males, respectively. Assume further that society accepts the proposition that $a_f < a_m$. Given that the optimal composition of accepted students requires the equalization of wages for the marginal male and female student accepted, the difference in intercept will have to be compensated for by differences in A. The value of A for the marginal male accepted will be lower than the value of A for the marginal female. This condition will be brought about by the acceptance of a share of females smaller than their share among the applying candidates.

Let

$$Ln \, W_f = a_f + bS + c \, A_f$$

A-(5a)

and

$$Ln \, W_m = a_m + bS + c \, A_m.$$

A-(5b)

The earnings of the marginal female and marginal male accepted (according to the level of A) must be equal:

$$Ln \, W_f = Ln \, W_m$$

A-(5c)

This will hold for

$$(A_f - A_m) = \frac{a_m - a_f}{c}.$$

A-(5d)

If $a_m > a_f$, the value of A_f of the marginal female will have to be larger than the value of A_m for the marginal male. If males and females applying to higher education have the same distribution of abilities, these conditions will hold if a share of females smaller than their share among the pool of candidates is accepted.

Obviously, the acceptance of the $a_f < a_m$ condition, crucial for this analysis, is philosophically quite debatable and is a subject we do not here address.

RELATIONSHIP OF v' AND v

Let

$$V = \text{vacancies,} \qquad\qquad\qquad \text{A-(5e)}$$

$$N_p = \gamma M + \gamma F, \qquad\qquad\qquad \text{A-(6)}$$

$$N = \gamma M + \pi \gamma F, \qquad\qquad\qquad \text{A-(7)}$$

$$v = V/N, \qquad\qquad\qquad \text{A-(7a)}$$

and

$$v' = V/N_p. \qquad\qquad\qquad \text{A-(7b)}$$

Therefore,

$$\frac{v'}{v} = \frac{V/N_p}{V/N} = \frac{\gamma[M + \pi F]}{\gamma[M + F]} \qquad\qquad \text{A-(7c)}$$

and

$$v' = \left[\frac{1 + \pi f}{1 + f}\right] v \qquad \text{where } f = F/M \qquad \text{A-(8)}$$

RELATIONSHIP OF v^* AND v

Let

$$v^* = V/N_p^* \qquad\qquad\qquad \text{A-(8a)}$$

Therefore,

$$\frac{v^*}{v} = \frac{V/N_p^*}{V/N} = \frac{N}{N_p^*} \qquad\qquad\qquad \text{A-(8b)}$$

where

$$N_p^* = \gamma 2M \qquad\qquad\qquad \text{A-(9)}$$

and

$$v^* = \left[\frac{M + \pi F}{2M}\right] v = \left[\frac{1 + \pi f}{2}\right] v \qquad\qquad \text{A-(10)}$$

Appendix B

CALCULATION OF THE PERCENTAGE CHANGE IN NET PRESENT VALUE OF ADDITIONAL EDUCATION (Δ)

The computation of Δ can be divided into three stages: (1) computation of dA, the change in mean level of ability resulting from a marginal ($\pi = 1$) or full increase in the participation of females ($\pi = 1, f = 1$); (2) determination of the value of c, or the effect of ability on the log of earnings; (3) computation of the $[1 - k/(b/r - 1)]^{-1}$ factor, adjusting for the fact that a fraction of the costs of schooling is not affected by dA.

Computation of $(dA)'$ and $(dA)^*$

In order to compute the change in the mean level of ability of the selected students, let us define

$$(dA)' = \hat{A}' - \hat{A} \qquad \text{B-(1)}$$

$$(dA)^* = \hat{A}^* - \hat{A} \qquad \text{B-(2)}$$

where the following are true:

Mean Level of Ability of Accepted Students	Status of the Educational System
$\hat{A}$	Present system, $\pi < 1$
$\hat{A}'$	$\pi = 1$, holding f constant
$\hat{A}^*$	$\pi = 1$, making $f = 1$

In order to compute $\hat{A}$, $\hat{A}'$, and $\hat{A}^*$, we need first to compute A_{mg}, A'_{mg}, and A^*_{mg} consistent with v, v', and v^*. Having obtained the ability of the marginal student, we can then derive the $\hat{A}$s, the mean level of ability of the accepted students.

The value for the marginal student is obtained by the conditions

$$\int_{A_{mg}}^{\infty} F(A)\, dA = v, \qquad \text{B-(3)}$$

$$\int_{A'_{mg}}^{\infty} F(A)\, dA = v', \qquad \text{B-(4)}$$

and

$$\int_{A^*_{mg}}^{\infty} F(A)\, dA = v^*, \qquad \text{B-(5)}$$

where $f(A)$ is the normal density function with mean $\bar{A}$ and standard deviation σ. Now that we have obtained A_{mg}, A'_{mg}, and A^*_{mg}, the mean for the selected students becomes

$$\hat{A} = \frac{1}{v}\int_{A_{mg}}^{\infty} A\ F(A)\ dA, \qquad\qquad\qquad \text{B-(6)}$$

$$\hat{A}' = \frac{1}{v'}\int_{A'_{mg}}^{\infty} A\ F(A)\ dA, \qquad\qquad\qquad \text{B-(7)}$$

and

$$\hat{A}* = \frac{1}{v*}\int_{A^*_{mg}}^{\infty} A\ F(A)\ dA. \qquad\qquad\qquad \text{B-(8)}$$

The values obtained can now be substituted into equations $B-1$ and $B-2$ to determine $(dA)'$ and $(dA)*$.

The first column of Table B9-1 shows values for πf and f for regional country groupings ranked according to the value of πf. The value of πf is derived from Appendix C. (It is assumed that π is equal to the ratio of females to males enrolled in higher education.) The value of f, the ratio of females *graduating* from secondary education, is assumed to be equal to the ratio of females *enrolled* in secondary education.

The second column of Table B9-1 shows the value of v, v', and $v*$. Two alternative initial values of v are used: .66 and .75, derived from Piñera and Selowsky (1976).

TABLE B9-1   CHANGE IN MEAN LEVEL OF ABILITY RESULTING FROM A MARGINAL ($\pi f \rightarrow f$) AND A FULL INCREASE IN THE PARTICIPATION ($\pi f \rightarrow 1$) OF FEMALES IN HIGHER EDUCATION

Region	πf (percent)	f	v	v' (percent)	$v*$	$\hat{A}$	$\hat{A}'$	$\hat{A}*$	$(dA)'$	$(dA)*$
				Africa						
I	7.8	20.8	66	59	36	108.2	110.0	116.0	1.8	7.8
			75	67	40	106.3	108.0	114.5	1.7	8.2
II	15.8	30.3	66	59	38	108.2	110.0	115.0	1.8	6.8
			75	67	43	106.3	108.0	113.9	1.7	7.6
III	23.5	32.8	66	61	41	108.2	109.5	114.2	1.3	6.0
			75	70	46	106.3	107.4	113.0	1.1	6.7
IV	41.0	49.0	66	62	46	108.2	109.3	113.0	1.1	4.8
			75	71	53	106.3	107.2	111.2	.9	4.9
				Latin America						
I	25.0	48.0	66	56	41	108.2	110.5	114.2	2.3	6.0
			75	63	47	106.3	109.1	112.8	2.8	6.5
II	33.2	47.2	66	60	44	108.2	109.7	113.4	1.5	5.2
			75	69	50	106.3	107.6	112.1	1.3	5.8
III	45.2	51.8	66	63	48	108.2	109.1	112.0	.9	3.8
			75	72	54	106.3	107.0	110.0	.7	3.7

(continued)

TABLE B9-1 *Continued*

Region	πf (percent)	f (percent)	v (percent)	v' (percent)	v^* (percent)	$\hat{A}$	$\hat{A}'$	$\hat{A}^*$	$(dA)'$	$(dA)^*$
					Asia					
I	12.0	19.0	66	62	37	108.2	109.3	115.7	1.1	7.5
			75	71	42	106.3	107.2	114.3	.9	8.0
II	25.4	32.3	66	62	41	108.2	109.3	114.2	1.1	6.0
			75	71	47	106.3	107.2	112.8	.9	6.5
III	33.0	68.5	66	52	44	108.2	111.5	113.4	3.3	5.2
			75	59	50	106.3	110.0	112.1	3.7	5.8

SOURCES: Values for πf and f from Appendix C. Values for v from Piñera and Selowsky (1976).

The third column shows the values for $\hat{A}$, $\hat{A}'$, and $\hat{A}^*$. In deriving these values, it is assumed that the normal distribution of $\hat{A}$ of the applicants has a mean $\bar{A}$ equal to 100 and a standard deviation of 15. This relationship between mean and standard deviation is supported by most studies dealing with the distribution of IQ in the population.

The fourth column shows the values for $(dA)'$ and $(dA)^*$. The value of $(dA)'$ ranges from .7 to 3.7. The value of $(dA)^*$ is much larger, a result of a much larger number of females now applying to higher education. The value ranges from 3.7 to 8.2, approximately three times as large as $(dA)'$.

The value of $(dA)'$ depends basically on the absolute deviation of πf from f. Africa I has the smallest πf, but f is large enough so as to make this deviation the largest of all groups. The value of $(dA)^*$ depends largely on how far is f from 1. Africa I and Asia I have the smallest values of f. A long-run reform making the number of females graduating from secondary schools equal to the number of males would have a strong effect on $\hat{A}$.

The Value of c

Three basic values for c, estimated for individuals in the United States with higher education, can be found in the literature: a value equal to .0132 from Rogers's sample; a value of .011 from Husen's sample 1; and a value of .0086 from the National Bureau of Economic Research (NBER)-Thorndike sample (see Hause 1972 for details of the three samples). In this essay we use a value of .01 for our calculations.[3]

The Value of $[(1 - k/(b/r - 1)]^{-1}$

In calibrating the value of $[(1 - k/(b/r - 1)]^{-1}$, we can use data on internal rates of return to higher education, which are by now available for several developing countries. The internal rate of return for one additional year of schooling can be written as

$$\rho = \frac{W_1 - W_0}{W_0 + K} = \frac{(W_1/W_0) - 1}{1 + k} = \frac{b}{1 + k}.$$

Solving for b and substituting in the expression for Δ, we get:

$$\Delta = \left[\frac{1}{1 - \dfrac{k}{(\rho/r)(1 + k) - 1}} \right] cdA. \qquad \text{B-(10)}$$

The value of the coefficient is now expressed in terms of the internal rate of return (ρ), the discount rate (r), and the value of k. If $\rho = r$, the value of Δ tends to infinity given that the initial present value of additional schooling becomes zero.

Table B9-2 shows data on ρ and k for developing countries from Psacharopoulos's (1973) survey. Except for Mexico and Venezuela, the value of ρ ranges between 8 and 17 percent. The value of k ranges between .50 and 4.1.

Table B9-3 shows the value of Δ for different values of ρ and k, given a discount rate, or social cost of capital, of .10. The results are sensitive to k but, in particular, they are extremely sensitive to the (ρ/r) ratio. This is quite important for the problem in question.

The value of Δ becomes particularly large and sensitive to the (ρ/r) ratio when this ratio approaches one (i.e., the internal rate of return becomes close to the relevant discount rate). What is interesting is that this is precisely the situation observed for higher education in most countries.

Internal rates of return to higher education are, for most countries, substantially lower than for other schooling levels and are quite close to what is usually considered the

TABLE B9-2   INTERNAL RATE OF RETURN
TO HIGHER EDUCATION AND VALUE OF *k*
FOR SELECTED DEVELOPING COUNTRIES
(IN PERCENTAGES)

Country	Rate of Return	*k*
Mexico	23.0	.50
Venezuela	23.0	—
Colombia	8.0	.90
Chile	12.2	1.00
Brazil	14.5	—
Greece	8.0	—
Turkey	8.5	—
Malaysia	10.7	4.1
Singapore	14.6	—
India	12.7	1.1
Philippines	11.0	—
Thailand	11.0	—
Nigeria	17.0	2.6
Ghana	16.5	3.1
Kenya	8.8	3.3

SOURCE: Psacharopoulos 1973.
NOTE: Mean = 13.3.

TABLE B9-3   VALUE OF Δ EXPRESSED IN TERMS OF *cdA*
($r = .10$)

	Internal Rate of Return (ρ)				
k	.10[a]	.11	.12	.15	.20
.5	∞	4.33 *cdA*	2.67 *cdA*	1.67 *cdA*	1.33 *cdA*
1.0	∞	6.00 *cdA*	3.50 *cdA*	2.00 *cdA*	1.50 *cdA*
2.0	∞	7.67 *cdA*	4.33 *cdA*	2.33 *cdA*	1.67 *cdA*
3.0	∞	8.50 *cdA*	4.75 *cdA*	2.50 *cdA*	1.75 *cdA*

NOTE: The internal rate of return for one additional year of school-ing is equal to ρ:

$$\rho = \frac{W_1 - W_0}{W_0 + K} = \frac{W_1/W_0 - 1}{1 + k} = \frac{b}{1 + k}.$$

Solving for b and substituting in the expression for Δ, we get:

$$\Delta = \frac{1}{1 - \dfrac{k}{(\rho/r)(1 + k) - 1}}\, cdA.$$

[a]Since $\rho = r$, the initial present value of additional schooling tends to zero, and $\Delta = \infty$.

discount rate in those countries. The mean internal rate for higher education in the countries listed in Table 9.2 is 13.3 percent; for the same countries the mean internal rates for primary and secondary education are 20.0 percent and 16.7 percent, respectively. This suggests that the value of (ρ/r) is much closer to one in the case of higher education (i.e., a higher participation of women would yield a larger value of Δ in the case of higher education).

Values of Δ

Tables B9-4 and B9-5 show values of Δ for the two types of increase in participation of females in higher education. For the marginal increase we have used $(dA)' = 1, 2, 3$; for the full increase we have used $(dA)^* = 4, 6,$ and 8.

TABLE B9-4   PERCENTAGE VALUES OF Δ WITH A MARGINAL ($\pi f \to f$) INCREASE IN WOMEN'S PARTICIPATION ($r = .1, c = .01$)

	$(dA)' = 1$			$(dA)' = 2$			$(dA)' = 3$		
k	$\rho = .11$	$\rho = .12$	$\rho = .15$	$\rho = .11$	$\rho = .12$	$\rho = .15$	$\rho = .11$	$\rho = .12$	$\rho = .15$
.5	4.3	2.7	1.7	8.6	5.4	3.4	12.9	8.1	5.1
1.0	6.0	3.5	2.0	12.0	7.0	4.0	18.0	10.5	6.0
2.0	7.7	4.3	2.3	15.4	8.6	4.6	23.1	12.9	6.9
3.0	8.5	4.7	2.5	17.0	9.4	5.0	25.5	14.1	7.5

TABLE B9-5   PERCENTAGE VALUES OF Δ WITH A FULL INCREASE ($\pi f \rightarrow 1$)
IN WOMEN'S PARTICIPATION ($r = .1$, $c = .01$)

	$(dA)^* = 4$			$(dA)^* = 6$			$(dA)^* = 8$		
k	$\rho = .11$	$\rho = .12$	$\rho = .15$	$\rho = .11$	$\rho = .12$	$\rho = .15$	$\rho = .11$	$\rho = .12$	$\rho = .15$
.5	17.2	10.8	6.8	25.8	16.2	10.2	34.4	21.6	13.6
1.0	24.0	14.0	8.0	36.0	21.0	12.0	48.0	28.0	16.0
2.0	30.8	17.2	9.2	46.2	25.8	13.8	61.6	34.4	18.4
3.0	34.0	18.8	10.0	51.0	28.2	15.0	68.0	37.6	20.0

If we use the mid value $\rho = .12$ and a range of k between 1 and 2, the value of Δ for the marginal increases ranges from 3.5 to 12.9 percent, depending on the value of $(dA)'$. If we use a range of ρ between .11 and .15 and a range of k between 2 and 3, the value of Δ fluctuates between 2.0 and 25.5 percent.

The results for a full increase in participation have less of a variation, since $(dA)^*$ has a smaller (percentage) range from $(dA)'$. For $\rho = .12$ and $k = 1, 2$, the range of Δ is from 14.0 to 34.4 percent. Using the three values of ρ and $k = 1, 2$, we obtain a range of Δ between 8.0 and 61.6 percent.

Appendix C

TABLE C9-1   FEMALES PER 100 MALES ENROLLED IN HIGHER
AND SECONDARY EDUCATION

	Region	Higher Education	Secondary Education
	Africa		
I	Chad	5	11
	Central African Empire	6	18
	Burundi	7	30
	Congo	8	35
	Ethiopia	8	28
	Guinea	8	21
	Mali	9	16
	Zaire	9	27
	Somalia	10	22
	Mean	7.8	20.8
II	Niger	11	27
	Malawi	12	27
	Cameroon	12	32

(continued)

TABLE C9-1 *Continued*

Region	Higher Education	Secondary Education
Africa		
Togo	14	23
Mauritius	15	44
Nigeria	15	33
Libya	16	31
Sudan	17	29
Senegal	17	28
Ivory Coast	17	21
Sierra Leone	18	39
Morocco	19	28
Uganda	19	24
Ghana	20	39
Mean	15.8	30.3
III Algeria	21	34
Liberia	22	25
Upper Volta	22	31
Zambia	24	33
Tunisia	25	32
Madagascar	27	42
Mean	23.5	32.8
IV Lesotho	41	56
Angola	41	42
Mean	41.0	49.0
Latin America		
I Panama	20	52
El Salvador	30	44
Mean	25.0	48.0
II Peru	32	43
Ecuador	32	45
Nicaragua	34	47
Chile	35	54
Mean	33.2	47.2
III Paraguay	42	50
Uruguay	44	54
Costa Rica	44	51
Venezuela	45	52
Brazil	48	52
Argentina	48	52
Mean	45.2	51.8

(continued)

TABLE C9-1 *Continued*

Region		Higher Education	Secondary Education
	Asia		
I	Yemen	10	12
	Bangladesh	10	21
	Afghanistan	13	13
	Saudi Arabia	15	30
	Mean	12.0	19.0
II	Turkey	21	30
	Syria	21	30
	Pakistan	24	24
	Korea	27	41
	Indonesia	28	37
	Iran	28	35
	Iraq	29	29
	Mean	25.4	32.3
III	Singapore	32	93
	Malaysia	34	44
	Mean	33.0	68.5

SOURCE: United Nations Educational, Scientific, and Cultural Organization (UNESCO), *Statistical Yearbook, 1976*.

NOTE: Within each region, countries are ranked according to ratio of females to males enrolled in higher education.

Notes

1. If years of schooling and early abilities are positively correlated, exclusion of the latter will yield positively biased estimates of the schooling coefficient.

2. Mincer (1974), using a schooling investment model, provided a theoretical justification for this semilog functional form. Heckman and Polacheck (1974) empirically verified this hypothesis by using the Box and Cox (1964) transformation to test for the correct functional form. Working with several sets of data they concluded that, under the normality assumption, the semilog form was the most appropriate simple transformation to be used in the specification of the earnings function. Neither Mincer's theoretical argument nor Heckman and Polacheck's empirical test explicity dealt with the preschool ability variable. Griliches (1970), however, concluded that the semilog form fitted the data best according to the "standard error in comparable units criterion."

3. These figures are as reported in Hause (1972). See also Piñera and Selowsky (1976), table 8.

10. Sex Differences in the Effects of Nutrition and Social Environment on Mental Development in Rural Guatemala

Patricia L. Engle, Charles Yarbrough, and Robert E. Klein

Evidence that early severe malnutrition in children retards the development of mental abilities has been accumulating (e.g., Monckeberg 1968; Brockman and Ricciuti 1971), and a number of studies have investigated whether comparable deficits in mental functioning are associated with mild to moderate levels of malnutrition (McKay et al. 1978; Mora et al. 1978; Chávez and Martínez 1979)—a condition affecting over half of the children in many developing countries. Malnutrition is believed to affect mental capacities both directly, through irreparable damage to the nervous system during brain growth (Winick 1976), and indirectly, by reducing the energy children require for the exploration of and interaction with the environment on which optimal mental development depends.

Social factors, too, appear to have a substantial impact on mental development. The deleterious effects of the cycle of poverty, including poor nutrition, poor health, and restricted educational and intellectual stimulation, have been well documented (Klein et al. 1975). These influences seem to function interactively, so that an adequate home environment can ameliorate to a large degree early severe nutritional stress (Winick 1975; Lloyd-Still et al. 1974). A rehabilitated child who is returned to a deprived environment will return to his former low level of functioning, whereas the rehabilitated child who is returned to a more supportive environment will conserve gains from treatment (Richardson 1976). An undernourished child's lack of receptivity to stimulation, coupled with poverty of environment, augers ill for the full development of his or her mental capacities.

Social factors may also affect nutritional input, and an examination of the interaction between nutritional treatment and the social context has been recommended (Pollitt 1980). Because of the important role that gender plays in defining an individual's social context, we might expect sex differences in the effects of malnutrition and its treatment on mental development. Few studies have examined this possibility, however. Most often, data are not reported by sex or only males are used (e.g., Hertzig et al. 1972; Richardson 1976; Satyanarayana et al. 1979; Graves 1976). Winick's (1975) analysis of Korean orphans adopted

198

by families in the United States is one of the few studies that used only females. Reasons given for studying only males have been as superficial as the ease of collecting urine specimens (S. A. Richardson, public lecture at the Institute of Nutrition for Central America and Panama in Guatemala City, 1974). In the traditional, rural villages usually studied, a girl's gender identity defines many aspects of her social environment (Whiting and Edwards 1973) that may limit the possibility of the development of her mental abilities more than they do that of boys. Also, changes in the social environment creating a more favorable climate for female achievement may have as great an impact on her mental development as changes in her nutritional status.

There are three mechanisms through which gender identity might alter the effects of malnutrition on mental development:

1. Biological effects. If malnutrition retards mental development through its effects on brain growth, then we might speculate that early nutritional insults would be felt more keenly by boys because they appear to be biologically at greater risk. Boys are "more susceptible to damage by a variety of noxious environmental agents, both prenatally and postnatally" (Maccoby and Jacklin 1974, pp. 350–51). There are indications that males are more affected by prenatal nutrition than females (Mora et al. 1979).

2. Intrafamilial differences in patterns of food allocation. Even if there are no sex differences in the impact of nutrition on mental development, the actual amount of food available for each sex may vary. Safilios-Rothschild (1980) and Horowitz (1979) both have found that in times of scarce food resources, families in some societies may distribute the food according to concepts of proportionality that favor men over women, adults over children, and boys over girls. Levinson (1974) attributes dramatic differences in nutritional status by sex, found in the Punjab region of India, to greater length of breast-feeding of males and greater care given to postweaning feeding of males in a society that values males more than females.

3. Interaction of social stimulation and nutritional input. A child who has relatively little energy available because of lack of nutrients will probably be unable to elicit as much caretaking and stimulation from providers as a well-nourished child. At the same time, the parents of undernourished children are themsleves less educated (e.g., DeLicardie and Cravioto 1974) and may be relatively less responsive to the children. If, in addition, the child is a girl, cultural attitudes toward proper female behavior and location (distance away from home) may limit her learning opportunities still further.

Sex differences in the effects of nutritional intervention on mental test performance of girls and boys in four traditional villages in rural Guatemala will be explored in this chapter. The data presented here indicate no differences in the effect of nutritional supplements on growth (biological) and no differences in food allocation by sex. These two hypotheses could not be adequately tested in this study, however, because (1) timing effects and the effects of prenatal supplement were not examined, and (2) since food was not extremely scarce in the villages studied, food allocation may not have varied by sex. The study does examine sex differences in test performance resulting from the interaction of social stimulation and nutritional input.

The description of the study design and the prestudy social environment of the villages, in the next section, is followed by an analysis of the empirical results of the intervention and discussion.

THE STUDY DESIGN

The study conducted by the Institute of Nutrition for Central America and Panama (INCAP), which is the subject of this essay, was a longitudinal, quasi-experimental intervention study. In 1969, four villages from an eastern, Spanish-speaking section of Guatemala, where moderate protein-calorie malnutrition is endemic, were matched with regard to a number of demographic, social, and economic characteristics. The intervention was differential supplemental feeding of two groups. Two villages (one large, with 1,200 residents; the other small, with about 800 residents) were selected as "experimental" villages, and a high protein–high calorie drink similar to a popular corn-base gruel (atole) was made available twice daily at a central dispensary for all residents. Two other villages (one large and one small) were selected as "control" villages, and a refreshing drink (fresco), containing no protein and about one-third the calories of atole, was made available. After 1971 both beverages contained enough vitamins and minerals so that none of these substances would be limiting in recipients' diets. In all villages, free preventive and outpatient medical care was provided throughout the study. Consumption of the supplement as well as attendance at the center and clinic was voluntary.

The design was also prospective. From February 1969 until March 1977, data on children's health, home environment, and food consumption, as well as cognitive development, were collected. In 1975, a study of fertility behavior in the four villages provided data on length of lactation and sex preferences. This sample was larger, since it included all mothers in the four villages. A census of all village residents was undertaken in the same year.

The Villages

The families who participated in the longitudinal study reside in four Spanish-speaking *Ladino* (non-Indian) communities. Virtually all of the families (83 percent) are engaged primarily in subsistence agriculture. The main crops are corn and beans. Cash crops in this arid region are limited to tomatoes, cassava, and tobacco. There is little continuous migration to or from the communities, although some men and families travel to the coastal zone once a year to harvest cash crops or go to work in other communities as short-term laborers.

The pervasive poverty of the study communities is evidenced by the fact that the median family income in 1975 was approximately $500 per year, less than half of it in cash. Families generally live in two-room houses constructed of local materials, mainly adobe. One room serves as a kitchen and the other serves as sleeping quarters for the whole family. Nearly all houses lack sanitary facilities. Clothing is simple; women wear plain dresses, and the wealthier individuals wear shoes and may have a sweater. Both infectious diseases and moderate protein-calorie malnutrition are endemic. The median number of living children per family is 4, with a maximum of 15. Many children die; 46 percent of the mothers reported having at least one child die. Those who die, die very young; 85 percent of these who die live less than a week, whereas only 2.4 percent die after the age of 3 years (see ethnographies of the villages in Nerlove et al. 1974 and Pivaral 1972).

The Subjects

Subjects in the study were all children who were under 7 years of age in February 1969, when the study began, or who were born in the communities between that date and March 1973. Data collection continued on this sample from March until September 1977, but no newborns were added. Each year of the program, children aged 3 through 7 years were tested. For instance, a child born in 1969 would be 8 years old at the end of the project (February 1977) and theoretically would have been tested all his or her life. Analyses of a single age-group, then, include children tested during each year of the project.

A 4-year age-group will include most, but not all, of the children who were in the 3-year age-group, due to attrition over time—that is, there is an overlapping cohort design. Thus the data do not, strictly speaking, form a time series of observations. A total of 1,235 children were tested once, and 671 were followed since birth. Nutritional and mental development measures were obtained for 95 percent of the children who were present in the villages at the time of each measurement.

Measures of Mental Development

Children were tested annually at ages 3 through 7. Twenty-three tests chosen to assess a variety of intellectual abilities, including reasoning, learning and memory, and perceptual analysis, constitute the Preschool Mental Development Test Battery. Of these tests, 13 were in the battery in 1969 and the remainder were added in 1971. Ten tests were administered at ages 3 and 4, and 22 tests were administered at ages 5, 6, and 7, reflecting the wider range of abilities of older children and the greater ease of testing them. A mental composite score was constructed for each child at each age by summing all of the cognitive tests in standardized form.

The testing houses were designed to be very comfortable for the children. Great care was taken to standardize the testers and to rotate them among villages. Details of the method are reported elsewhere (Engle et al. 1979; Martorell, Klein, and Delgado 1980).

Measures of the Home Environment

The quality of the child's home environment was measured and scored for each family by five socioeconomic status (SES) indicators: the quality of the family's house; parents' clothing quality; the extent of familial teaching of preschool children; a composite scale of the mother's vocabulary, literacy, years of school passed, and modernity (Inkeles and Smith 1974); and a measure of the visual stimulation and the presence of reading matter in the home. The parity of the child was also recorded. The mother's composite scale was not available for 19 percent of the subjects (those children who had been participants during the early years of the study) since these data were not collected until 1975, by which time these subjects had graduated from the sample.

The Nutritional Supplement

The project was initially designed to test the effects of protein supplementation on mental development. Fresco, with no protein and only about one-third the calories of atole, was to be a control beverage. It now appears, however, that calories rather than protein were inadequate in the children's diets (Martorell, Klein, and Delgado 1980).

The children's supplement ingestion and home diet were assessed, but the only independent variable used here was calories of supplement ingestion, a highly reliable value. Home diets were not used in testing the main hypothesis, because data on diet could only be gathered by asking each mother to recall what her child ate the day before and the answers tended to be unreliable.

Sex Differences in Nutrient Ingestion

Prior to the inception of this longitudinal study, baseline data on the home diets of boys and girls showed no significant difference in the amount of calories or protein ingested by kilogram of body weight for boys or girls. The diet of both boys and girls was inadequate in caloric intake but was quite adequate in protein. Boys' and girls' home diets continued to be equivalent after the supplement was made available (Martorell, Klein, and Delgado 1980). The amount of supplement ingested did not affect the home diet (Martorell and Klein 1980). Over the period of the study, boys ingested more of the supplement than girls between the ages of 2 and 3 ($t = 4.07$, $df = 1/727$, $p < .04$), but no differences in supplement ingestion by sex were found for older children. Data for children under 24 months were not examined.

Sex differences in nutrition from several other sources were examined. Duration of breast-feeding, another important source of nutrition in this population did not differ by sex; both girls and boys were breast-fed for an average of 18 months, according to their mothers' reports. Incidence of diarrhea, which reduces nutrient availability, *was* more frequent in males at ages 4 and 5 years ($t = 1.96$, $df = 65$, $p < .05$; $t = 1.96$, $df = 600$, $p < .05$). These results suggest that families do not appear to be feeding boys more than girls, although our measures are far from precise. This conclusion is corroborated by a recent anthropological observation of 10 families in one of the four villages in the INCAP study (Bratton-Kearns 1979). The investigator was specifically looking for differential feeding patterns by birth order. Rather than finding that the youngest child in a large family was receiving less food, she noted that food was being distributed equally. The only children who received less were the oldest children, particularly the females, who often missed meals because household duties were not yet completed. We must recall that food was not as scarce in these villages as in many other cultures studied.

Sex preference for males was also not as strong in these villages as in other cultures studied. Despite the traditional Latin notion of machismo, Pebley, Delgado, and Brineman (1978) note little evidence of strong son preference in this sample. Children of both sexes are seen as useful. Pebley, Delgado, and Brineman (1978) analyzed the responses of mothers and fathers in the four villages to three questions about preferences for and usefulness of boys and girls. Many mothers and fathers regard boys and girls as equally useful when young, but, when there is a difference, mothers perceive girls as more useful and fathers perceive boys as more useful. In the older age-group, boys are seen as more useful by both mothers and fathers. The reasons differ by sex; young girls are seen as more helpful by both mothers and fathers because they are around home more and are willing to do simpler work. Both mothers and fathers see boys as more useful when they are older because they can earn more.

Sex Differences in Growth

Physical size differed by sex in this population. Boys were taller and heavier than girls from birth through age 7 (Yarbrough et al. 1975). Differences in growth between sexes were greatest at 30 months and decreased after 4 years of age. Deficits in growth (the difference between mean height of the Guatemala sample and mean height of well-nourished children in the United States) were similar for boys and girls (Yarbrough et al. 1975). The effect of both atole and fresco ingestion on growth in height and weight were significant, particularly

204 / Patricia L. Engle, Charles Yarbrough, and Robert E. Klein

from birth up to 3 years of age. These effects appeared to be very similar for boys and girls (Martorell, Klein, and Delgado 1980). There is no biological evidence that the nutritional supplement had different effects on boys' or girls' physical growth, however.

Sex-Role Stereotypes in the Social Environment

In the traditional rural villages of this study, sex-appropriate behavior is well defined. This stereotyping is seen both in children's play and work, and in their attitudes toward typical male and female adult roles.

In these rural villages, some tasks are clearly assigned on the basis of sex, whereas others are shared. In her ethnography of the villages, Nerlove (1974b) describes the patterns as follows: "Girls are more often found playing in home environments—houses or patios—than are boys. The more mature and active boys who are not yet involved in work with their fathers are quite independent and participate in play that may take place quite far from their homes, like bathing in the river or picking fruits. Both sexes enjoy many of the same activities; other activities are clearly sex-typed" (p. 274).

The sex differences in children's movement away from home are striking. Girls are much more likely to be near or at home, whereas boys are often farther from home because of work or play activities. In her study, Nerlove observed 31 boys and 31 girls aged 5 to 8 years on 20 occasions. Girls rarely went outside the community, whereas many times the boys went far from home. This difference was salient in the villages. Mothers commented that girls are useful because they stay near home.

The Woman's Role

Women in this culture also center their activity in the home. The major household structure is nuclear; 73 percent of the 484 women in the fertility study sample reported living alone with husband and children; 23 percent lived with the family of one spouse or the other; only 3 percent were women living alone with children. This nuclear family pattern may accentuate sex-typing of adult roles (Romney 1965) and may increase the likelihood of women having low status in the community (Giele and Smock 1977b).

Women's work experience tends to be limited. Thirty-one percent of the women in the life history sample had not done any work outside the home since the age of 15. At the time of the interview, 69 percent were not working at all for pay. Of those currently working, 50 percent were engaged in a home craft. All but one of the latter group resided in one village (the small, fresco village) and were making straw hats at home. In that village, 80 percent of the mothers worked for pay, whereas in the other three villages, from 13 percent to 24 percent of the women worked for pay.

When asked if they would like to work more for earnings, 64 percent of the women replied that they would; popular choices were domestic work for money (ironing, mending, washing) and selling wares outside the villages. But 74 percent of the husbands were opposed to their wives' (and, in fact, to all wives') working. These mens' attitudes probably represent a powerful social limitation on the woman's capacity to develop her working potential.

Schooling tends to be limited for these mothers. Forty-nine percent of the 484 women in the life history sample never attended school, and only 2 percent attended for 6 years; most who attended went for 1 or 2 years only. Although women and men are about equally likely to attend school, women tend to stay in school fewer years and are less likely to be able to read as adults. In the census, 22 percent of the women and 39 percent of the men said that they could read. The message daughters might be getting is that schooling does not really contribute to literacy, that wage earning is not a likely alternative, and that men believe that women should not be participating in activities on the side to earn a little more.

EMPIRICAL RESULTS

Differences in Test Scores by Sex

Sex differences in test performance were not expected because of the initial standardization process used in the study. The current literature, however, indicated that girls would show initial precocity in verbal abilities and would be less impulsive than boys. When simple *t* tests were computed to compare mean test scores for girls and boys, significant differences were found. At age 3, girls did, in fact, have higher scores than boys on the Digit-Memory Test of verbal ability (significant at .03 level), but they were not found to be less impulsive than boys. On two tests that presumably measure a child's ability to inhibit impulsive responding, the Embedded Figures Test and Draw-a-Line-Slowly, boys showed a clear superiority at most ages.[1] Finally, boys had higher verbal reasoning scores at age 7 (significant at .01 level).

It has often been hypothesized that boys' scores are more variable than the scores of girls. Two kinds of variability were examined: variability between test scores for all boys and for all girls within an age-group, and variability within a single child's test scores. No sex differences in within-child variability were found at any age. Differences between boys' and girls' variance within an age-group were generally insignificant.

There were no sex differences in years of school attended in these villages (Irwin et al. 1978) nor in a neighboring village (Engle et al. 1977).

Effects of Supplement Ingestion on Mental Test Scores

To test the association between level of nutritional supplementation and test performance, a regression predicting test scores from total supplement ingestion over the child's lifetime was performed for boys and for girls in the two atole and in the two fresco villages. If supplementation affects mental development, increased levels of test performance should be associated with increased levels of supplement ingested. Regression coefficients are presented in Table 10.1, in the columns headed (1). Data are presented only for children up to their sixth birthday because very few children in the 7-year age-group had received early supplementation.

The most striking finding was a lack of association between test performance and supplement ingestion for girls. The coefficients for the effect of total supplement ingestion on the mental composite were positive and significant or approaching significance for boys in both the fresco and atole villages. If the supplement caused increased mental development, a boy who has ingested an extra 200 calories per day since the program began, or about 1¼ cups of atole a day, should increase his composite score by between one-third and one-half of a standard deviation. This would be roughly similar to a change in IQ score on a standardized test, like the Wechsler Intelligence Scale for Children, of one-half of a standard deviation, or 8 points (e.g., from 100 to 108). For the atole girls, on the other hand, the coefficients were close to zero at ages 3 and 4 and negative at ages 5 and 6. Coefficients for the fresco girls were significant only at age 3.

Could the absence of an effect of supplement ingestion on the test performance of girls be attributed to a lack of difference between well- and poorly supplemented girls' nutrient intake? We suspect not, because other studies have shown that all supplement intake affects the physical growth of both boys and girls (Martorell and Klein 1980). A second possibility is that the girls who received more supplement had lower SES indicator scores, which offset the improvement in mental test scores resulting from the nutrition supplement. To test this hypothesis, a regression was performed controlling for SES and other possible relevant variables before examining the effects of nutrition on test performance. These other variables were birth order, number of months breast-fed, whether the child lived in the larger or the smaller of the two villages in each pair (fresco and atole), and the number of months after the inception of the project (February 1969) that the child was tested. (Secular time was used as a control measure).

Because, as noted previously, the mother's composite scale was missing for some of the children, the sample size for this regression is smaller than the sample size for the first regression—see Table 10.1, columns headed (2). Controlling for the additional variables generally either had no effect on the coefficient of the effect of supplement ingestion on test performance or increased the size of the coefficient of the effect of supplement ingestion on mental test performances for both fresco boys and girls, and for atole boys. This is not

TABLE 10.1 REGRESSION COEFFICIENTS: EFFECT OF NUTRITIONAL SUPPLEMENTATION AND SOCIOECONOMIC VARIABLES ON MENTAL COMPOSITE TEST SCORES

Independent Variable	Age 3 yrs.		Age 4 yrs.		Age 5 yrs.		Age 6 yrs.	
	(1)	(2)	(1)	(2)	(1)	(2)	(1)	(2)
Atole Girls								
Amount of supplement	.01	−.04	.01	−.04	−.02	−.08	−.02	−.07
House quality		.98*		.54		.78		2.06**
Parental teaching		.87		1.11**		.45		1.91
Clothing quality		−.84		.32		.38		−.61
Reading materials		−.04		−.09		.45		.36
Maternal intellectual characteristics		.16		.03		.26		.68*
Village size		1.12		1.39**		1.71		2.72*
Months of lactation		.05		.10		.19		.21
Birth order		−.17		−.19*		−.42*		−.53**
Month in project		.05**		.05**		.08**		.08**
n	(161)	(136)	(187)	(158)	(190)	(156)	(178)	(145)
Atole Boys								
Amount of supplement	.05	.02	.07**	.05	.08	.11	.08*	.19**
House quality		.18		.28		.69		.55
Parental teaching		.84		.22		1.90*		2.03
Clothing quality		.26		.90*		−2.54**		1.37
Reading materials		−.04		.29		.17		.75
Maternal intellectual characteristics		.25		.04		.45		.43
Village size		.49		−.19		−.94		−2.47
Months of lactation		−.02		.06		.09		.02
Birth order		−.17		−.04		−.07		−.25
Month in project		.03		.02		0		−.06
n	(174)	(146)	(207)	(168)	(195)	(152)	(171)	(129)

(continued)

TABLE 10.1 Continued

Independent Variable	Age 3 yrs.		Age 4 yrs.		Age 5 yrs.		Age 6 yrs.	
	(1)	(2)	(1)	(2)	(1)	(2)	(1)	(2)
Fresco Girls								
Amount of supplement	.25**	.30**	.09	.14	.17	.27*	.10	.21
House quality		−.31		.31		−.92		−1.58
Parental teaching		−.41		−1.34**		−1.33		.31
Clothing quality		.26		.49		.30		2.28
Reading materials		.11		.15		.72**		.69*
Maternal intellectual characteristics		.11		.26		.55		.61
Village size		1.27*		1.30*		3.26**		1.80
Months of lactation		.02		.02		.22		.15
Birth order		−.02		.02		.09		.17
Month in project		.03		.02		.01		.02
n	(170)	(150)	(202)	(168)	(198)	(160)	(198)	(158)
Fresno Boys								
Amount of supplement	.16	.15	.08	.10	.24*	.20	.18**	.21*
House quality		−.71*		−.94**		.24		.18
Parental teaching		.25		0		1.91*		2.42*
Clothing quality		.98*		1.20**		1.31		2.90**
Reading materials		.24		.19		.38		.54
Maternal intellectual characteristics		−.03		.35**		.25		DNE
Village size		.16		−.98		0		.84
Months of lactation		.13*		.14**		.21		.02
Birth order		.24*		.12		.17		.10
Month in project		.02		.01		.01		−.01
n	(196)	(176)	(238)	(205)	(222)	(182)	(217)	(173)

NOTES: Column 1: equation with supplement alone entered.
Column 2: multiple regression equation after all variables are entered.
DNE = did not reach tolerance level to enter.

**Significant at .01 level.
*Significant at .05 level.

208

surprising, since supplement ingestion and SES indicators were sometimes found to be negatively related for the boys but not for the girls. The continued lack of effect of supplement ingestion on the test performance of the atole girls and the older (i.e., older than 3 years) fresco girls was suprising, however. We looked within the regression to see what variables *were* related to the mental composite scores.

The relationships between the SES indicators and mental test performances were generally positive and significant or almost significant. No clear or consistent sex differences or atole/fresco differences as to which SES indicator was most related to the test scores appeared. Several other sex-specific influences on test performance were noted. Girls living in the larger of the two villages tended to score higher than the girls living in the smaller of the two villages, for *both* the fresco and the atole village pairs. The scores of boys, however, were either the same or higher in the smaller villages. Because these village differences appeared even after our social and nutritional variables were controlled for, it is possible that this difference may be the result of different social factors affecting boys' and girls' development in each village, such as degree of heterogeneity in the population or more market activity.

A longer length of lactation was associated with higher test scores for both boys and girls. Early-borns tended to score higher than later-borns, although simple correlations of birth order with the composite were very low. Yet the coefficients were occasionally significant when the other variables were controlled for.

Effects of Secular Time

In order to see whether scores had changed over the time of the project, secular or calendar time was entered into the equation. Surprisingly, the coefficient of secular time, that is, the number of years between project inception and testing of children, was highly significant for atole girls at all ages, even after all other variables were controlled for. It was also marginally significant and positive for 3-year-old and 4-year-old atole boys and 3-year-old fresco girls.

The significant effect of secular time on the test performance of the atole girls contrasts with the lack of effect of supplementation. The coefficients of secular time on test performance continued to be significant when all other SES variables were controlled for; there was no comparable effect of secular time for boys. What can these changes be attributed to? The most obvious possibility is that simply attending the supplementation center improved their scores; children who attended probably became acquainted with the staff members and benefited from the social stimulation in the center and from spending time in the streets of the village. If so, we would expect to see higher scores in the later years of the project only for the supplemented groups.

To test this hypothesis, we split the atole children into two groups: a least supplemented group (less than 50 calories per day), and a more supplemented group. The correlation between supplement ingestion and days of attendance was found to be high (r = approximately .80) but not unitary, since children may ingest differing amounts of supplementation at each visit. The fresco children could not be split into the same calorie ingestion groups; instead, two approximately equal groups with attendance levels similar to those of the atole groups were defined.

Within these four groups, test scores of children from the initial half of the study (first 4 years) were compared with test scores of children tested in the last half of the study. As explained earlier, because of the overlapping cohort design, these were not always the same children. Correlations between secular time in months and composite test scores were also computed for the atole group. (The sample sizes for the fresco group were too small to allow this computation.) These figures are presented in Table 10.2.

In the atole group, least supplemented boys' scores were never significantly higher in the second half of the study than in the first half; instead, they were the same as or lower than scores of boys tested in the first half of the study. Correlations of secular time and composite test scores were not significant and often negative for the atole boys. The scores of least supplemented atole girls, however, were higher for those tested in the second half of the study than for those tested in the first half of the study in all five age-groups—they were significantly higher in the 3-year age-group, and marginally higher in the 4- and 5-year age-groups. Correlations of secular time and test performance were positive and significant for the 3- and 4-year age-groups as well. Among the more supplemented atole children, girls' scores, again, improved more than boys' scores over time.[2] Atole girls' scores, evidently, improved over time apart from the supplement effect.

In the fresco group, least supplemented 3-year-old girls' scores were higher in the second half of the study than in the first, whereas the boys' scores were significantly lower in the second half of the study for two age-groups, 5- and 7-year-olds. In the more supplemented, higher attendance group, results were similar to those for the more supplemented atole group: Significantly higher scores were noted in the second half of the study for 3-, 6-, and 7-year-old males and for 3-, 4-, and 5-year-old females.

These results do not indicate that changes in the girls' scores over time were the result of ingestion of the nutritional supplement or attendance at the supplement center. To examine the process of change in scores, we referred to the individual test results to determine what kinds of mental abilities (verbal and nonverbal) were changing. The individual test scores were correlated with secular time in three groups: atole less supplemented, atole more supplemented, and all fresco. Correlations with secular time for boys (not reported herein) were most significant for response time on the Embedded Figures Test and Discrimi-

TABLE 10.2 MEANS AND STANDARD DEVIATIONS OF MENTAL COMPOSITE TEST SCORES FOR EARLY- AND LATER-TESTED SUBJECTS, BY SEX AND SUPPLEMENTATION GROUP

		Fresco							Atole									
		Least Supplemented[a]			More Supplemented			Least Supplemented[b]				More Supplemented						
Age		n	X̄	SD	n	X̄	SD	n	X̄	SD	r^c	n	X̄	SD	r^c			
Males																		
3		E55	−.70	2.98	51	−.139	3.26	33	−.322	2.87	−.13	52	−.478	3.57	.21‡			
		L55	−1.02	3.94	47	1.61	4.03*	13	−1.343	3.04		76	.828	3.73**				
4		E41	−.50	3.52	59	−.25	3.65	43	−1.101	3.80	.06	48	.397	4.47	.15†			
		L53	−1.56	4.88	85	.88	3.79	14	−1.025	3.71		101	.939	3.58				
5		E36	−.48	6.16	59	−.33	6.58	43	−.818	5.33	−.07	43	.414	8.82	.12			
		L28	−5.09	10.35**	99	1.06	8.49	21	−1.45	6.91		88	1.119	8.96				
6		E34	−1.91	5.60	54	−.84	5.47	43	−.948	5.35	−.15	41	.150	7.01	−.04			
		L29	−1.87	13.79	100	2.17	9.28***	19	−3.73	10.64		68	1.62	9.43				
7		E35	−1.38	4.74	49	−.16	7.90	42	−.83	6.66	0	26	.44	6.82	−.03			
		L20	−7.32	11.11**	93	2.39	10.40*	20	.52	11.40		74	.99	9.38				
Females																		
3		E56	−1.75	3.44	38	−1.12	3.02	26	−.046	3.00	.36‡	53	.018	3.82	.27‡			
		L41	−.17	3.81**	35	1.41	3.77***	22	1.741	3.05**		60	.973	3.53				
4		E38	−1.75	3.04	57	−.71	3.14	<10	−.864	2.64	.29‡	44	−.503	3.44	.19‡			
		L40	−1.20	3.97	67	1.06	4.64***	15	.768	3.26***		88	1.297	4.07**				
5		E31	−2.39	6.42	61	−1.68	6.36	47	−.63	5.51	.18	43	−1.00	6.28	.18‡			
		L31	−1.42	9.55	75	.58	9.48*	15	2.70	7.53		85	2.58	7.76***				
6		E38	−1.33	7.39	62	−1.91	6.65	39	.51	7.14	.09	38	−.08	5.92	.19‡			
		L21	−2.11	12.54	77	.16	9.99	19	1.24	9.30		82	1.83	8.35				
7		E36	−1.08	6.27	63	−.63	6.77	36	.15	6.30	.13	33	−.47	8.24	.21‡			
		L10	−6.64	16.33	89	−.23	9.79	20	1.44	11.00		70	2.59	9.19				

NOTE: Early (E) = 1969 to 1972; later (L) = 1973 to 1976.

[a] Attendance levels similar to those of Atole group.

[b] Supplement less than 50 calories/day.

[c] Coefficient of correlation between test scores and secular time.

*** Difference between means significant at .01 level.

** Difference between means significant at .05 level.

* Difference between means significant at .10 level.

‡ Correlation significant at .01 level.

† Correlation significant at .05 level.

nation Learning, two measures of nonverbal abilities. For girls, the tests with the highest frequency of significant correlations were verbal: Naming, Verbal Inferences, and Memory for Sentences. Because the patterns of correlations differ by sex, we can suggest that these improvements in girls' test scores may be the result of changes unique to them and not shared by the boys.

Finally, it appears that girls' scores increased relative to boys' scores over the period of the study. Table 10.3, which presents individual test score means, shows significant differences in mean scores. In the first 4 years of the study, boys scored higher on several measures: Digit Memory in the 4- and 5-year age-groups and Verbal Inferences in the 5- and 7-year age-groups. Boys in all age-groups showed more motor inhibition (i.e., their response times were higher, or longer) in the Embedded Figures Test, and they drew more slowly in the Draw-a-Line-Slowly Test. In the second half of the study, the girls scored higher on several measures: Digit Memory in the 3-year age-group, Memory for Sentences in the 3- and 4- year age-groups, and Naming in the 4-year age-group. Boys continued to show longer response latencies in the 6- and 7-year age-groups in the Embedded Figures Test and scored higher on Verbal Inferences in the 7-year age-group. The improvement in girls' scores relative to those of boys was most noticeable in the younger age-groups and in verbal measures.

DISCUSSION OF RESULTS

The results of the study indicate that supplement ingestion had a positive, significant effect on mental composite test scores of boys in both fresco and atole (calorie and protein-calorie) villages, but little or no impact on the scores of girls in atole villages. The effect on fresco girls' scores was similar to that on fresco boys' scores in the 3-year age-group, but only boys' scores were significantly related to ingestion of supplement in the 6- and 7-year age-groups.

Some birth-order effects on scores were seen, favoring early-borns, and longer breast-feeding was associated with higher test scores. Scores of girls from the two larger villages were higher than those of girls from the smaller villages, whereas scores of boys from the larger villages were equal to or lower than those of boys from the smaller villages.

Girls' scores were higher at the end of the project than at the beginning, particularly in the atole villages. A similar but much weaker trend was observed for boys in the atole villages. These changes in test scores may have been the result of changes in the social environment that encouraged girls' cognitive development over the period of the study.

A number of social changes could be related to the increase in girls' scores. Girls' scores could have improved because of (1) repeated mental testing, (2) the presence of the program in the villages, or (3) other changes that occurred within the villages. We can eliminate the possibility that these improvements were the

TABLE 10.3 MEANS, BY SEX, OF INDIVIDUAL TEST SCORES IN FIRST HALF AND SECOND HALF OF PROJECT

Test	Sex	First Half					Second Half				
		Age 3 Yrs.	Age 4 Yrs.	Age 5 Yrs.	Age 6 Yrs.	Age 7 Yrs.	Age 3 Yrs.	Age 4 Yrs.	Age 5 Yrs.	Age 6 Yrs.	Age 7 Yrs.
Embedded Figures Test (correct responses)	Male	9.74	2.84	4.08	5.77	7.25	10.03	2.86	4.45	6.46	7.51
	Female	9.27	2.84	4.08	5.79	7.27	10.50	2.88	4.85	6.06	7.38
Embedded Figures Test (response time)	Male	3.25	3.11	3.47	3.86	4.19	3.12	3.52	3.58	4.06	4.01
	Female	3.12	3.08	3.28	3.52*	3.59**	2.91	3.35	3.38	3.57**	3.57**
Digit-Memory	Male	10.07	22.78	37.53	41.32	48.38	10.35	21.84	34.87	42.14	45.98
	Female	10.72	19.32**	34.00*	42.08	47.82	12.62*	22.42	34.85	41.84	46.08
Memory for Sentences	Male	11.74	32.78	52.66	64.33	80.86	13.50	33.43	52.23	68.36	79.89
	Female	13.11	30.35	48.39	63.40	76.95	16.48*	37.71*	55.30	68.37	77.77
Discrimination learning (trials to criterion)	Male	12.68	10.55	11.53	10.73	9.51	12.93	9.29	10.89	9.60	8.35
	Female	13.91	10.48	12.20	10.83	10.00	12.37	9.54	10.98	9.55	9.28
Naming	Male	6.65	12.24	17.50	20.76	23.49	7.46	13.23	17.88	21.71	24.26
	Female	6.63	12.08	17.41	20.55	23.20	8.22	14.35*	18.31	22.12	24.25
Verbal Inferences	Male	1.23	2.74	4.24	5.52	7.20	2.36	3.26	4.36	5.82	7.20
	Female	1.03	2.73	3.80*	5.31	6.63	2.31	3.30	4.38	5.53	6.62**
Draw-a-Line-Slowly (velocity)	Male	.954	.580	.35	.22	.15	.93	.62	.37	.23	.16
	Female	1.106**	.709**	.44**	.25	.17	.95	.63	.39	.23	.18

NOTE: First half = 1969 to 1972; second half = 1973 to 1976.
**Difference between means significant at .01 level.
*Difference between means significant at .05 level.

213

result of increased familiarity with the test materials, because significant improvements appeared in the younger age-groups, for whom the test materials were either completely novel (age 3) or still relatively novel (age 4). If the testers had changed their methods of administration, which we believe did not happen to any degree, differences should have been seen for both boys and girls. The hypotheses that with time, little girls became less shy and could perform closer to their potential, that the testers began to favor the little girls more than the little boys, or that the changes in the ambience of the villages stimulated girls to perform better may all be correct. All three imply that the social context of the villages was increasingly supportive of female competence. New social stimuli were present in the villages because of the project, even though every attempt was made to keep the INCAP profile low.

Another aspect of the INCAP project that may have had a greater impact on girls than on boys was the presence of new female role models. Every day one or two cars appeared carrying the project personnel. The vast majority of the personnel were women (one man daily and several other men who appeared periodically, compared with about 6 women who were present every day). These women were unlike the village women. They were obviously employed, well educated, well dressed, and in positions of power (a nurse, supervisors who visited the village regularly, etc.). They had a lot of contact with the villagers; each house was visited at least once every 2 weeks, and other contacts were made in the clinic and at the supplementation center. Children were tested and measured regularly by these personnel.

Nerlove et al. (1974) observed social role playing of various kinds, including "pretending to be INCAP project personnel with people in the community as their 'subjects'" (p. 275) and "pretending to be a *citadora* from INCAP (one who makes appointments for tests of various kinds with members of sample families who are part of the longitudinal study), making soft drinks in imitation of INCAP supplementation" (p. 283). The *citadora* was a girl of about 15, hired from the village; here was a specific work opportunity for a girl from this village who could read and write to earn money. Other young women prepared the supplement, and some served the city folk tea and lunch. In this culture in which parents value girls because they stay at home and do simple work and see girls as weaker, the presence of these people may have opened a new world of possibilities.

Another new influence was the regular (biweekly) visiting and interviewing of mothers to request their opinions about their own and their children's illnesses. Most mothers attended the supplementation center, where they visited with the personnel and other mothers. Mothers themselves may have changed their behavior or their attitudes because of the attention they were receiving. Some may have begun to think of themselves as more important, or of their children as more important and deserving of more attention because of the energy directed to testing and measuring them. For girls, who regularly stayed at home, an increase in mobility and social contact probably occurred as a result of visits to the center and clinic.

Thus, the strength of the effect of social change over time may have masked the effects of the nutritional supplements on girls' scores, by increasing the scores of the less supplemented children. Plots of these changes in girls' test performance over time indicate that most of the changes occurred in the first 4 years of the project. Analyses of the second 4 years of the intervention, currently under way at INCAP, may show nutritional effects to be equivalent for boys and girls.

What are the long-term implications of interventions that, through either nutritional or social impacts (or both), positively affect the mental development of girls? Mental development will open up educational and economic opportunities for both sexes, but mental ability may be more critical for girls than for boys. For example, in a study of schooling in the same four villages, Irwin et al. (1978) found that girls' years of school attendance were related to their mental test scores at age 7—even when the socioeconomic characteristics of the family were controlled for—whereas for boys, success in school was much more related to these socioeconomic characteristics. It seems that boys are sent to school as a function of the family standing, whereas a girl may be sent, or may choose to stay, only if she is smart enough. Whether schooling decisions for girls will be altered in the next few years as a result of the project is a matter of great interest.

Evidence of the powerful impact that awareness of new social options may have on the mental development of poor girls is the salient finding of this study for policymakers, and one that should encourage the introduction of positive role models for females in development programs.

Notes

1. Embedded Figures Test time: $t = 1.93$, $df = 698$, $p < .05$ at 3; $t - 2.17$, $df = 800$, $p < .03$ at 5; $t = 4.44$, $df = 734$, $p < .00$ at 6; and $t = 5.73$, $df = 700$, $p < .00$ at 7. Draw-a-Line-Slowly Test time: $t = 2.59$, $df = 667$, $p < .01$ at 3; $t = 2.12$, $df = 806$, $p < .04$ at 4; $t = 2.25$, $df = 750$, $p < .03$ at 5; $t = 2.20$, $df = 602$, $p < .03$ at 7.

2. For the boys, the difference in scores between those tested earlier and those tested later was significant only for the 3-year age-group (significant at .05 level) and correlations between secular time and composite scores were significant for the 3- and 4-year age-groups. For the girls, the differences in scores were significant for the 4-year, 5-year (.05 level), and 7-year (.10 level) age-groups; correlations between secular time and scores were significant at or beyond the .05 level for all five age-groups.

SECTION 3 Women and Alternative Household Structures

11. Establishing the Economic Condition of Woman-headed Households in the Third World: A New Approach

Nadia H. Youssef and Carol B. Hetler

The rapid growth of households headed by women in parts of the developed world has been well documented at national and sometimes regional levels since the early 1960s (United Nations 1973; United Nations 1981a; Sawhill and Ross 1976; United States Bureau of the Census 1980; Pearce and McAdoo 1981; Rawlings 1980). What is less well documented, due to a lack of national-level data, is the emerging phenomenon of woman-headed households in those countries that are experiencing rapid social change in the context of economic development efforts (Buvinić and Youssef 1978; Youssef and Hetler, forthcoming). Scattered sample surveys and a few in-depth analyses indicate, however, that their incidence is high (Tienda and Salazar 1980; Kerven 1979; Rogers 1979; Visaria 1980a, 1980b; Ahmad and Loutfi 1981; Kusnic and DaVanzo 1980; and Chap. 12 in this volume).

This essay represents a preliminary assessment of some of the methodological and conceptual obstacles to obtaining reliable information on the incidence and economic conditions of woman-headed households in developing countries. It stresses the need for a more in-depth understanding of qualitative variations among these woman-headed households, which, in different social contexts, affect their economic standing.

THE MEASUREMENT ISSUE

The major problem in attempting to determine how many households are headed by women in the developing countries is that official census and national survey documentation of the incidence of woman-headed households, although available and relatively accurate in the developed world, is generally unavailable

216

or inaccurate in the less developed world (United Nations 1973; United States Bureau of the Census 1980).

Availability of Data

There are few sources of data on how many households in the Third World have de jure woman heads (i.e., defined as such by national censuses), and data on how many households have de facto woman heads are almost nonexistent. Of the small number of developing countries that include specific tabulations of household heads by sex in their national census data, only a few cross-tabulate this information by marital status, age, economic activity, rural/urban residence, or household size.

Table 11.1, taken from a 1973 United Nations review of census documents, summarizes by country and region the availability of statistics on households and families, household headship by sex and age, and household/family size in national censuses taken principally from the 1960 round of censuses.[1] Of the 26 African censuses reviewed, not one made available headship data by sex and age. In Northern and Middle America and the Caribbean, of the 29 censuses investigated, 16 made available such data—2 in 1950, 1 in 1967, and the rest in 1960. Of the 12 South American censuses reviewed, only 2 reported headship data by sex and age—one in 1950, the other in 1960. In Asia, of the 23 censuses reviewed, only 3 made available such data. In Europe, of 32 censuses reviewed, 17 reported data on headship by sex and age. In Oceania, 1 out of 9 censuses reviewed reported such data. The Soviet Union reported no such data. Thus, in only 2 of the 7 regions did more than 50 percent of the reviewed censuses report headship data by sex and age. Generally, sex-specific headship data were more often available in the censuses of developed countries than in those of the less developed countries.

In an effort to determine whether progress had been made in the collection and analysis of census data on women in the developing world, the United States Bureau of the Census reviewed the most recently available census documents (and, in some instances, major surveys) to determine which developing countries had, as of the fall of 1979, identified woman-headed households.[2] This review indicates that there has been some improvement in the distribution of countries that collect data on heads of household (see Table 11.2 for a summary of the data available).[3] In Asia, of the 9 censuses reviewed, that of Indonesia now makes data available on heads of household by sex, age, and urban/rural residence. Of 10 censuses reviewed in the Middle East, 4—those of Israel, Morocco, Syria, and Tunisia—reported some data on heads of households; however, censuses of 9 countries in the region did not define the "head of household" category, and none of the censuses provided an ideal amount or breakdown of data. Of the 14 Latin American censuses reviewed, 8 provided data on age or urban/rural residence by sex of the household head.

TABLE 11.1 AVAILABILITY OF STATISTICS ON HOUSEHOLDS AND FAMILIES AND SEX/AGE-SPECIFIC HEADSHIP DATA IN THE 1960 ROUND OF POPULATION AND HOUSING CENSUSES IN COUNTRIES AND TERRITORIES OF THE WORLD

Continent and Country or Territory	Census Year	Household Statistics		Distribution of Households and Families by Size	Family Statistics	Family Nucleus Data	Headship Data by Sex and Age
		Housekeeping Unit Concept	Household-Housing Unit Concept				
Africa							
Algeria	1960	x	—	—	x	—	—
Angola	1960	—	x	—	x	—	—
Basutoland (now Lesotho)	1956	—	x	x	x	—	—
Cameroon	1957	...	...	x	—	—	—
Congo (Brazzaville) (now Congo)	1958	...	...	—	—	—	—
Dahomey	1961	—	—	x	—	—	—
Ethiopia	1961	—	x	—	—	—	—
Gabon	1960/61	x	—	x	—	—	—
Ghana	1960	—	x	—	—	—	—
Ifni	1960	x	—	—	—	—	—
Ivory Coast	1956/58	...	...	x	x	—	—
Kenya	1962	x	—	x	—	—	—
Libya	1964	—	x ...	x	—	—	—
Mali	1960/61	...	—	x	—	—	—
Mauritius	1962	x	—	—	—	—	—
Morocco	1960	...	...	x	—	—	—
Mozambique	1960	—	x ...	x (1950)	—	—	—
Réunion	1961	...	—	x	—	—	—
Seychelles	1960	x	x	x	—	—	—
Sierra Leone	1960	x	—	x	—	—	—
South Africa	1960	—	x	x	—	—	—
Southern Rhodesia	1962	—	x	x	—	—	—

Country	Year						
Sudan	1960	x	—	—	—	—	—
Togo	1958/59	—	x	—	—	—	—
United Arab Republic (now Egypt)	1960	x	x	x	—	—	—
Zambia	1961	x	—	—	—	—	—
Northern and Middle America and the Caribbean							
Bahamas	1963	x	—	—	∶	—	—
Barbados	1960	x	x	x	x	—	x
Bermuda	1960	x	x	x	—	—	—
British Honduras	1960	x	—	x	—	—	x
Canada	1961	—	x	x	x	x	—
Cayman Islands	1960	x	—	x	—	—	x
Costa Rica	1963	x	—	x	x	—	x
Dominica	1960	x	—	x	x	—	—
Dominican Republic	1960	—	x	x	x	—	x
El Salvador	1961	—	x	x	—	—	—
Greenland	1960	x	—	x	x	x	x
Grenada	1960	x	—	x	x	x	x
Guadeloupe	1961	x	—	x	—	—	x
Guatemala	1964	—	x	x	x	—	x (1950)
Haiti	1950	x	—	x	x	—	x
Honduras	1961	—	x	x	x	—	—
Jamaica	1960	x	—	x	—	—	—
Martinique	1961	x	—	x	—	—	x
Mexico	1960	x	—	x	x	—	—
Nicaragua	1963	—	x	x	x	—	x (1950)
Panama	1960	—	x	x	x	x	x
Puerto Rico	1960	x	x	x	x	x	x
St. Lucia	1960	x	—	x	—	—	—
St. Pierre and Miquelon	1957	x	—	x	x	x	x (1967)
St. Vincent	1960	x	—	x	x	—	—

(continued)

TABLE 11.1 *Continued*

Continent and Country or Territory	Census Year	Household Statistics		Distribution of Households and Families by Size	Family Statistics	Family Nucleus Data	Headship Data by Sex and Age
		Housekeeping Unit Concept	Household-Housing Unit Concept				
Trinidad and Tobago	1960	x	—	x	x	—	x
Turks and Caicos Islands	1960	x	—	x	—	—	—
United States of America	1960	—	x	x	x	x	x
United States Virgin Islands	1960	—	x	x	x	x	—
South America							
Argentina	1960	—	x	x	x	—	x
Brazil	1960	—	x	x	x	—	x (1950)
British Guiana (now Guyana)	1960	x	—	x	x	—	—
Chile	1960	—	x	x	x	—	—
Colombia	1964	x	—	x	x	—	—
Ecuador	1962	x	—	x	x	—	—
French Guiana	1961	—	x		x	—	—
Paraguay	1962	—	x	x (1950)	x	—	—
Peru	1961	⋮	x	x	x	—	—
Surinam	1964	—	x ⋮	x	—	—	—
Uruguay	1963	—	x	—	—	—	—
Venezuela	1961	x	—	x	—	—	—
Asia							
Brunei	1960	x	—	x	—	—	—
Cambodia (now Khmer Republic)	1962	⋮	⋮	x (1958)	—	—	—
Ceylon	1963	x	—	x (1953)	—	—	—
Cyprus	1960	x	—	x	—	—	—
Hong Kong	1961	x	—	x	—	—	—

India	1961	x	—	x	—	—	—
Iran	1956	—	x	x	—	—	—
Iraq	1957	…	…	x	—	—	—
Israel	1961	—	x	x	—	—	x
Japan	1960	x	—	x	x	x	x
Jordan	1961	x	—	x	—	—	—
Korea, Republic of	1960	x	—	x	x	—	—
Macau	1960	—	x	x	x	x	—
Malaysia Federation of Malaya (now West Malaysia)	1957	x	—	x	—	—	—
North Borneo (now Sabah)	1960	x	—	x	—	—	—
Sarawak	1960	x	—	x	—	—	—
Pakistan	1961	x	—	x	—	—	—
Philippines	1960	x	—	x (1957)	—	—	—
Ryukyu Islands	1960	x	—	x	—	—	—
Singapore (sample survey)	1966	x	—	x	x	x	x
Syria	1960	—	x	x	x	—	—
Thailand	1960	—	x	x	x	—	—
Turkey	1960	x	—	x	—	—	—
Europe							
Albania	1955	—	—	x	x	—	—
Austria	1961	x	—	x	x	x	x
Belgium	1961	x	—	x	x	x	x
Bulgaria	1956	—	—	x	x	—	—
Czechoslovakia	1961	—	x	x	x	x	x
Denmark	1960	x	—	x	x	x	x
Finland	1960	x	—	x	x	x	x
France	1962	—	x	x	x	x	x
Germany, Federal Republic of	1961	x	—	x	x	x	x
Germany, West Berlin	1961	x	—	x	x	x	…

TABLE 11.1 *Continued*

Continent and Country or Territory	Census Year	Household Statistics		Distribution of Households and Families by Size	Family Statistics	Family Nucleus Data	Headship Data by Sex and Age
		Housekeeping Unit Concept	Household-Housing Unit Concept				
Gibraltar	1951	x	—	x	—	—	—
Greece	1961	x	—	x	—	—	—
Hungary	1960	x	—	x	x	x	x
Iceland	1960	x	—	x (1950)	—	—	—
Ireland	1961	x	—	x	—	—	—
Italy	1961	x	—	x	x	x	x
Jersey and Guernsey	1961	x	—	x	—	—	—
Luxembourg	1960	x	—	x	x	x	x
Malta and Gozo	1957	x	—	x	—	—	—
Monaco	1962	...	...	x	—	—	—
Netherlands	1960	x	—	x	x	x	x
Norway	1960	x	—	x	x	x	x
Poland	1960	x	—	x	x	x	—
Portugal	1960	x	—	x	x	—	—
Romania	1965	—	—	—	x	—	—
Spain	1960	x	—	—	x	x	—
Sweden	1960	—	x	x	x	x	x
Switzerland	1960	—	x	x	x	x	x
United Kingdom							
England and Wales	1961	x	—	x	x	x	x
Northern Ireland	1961	x	—	x	x	x	x
Scotland	1961	x	—	x	x	x	x
Yugoslavia	1961	x	—	x	x	x	—
Oceania							
American Samoa	1960	—	x	—	x	x	—

Australia	1961	—	x	x	—	—	x
Christmas Islands (Australia)	1957	⋯	⋯	x	—	—	—
Fiji	1956	x	—	—	—	—	—
Guam	1960	—	x	—	x	x	—
New Zealand	1961	x	—	x (1956)	—	—	—
Niue	1961	⋯	⋯	x	—	—	—
Pacific Islands	1958	⋯	⋯	x	—	—	—
Western Samoa	1961	—	x	—	—	—	—
USSR							
USSR	1959	—	—	x	x	—	—
Byelorussian SSR	1959	—	—	x	x	—	—
Ukrainian SSR	1959	—	x	x	x	—	—

SOURCE: United Nations, Department of Economic and Social Affairs, *Methods of Projecting Households and Families*, Manual VII, 1973.

NOTE: x indicates that data were available or that category concerned was relevant.

— indicates that data were not available or that category was not relevant.

⋯ indicates that some statistics on households were available, but the definition was vague or unobtainable.

TABLE 11.2   SUMMARY OF AVAILABLE CENSUS DATA ON "HOUSEHOLD HEADS,"
10 YEARS OLD AND OVER, BY AGE, SEX, AND URBAN/RURAL RESIDENCE,
FOR MAJOR REGIONS OF THE DEVELOPING WORLD
AND FOR SELECTED COUNTRIES, 1980

Region or Country	Total Countries Reviewed	Data on Sex of Head Available[a]		Head Defined		Constraints on Data
		Yes	No	Yes	No	
Asia	9	1	8	0	9	—
Indonesia		x			x	STD
Middle East	10	4	6	1	9	—
Israel		x		x		AG/UR
Morocco		x			x	AG
Syria		x			x	TOT
Tunisia		x			x	AG
Latin America	14	8	6	8	6	—
Costa Rica		x		x		AG
El Salvador		x		x		AG
Guatemala		x		x		TOT
Guyana		x		x		AG/UR
Honduras		x		x		TOT
Jamaica		x		x		AG/UR
Panama		x		x		AG
Peru		x		x		SG/UR
Africa	36	13	23	9	27	—
Benin		x			x	AG
Burundi		x			x	AG/UR
Chad		x			x	AG
Ghana		x		x		STD
Guinea		x		(x)[b]		AG
Liberia		x		x		STD
Malawi		x		x		STD
Mali		x		(x)[b]		AG
Mauritania		x			x	RC
Mauritius		x		x		AG/UR
Niger		x			x	RC
Sudan		x		x		TOT
Upper Volta		x		(x)[b]		AG
Ivory Coast			x	x		ND
Total	69	26	43	18	51	—

SOURCE: United States Bureau of the Census, International Demographic Data Center,
unpublished data from the Women in Development Data Base, 1980.

NOTE: STD = data conform to "ideal" distinctions; TOT = tables lack age breakdowns
and contain column or row totals only; UR = urban/rural (total or partial) not available; AG =
age categories differ from standard format; RC = row and/or column deviation from standard
format (other than UR, AG); ND = search conducted, no data found.

[a]At least totals by sex are available.

[b]Definition of head is not directly stated, but sex is implied as male.

In the African countries, there has been a significant increase in the availability of census data on households reported by the sex of the head. Of the 36 African censuses reviewed, 13 reported some data by sex of head, and 3 of them—Ghana, Liberia, and Malawi—met the United States Census Bureau's "ideal" format standards. Ghana, for instance, reported no sex-specific headship data in its 1960 national census, despite the fact that a high level of male migration made the existence of many woman-headed households very likely. By 1970, however, a question on the sex of the household head had been incorporated into the census questionnaires and the government subsequently published detailed tables on household size and age composition, cross-classified by the sex of the head. According to the 1970 Ghana census, fully 29 percent of the total number of reported households were woman-headed. In urban areas, woman-headed households made up 31 percent of all households; in rural areas, the proportion was 28 percent.

Even with the clear improvement since 1970 in the collection of statistics on woman-headed households, the availability and completeness of such data continue to vary from country to country. Only 4 of the 69 countries reviewed by the United States Census Bureau reported a complete breakdown of data on household heads (by age, sex, and urban/rural residence) in a standardized format.[4]

Quality of Data

Even when questions on the sex of the household head are incorporated into data collection procedures, there are still major obstacles to determining the incidence of woman-headed households because of the definitions, or lack of definitions, of "family" and "household head" in censuses and surveys.[5]

The United Nations recommends that the person reported as the *family head* be "either (a) that person who is acknowledged as such by the other members of the census family or of the family nucleus . . . or (b) the member of the family or of the family nucleus who meets specified requirements" (United Nations 1969, para. 266). The United Nations further recommends that "if the first definition is used, the head of the family must be identified by means of a direct question at the enumeration. If the second definition is employed, the head of the family can be identified at the processing stage on the basis of such characteristics as sex, age and marital status, or simply by virtue of being the head of a one-person household" (United Nations 1973, p. 11).

The United Nations suggests, however, that the more desirable definition is the one that further specifies the role of the household head, by designating the head of the household as "the person who bears the chief responsibility for the economic maintenance of the household, [although] it is not recommended that this definition be applied because of the difficulty of collecting the information needed to determine economic responsibility" (United Nations 1969, para. 269).

Few countries adhere to these guidelines. A review of the international census literature and the literature on cross-cultural comparisons of family and household structure indicates that there is a wide range of definitions of the terms ''family head'' and ''household head'' and that these terms are often assumed to be commonly understood and so are not formally defined.

The United Nations review of census documents just mentioned (United Nations 1973, p. 11) reports that only 36 countries explicitly defined headship; their definitions were of three types:

- Those which defined the head (of the household or of the family) as the one who reports himself as such or is so reported by another member of the household or family (23 censuses)
- Those which defined the head as a person who controls the maintenance of the household—that is, exercises the authority to run the household (7 censuses)
- Those which defined the head as the ''main supporter'' (chief earner) of the household (6 censuses)

It appears that, for the most part, the definitions used were not based upon any economic or sociological criteria. The United Nations has concluded that neither the definitions adopted for ''head of household,'' nor the differences among the definitions, are clear.

As can be seen from Table 11.3, many of the 36 countries using a definition, however unclear, were in Western Europe and Northern or Central America. Twenty of them were developed countries. Only 3 of the countries were in Asia, and only 2 were in South America; none was in Africa.

A comparison of the United States Census Bureau summary (1980) with United Nations data (1973) indicates that there has been an increase in the number of developing countries that have adopted explicit definitions of heads of household (compare Tables 11.3 and 11.4). The Caribbean and Latin American countries had already adopted definitions of head of households for their 1950 and 1960 rounds of censuses, but this was not true in Asia and Africa. The United States Census Bureau survey indicates that some African countries (9 out of the 36 surveyed) have now begun to use definitions of household head (most of them in time for the 1970 round of censuses). Asian countries had yet to adopt a definition of household head by the late 1970s. Of the 69 countries reviewed by the Census Bureau, more countries *reported data* on household heads than *defined* the head of household. Of the 18 countries that had adopted some kind of definition of household head,[6] 15 used definitions that were reasonably well specified and similar to one of the 3 definitions recommended by the United Nations; the other 3 countries used implicit definitions—that is, indirectly derived from the definition of ''household.'' Of the 15 explicit definitions, 12 relied upon the reporting of ''head of household'' by respondents (either the head or other members of the household), and 2 designated as head the person who exercised authority in running the household. Only one country defined household head principally on the basis of the degree of economic support provided by that person. In the 3 cases in which the definition of household head was implicit, the definition presumed that the household head was male.

The use in censuses of biased and inconsistent definitions of the head of household (or family), as well as cultural preferences for males to be designated as heads (regardless of their actual roles in households), results in a situation

TABLE 11.3   DEFINITION OF "HEAD OF HOUSEHOLD" (OR FAMILY) IN THE 1960 ROUND OF CENSUSES IN 36 COUNTRIES AND TERRITORIES WHERE HOUSEHOLD (OR FAMILY) DATA HAVE BEEN TABULATED AT LEAST BY SEX AND AGE

Country or Territory	Head of Household Reported by Respondents as Such (Either by Himself or by the Other Members)[a]	Person Who Controls the Maintenance of Household (Exercises the Authority to Run the Household)	Main Supporter and Others
Northern and Middle America and the Caribbean			
Barbados	—	—	x
Canada	x	—	—
Costa Rica	x	—	—
Dominican Republic	x	—	—
Grenada	—	—	x
Guadeloupe	x	—	—
Guatemala	x	—	—
Haiti	—	x	—
Martinique	x	—	—
Nicaragua	x	—	—
Panama	x	—	—
Puerto Rico	x	—	—
St. Pierre and Miquelon	—	x	—
Trinidad and Tobago	—	x	—
United States of America	x	—	—
South America			
Argentina	x	—	—
Brazil	x	—	—
Asia			
Israel	x[b]	—	—
Japan	x	—	—
Singapore	x	—	—
Europe			
Austria	x	—	—

(*continued*)

TABLE 11.3 *Continued*

Country or Territory	Head of Household Reported by Respondents as Such (Either by Himself or by the Other members)[a]	Person Who Controls the Maintenance of Household (Exercises the Authority to Run the Household)	Main Supporter and Others
Belgium	—	x	—
Czechoslovakia	—	x	—
Denmark	—	—	x
Finland	—	—	x
France	x	—	—
Germany, Federal Republic of	x	—	—
Hungary	—	—	x
Italy	x	—	—
Luxembourg	—	x	—
Netherlands	x	—	—
Norway	—	—	x
Sweden	—	x	—
Switzerland	x	—	—
United Kingdom	x	—	—
Oceania			
Australia	x	—	—
Total	23	7	6

SOURCE: United Nations, Department of Economic and Social Affairs, *Methods of Projecting Households and Families,* Manual VII, 1973.

[a]In some instances, even when no definitions were given in the census reports, the census questionnaires included a question on the relationship of the household or family members to the head, and hence it was concluded that the head of the household or family was reported or designated as such either by himself or by the other members.

[b]When identification was difficult, the oldest member of the household was designated.

where women who are heads of household, in terms of decision making and provision of economic support, are not reported as such.

When the definition of head is not explicit, census enumerators and/or respondents may themselves determine headship by whatever means they choose. Male headship is often assumed. When headship is determined by means of demographic criteria (age, sex, marital status) rather than direct inquiry, the likelihood of accurate reporting of the incidence of woman headship decreases dramatically (Buvinić and Youssef 1978).[7]

Furthermore, even when the definition of household head is unbiased and fairly accurate data on the incidence of woman-headed households are collected, the data are seldom made available in a form useful for the analysis of the economic and social situation of these households relative to male-headed households—that is, there is little effort to publish the data in a format that allows for the comparison of household characteristics (size, composition, etc.). In addition, the data are rarely reported by geographic regions within a country or an urban/rural area.

TABLE 11.4 SUMMARY OF DIRECT AND INDIRECT DEFINITIONS OF "HOUSEHOLD HEAD" USED IN MAJOR REGIONS OF THE DEVELOPING WORLD AND IN SELECTED COUNTRIES, 1980

| Region or Country | Total Countries Reviewed | Total Countries Having Definition | Direct Definition | | | Indirect (Implied) Definition | Male Is Identified as Head |
			Reported as Such	Makes Decisions	Main Support		
Asia	9	0	—	—	—	—	—
Middle East	10	1	—	—	1	—	1
Israel					x		x
Latin America	14	8	8	—	—	—	—
Costa Rica			x				
El Salvador			x				
Guatemala			x				
Guyana			x				
Honduras			x				
Panama			x				
Peru			x				
Jamaica			x				
Africa	36	9	4	2	—	3	5
Malawi				x			
Ghana				x			x
Mauritius			x				
Sudan			x				
Liberia			x[a]				x
Guinea						x	x
Ivory Coast			x				
Upper Volta						x	x
Mali						x	x
Total	69	18	12	2	1	3	6

Source: Adapted from United States Bureau of the Census, International Demographic Data Center, unpublished data from the Women in Development Data Base, 1980, tables 12 and 13.

[a]Head was determined by the enumerator, who was instructed to designate a male as head, if a male was present.

The Survey Approach

It is difficult to determine the degree of inaccuracy of census data on woman-headed households. Area or regional surveys, however, as well as in-depth anthropological studies, suggest that in certain areas and countries the incidence of woman-headed households is higher, and their economic status more marginal, than officially reported. Although some of these studies do not use rigorous sampling methods, they nonetheless indicate that woman-headed households do exist in substantial numbers and that their incidence may be surprisingly high both in urban slums and in remote agricultural districts. Since census data fail to report the incidence or economic plight of these households, they would remain a part of the "invisible poor" were it not for the evidence of their existence and economic condition presented in surveys and case studies.

A comparison between census data and the findings of some microstudies highlights the limited usefulness of aggregate national census data for the study of poor women in particular. For example, the 1973 Costa Rican census indicated that only 6.4 percent of all households were headed by women and that only 5.3 percent of the total economically active woman heads of household held jobs similar to those held by the total number of economically active females. Like economically active women in general, woman heads of household provided personal services and worked as professionals, administrators, and office workers—although twice as many of them were seeking their first jobs as were economically active women in general.

In contrast, a small-sample study of women of low socioeconomic status, conducted by a Costa Rican anthropologist using the technique of biographies, indicated that 51 of 82 women surveyed were de facto heads of households. Fifty-five of the women lived in a matrifocal family structure where economic responsibility for family survival is assumed by the mother. These poor women and their children worked most often in marginal occupations that did not provide them with a fixed wage; therefore, they did not get counted as "economically active" (de Piza 1977).

The Asian countries of India, Nepal, Sri Lanka, and Malaysia do not report the incidence of woman-headed households in their censuses (United Nations 1973, pp. 8–9; United States Bureau of the Census 1980). Sample surveys undertaken in those countries and reviewed by the World Bank, however, found significant proportions of households headed by women (Visaria 1980b, p. 57). In India, in the state of Gujarat (1972–73), 6.2 percent of all rural households sampled and 7.6 percent of all urban households sampled were headed by women—sample sizes (n) were 5,560 and 3,545 households, respectively. In the state of Maharashtra (1972–73), 10.4 percent of rural households and 7.4 percent of urban households ($n = 5,314$ and 11,103) were woman-headed. In two surveys of towns in Nepal (11 towns in 1973–74 and 9 towns in 1974–75), woman-headed households represented between 9 and 10 percent of all households ($n = 4,392$

and 2,253). In Sri Lanka in 1969–70, woman-headed households represented 12.4 percent of all households ($n = 9,664$). Finally, a major survey in Peninsular Malaysia in 1973 found that over 18 percent of all households were headed by women ($n = 7,273$).

There are, however, cases where census data and microsurvey data converge. A study conducted in 1971 in Caracas, Venezuela, that compared barrio households with regard to the employment and labor force status of the household head, showed that approximately one-fourth of Venezuelan households were woman-headed. This finding is in accord with 1961 census data and with the findings of a 1971 housing study undertaken by the National Bank of Venezuela (Blumberg and García 1977). Another survey of a representative sample of 2,245 households in the metropolitan area of Belo Horizonte, Brazil, found that 19 percent of the households were headed by women (Merrick 1977), as the census for that region reported. Usually, however, census data and small-sample survey findings are not compatible.

In summary, it appears that if censuses and surveys are going to report meaningful and comparative information, the conceptualization and definitions of the terms "household" and "head of household" must be standardized. In addition, in order to increase our understanding of the structure and economic condition of woman-headed households and the ways in which members of these households interact with each other and with other residence groups, priority should be given to conducting intensive surveys and microstudies in areas where the incidence of such households is likely to be high.

VARIATIONS IN THE CHARACTERISTICS OF WOMAN-HEADED HOUSEHOLDS

Although data on woman-headed households have several shortcomings, as has been discussed in this chapter, they do provide evidence, however fragmented, that woman-headed households are not undifferentiated and should not be treated as such. It fact, it appears that these households vary substantially in those characteristics that may affect the economic condition of the household in general. Thus, differing findings on the situation of woman-headed households may not be contradictory but may instead underscore the need to clarify our conceptual and methodological approach to a complex subject of investigation.

In Chapter 12, for example, Merrick and Schmink report that data from urban Brazil point distinctly to the severely disadvantaged condition of woman-headed households. Evidence of the poverty of woman-headed households has also been found by Buvinić and Youssef (1978) and Kusnic and DaVanzo (1980). On the other hand, the claim that woman-headed households are *not* as disadvantaged as previously reported, and are not more likely than male-headed households to be poor, has been made in a World Bank review of national income and expenditure surveys in Asian countries (Visaria 1980*a,* 1980*b*). We suggest that priority should be given to highlighting the variability in characteristics of woman-headed households, as a means of understanding the basis for this diversity of opinion on the economic status of these households.[8]

Some of the more important considerations in determining the different types of woman-headed households—considerations that are closely linked to the economic status of these households—are:

- De jure and/or de facto female headship
- The social context of female headship
- The marital status of the woman household head
- Access to productive resources and income
- Household size and composition

De Jure and/or De Facto Female Headship

Differentiation among types of woman-headed households naturally requires the identification of those households that are headed by women. A household may be designated as woman-headed, de jure, or de facto, or both. There are five broad categories of de jure and/or de facto woman-headed households:[9]

1. Households with no male spouse or partner present at any time, which include households headed by single mothers, divorced or widowed women who have not remarried, women who are separated, women whose nonlegalized unions have been dissolved, and wives who have been deserted by their husbands (de jure woman-headed households)

2. Households where the male partner is a transient resident, which include households headed by women who have temporary liaisons with men but cannot count on these partners as regular household residents who will provide economic support (de jure woman-headed households)

3. Households from which the male spouse or partner is temporarily absent, such as households headed by married women whose husbands are away for unspecified periods (de facto woman-headed households)

4. Households in which the male spouse or partner is present, but his contribution to the economic maintenance of the household is marginal (because of unemployment, disability, illness, etc.) (de facto woman-headed households)

5. Households from which the male spouse or partner is absent, but one or more adult males are in residence (de facto and/or de jure woman-headed households)

The Social Context of Female Headship and Marital Status

It is important to note that widowed, divorced, or separated women and single mothers do not automatically become de jure heads of household; wives of migrants do not all assume de facto headship, in the sense of becoming sole/major economic providers. Instead, whether or not women assume headship (de jure or de facto) depends on the socioeconomic position of the household in question, the status of women in the familial structure, and the ability and willingness of the larger family unit (or society) to extend financial assistance to women. Thus, whether or not independent households headed by women are formed in structural/economic terms is determined by specific culturally defined provisions for women and their households, following divorce, separation, death of spouse, or single motherhood. Such provisions can consist of (1) explicit obligations (lack of obligations) on the part of the larger family to absorb the divorced, widowed, or abandoned women into the affinal household and/or explicit provision (or lack of provision) for her economic support; and (2) societal and/or legal stipulations regarding remarriage.

Widows and Divorced Women

Remarriage possibilities for widows and divorced women are strongly conditioned by demographic characteristics. Even when remarriage is culturally or legally permissible, widowhood can become a permanent status because of the interaction between sex differentials in mortality rates (men die at younger ages than women) and age differentials between spouses (men typically marry women considerably younger than themselves). This interaction often creates a large pool of older, unmarriageable women among the divorced or widowed.[10]

When such a pool exists and families are unable or unwilling to provide economic support to their female kin, women are likely to assume household headship and the sole or major responsibility for the economic support of their households. The demise of the traditional family-based support system in many developing countries will undoubtedly lead to this very situation. Women, more than men, have been losing a great deal of the economic and emotional security previously extended to them by kinship groups. Not only widows and divorcees, but married women as well are affected, since this waning support has meant a parallel decline in marital obligations.

In India, joint-family norms requiring the absorption of widowed daughters-in-law into the husband's family are no longer always followed. Instead, widowed women often return to their own families or set up separate households with their children. In some cases widowed mothers and widowed daughters live together (Shah 1976). Men in Upper Volta find it increasingly difficult to maintain the prescribed custom of incorporating widows into affinal households. As a result, widows are being left on their own to provide for their own support and that of their children (Correze 1977). In Morocco, poverty compels extended families to abandon widows, separated women, and single mothers (Ahmad and Loutfi 1981). Swazi women are finding considerable economic insecurity in marriage because men now find it easier to leave their wives on their own, responsible for their own support (Ferraro 1980). In Zambia, widows and divorced women have to rely on nonkinship groups to extend assistance (BAM Zambia 1981).

Married Women

When a married woman assumes de facto headship by default because her husband is unable to maintain his economic obligations to the household, she is obligated to assume economic and decision-making responsibilities—although the husband may still make some decisions or advise his wife. This type of household is in large part "invisible." Often, the husband in such a household is classified as "head" when he might more accurately be described as dependent on his wife (Rogers 1979).

The headship status of married women whose husbands are migrant laborers has been the subject of some controversy (Wiest 1973). The postulated linkage between male out-migration and the formation of woman-headed households has been questioned with respect to whether male absenteeism necessarily produces a change in the economic structure of the rural household that warrants a redefinition of household headship. Insofar as absent men continue to provide economic support and women "left behind" continue to have access to economic resources (especially land) and support (labor, economic assistance) of kinship groups, there is no reason, it is sometimes argued, for women to be designated as either de jure or de facto household heads, even on a temporary basis.

This argument suggests the need to differentiate further the status of women in rural households characterized by the temporary absence of the male. Investigations of the roles and responsibilities of rural women left behind have tended to neglect the distinction between the domestic and income-earning work load/ responsibility assumed by women, the proportion of household income that women contribute, and the degree of control over property and decision making exercised by women in their husbands' absences.[11]

Field studies in some countries have shown that women left behind bear the major, if not complete, responsibility for agriculture and livestock production *and* management of the farm during the men's absence. The male often returns at harvest time, however, to sell the crops; he retains full control over farm income and makes any major decisions about farm and domestic matters (Ferraro 1980; Kerven 1979; BAM Zambia 1981; Ahmad and Loutfi 1981; Staudt 1978; World Bank 1980; Wiest 1973; Moses 1977; Birks and Sinclair 1977; Lubell 1974).

In other countries (Mali, Ghana, Brazil, Togo, Liberia, Nigeria, Swaziland), women left behind become the major, if not the sole, supporters of the rural household. Some of these women (Togo, Liberia) cannot rely on husbands' earnings and may undertake cash cropping or resort to trade in order to pay land taxes and agricultural labor costs.

In some countries, women do not receive remittances from the absent males at all; in others (Pakistan, India), remittances are sent not to the women themselves, but to extended/joint-family male members. Remittances may then be spent on larger family obligations (land debts, marriage festivities), rather than on direct nuclear household consumption. This usually means that women have to generate their own incomes.

There are other instances where women farmers end up supporting their husbands in the city (Swaziland) and where they exercise considerable independence in decisions related to the economics of the farm and property (Yemen, Turkey) (see Ahmad and Loutfi 1981; Handwerker 1974; Ross 1977; Ferraro 1980).

In rural settings, one "benefit" for married woman heads of household is that they may have individual or joint ownership of cattle and may be better able to demand assistance from the husband's family than widowed or divorced women. Rural women whose husbands are temporarily absent have an advantage over women who are no longer, or who have never been, married *only* if their husbands are absent for a relatively short period, regularly send cash remittances sufficient to support the household, and return regularly to assist in farm labor. If such conditions do not exist, married woman heads of household may find themselves in the same predicament as women residing with men whose economic support is marginal and women who do not reside with male partners at all.

Single Mothers

The position of single mothers as household heads has been best documented for Central and South America, where their incidence is particularly high in urban areas. The preponderance of young single women in rural-to-urban migratory flows has created an oversupply of younger women relative to men in major urban areas and caused a consequent rise in temporary and sporadic sexual unions. When such unions are dissolved, women are often left on their own to support themselves and their dependent children.[12] They very rarely live with their parents and receive no institutional assistance (from government or place of employment) when they attempt to combine their motherhood and work roles.[13]

In rural Latin America, there are also significant proportions of single mothers who are household heads. In-depth studies in Guatemala indicate that the majority of single mothers come from rural areas. In Honduras, rural single mothers have a higher rate of fertility than their urban counterparts. In Peru and in Colombia, the proportion of single mothers in the single adult population is higher in rural areas than in the cities (Buvinić and Youssef 1978).[14]

Single motherhood is not uncommon in other regions of the world. In Africa, for example, in both Botswana and Mozambique the number of single mothers is high.[15] Fieldwork in South Cameroon, Ghana, Niger, and Upper Volta has revealed increases in the number of women who have borne children outside marriage (Weekes-Vagliani 1976; Poole 1972).[16]

Not much is known of the social context in which reproduction takes place in Africa, nor of the immediate economic consequences of reproduction for women. Customary law in some African societies gives women the right to head their own households without male guardianship. Interest in retaining this right, which includes the right to keep their children, has prompted women in some African countries to avoid formal marriages. Unmarried mothers surveyed in Botswana and Zambia stated that they would rather not marry the fathers of their children because the fathers had provided no financial assistance (Kerven 1979; BAM Zambia 1981).

In some rural areas of Africa, women heads of household who are unmarried mothers (who may or may not have formed temporary liaisons), and divorced or deserted wives, are the women least able to depend on agriculture as a means of livelihood. These are also the groups of women least likely to receive cash remittances or to have free labor available to them or the cash to hire laborers; they are the least likely to own cattle or to have the social right to demand assistance from relatives. Some of these heads of household are forced to sell what few assets they own in order to pay for agricultural labor, food, and taxes. In Botswana and Zambia, the situation of rural single mothers and of divorced or widowed women is growing worse; many of them have been forced to become dependent on their communities (Kerven 1979; BAM Zambia 1981).

It is often widowed woman heads of household who are the most advantaged, since they may inherit their deceased husbands' land or cattle. Sometimes, however, widowed women are barred from inheriting their husbands' land holdings with the result that they are forced into dependent positions (Kerven 1979)—though in general, traditional kinship obligations to dependents appear to operate favorably for the widowed woman as opposed to the woman who is divorced, deserted, or an unmarried mother (Youssef 1974).

Access to Productive Resources and Income

The literature includes numerous investigations of the relationship among women, work, and productive resources in developing economies (International Center for Research on Women 1980a, 1980b; Dauber and Cain 1981). This relationship is extremely important for woman-headed households whose economic success or failure often depends on their differential access to, and utilization of, productive resources, on the availability of different sources of income, and on the regular receipt of that income.

Productive Resources

Productive resources are needed for on-farm and off-farm work in both rural and urban areas. Resources necessary for on-farm production include land, cattle, labor, credit, tools, and technology. Off-farm (rural *and* urban) productive resources include access to wage labor and employment, access to training and technical assistance, credit, appropriate work facilities, adequate transportation, and markets. Some of the more critical of these resources are discussed in the following paragraphs.

Land. A clear distinction must be made between ownership of and access to productive resources, since there is greater security and greater possibility of profit when full title to a resource is held. In agricultural economies the principal productive inputs are land, draft animals, plows, and irrigation systems or access to water. Ascertaining "ownership" of these primary resources may sometimes be difficult, and different types or degrees of ownership may exist. In some settings, notably in Africa, these resources are shared in complex agreements that take the form of kin-based or semicontractual reciprocal agreements. It is important to give consideration to the issue of land ownership versus access to land in regions where title to land is typically held by individuals and inheritance laws exist. In these regions it is important to determine whether women, and particularly women who head households, are allowed to hold clear title to farmland; if they only have access to the land, their economic security may be in question.

Ownership of land carries with it a set of rights and expectations very different from those which accompany mere access to land through rental or sharecropping agreements. Landowners acquire access to the secondary factors of production—for example, land may serve as collateral for both short- and long-term loans that are used to finance acquisition of other agricultural inputs such as tools, draft power, fertilizers, sprays, and irrigation. Land ownership may also bring with it membership in cooperatives, access to an agricultural extension service, and even participation in local government. It is critical, therefore, that land owned by women be held in their names so that woman heads of household may have direct access to both the primary and secondary inputs to agricultural production. When women are prevented from holding legal title to their own farms or, as in some cases, from even having access to land, they are in danger of being denied the principal source of their agricultural income in the event of divorce or separation from their husbands who do hold title to the land.[17]

Access to credit. Whether or not woman heads of household have access to financial institutions in seeking credit can have important consequences for income distribution. Credit plays an important role in the mobilization of productive resources and can be used by woman household heads as a means of raising productivity. Capital inputs to home production can increase efficiency and can free women to spend time earning cash income. In rural areas, credit for cash crop investments (such as the purchase of equipment) is needed to generate income. In urban areas, loans to small-scale interprises may create opportunities to generate income through participation in new activities.

Access to appropriate training and technical assistance. Women's capacity to increase household income, both in rural and in urban areas, is influenced to a large degree by their opportunities to participate in programs that teach industrial, technical, entrepreneurial, and mechanical skills. The tendency has been to promote women's training programs that focus on activities that yield little or no income, such as cooking and handicrafts (e.g., sewing and embroidery).

In rural areas, inequities in the delivery of agricultural extension programs to women who are farm managers and heads of household have reinforced the disadvantaged position of these women (Kerven 1979; Ahmad and Loutfi 1981). The preferential treatment given by extension workers to wealthier farmers and to farms managed exclusively by male farmers (or jointly with their wives) is a form of discrimination against woman heads of household because of their poverty, sex, and marital status. In Kenya, great disparities have been found in the delivery of services to farms managed only by women versus those managed, at least in part, by men. Women's access to technical information, training, and loans continued to be restricted even when rules were introduced instructing extension agents to disregard economic standing and land size in making their programs available. There were obvious negative effects on women's productivity (Staudt 1976, 1978).

Access to wage labor and employment. Wage labor and employment in the modern sector are extremely important for all women, particularly for woman heads of household, for several reasons:

- Women (excluding widows) are less likely than men to own land or to have legal rights to land.
- Land redistribution schemes often grant land titles to male household heads only.
- Women agricultural laborers earn less per day than males, and they are more likely to be seasonally employed.
- Women often remain in villages while their male partners migrate. When regular remittances are not forthcoming, their need for income increases.
- Women are subject to eviction from homes and farms at the time of divorce, desertion, or widowhood.
- As men gain control over new technology, there is a widening gap between men's and women's productivity and income-earning capacity.
- Women's traditional jobs are often low-paying and of low status, with little or no opportunity for advancement (Dixon 1979).

Access to nonagricultural sources of income assumes great significance in rural areas for woman household heads in the landless and near-landless classes because their agricultural resource base is small, whereas their economic obligations may be substantial. This is particularly true in households where women are the primary economic providers and lack support from secondary earners. In regions where heavy out-migration of men leaves women as de facto heads of households and where remittances are uncertain or irregular, the availability of other bases of support is critical (Dixon 1979).

In urban areas, where woman heads of household appear to be restricted to working in low-level service jobs in the informal sector, access to employment in modern-sector activities and/or small-scale enterprises can result in a substantial improvement in the economic status of their households.

Household Income

The economic organization of woman-headed households may be differenti-
ated according to the sources of income at the household's disposal, the household's total observable income, and the pattern or regularity of receipt of income.

Sources of income. Household income is derived from several sources,
among which are:

1. Income of household head—derived from wage employment and/or self-
   employment
2. Income of resident household members—derived from wage employment
   and/or self-employment
3. Remittances—derived from absent spouse and/or adult children
4. In-kind income, goods, and/or services—derived from local nonresident
   kin (excluding remittances)

Other sources of support, including returns on accumulated wealth, such as
savings, and governmental or quasi-governmental assistance, are available to
some woman-headed households. Typically, however, these other sources contribute little.

Total observable income. A number of difficulties are encountered in attempting to determine household income; only those specifically related to the incomes
of women and woman-headed households are mentioned here.[18] The principal
problem is to determine the "value" of women's input into the household
economy. Accurate data on women's work participation and earnings are scarce;
labor force statistics ignore the economic/income-earning activities in which
women are engaged in the informal sector and/or neglect to consider women's
productive role in agricultural subsistence and unpaid family labor. In addition,
there is controversy regarding the appropriateness of counting certain activities
and means of payment (i.e., home production and in-kind transfers) in the
determination of total household income. It is not clear how one should assess
the cash value and the relative contribution to household living standards of such
activities and payments.

The pattern or regularity of receipt of income. When woman-headed households rely upon several sources of income, these sources typically differ in
importance and provide income at different times. Such households are often as
dependent upon the *regularity* of receipt of income as upon the *amount* of income
received. When income is received sporadically or when there is great uncertainty as to when income such as remittances can be expected, the household may be
classified as economically unstable.[19]

Household Size and Composition

Only since the mid-1970s has the usefulness of distinguishing the demographic characteristics of households as a means of differentiating among types of

households been recognized, both in theory (Kuznets 1976) and in application (Youssef and Hetler, forthcoming). In an effort to "disaggregate" the poor, recent studies have focused on differences among households in the characteristics of members (such as age, sex, education, marital status, and dependency burden) that affect the relative income levels and expenditure patterns of households. In woman-headed households, these characteristics may determine the potential ability of woman heads to devise adaptive strategies for their households' survival (Cain 1977; DaVanzo and Lee 1978; Deere 1978; Sant'Anna, Merrick, and Mazumdar 1976; Mueller 1979; Nieves 1979; Tienda and Salazar 1980; Visaria 1979, 1980a, 1980b; and Chap. 12 in this volume).

Mueller (1979) has shown that demographic variables related to the income-earning abilities of households in Botswana include the number, ages, and sex of children; the presence of adult males; household size; and sex of the head. Identifying differences in the work patterns of individual household members in man- and woman-headed households, she reports that young males (ages 7 to 19) and children of either sex in woman-headed households worked *shorter* hours than they did in households headed by a man. This was because woman-headed households had, on the average, less cattle, the care of which is undertaken by young males. The work activities of women in woman-headed households were influenced by the presence or absence of a female adolescent. Woman aged 25 to 29 years worked considerably more hours in market activities when a younger woman aged 15 to 19 years was residing in the household and engaging in housework, child care, and home production activities. The presence in the household of young men of similar ages did not affect the amount of time women spent in market-oriented activities, since these young men did not take over "women's tasks."

The important role of children in the economy of urban households characterized by the absence of a resident male is borne out by data from Venezuela. In 1971 only 24.5 percent of woman heads with an unmarried eldest child aged 14 to 19 were employed, but 54 percent of woman heads whose eldest child was single, but 20 years of age or older, were employed. Woman household heads appear to benefit from the earnings of employed children, but only when these children are aged 14 to 19 years. Children aged 20 or older, if not living at home, do not appear to contribute to the mother's support (Blumberg and García 1977).

Tienda and Salazar (1980) further demonstrate the link between demographic characteristics and income, using data from rural and urban Peru. Peruvian woman heads of household, particularly older widows and divorcees, incorporate nonnuclear relatives into their homes more frequently than do Peruvian male heads of household. These nonnuclear relatives are expected to work and to contribute to household income. The incorporation of additional members into the household is apparently an attempt to compensate for the lack of an adult male principal earner.

Attempts to determine the link between demographic variables and the relative economic condition of woman-headed households are, of course, worthwhile.

They depend, however, on first *identifying* woman-headed households and ascertaining their income levels. As discussed earlier, such identification can be quite difficult due to the unavailability of accurate data. The productive inputs of women continue to be characterized as minor, and data on their employment status, occupation and earnings, and economic "worth" are often misleading or unavailable. Since the sex of the head of household is only rarely tabulated, there is generally little information on the work efforts of woman heads. When woman heads are identified, it has been shown that they are generally underreported (Buvinić and Youssef 1978). The work efforts of de jure woman heads may be reported under the category of "household head," but the work efforts of de facto woman heads are usually reported as "unpaid family work," "farm family labor," and so on. Further, in instances when the productive work activities of woman household heads are reported, but where remuneration is sporadic or in kind, the woman head's economic contribution to the welfare of her household and thus the actual total income of the household may be unknown.

CONCLUSION

One of the objectives of this essay has been to assess the quality and validity of official census data on woman-headed households in the Third World. As a result of this tentative assessment, we conclude that the shortcomings of the data are of serious magnitude in all regions of the developing world. Only in the censuses of 4 of the 69 countries reviewed (Ghana, Liberia, Malawi, and Indonesia) are household headship data available by age, sex, and urban/rural residence. There has been some increase since 1970 in the availability of statistics on woman-headed households. This availability continues to be scattered, however, and the quality of the data is uneven. Even when official data report the incidence of woman heads of household, serious questions regarding the accuracy of these reports remain. Biases at the conceptual and methodological levels constrain attempts to identify and enumerate woman household heads. There is a wide range of variation in the definitions of the terms "family head" and "household head"; often the meanings of these terms are assumed to be commonly understood, and thus the terms remain undefined. Distinct cultural preferences for designating males as household heads produce a situation where women who function as heads of household in an economic provider/decision maker capacity are not so designated. Further, data on household characteristics are not often cross-tabulated by the sex of the head of household.

The second objective of this study has been to challenge the view that woman-headed households are undifferentiated in socioeconomic and demographic characteristics. Controversy in the literature surrounding the economic condition of woman-headed households relative to those headed by men leads us to conclude that woman-headed households may vary significantly in those characteristics which affect the economic condition of the household. We suggest that the identification of woman-headed households according to de jure or de facto female headship status, the social context of female headship, the woman's marital status, her access to productive resources and income, and the household composition, is crucial to the determination of the economic condition of these households and variations in that condition. Ultimately, such differentiation may be used to assess the link between woman-headed households and poverty.

Notes

1. The United Nations review did not indicate whether data on household size were cross-tabulated by sex of the household head.

2. The review was undertaken by contract with the Office of Women in Development, United States Agency for International Development.

3. Due to differences in the number and choice of individual countries reviewed in the 1973 United Nations report and in the 1970 United States Census Bureau analysis, the two are not strictly comparable.

4. The countries in the Commonwealth Caribbean, not included in the United States Census Bureau survey, published two volumes of relevant information from their censuses on the population. The union status of the population is included in order to specify family typologies; it is perhaps the best available type of census information on women who are de facto heads of households.

5. This is particularly true in those surveys which are national in scope, typically sponsored by the government, the United Nations, or other international agencies.

6. The number would be slightly higher if all those countries identified by the 1973 United Nations survey as having a definition were combined with those of interest to the United States Census Bureau and the United States Agency for International Development.

7. The United Nations has published *Estimates and Projections of the Number of Households by Country, 1975–2000* (ESA/P/WP .73, 1981*a*), which is based on the 1978 assessment of population estimates and projections. These estimates and projections are sex- and age-specific with regard to household headship and include all the more and less developed regions and eight major areas (their table 11). It is interesting to note the assumptions used in these calcuations for the developing regions where data are scarce.

8. We are indebted to the work of Kerven (1979), which develops a typological classification of both urban and rural woman-headed households in Botswana and assesses their dependence on different sources of income and productive resources.

9. These types are not necessarily mutually exclusive, nor "stable" over time. For heuristic purposes, however, they are used as a means of initially identifying and distinguishing the nature of female headship.

10. Cameroon is a prime example of this interaction. Only 1 percent of the men aged 45–54 are widowers, whereas among women in the same age-group, 19 percent are widows, despite nearly universal marriage. This suggests that the age differential between the sexes at first marriage remains significant in subsequent marriages. It has been estimated that in rural Nigeria, where large age differentials are common, if a 15-year-old girl marries a 25-year-old man and survives to age 50, the chances are only 50 percent that he will have survived also. Momeni (1976) cites evidence that average husband-wife age differentials in Iran are almost twice as large as the average of 55 countries studied. He reports that the larger these age differences, the higher the chance for marital dissolution, and that the younger the bride, the greater the age difference between bride and groom. The chance of her surviving into old age as a widow or divorcee is therefore great.

11. Birks and Sinclair (1977) note that in some areas (such as Oman), migrant husbands increasingly view a return to their homes as a "vacation" and are unwilling to participate in farm chores even when they stay for several months. Furthermore, even when remittances are received regularly, the intrahousehold allocation of these funds may not directly contribute to basic household welfare. In Turkey, electrical applicances (considered status symbols in villages with no electricity) were purchased with remittance money (Kudat 1978). Singh (1977) reports that in India, remittances were not necessarily spent for daily needs of the household and sometimes went toward marriage festivities, dowries, and debt repayments.

12. Of all single women aged 15 and over, 43 percent in Chile, 27 percent in Guatemala, 25 percent in Peru, 48 percent in Colombia, and 50 percent in the Commonwealth Caribbean, as of 1973, had from 1 to 10 children (Youssef 1973).

13. Interviews with 100 single mothers in a maternity ward in Guatemala City revealed great anxiety with respect to their parents' anger and an awareness of the rejection they faced as a result of their pregnancies. None of these women lived with their parents (Villalta 1971).

14. Referring to single mothers working on a coffee plantation in Sierra Juarez, Oaxaca (Mexico), Kate Young says: "Single mothers have usually been disinherited or abandoned by their families. Always beholden to landowners' wives who employ them fully at harvest to pay off 'gifts' received during the year, their needs are the greatest, their means are the least" (Palmer 1976, quoting Kate Young).

15. Twenty percent of all adult single women in Mozambique and 45 to 54 percent of those in Botswana have children. On the average for the two countries, the child-to-single mother ratio is between 2.6 and 2.9. A household study conducted in South Cameroon revealed that two-fifths of the newly married women averaged between two and three children (Weekes-Vagliani 1976).

16. Inaccuracies in the enumeration of single mothers in statistics may be partly a definitional issue. Some births may be taking place in customary marriages that, because the bride price or dowry has not been paid, may not be recognized as legal. In such instances, women may be classified in the statistics as "single" although they are living in de facto stable unions. When childbearing takes place outside marriage, one may assume that women are de jure heads of household with major economic responsibilities.

17. A study in Botswana showed that among all women, divorced and separated women and single mothers were the least able to make a livelihood from agriculture. Widowed women were in a relatively better position since some provisions for their ownership/access to land had been made (Kerven 1979).

18. For a discussion of these problems, see Christiaan Grootaert, "Selected Problems in the Implementation of Household Surveys," in Christopher Saunders and Christiaan Grootaert, eds., *Reflections on the LSMS Group Meeting,* Living Standards Measurement Study Working Paper no. 10, World Bank, October 1980.

19. Sporadic receipt of income also leads to difficulty in accurately recounting earnings, since amounts vary weekly or even daily. Placing a value on in-kind transfers of goods and services when no actual cash is exchanged is also difficult, especially in rural areas where little is known of local price structures. When woman-headed households rely on informal-sector sources of income, these households may predictably have difficulty in accurately assessing total income, leading to both over- and underestimation. If the earners are illiterate, the problem is compounded.

12. Households Headed by Women and Urban Poverty in Brazil

Thomas W. Merrick and Marianne Schmink

Close analysis of data obtained in surveys of poor families of the Third World reveals important diversity among groups that share the common characteristics of poverty: low income, poor health and nutrition, and lack of basic needs. Failure to consider such diversity can result in a misleading assessment of the roots of poverty and of programs required to combat it. Special attention to specific poverty groups is becoming recognized as a major requirement for both the assessment and the alleviation of poverty, and the study reported here is based on the working premise that a focus on household structure (composition by member age, sex, and marital status) and on poverty as a women's issue contributes to this goal.

In this essay we utilize survey data on households headed by women in Belo Horizonte, Brazil, as the basis for an analysis of the relationship of household structure, human capital endowments (such as education), and earning capacities. The reasons for using the household, rather than the individual, in analyzing income inequalities are outlined in the first section, which is followed by a brief discussion of households headed by women in Brazil and the labor market conditions faced by these women. Having outlined this broader environment, we present the evidence from the Belo Horizonte survey data. A description of the socioeconomic and demographic characteristics of female- and male-headed households is followed by an analysis of the earnings differentials and work status of other household members, a discussion of the urban services available to women heads of households, and a concluding section on the policy implications of the findings.

HOUSEHOLD STRUCTURE AND POVERTY

Kuznets (1976) argues that for an analysis of income inequality to be meaningful, the recipient unit has to be the family or household and not the individual and that even then, account must be taken of the effect of differences in household size and structure and of different phases of a family's life cycle on its capacity to

244

generate income. He finds that the failure of conventional measures to account for differences in household structure obscures comparisons of income inequality. Although his work consists for the most part of empirical illustrations of how distributions were affected by the type and size of household and by the age of household heads (as an index of the phase in families' income-generating life span), it points clearly in the direction of dealing with income inequality and poverty questions in terms of specific types of households.

If the issue is viewed from the broader conceptual perspective of "full income," an even more compelling case can be made for focusing on the household as the unit of analysis. Studies of time and labor investments have demonstrated the importance, particularly for poor populations, of home production activities that directly satisfy family consumption and reproductive needs (see Chaps. 3, 4, and 6 in this volume; see also Cain 1977; Stoler 1978; Szalai 1972). Although such activities are most extensive and visible in rural settings, child care, home maintenance, and related tasks also occupy a large proportion of household labor time in cities (Szalai 1972; Schmink 1979). The measurement of a household's full income should thus be based on returns from both home and market production activities, and household economic strategies should direct the allocation of resources and personnel to activities that are related to *both* components of full income.

Since many productive activities in both home and market settings demand laborers with specific age and sex characteristics, the success or failure of a household's income generation will be influenced by the "fit" between household composition and the labor demand structure in both home and market production. Whereas demand is a product of macro-level economic and policy trends and tends to shift only gradually, household structures are highly variable over the family life cycle. Furthermore, many households, especially in low-income groups, do not conform to the nuclear family model; their composition may frequently change. Within a given labor demand structure, therefore, the least successful households may be those whose composition is ill-suited to carrying out necessary productive activities in both home and market.

An earlier study of Brazilian income inequality and urban poverty (Sant'Anna, Merrick, and Mazumdar 1976) that used the same survey data from Belo Horizonte used in this essay adopted the household as a focus of analysis. That study attempted to determine the extent to which differences in household standards of living can be explained by differences in demographic factors (which determine the potential stock of workers and the dependency burdens in households) and in economic factors (which influence the participation of adults in market activities and their levels of earnings). Analysis of households by income level showed that economic factors had a greater effect on the household's standard of living than demographic factors. Although the dependency burden was higher at the lower end of the income scale (because low-income families tend to include relatively large numbers of children), the potential stock of adult workers was also significantly larger. Poor households were poor partly because they were unable to utilize as much of this stock as the richer households. Poor households were characterized by a relatively low level of utilization of principal earners (heads) and a particularly low level of utilization of female secondary earners.

One of the most important conclusions of the 1976 analysis was that differences in earnings per worker were quantitatively much more important in explaining differences in the standard of living than were variations in employment rates of household numbers. Yet these differences in earnings per worker could be explained only in part by earning functions within the human capital framework, suggesting that other aspects of household structure affected the determination of employment and earnings in ways that could not be attributed to human capital endowments in their strictly economic sense. This ambiguity of the findings pointed again to the need to look more closely at specific household types within the broad array of poverty-level households, and a principal objective of this essay is to reexamine the relation between household structure and poverty, using the Belo Horizonte data and viewing households headed by women as a distinct household type.

Households headed by women are vulnerable to poverty because unpartnered women usually retain the primary responsibility for child care and home maintenance tasks; in the absence of a male breadwinner, they face the challenge of making market-oriented activities compatible with domestic responsibilities. Because women are usually socialized primarily for family roles and not for an economically active life, they often lack a primary identification with market work roles as well as the training required to obtain comfortable and challenging jobs. How successful unpartnered women will be in responding to the challenges of a dual role will depend upon what jobs are available to household members, how much they pay, and how compatible they are with home production needs.

CHANGING TRENDS IN THE INCIDENCE OF HOUSEHOLDS HEADED BY WOMEN

Brazilian census publications provide only very sketchy information on households headed by women, and as far as we know, no one has worked with special tabulations having this particular focus. Published summary tables include sex of head as a control variable, but it is cross-tabulated with only one other variable at a time, which severely limits analytical work. Table 12.1 summarizes data on the number of households with female heads reported in the 1950, 1960, and 1970 population censuses. The data are broken down by rural and urban residence and by region.

In 1970, 13.0 percent of households were headed by women, with urban households much more likely to be headed by women than households in rural areas. The 1970 figure is an increase over the 10.7 percent reported in 1960;

TABLE 12.1 TRENDS IN FEMALE-HEADED HOUSEHOLDS IN BRAZIL, BY RURAL/URBAN RESIDENCE AND REGION, 1950–70

	1950			1960			1970		
	Number of Households (Thousands)	Female-Headed Households (Thousands)	Percentage	Number of Households (Thousands)	Female-Headed Households (Thousands)	Percentage	Number of Households (Thousands)	Female-Headed Households (Thousands)	Percentage
Residence									
Urban	—	—	—	6,374.6	890.1	14.0	10,904.3	1,714.5	15.7
Rural	—	—	—	7,157.5	559.2	7.8	7,650.1	702.1	9.2
Total	10,046.2	1,219.0	12.1	13,532.1	1,449.3	10.7	18,554.4	2,416.6	13.0
Region									
North	346.9	43.3	12.5	448.8	48.4	10.8	631.7	79.0	12.5
Northeast	3,569.7	554.0	15.5	4,239.8	569.1	14.1	5,380.8	860.7	16.0
Southeast	4,333.6	452.4	10.5	6,093.0	597.9	9.8	8,328.9	1,071.0	12.9
South	1,467.0	125.5	8.6	2,211.9	155.9	7.0	3,256.8	298.5	9.2
Central-West	328.9	42.8	13.0	538.7	51.0	9.5	956.3	108.3	11.3

SOURCE: Brazilian population censuses, 1950, 1960, 1970.

however, the latter figure represents a decline compared with 1950. The decline may have resulted from changes in the reporting of marital status and headship. About 15 percent of the female heads of household in 1950 were reported in the census as married. Starting in 1960, married women no longer were classified as heads of household, so that the numbers of female heads reported in 1960 and 1970 are lower than they would have been if married women had been considered heads. It is likely that some separated female heads of household were considered "married" in 1950 but classified as "separated" later on, as reporting practices changed. The census volumes do not specify the change in procedure. If we assume that the proportion of married female heads in 1970 was the same as in 1950, then the 1970 proportion of female heads increases to 14.8 percent.

The relative increase of female-headed households from 1960 to 1970, a period for which the data are more comparable, indicates that female-headed households were responsible for about 18 percent of the increase in the number of households in that decade. If we add the number of households headed by married women, which may have been omitted in 1960 and 1970, then one out of every five households added between 1960 and 1970 was headed by a female.

If we regard the change in the "married" category as definitional and omit it, the increase in the number of female-headed households between 1950 and 1970 is distributed as indicated in Table 12.2. (The marital status distribution was not available for 1960.)

The "separated or divorced" category immediately stands out. Less than 1.0 percent of the female heads of household were separated/divorced in 1950, but 25.2 percent were in that category in 1970. Some of this increase may have resulted from the change in reporting practice already discussed, but setting that aside, the figures still indicate that the·"separated or divorced" group contributed much more than its proportional share of the growth of female-headed households. This change, whatever its "cause," was the main factor in the overall increase in the number of women heads of household. Increases in the other two groups (single and widowed) were less than proportional to their shares in the total number of households headed by females. Other factors—increases in female labor force participation (from 13.6 percent in 1950 to 18.4 percent in 1970) and a growing differential between male and female life expectancy (from a 3.6-year advantage for females in 1950 to a 4.3-year advantage in 1970)—also contributed, but less than did the increase in dissolution of marital unions by divorce or separation.[1]

Data from Brazilian National Household Sample Surveys (PNAD) carried out in 1973 and 1976 suggest that these trends have continued into the 1970s, with female-headed households accounting for 15 percent of the total in 1976. Barroso (1978) found that the proportion of families headed by women systematically increased each survey year in all five regions (see Table 12.1), with the highest percentage (15.9 percent) in the northeast and the lowest percentage (9.7

TABLE 12.2 PERCENTAGE DISTRIBUTION
OF FEMALE-HEADED HOUSEHOLDS IN 1950 AND 1970,
BY MARITAL STATUS OF HEAD

Marital Status	Percentage Distribution		Percentage Distribution of Absolute Increase, 1950–70
	1950	1970	
Single	27.1	19.6	13.8
Separated or divorced	.9	25.2	43.6
Widowed	72.0	55.2	42.6
Total	100.0	100.0	100.0

SOURCE: Brazilian population censuses, 1950, 1960, 1970.

percent) in the more developed south. Proportions of households headed by women were consistently higher in urban areas, reaching 22.7 percent in the northeast region in 1976 (compared with 13.5 percent of rural households).

It is difficult to determine the effect of increases in the number of households headed by females on the overall level of poverty in Brazil, because the published census data do not lend themselves to the kind of analysis (which should control for age, marital status, and labor force participation) required in order to identify specific factors. Income data are given only for heads of household, not for the entire household. It can be seen from the census data, however, that a substantially higher proportion of female heads of household report no income (39.8 percent) than do male heads of household (2.5 percent). Of those who reported income, 49.5 percent of the women heads of household fall in the two lowest income classes, compared with 26.6 percent of the men. Although income from secondary earners and nonsalary income could reduce some of the difference between women and men, every indication is that the households headed by females are an important poverty group in Brazil. A brief look at the situation women face in the labor market will provide an indication of some of the reasons for their relative poverty.

LABOR MARKET CONDITIONS AND WOMEN IN BRAZIL

At the beginning of the twentieth century, women constituted 45 percent of Brazil's reported labor force, concentrated in home-based textile industries, domestic-servant activities, and agriculture; by 1920 women constituted only 15 percent of the total labor force. Although a substantial part of this "decline" is related to a change in the way in which domestic-servant activities were reported, there is also evidence that early industrialization had an adverse effect on female labor force participation. The proportion of females among manufacturing workers fell from 63 percent in 1900 to 12 percent in 1920. The low figure for 1920 may also be related to changes in reporting practice (Merrick and Graham 1979, p. 150). These trends continued through the accelerated phase of industrial expansion stimulated by government policies in the 1950s. During this period, Brazil's labor force in both urban and rural areas began to change rapidly. In regions where industry grew, the urban labor force expanded and became more male-dominated, leaving a higher proportion of women workers in agriculture, primarily as unpaid family workers in subsistence production (Lewin, Pitanguy, and Romani 1977, p. 89; Madeira and Singer 1973, p. 53; Saffioti 1969, p. 255; Oliveira 1978, pp. 5–6).

In the cities, women were intially drawn to textile factories but were absorbed less and less as the industry was transformed as a result of technological investment (Madeira and Singer 1973, pp. 34–37). Between 1950 and 1970, the textile industry dispensed with one-quarter of its female workers, while nearly doubling the number of its male workers (Lewin, Pitanguy, and Romani 1977, pp. 110–111). The proportion of women workers employed in this industry in this period fell from 15.6 percent to 8.9 percent (Bruschini 1978, p. 13). Similarly, women employed in the food- and beverage-processing industries declined from 2.7 percent to only .3 percent in this period; the proportion of women in manufacturing overall fell from 18.6 percent to 11.0 percent.

Instead of being absorbed by the dynamic capitalist sector, female workers moving out of agriculture in the 1950s were employed increasingly in a few "female" occupations in the service and commerce sectors of the economy: primary-school teachers, office workers, salesclerks, seamstresses, and domestics (Abreu 1977, p. 16). This concentration was accentuated rather than lessened by two decades of economic development (Bruschini 1978). In the 1970s, nearly one out of three women workers was some kind of domestic servant (Saffioti 1978). Probably another 25 percent were self-employed or unpaid family workers. With only 20 percent of women working overall, this means that probably less than 10 percent of all women in Brazil participate directly as workers in the formal sector of the economy. In fact, Brazil has one of the most "masculine" labor forces in the world (Lewin, Pitanguy, and Romani 1977).

The segregation of women in occupations distinct from those occupied by male workers is linked to male/female earnings discrepancies. Even the highest status female jobs, such as schoolteaching, are extremely low-paying, despite the relatively large investment in education they require. Women's earnings rise much less with education than do men's, so that salary differences between the two sexes increase systematically with women's educational levels (Abreu 1977, pp. 5–19; Barrera 1978; Saffioti 1969). Lower status female occupations and informal-sector jobs are particularly low paid, despite the bed-and-board benefits that often are the domestic servant's indirect wage.

These patterns represent special hardships for women in poor households who are often forced to work in order to supplement family income. Despite their greater disadvantages, poor women in general have a much more permanent—if irregular—link to the labor market than do higher income women. It is for this reason that some studies of poor populations find their participation rates to be *higher* than the average, in contrast to the usual trend for rates to increase with aggregate income (Bittencourt 1979; Schmink 1980). If official data collection techniques were better suited to capturing women's irregular work activities, this contrast would undoubtedly be more accentuated.

EVIDENCE FROM SURVEY DATA: BELO HORIZONTE

The data used here were obtained from a survey of a representative sample of 2,445 households in the Belo Horizonte metropolitan area in 1972. Detailed descriptions of Belo Horizonte, the study population, and the sample survey are reported elsewhere (Merrick 1976; Sant'Anna, Merrick, and Mazumdar 1976). In analyzing the data, we stratified households into four household income groups according to the level of household income per adult equivalent consumer. This measure of income attempts to treat household income on a per capita basis, while explaining differences in consumption needs arising from household structure. The technique that was employed is described in Sant'Anna, Merrick, and Mazumdar (1976).

Of the 2,445 households in the sample survey, 158 consisted of a single individual. To avoid distortion, this discussion is limited to the remaining 2,287 households with two or more individuals. Table 12.3 presents a distribution of these households by sex and marital status of heads, and by the level of household income per equivalent consumer. Three household income classes are utilized: the poor, whose income per consumer averaged less than 100 cruzeiros (Cr$) per month (in 1972, equivalent to about U.S.$16—at the time, a kilogram of rice cost about 30 cents and an inexpensive pair of shoes about $5), representing 30 percent of all households; low-income families, with income per consumer between Cr$100 and Cr$368, representing 46 percent of all households; and middle/upper-income classes with income per consumer of Cr$369 or more, representing 24 percent of households. The "poverty" cut-off was the same as the standard used by Brazilian authorities in determining a legal minimum salary based on consumption needs, but it should be noted that this cut-off was very low even by Brazilian standards.

Of the households shown in Table 12.3, 379 (16.6 percent) were headed by women. This is somewhat higher than the proportion for urban Brazil as a whole, but it is less than the 18.8 percent that is the figure when households consisting of a single individual are included. (A higher proportion of these individuals are women.) Households headed by women show a relatively higher incidence of poverty, with 44.9 percent falling below the poverty line, compared with 27.4

TABLE 12.3   DISTRIBUTION OF HOUSEHOLDS IN BELO HORIZONTE IN 1972,
BY SEX AND MARITAL STATUS OF HEAD AND HOUSEHOLD INCOME CLASS

Income Class, by Sex	Single[a]	Married	Separated	Widowed	Total	Percent
Male						
Poor	30	481	9	2	522	27.4
Low	86	801	16	4	907	47.5
Middle/high	34	438	7	0	479	25.1
Total	150	1,720	32	6	1,908	100.0
Female						
Poor	42	27	75	26	170	44.9
Low	52	25	65	8	150	39.6
Middle/high	24	8	18	9	59	15.6
Total	118	60	158	43	379	100.0

SOURCE: Tabulations of survey data from 1972 Plan for Metroplitan Belo Horizonte (PLAMBEL) (see Sant' Anna, Merrick, and Mazumdar 1976).
[a]Excludes single-person households.

percent of the households headed by males. Although one in every six households in Belo Horizonte has a female head, females count for one in every four of the poverty households.

As the breakdown by marital status shows, the proportion of poor, woman-headed households is the lowest for households headed by single women, 36 percent. Of the 261 households headed by married, separated, and widowed women, the poverty group accounts for 49 percent; 60 percent of the women in the widow group live at poverty level (Table 12.3).

Age is another important aspect of the poverty observed among households headed by females. A substantial proportion of the female heads of poor households are in the "prime" working ages (25–59). When single-person households are excluded, 80 percent of female household heads fall in this age-group. Of these, 47 percent are poor. When single heads of household are excluded, the poverty proportion increases to 54 percent. The comparable figure for males is only 27 percent.

The fact that the proportion of poverty-level households headed by females is higher still among the prime working age-group is significant, since in this period of the life cycle of the head, the burden of household dependency is likely to be greatest. Clearly, such households are particularly vulnerable when the head is a woman, and it is on the earning capacities of households whose heads are in the prime working age-group that we focus subsequent analysis.

One reason for the increased incidence of poverty among households headed by women could be a higher dependency burden—that is, a higher ratio of nonworkers to workers than in male-headed households. Table 12.4 shows that this is not true. Dependency in poor households is, in fact, slightly higher in households headed by males. Despite the fact that increased dependency does not explain male-female differences, its role in poverty is clearly important. When we compare poor households with households in the higher income groups, especially the adjacent low-income group, we find that the differences are striking. Additional workers *do* make a difference in the comparative economic situation of the poor and low-income groups. One of the principal findings of the 1976 analysis of these data was that low-income households, although similar in many respects to their poor counterparts, were able to break through the poverty threshold because of the added earnings of a secondary worker.

The importance of income other than the head's salary is shown in Table 12.5, in which household income is divided according to three sources: head's earnings, other earnings, and unearned income (pensions, rental income, other transfers). The distributions are cross-tabulated by household income level and by the sex and marital status of heads. Several differences stand out. Except for single persons, the earnings of female heads constitute a much lower proportion of household income than those of male heads. This suggests that other income sources (earnings of other workers and unearned income) are important in explaining household income differences. Indeed, the proportion of these other sources is higher for female heads in the *low*-income category than for female heads in the *poor* group. The same is true for male-headed households, but the difference is less significant because of the lower weight of income from other sources when compared with the head's earnings.

Unearned income is more important for the separated/widowed marital status group. It is 4.3 percentage points higher for women in the low-income category

TABLE 12.4 DEPENDENCY RATIOS (NONWORKERS/ WORKERS), BY SEX AND MARITAL STATUS OF HEAD AND HOUSEHOLD INCOME CLASS, FOR HOUSEHOLDS WITH A HEAD AGED 25–59 YEARS, 1972

Income Class, by Sex	Single	Married	Separated or Widowed
Male			
Poor	2.6	4.0	3.6
Low	1.2	2.2	1.7
Middle/high	.7	1.7	.6
Female			
Poor	2.3	3.8	2.6
Low	.9	1.3	1.5
Middle/high	1.0	1.0	1.3

SOURCE: Tabulations of survey data from 1972 Plan for Metropolitan Belo Horizonte (PLAMBEL) (see Sant' Anna, Merrick, and Mazumdar 1976).

TABLE 12.5 PERCENTAGE DISTRIBUTION OF SOURCES OF HOUSEHOLD INCOME IN 1972, BY SEX AND MARITAL STATUS OF HEAD AND HOUSEHOLD INCOME CLASS, IN HOUSEHOLDS WITH A HEAD AGED 25–59 YEARS

Income Source, by Income Class	Single		Married		Widowed or separated	
	Male	Female	Male	Female	Male	Female
Poor						
Head's earnings	59.1	74.5	71.4	43.0	56.8	32.8
Other earnings	19.1	8.7	14.9	23.0	11.4	30.1
Unearned income	21.8	16.8	13.7	34.0	31.8	37.1
n	(10)	(26)	(414)	(25)	(9)	(89)
Low						
Head's earnings	51.2	43.0	68.6	40.8	41.4	25.5
Other earnings	37.5	47.0	22.4	40.8	39.8	33.1
Unearned income	11.3	10.0	9.0	18.4	18.8	41.4
n	(30)	(39)	(690)	(23)	(12)	(53)
Middle/high						
Head's earnings	45.1	47.4	70.6	31.0	40.3	37.5
Other earnings	33.1	33.0	21.7	28.8	27.2	30.5
Unearned income	21.8	19.6	7.7	40.2	32.5	32.0
n	(24)	(22)	(379)	(7)	(4)	(16)

SOURCE: Tabulations of survey data from 1972 Plan for Metropolitan Belo Horizonte (PLAMBEL) (see Sant' Anna, Merrick, and Mazumdar 1976).

than in the poor group, but the differential does not appear to be significant in other marital-status categories. The survey data report income from other sources but do not provide enough information to determine the reasons for differences other than the obvious ones—age, marital status, and income level. For this reason, we concentrate our attention on the work and earnings status of household members.

Table 12.6 presents a breakdown of the economic activities of adult members of households headed by women. Table 12.7 shows comparable data for households headed by men. For each marital status and household income category (the columns of the table), an inventory of the potential earners in the households in each group is shown, starting with heads and followed by other adult males and other adult females in the household. The percentage actually working is shown for each, and of those working, the percentage employed in the so-called informal sector is given.

An explanatory note concerning the informal sector is required. Belo Horizonte's urban labor market, like that of other large cities in Brazil, is highly segmented. Because of the wage policy and the technology employed in recent industrialization, the number of jobs available in more highly capitalized establishments is limited. Such jobs require a higher level of skill but pay more and

TABLE 12.6 EMPLOYMENT IN HOUSEHOLDS HEADED BY FEMALES AGED 25–59 YEARS, BY MARITAL STATUS AND HOUSEHOLD INCOME GROUP, 1972

	Poor			Low			Middle/High		
	Single	Married	Widowed or Separated	Single	Married	Widowed or Separated	Single	Married	Widowed or Separated
Number of households (n)	(26)	(25)	(89)	(39)	(23)	(53)	(22)	(7)	(16)
Working heads (percentage)	84.6	84.0	69.7	94.9	73.9	60.4	86.4	71.4	68.8
Informal-sector employment (percentage of workers)	77.3	85.7	85.5	18.9	35.3	50.0	0	—	9.1
Other adult males (n)	(11)	(87)	(83)	(34)	(34)	(46)	(8)	(8)	(16)
Working (percentage)	18.2	29.9	32.5	64.7	61.8	56.5	12.5	37.5	37.5
Informal-sector employment (percentage of workers)	—	50.0	74.1	13.6	28.6	15.4	—	37.5	0
Other adult females (n)	(18)	(74)	(121)	(76)	(27)	(65)	(33)	(3)	(16)
Working (percentage)	27.7	5.4	33.9	44.7	51.9	35.4	27.3	—	37.5
Informal-sector employment (percentage of workers)	—	50.0	92.7	20.5	28.6	52.2	0	—	16.7

SOURCE: Tabulations of survey data from 1972 Plan for Metropolitan Belo Horizonte (PLAMBEL) (see Sant' Anna, Merrick, and Mazumdar 1976).

NOTE: Dash (—) indicates that there were 5 or fewer cases in denominator of ratio.

TABLE 12.7 EMPLOYMENT IN HOUEHOLDS HEADED BY MALES AGED 25–59 YEARS,
BY MARITAL STATUS AND HOUSEHOLD INCOME GROUP, 1972

	Poor			Low			Middle/High		
	Single	Married	Widowed or Separated	Single	Married	Widowed or Separated	Single	Married	Widowed or Separated
Number of households (n)	(10)	(414)	(9)	(36)	(690)	(12)	(24)	(379)	(4)
Working heads (percentage)	80.0	82.1	66.7	94.4	91.7	75.0	91.7	96.3	—
Informal-sector employment (percentage of workers)	25.0	23.2	33.0	26.5	10.7	22.2	0	2.7	—
Other adult males (n)	(9)	(278)	(7)	(33)	(327)	(21)	(19)	(128)	(9)
Working (percentage)	0	27.3	0	57.6	51.1	61.9	68.4	40.6	55.5
Informal-sector employment (percentage of workers)	—	48.7	—	15.8	35.3	46.2	23.0	13.5	—
Other adult females (n)	(20)	(826)	(13)	(65)	(1,270)	(15)	(44)	(597)	(0)
Working (percentage)	15.0	10.7	15.4	26.7	19.7	26.7	34.1	32.8	—
Informal-sector employment (percentage of workers)	—	90.9	—	52.9	51.6	—	13.3	16.8	—

Source: Tabulations of survey data from 1972 Plan for Metropolitan Belo Horizonte (PLAMBEL) (see Sant' Anna, Merrick, and Mazumdar 1976).

Note: Dash (—) indicates that there were 5 or fewer cases in denominator of ratio.

offer a greater degree of employment and income security, including protection under Brazilian labor law. Although it is difficult and misleading to group all workers into "formal" and "informal" categories, the division is useful for understanding differences in employment and earnings opportunities at various levels in Brazil's urban labor market. The criterion for distinguishing formal and informal employment here is payment of social security taxes, which is shared by employer and employee. These taxes have been shown to be the best screening measure for identifying self-employment or loose employment arrangements, lack of minimum-wage protection, and other features of informal employment (Merrick 1976).

Informal employment plays a major role in labor absorption in Belo Horizonte. Although informal employment is more abundant and is often preferred by employers who are interested in keeping labor costs down, workers who get informal jobs have limited bargaining power and job protection, so that wages are low and labor turnover is high. Employment as a domestic is by far the most important form of informal activity for females in Belo Horizonte, which is typical of many Latin American cities in this respect (Jelin 1977). Nearly all (85 percent) of the married, widowed, or separated female heads of poor households are employed in informal activities. For male heads, the figure is approximately 25 percent. Informal employment is also important for other workers in poor households, though their limited number makes comparison difficult.

As Table 12.6 shows, the availability of secondary workers, as well as the sex of such workers, is a major point of contrast between poor and low-income female-headed households. Females tend to outnumber males in most households headed by women, but in low-income households the proportion of male secondary earners (60 percent) is about double that of poor households (30 percent), suggesting that male secondary workers make an important difference in the income status of these households. The differences in numbers of other female workers are not outstanding. These workers may be less important in determining income differences because it is other males who work in the low-income class who are more likely to secure formal-sector jobs with higher and more steady earnings for these households.

These differences between work patterns in poor and low-income households headed by women are similar in most respects to the differences reported for comparable households headed by men, except that the former are more pronounced. One important exception is that in general, a higher proportion of female heads in poor households work than in other income classes, whereas the reverse is true for male heads. This means that the type of job found and the earnings generated by it are critical for the survival of households headed by females. Another exception is that comparatively few male secondary workers are found in poor households headed by females, so these households are more dependent on earnings of other females. Two analytical questions are thus raised: (1) Why are the earnings of poor women household heads so low? (2) Why do so few other adults, particularly males, contribute to household income in poor households headed by females?

Earnings of Male and Female Household Heads

Since the income of poor households depends to a large extent on the earnings of the head, the head's earning capacity is a key variable in the economic status of those households. Comparative analysis of the earnings of male and female household heads shows that although human capital variables (age and education) are important determinants of the general level of earnings, labor market structure (principally the jobs open to women) explains most of the differential earnings between male and female heads.

Table 12.8 presents a comparative analysis of the earnings of prime-age male and female heads of household in the Belo Horizonte survey. Separate multiple regression results for the logs of earnings are shown, along with the percentage of the population of male and female heads in each category of the variables included in the analysis. The independent variables in the regression are dummy variables, which take the value of one when the socioeconomic category applies

TABLE 12.8 MULTIPLE REGRESSION ANALYSIS: LOGS OF EARNINGS
OF PRIME-AGE (25–39 YEARS) MALE AND FEMALE HEADS OF HOUSEHOLD

Variable	Males		Females	
	Regression Coefficient	Percentage of Population in Category	Regression Coefficient	Percentage of Population in Category
Age 40+	.160	47.0	.149*	50.4
Education (did not complete primary)	−.586	38.4	−.460	44.7
Education (completed secondary and above)	1.061	18.5	.587	17.7
Informal-sector employment	−.462	12.5	−.993	53.1
Small children in household	.113	82.2	.166*	53.5
Constant (aged 25–39, completed primary education, formal-sector employment; no small children)	6.42		5.87	
R^2	.44		.43	
F	220.0		35.2	
(Degrees of freedom)	(1414,6)		(220.6)	

SOURCE: Tabulations of survey data from 1972 Plan for Metropolitan Belo Horizonte (PLAMBEL) (see Sant' Anna, Merrick, and Mazumdar 1976).
*Significant at .10 level. All other coefficients significant at or above .01 level.

TABLE 12.9   MALE/FEMALE AND FORMAL/INFORMAL-SECTOR
DIFFERENTIALS IN AVERAGE MONTHLY EARNINGS
(IN CRUZEIROS) OF PRIME-AGE (25–39 YEARS)
HOUSEHOLD HEADS

Sector	Male	Female	Male/Female
Formal sector	614	354	1.7
Informal sector	387	131	3.0
Formal/informal sector	1.6	2.7	—

SOURCE: Derived from regressions in Table 12.8.

and are zero otherwise. Regression coefficients represent deviations of the log of earnings from the mean value indicated by the constant term (working heads of household aged 25 to 39 years who have completed primary education, have no small children less than 6 years old in the household, and hold a formal-sector job).

A sex differential appears even in this mean value, which is 6.42 (Cr$614) for males and 5.87 (Cr$354) for females. Male and female heads do not differ markedly in either their age or educational characteristics. About 50 percent of both are over age 40 and about 40 percent have less than a primary education. Age and education have a significant effect on male, but almost no effect on female, earnings. Small children in the household, who might restrict the activities of female heads, do not appear to have a statistically significant effect— in fact, their influence is closer to being significant for males.

The most striking sex differential is in type of employment, as indicated by the proportion of workers whose jobs are in the informal sector: 53.1 percent of the females have jobs in the informal sector, compared with 12.5 percent of the males. Further, the differential in informal-sector earnings for female heads of household is large in reference both to female heads with formal-sector jobs and to male heads in the informal sector. Interpretation of the regression gives the averages shown in Table 12.9.

Clearly, a major part of the disadvantaged earnings position of working female heads of household derives from a comparative lack of access to formal-sector jobs, and their benefits, in the urban labor market. Admittedly, it is difficult to isolate the effects of informal employment from age and educational characteristics, which themselves correlate highly with informal employment (Merrick 1976), yet the male/female differential appears to be little affected by this interaction. The advantages and disadvantages of high and low educational attainment have a marked effect on male earnings differentials, whereas this effect is less significant for female earnings. Simply being a female, however, increases the likelihood of being in the informal sector and having low earnings.

Earnings Differentials and Work Status of Other Adult Household Members

Another major issue is the work of household members other than the head. These household members' earnings generally follow the patterns described in the preceding section, especially with regard to sex differences, so that the effect of other workers on household income is largely determined by whether or not they work. Here we seek to determine the extent to which household structure (composition by member age, sex, and marital status) and human capital endowments (particularly education) interact in determining the work status of these other members. Work status is treated as a dichotomous variable, with all other adult household members classified as either working or not working. Besides the four variables just mentioned, the other explanatory variables are the sex of the head of household, the household's income level, and the work/earnings status of the head. The symbols for variables and their descriptions are shown in Table 12.10.

Hierarchical log-linear models are used here to analyze relations between the variables and their effects on work status. Log-linear models are similar in many respects to multiple regression with dummy variables but have several advantages over multiple regression when the dependent variable is also dichotomous.

TABLE 12.10 VARIABLES USED FOR ANALYSIS OF WORK STATUS
OF ADULT HOUSEHOLD MEMBERS OTHER THAN HEADS

Variable Name and Symbol	Number of Categories	Description of Category and Symbol
Work status (WS)	2	Working/not working (W/NW)
Age (A)	3	15–24/25–59/60+
Sex (S)	2	Female/male (F/M)
Education (E)	3	Incomplete primary/complete primary/complete secondary (IP/CP/CS)
Marital status (MS)	2	Married/single/separated/widowed (M/NM[a])
Sex of household head (SH)	2	Male/female (M/F)
Work/earnings status of head (WE)	4	W_1: Not working W_2: Working, earning less than one minimum salary (MS) W_3: Working, earning 1–3 MS W_4: Working, earning more than 4 MS
Income level of household (Y)	3	Poor/low/middle-high (P/L/M-H)
Total number of cells	(1,728)	
Total number of individuals	(3,011)	

[a]NM category includes all unpartnered women.

Dummy variable coefficients estimated by ordinary least squares in multiple regression will "predict" values less than zero or greater than one when the expected proportions deviate substantially from .5, as they do here. They also assume that the effects of variables are additive, which is unlikely when interactions are present. To cope with these problems, a range of techniques is now available, including log-linear models that employ maximum likelihood estimation of the logarithms of cell frequencies of multidimensional tables (into which the original data are transformed) to determine interaction models and the effects implied in them. Calculation of these effects is based on the amount of variation from the grand mean deriving from an individual's belonging to a particular category of a variable. In relation to a dependent variable (e.g., work status), interaction effects can be compositional or direct. "Composition effects" refers to the interactions among independent variables and to the composition of the sample population exhibiting such interactions. Direct effects are the interactions between one or more independent variables and the dependent variable (e.g., work status; see Reynolds 1977; Bishop, Feinberg, and Holland 1975; Soldo 1977).

Table 12.11 presents a frequency distribution of other adult members of households in the sample by their sex, the sex of the head of household, their work status, and household income level. The logs of cell frequencies and their means are also shown in the table. To compute the main effects (expected cell frequencies) for the two categories of work status, we subtract the grand mean from the cell means (for example, with WS = W: $3.90 - 4.24 = -.34$). To compute a two-way interaction, such as the effect of sex on work status when sex = F, we subtract from the average of their means the sum of the grand mean and their individual deviations from the grand mean $[(4.93 + 3.41)/2 - (4.24 + (3.90 - 4.24) + (4.67 - 4.24)) = -.16]$. Higher level interactions, though computationally more complex, follow the same logic. When all possible interactions are calculated, the model is said to be saturated. In testing hypotheses, the objective is to estimate cell frequencies using as few interactions as possible. To accomplish this, maximum-likelihood estimates of expected logarithms of cell frequencies are compared with observed frequencies by means of the chi-square likelihood ratio goodness of fit statistic. Hypotheses concerning the relation of household characteristics and other variables to the work statuses of other adults are evaluated sequentially until no further significant improvements in the estimates are possible.

A selection of the log-linear models tested is presented in the Appendix. The specific sequence of models tested starts with three independent variables (sex, sex of head, household income); then the marginal effects on work status of age, education, marital status, and work/earnings status of the head are tested, followed by the various sets of interactions among the independent variables and their joint effects on work status. The tests described in the Appendix reveal that the composition effects of household structure variables (i.e., members' age,

TABLE 12.11   FREQUENCY DISTRIBUTION OF OTHER ADULT HOUSEHOLD
MEMBERS, BY SEX OF HOUSEHOLD HEAD, SEX OF MEMBERS, THEIR WORK STATUS,
AND HOUSEHOLD INCOME LEVEL (ABSOLUTE AND LOG FREQUENCIES)

Other Household Member	Poor		Low		Middle-High		Work Status Mean
	n	log	n	log	n	log	
Male Household Head							
Female							
Working	58	4.06	174	5.16	271	5.60	4.93
Not working	472	6.16	709	6.56	309	5.73	6.15
Income-level mean		5.11		5.86		5.67	5.54
Male							
Working	47	3.85	127	4.84	50	3.91	4.20
Not working	135	4.91	116	4.75	59	4.08	4.58
Income-level mean		4.38		4.80		4.00	4.39
Female Household Head							
Female							
Working	30	3.40	44	3.78	21	3.04	3.41
Not working	97	4.57	77	4.34	35	3.56	4.16
Income-level mean		3.99		4.06		3.30	3.79
Male							
Working	25	3.22	45	3.81	8	2.08	3.04
Not working	55	4.01	30	3.40	17	2.83	3.41
Income-level mean		3.62		3.61		2.46	3.23

Summary:	Grand Mean	Sex of Head	Sex	Income Level	Work Status
	4.24	F = 4.97	F = 4.67	P = 4.28	W = 3.90
		M = 3.51	M = 3.81	L = 4.58	NW = 4.58
				M-H = 3.86	

sex, and marital status) explain most of the variation in the work status of other adult members in female-headed households.

Table 12.12 summarizes these interactions. In the first three columns, the composition effects of sex, age, education, marital status of adult household members, and the head's work/earnings status on each other are summarized. Among all households, in the two-way interactions, other females ($S = F$) are more likely to be in the 25–59 age category, in the two extreme educational groups, married, and in male-headed households. In households headed by females, other adults are more likely to be older and unmarried. Female heads are likely to be nonworking or earning less than the minimum wage if working. Other adults in households headed by women are more likely to be older or younger unmarried females (and not members of the prime working age-group most likely to work when single).

TABLE 12.12 SUMMARY OF RELATIONS BETWEEN EXPLANATORY VARIABLES AND WORK STATUS: HOUSEHOLD COMPOSITION EFFECTS AND DIRECT EFFECTS

Household Composition Effects	Effect	Standardized Effect
S,A = F, 15–24	−.051	−1.16
F, 25–59	.188	4.09
F, 60–64	−.137	−2.62
MS,A = M, 15–24	.539	12.23
M, 25–59	−.371	−8.07
M, 60+	−.168	−3.24
S,E = F,IP	.019	.41
F,CP	−.059	−1.30
F,CS	.078	1.54
S,MS = F,M	.140	4.95
SH,MS = F,NM	.096	2.87
S,SH = M,F	.166	4.95
SH,A = F, 15–24	−.173	−3.92
F, 25–59	−.158	−3.47
F, 60+	.332	6.35
SH,WE = F,NW	.199	3.50
F,W_1	.288	4.81
F,W_2	−.306	−6.10
F,W_3	−.181	−2.78
S,MS,A = F,NM, 15–24	.033	.76
F,NM, 25–59	−.238	−5.19
F,NM, 60+	.205	3.92
S,SH,A = F,F, 15–24	.164	3.72
F,F, 25–59	−.311	6.78
F,F, 60+	.147	2.82
SH,Y = F,P	.092	1.90
F,L	−.087	−1.96
F,M-H	−.005	−.10

Direct Effects	Effect	Standardized Effect
WS,S,A = W,F, 15–24	.006	.143
W,F, 25–59	−.042	−.904
W,F, 60+	.035	.674
WS,MS,A = W,M, 15–24	.050	1.14
W,M, 25–59	−.152	−3.31
W,M, 60+	.102	1.94
WS,S,E = W,F,IP	.063	1.34
W,F,CP	.031	.69
W,F,CS	−.093	−1.90
WS,S,MS = W,F,M	−.018	.52
WS,MS,SH = W,NM,F	.081	2.41
WS,SH,WE = W,F,NW	.021	.37
W,F,W_1	−.066	−1.10
W,F,W_2	.035	.70
W,F,W_3	.010	.15
WS,S,MS,A = W,F,NM, 15–24	.053	1.21
W,F,NM, 25–59	.030	.64
W,F,NM, 60+	−.083	1.59
WS,SH,Y = W,F,D	−.058	−1.19
W,F,L	−.069	−1.55
W,F,MH	.126	2.53

The last three columns of Table 12.2 show the direct effects of the household composition variables in the first three columns of the table on work status. In comparison with composition effects, the direct effects of these interactions are not as strong (when the standardized effects are used as the basis of comparison). The interaction of age and marital status is confirmed, as is the negative effect of being a married female. Tests of models that related sex of head to work status did not show an improvement over those which related sex of head to household composition—principally sex and age of other adults, which themselves *did* affect work status.

The tests indicate that once account is taken of differences in the marital status of other household members (male household heads typically have a spouse who is less likely to work), the work potential (i.e., the likelihood of being employed) of other members of households headed by women is less because these other members, although more likely to be unmarried, are also likely to be younger or older than the prime-age adults who are most likely to be secondary earners. Thus, the effects of age, sex, and marital status on work status are direct and interdependent but are conditioned by the sex of the household head. Such household composition effects, in combination with the lower overall frequency of secondary workers in poverty households and the greater likelihood of females' earnings being lower than males', complete the description of the economic bind in which these households find themselves and explain why the likelihood is high that a household headed by a woman will be poor.

Comparing these findings with those of the report on poverty that used the Belo Horizonte data (Sant'Anna, Merrick, and Mazumdar 1976), we find that household demographic factors play a more important role when attention is focused on a specific subgroup of the poverty population, in this case households headed by women. The earlier study emphasized the importance of economic factors, particularly the earning capacity of secondary workers, in determining differences between poor and low-income households. The earning capacity of secondary workers also determines differences between poor and low-income households headed by women; but beyond this, the composition of households headed by women leaves these households comparatively worse off because they have fewer other adult members who possess the characteristics that might enable them to improve the household's situation by becoming a secondary worker in that household.

URBAN SERVICES FOR FEMALE-HEADED HOUSEHOLDS

Additional tabulations from the Belo Horizonte survey were used by Schmink (1980) to compare access to health and educational services by low-income households headed by men and by women. The findings suggest that not only are female-headed households particularly disadvantaged in their income-earning possibilities, but they also have less access to basic services when compared with male-headed households in the same income group. This hardship is, as was shown in Tables 12.8 and 12.9, closely tied to these households' limited incorporation into the formal labor market with its associated benefits.

Belo Horizonte data showed that in 1972, households headed by women were much less likely to have access to the main government-sponsored health program, Instituto Naçional de Previdencia Social (INPS), than were those with male heads in *all* income groups; in the lowest income category, male-headed households were more than four times as likely to have access to this program. As a consequence, male-headed households were about twice as likely to use INPS medical, laboratory, and hospitalization services, whereas those headed by women were twice as likely to use services provided by religious and charity organizations or other health posts. Households headed by women were also less likely to turn to a pharmacist and more likely to resort to a friend or relative or a ritual curer. This pattern probably reflects the differential cost of these services and may also suggest a preference for community-based health practitioners.

Similar findings emerge with regard to access to education for children in households headed by women. In the poor income group, female-headed households were more likely than male-headed households to have no children registered in school and much more likely to cite financial problems as the reason; they were also less likely to have their children in desired schools. Thus, the need for multiple earners in female-headed households appears to affect the extent to which future generations of workers are able to take advantage of educational services in urban areas. The lack of effective access to services, coupled with the disadvantaged economic position of these households, has potentially serious consequences for the future of children raised in households headed by women— particularly the female children in these households. One study of female-headed households in the city of Salvador, Brazil, found that female children were given work responsibilities at an earlier age and were more likely to be kept out of school for this purpose than were their brothers (Machado Neto 1978, pp. 17–18). Young girls were enlisted to help with both domestic and outside work, although they were rarely paid in money for their labor.

The important role played by female children in households headed by women is strongly tied to the lack of day-care facilities for working women. Brazil lacks preschool facilities to serve the approximately 35 million children who lived in female-headed households in 1980 (Egger-Moelwand and Raucci, 1979; Bittencourt 1979). The only legislation dealing with this population is the Labor Law of 1943, which requires that firms employing at least 30 women provide a day nursery where female employees may leave their children during the nursing period (ages 1 to 6 months). The law permits the contracting of services to facilities distant from the workplace, however, creating a serious problem of transportation for working mothers. The law is not enforced and the fine for violating it is insignificant (Campos 1977; Egger-Moelwand and Raucci 1979).

Further, many day-care facilities are privately run, expensive, and accessible only by middle- and upper-class families; the majority of working mothers must find individual solutions to their work/home responsibilities. Even in the relatively well-served state of Sao Paulo, only 1 percent of working mothers surveyed in 1970 left their children in day-care institutions; nearly half (46.6 percent) left them with relatives, and 21.6 percent left them unattended in the home (Secretaria do Trabalho e Administracão 1970).

POLICY IMPLICATIONS

The findings of the Belo Horizonte survey indicate that the hardships faced by female-headed households in Brazil are multiple and far-reaching. First, there is a distinctly higher probability that they will be poor, when compared with households headed by men. Even within poor populations, however, households headed by women suffer additional relative deprivation. Their heads and other members are less likely to be employed in formal-sector jobs that assure a regular minimum salary and institutional health benefits, yet poverty forces these households to rely on the unpredictable and low earnings of as many members as possible in order to survive. Women who head households may be forced to work despite the lack of day-care services for their young children; this dilemma is often resolved by substituting daughters for the mother either in the home or in the workplace, thus disrupting their educational progress. As a consequence, families without a primary male breadwinner may suffer from low monetary income and an inadequate nutritional level and may also have less access to what minimal urban services may exist, so that efforts to improve their welfare are further obstructed. This complex of problems has the potential for perpetuating a situation of deprivation for future generations of families headed by women. A compelling argument can therefore be made for developing policies to deal with the specific employment and service needs faced by the growing segment of the urban poor living under these conditions.

From a policy standpoint, it is useful to point out that the growing incidence of households headed by women appears to be linked to a particular sort of poverty—that associated with developmental change rather than stagnation. Buvinić and Youssef (1978, p. iii) postulate that the most important factors stimulating the increase in female-headed households include migration, mechanization and capitalization of agriculture, urbanization, and the marginalization of low-income workers—all changes that accompany the modernization process. Certainly Brazil is an example of a rapidly developing economy in which these processes have contributed to recent growth in the proportion of poor households with female heads.

From this standpoint, the problem of female-headed households cannot be understood without considering the overall impact of different styles of development. The fate of this subgroup of the urban poor is but one aspect of the broader analysis of the impact of development policies on Third World populations that has stimulated a new emphasis on the "basic needs" of the poor. So far, global planning efforts have rarely focused on the specific needs of families headed by women with respect to vocational training, employment opportunities, day care, and other essential urban services. Indeed, information about these needs is only beginning to appear. If the social and economic goals implied by the new development concepts are to be met, findings such as those generated by this study, which points out the multiple disadvantages faced by families headed by women, must be addressed specifically by planners.

Appendix A

Table A12-1 presents the stepwise sequence of models tested in the analysis of the work status of other adult household members. Each step is denoted by an alphabetical letter and a panel heading. The first column in the table describes the model being tested, using standard notation. Only parameters indicated for the specific model are included, with the remainder set equal to one, or having no effect. The second column shows the goodness of fit statistic, X^2_{LR}, and the third column shows the degree(s) of freedom (df) available in each specific test. Because X^2_{LR} should not be used with large samples to indicate goodness of fit, an index of dissimilarity was obtained (the percentage of cases that are misclassified under the hypothesis being tested, Δ) and is given in column four.

Panel A tests the model (A2) incorporating only two-way interactions of sex, sex of head, and household income level with work/earnings status. In comparison with the null hypothesis (model A1, no significant effects), model A2 improves X^2 by 233.58, or 58.4 per df, which is a significant change (for significance test statistics, see Joreskog and Sorbom 1976). In panel B, the effects of age, education, marital status, and head's work/ earnings status are shown to be significant, although those of age and education are only marginal. Further tests, however, revealed that the effects of age and education on work status are primarily joint effects, in combination with other variables.

Underlying these bivariate relations between work status and the independent variables are a number of important relations among the independent variables themselves. As seen in panel C, the work/earnings status of heads and household income level are closely related, as are sex and marital status, and marital status and the sex of head (e.g., the proportion of married females is likely to be higher in male-headed households). Model C7 incorporates these interactions and yields a considerable improvement in goodness of fit (reduction in $X^2_{LR} = 1,562$ for 8 df).

Panel D explores the interaction effects of sex and marital status (S, MS), sex and sex of head (S, SH), and their effect on work status; both three-way interactions yield significant improvement in goodness of fit. Panel E explores further interactions of age, sex, and marital status and shows that whereas age, by itself, does not have major effects on work status, age/sex and age/marital status composition of households have an important influence on the work status of other household members (X^2_{LR} reduced by 1253.53 for 12 df).

TABLE A12-1   SELECTED LOG-LINEAR MODELS OF THE RELATION BETWEEN WORK
STATUS OF OTHER ADULTS AND HOUSEHOLD STRUCTURE VARIABLES

Model	X^2_{LR}	df	Δ
A. Marginal effects on work status of sex, sex of head, and household income with added variables: age, education, marital status, work/earnings status of head			
1. WS,S,SH,Y,A,E,MS,WE	5,481.85	1,714	47.0
2. WS,S,WS,SH,WS,Y,A,E,MS,WE	5,248.27	1,710	46.1
3. A1 − A2	233.58	4	
B. Marginal effects on work status of age, education, marital status, and head's work/earnings status			
1. A2 + WS,A	5,241.05	1,708	46.1
2. A2 − B1	7.22	2	
3. A2 + WS,E	5,233.88	1,708	46.1
4. A2 − B3	14.39	2	
5. A2 + WS,MS	5,180.47	1,709	46.0
6. A2 − B5	67.8	1	
7. A2 + WS,WE	5,200.07	1,707	46.1
8. A2 − B7	48.2	3	
9. A2 + WS,A + WS,E + WS,MS + WS,WE	5,110.66	1,702	45.9
C. Composition effects: interrelations between sex and sex of head, sex of head and marital status, head's work/ earnings status and household income			
1. B9 + WE,Y	3,885.53	1,696	41.2
2. B9 − C1	1,314.54	6	
3. B9 + S,MS	4,872.81	1,701	45.2
4. B9 − C3	327.26	1	
5. B9 + MS,SH	5,011.66	1,701	45.6
6. B9 − C5	188.41	1	
7. B9 + WE,Y + S,MS + MS,SH	3,548.71	1,694	39.6
D. Interaction effects of sex, marital status, sex of head			
1. C7 + WS,S,MS	3,533.71	1,693	39.5
2. C7 − D1	15.00	1	
3. C7 + WS,MS,SH	3,520.96	1,693	39.4
4. C7 − D3	27.75	1	
5. C7 + WS,S,MS + WS,MS,SH	3,506.15	1,692	39.3
E. Interaction effects of age with sex, marital status			
1. D5 + WS,A,S	3,212.91	1,688	37.4
2. D5 − E1	293.24	4	
3. D5 + WS,A,MS	2,447.48	1,688	30.6
4. D5 − E3	1,058.67	4	
5. D5 + WS,A,S + WS,A,MS	2,329.82	1,684	29.5
6. D5 − E5	1,176.33	8	
7. D5 + WS,A,S,MS	2,252.62	1,680	29.1

(*continued*)

TABLE A12-1 *Continued*

Model	X^2_{LR}	df	Δ
F. Interaction effects of head's sex, work/earnings status, and household income			
1. E7 + SH,WE	1,974.28	1,677	26.7
2. E7 − F1	278.34	3	
3. E7 + SH,Y	2,213.90	1,678	28.8
4. E7 − F3	38.73	2	
5. E7 + SH,WE + SH,Y	1,971.66	1,675	26.7
6. E7 − F5	280.96	5	
7. E7 + SH,WE + WS,WE,Y	1,928.86	1,671	26.3
8. E7 − F7	323.76	9	
9. F7 + WS,S,E	1,896.78	1,664	26.1
10. E9 − F9	355.84	16	
11. F10 + WS,SH,WE,Y	1,758.50	1,648	25.2
	494.12	32	
G. Interaction effects of age, sex of head, and household income			
1. F10 + A,Y	1,734.17	1,644	25.1
2. F10 − G1	24.33	4	
3. F10 + S,Y	1,728.47	1,648	24.9
4. F10 − G3	30.17	2	
5. F10 + A,S,Y	1,708.83	1,638	24.7
6. F10 − G5	49.67	10	
7. F10 + A,SH	1,637.15	1,646	24.3
8. F10 − G7	121.35	2	
9. F10 + S,SH	1,708.55	1,647	25.0
10. F10 − G7	49.95	1	
11. F10 + A,S,SH	1,496.03	1,643	23.3
12. F10 − G11	262.47	5	

Panel F focuses on the strong relation between head's work/earnings status and household income found in model C1 and explores its relation to the head's sex (models F1 and F3) and the combined effect of these interactions on work/earnings status (F7). Both of the hypothesized two-way relations are supported, but only WS, WE, Y brings a sizable reduction in chi-square. Finally, model F9 (the interaction of education with sex) and model F11 (the further interaction of head's sex with WS, WE, Y in model F7) are tested. Both bring further reductions in chi-square but require a considerable reduction in the degrees of freedom to do so.

The last panel (G) in Table A12-1 focuses on the relation between household composition and the sex of the household head and the household income level. Previous models have shown that age and sex have an important effect on work status. To what extent is the potential to have additional workers who can contribute in households headed by females (and specifically poor households headed by females) affected by age/sex composition?

Models of G1 to G5 explore the relation of age and sex to household income, and models G7 to G11 explore the relation of age and sex to sex of head. Comparing the composition effects associated with household income level with those associated with sex of head, we see that the latter are clearly the stronger (reducing X^2_{LR} by an average of 50 per df compared with 5 per df for the age, sex, household income interaction). Model G11 has improved the "fit" of the original model, reducing the index of dissimilarity from 47.0 percent to 23.3 percent. Further tests yielded no significant improvement, and this model will be employed in studying the effect parameters of particular categories of the variables.

Table A12-2 presents the direct-effect parameters of variables and their interactions on work status from model G11. Although this model is less complex than the fully saturated model (preserving 1,643 of the original 1,728 df), it still includes a large number of higher order terms, and only a sample of them can be shown in the table. What, then, does the model tell us about the relation of the work status of other household members to household structure? The left-hand column of Table A12-2 lists variables and categories for which effects are being reported. For dichotomous variables WS, S, MS, and SH, the effect is shown only for one category, since the effect parameters are symmetric (e.g., WS, S for W, F $= -.166$ and for W, $^M = .166$) in the additive logarithmic form. The multiplicative effects (antilogs of the additive) are multiplied by, rather than added to, the

TABLE A12-2   MARGINAL FREQUENCIES AND DIRECT-EFFECT PARAMETERS OF MODEL G11 IN TABLE A12-1

Variable	Marginal Frequency Effect (a)	Standardized Effect (b)	Association with WS, Assuming No Interaction (B9) Effect (c)	Standardized Effect (d)	Association with WS, Assuming Interactions (G11) Effect (e)	Standardized Effect (f)
WS = W	−.113	−3.36	—	—	—	—
A = 15–24	.450	10.20	.007	.19	−.069	−1.56
= 25–59	.136	2.96	−.069	−1.89	.098	2.13
= 60+	−.586	−11.22	.062	1.21	−.029	−.56
S = F	.306	9.09	−.166	−5.64	−.153	−4.56
E = IP	.020	.25	.058	1.41	.031	.65
= CP	.206	4.58	.037	.93	.016	.36
= CS	−.218	4.30	−.095	−2.20	−.047	−.92
MS = NM	.264	7.84	.142	4.82	.031	.93
SH = M	.245	7.29	−.114	−3.88	−.072	−2.16
WE = NW	−.115	−2.02	.024	.43	−.007	−.13
= W_1	−.083	−1.39	−.007	−.12	.015	.25
= W_2	.460	9.18	−.156	−3.66	−.096	−1.92
= W_3	−.263	−4.05	.138	2.78	.088	1.36
Y = P	−.029	−.06	−.224	−5.21	−.153	−3.16
= L	.233	5.26	−.030	.77	.007	.14
= M-H	−.204	−4.10	.254	5.95	.146	2.93

grand mean. As in the case of conventional regression coefficients, the effect parameters indicate the contribution of a specific category of a specific variable or set of variables to deviations from the grand mean when the variable is included. Columns a and b report marginals of all variables (the logs and their standardized values), that is, the expected marginal frequencies generated with model G11 in the contingency table (Table A12-1). Columns c to f show the association between work status and the independent variables. The magnitude and direction of this association or "effect" depend upon the model according to which it is estimated. Columns c and d show bivariate relations to work status when no interactions are assumed (as in model B9), whereas in columns e and f it is assumed that the interactions of model G11 are present.

Comparing the results with and without interaction, we see that the effect of age shifts from negative to positive for the prime working age-group (ages 25-59) principally because of the interaction of sex and marital status, since married females in this category are less likely to be working than unmarried males. Females are less likely to be working than males. The less educated are more likely to work than the more educated, though the education effect is less when interactions are taken into account. Similarly, unmarried individuals appear more likely to work without interactions but this is not true when interactions are included. A complex set of interactions affects the relation between the work/earnings status of adults other than the head and the work/earnings status of the head, especially in the higher income categories for the head. This is further related to household income level, since there is a strong positive association between work/earnings status and household income.

In comparing these results with what is typically found in the literature on human capital (specifically, on labor force participation), it should be recalled that these data embrace a much wider range of variation than is usually found in that literature, which is usually focused on married women with husbands present. Restricting ourselves to that more limited subset of the data would yield results with positive effects on work status for education and head's earnings, but it would prevent us from looking at the larger question of how household structure affects the operation of these variables in female-headed households. Controlling for household structure (by way of interactions among sex, sex of head, head's work/earnings status, and household income) does yield the expected pattern of participation by secondary workers to supplement household income when the primary earner's wages are lower for male-headed households.

Note

1. These data are reported in Merrick and Graham (1979). Although less dramatic, the trend in Brazil is similar to that in the United States. According to Ross and Sawhill (1975, p. 1), the rate of growth of the number of households headed by females in the United States from 1965 to 1974 was 10 times that of two-parent households. The precarious financial status of households headed by women has generated growing concern, for whatever their prior income status, there is a high risk of poverty for households without a male wage earner. According to Ross and Sawhill (1975, p. 3), almost half of these households are indeed poor, and the same proportion spends some time on welfare.

SECTION 4 Measurement of Women's Work and Welfare

13. Measuring Women's Poverty in Developing Countries

Eva Mueller

It is widely agreed that more and better statistical information about the economic status of women is needed, but there is less agreement on specifically what kind of information is required. This is in part due to the fact that much of the research and writing on poverty among women in developing countries has taken a qualitative sociological approach; little of it has used a quantitative economic perspective (a notable exception is Boserup 1970 and 1975).

Using the latter approach, this essay identifies the data needed to measure the incidence and extent of women's poverty in developing countries. Specific categories of information needed are derived from an operational definition of poverty among women, since a problem must be well defined before it can be measured or before its causes and consequences can be analyzed statistically.

The essay first presents a conceptual framework within which is developed an operational definition of the concept of women's poverty that includes three central aspects. After a brief discussion of the sample survey methods of collecting data on poverty, the measurement of the three central aspects of women's poverty—unemployment problems, support systems, and social attitudes—is addressed. Next, the collection of data on background variables is discussed and is followed by concluding remarks.

CONCEPTUAL FRAMEWORK

A person may be viewed as poor when he or she does not have adequate access to the necessities of life (recognizing that "necessities" are defined differently at successive stages of economic development and in different cultures). People gain access to the necessities of life primarily by two means. First, they gain access by means of work, paid either in cash or in kind. The productivity of work depends on the capital (land, tools, equipment, animals) and technology that a worker has at his or her disposal; it also depends on the worker's human capital assets (health and education). The inadequacy of these capital and technological inputs is as much a cause of women's poverty as are the insufficient numbers of jobs available to women and the social restrictions on women's labor force participation.

Second, people gain access to the necessities of life by means of the "support system." Support systems may be private (economic assistance from kinship groups, friends, or other mutual help networks) or public (social security, welfare, school lunches, free medical care). Support may take the form of transfers of money, goods, labor (help in the fields, for example, or with child care), or other services. These transfers may occur regularly—as when migrants remit money to family members left behind in rural areas, when children help to support aging parents, or when a man provides regular support for a widowed or separated sister. Support may also be given irregularly, taking the form of large or small gifts for special occasions (weddings, birthdays, harvest time) or when the donor has a surplus.

Because of their childbearing and child-rearing responsibilities, their greater longevity, and the social restrictions on their labor force participation, women tend to be more dependent on the support system than men. One of the problems that women in developing countries face is the deterioration of the private support system under the influence of ongoing economic and cultural changes. These countries in which familial obligations are weakening have not yet reached a level of development at which they can afford and can organize public support systems.

Uncertainty regarding access to the necessities of life is likely to affect women's social attitudes. It is commonly held that insecurity may generate fear of deprivation, inability to take risks, willingness to subordinate oneself to others, and a desire to strengthen family ties and to have large families. Although such attitudes can result, in part, from poverty, they can also contribute to poverty by preventing women from taking action to strengthen their economic position. Examples of such action are obtaining more education; taking a more active role in decision making within the household; forming voluntary associations of women; being politically active; demanding access to vocational training, credit, and child care facilities; and taking more economic risks.

We know very little about poverty-related attitudes among women in developing countries, however. For instance, whereas one hypothesis suggests that the weakening of familial support systems fosters traditional attitudes, another states that it frees women from familial constraints, inducing them to pursue employment opportunities more vigorously and to seek more equal roles in the family and the community (Youssef 1974).

In sum, an operational definition of the concept of women's poverty should include three *measurable* aspects that require study at the micro level: women's employment problems, women's support systems, and women's social attitudes. Figure 13.1 depicts the relationships among these three aspects of women's poverty and their origins and effects. Employment problems and support systems affect women's standard of living, which is the result of women's earnings and/

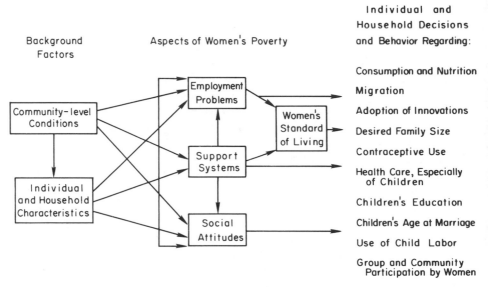

FIGURE 13.1. Women's poverty: a conceptual framework.

or the income women receive from other family members. Women's standard of living and the three aspects of women's poverty affect important individual and household decisions and behaviors, listed on the right side of Figure 13.1. Data on employment problems, support systems, and social attitudes (in the center of Figure 13.1) should enable us to measure *the incidence and extent of poverty among women*. (Data on the consequences of female poverty cannot be discussed within the scope of this essay.)

Descriptive data on the economic status of women can be useful as a means of drawing the attention of the general public and of policymakers to poverty among women (United Nations Economic Commission for Africa 1974). Such data also should enable us to analyze the causes and consequences of female poverty, a necessary first step toward making policy changes. Since the poverty of women has many causes and consequences, it is not possible to deal with the measurement of all of them. This essay focuses on the measurement of the three central aspects of women's poverty and then discusses more briefly the collection of background data.

Sample Survey Methods

Data on economic variables are gathered in censuses; government surveys with large samples, intended primarily for time-series analysis of variables such as employment and unemployment or agricultural output; anthropological studies of particular villages or population subgroups within these villages; case studies made at the macro or micro level; and the like.

Censuses and government surveys generally reflect the inferior economic role assigned to women. Official statistics focus on household income and consumption and on the economic activities of the chief earner of the household (who is most often a male). The economic activities, hours, and pay rates of women and other secondary earners, particularly those of unpaid family workers, often are neglected. Therefore, much of the economic information that is available about women relates to women as individuals rather than as members of households, and although official statistics may show what proportion of women work, it is seldom possible to analyze the incidence of female employment by husband's income, or by marital status and number of children simultaneously (see Youssef 1974, p. 72). Likewise, it is difficult to analyze women's earnings in the context of the earnings of other family members.

In official censuses or surveys, data about women often are obtained from male members of the household. This procedure is unsatisfactory for studies of women. In the first place, women are likely to know more about their own work and support systems than do male household members. This may be particularly true of women who live in consensual unions and women other than the respondent's wife in an extended family. It should also be true in some African societies, where women keep their economic affairs quite separate from their husbands'. Second, in some cultures, men may be embarrassed about their wives' work and thus may underreport it. Third, attitudinal data must be obtained from the women themselves, since no one can reliably report the attitudes of another individual.

This essay describes more appropriate kinds of data that may be collected from moderate-sized, representative samples of households (perhaps 2,000–4,000) or representative samples of women, in both cases by personal interview surveys. It is highly desirable, and in some cultures necessary, to use women interviewers to carry out these personal interviews of women (Papaneck 1979, pp. 412–15).

Moderate-sized sample surveys are a suitable method for supplementing the tabulations available from official statistics. In contrast to small-village studies, such surveys permit generalizations to a larger population, of which the sample is representative. They also permit multivariate analysis of important relationships among the variables covered by the survey.

Surveys of representative samples of women also enable us to deal with the heterogeneity of women's economic status, even within the same country. One important contrast that needs study is that between upper-class, well-educated women who can obtain satisfying professional employment, or wives of wealthy men; and very poor women who are forced to do the most menial and underpaid kinds of work—although the changing economic status of middle-class women is also of interest. Economic class, however, is not the only factor that creates differences in the economic status of women. The economic characteristics of the place in which women live, their age, family characteristics, and ethnic differences also have a bearing on women's economic status. Macro or grouped data hide many of these differences and make it difficult to explore them analytically.

A primary requirement of surveys that focus on women is that a sample be drawn that is representative of *all kinds* of women. The women who are most likely to have economic problems are women who are *not* wives of male household heads. Thus, the sample must be designed to give adequate representation to the following groups: female heads of household (distinguishing among the never-marrieds, separated, divorced, and widowed); unmarried daughters of working age (over 14 years old) who live in nuclear or extended families; mothers or mothers-in-law and other female relatives of the household head; female servants living in the employer's household; and, in urban areas, women who live in rented rooms, rooming houses, or dormitories. Since in many countries women in some of these categories constitute a small proportion of the population, they may have to be oversampled in order to obtain sample sizes large enough for analysis.

One word of caution is needed at this point. Developing countries differ considerably among themselves: Their economies are organized in different ways, their cultures and family systems are quite diverse, and the status and economic roles of women differ. Thus, whatever is suggested about data requirements in the remainder of this chapter must be modified to fit the conditions prevailing in a particular country.

ASPECTS OF WOMEN'S POVERTY

Employment Problems

Conventional employment statistics in developing countries fail to report accurately women's work, wage rates, and earnings and do not provide information on constraints on women's economic opportunities—that is, limited access to capital and technology and dual housework and child care responsibilities.

Women's work is misreported because of the short time perspective of conventional surveys and their disregard of secondary occupations and unpaid family work. The conventional employment statistics report work experience in the week preceding the interview. The short length of the reference period enhances the accuracy of recall, but for purposes of analysis, data collected for a week-long (or even a month-long) reference period are not meaningful. In developing countries and particularly in rural areas, work is highly seasonal and for other reasons as well may be available only intermittently. In many countries, women as well as children are the reserve work force. They are called upon to participate in market work primarily when seasonal labor demands are high. In addition, the prevailing division of labor may assign to women certain tasks (weeding, rice transplanting, work in a canning factory) that are of limited duration. A woman who happened to work during the reference period may work only 2 or 3 weeks (months) during the year, or she may have year-round employment.

In order to assess accurately the employment situation of women and their productive contribution, it is important to determine the approximate amount of time women devote to market work over the period of a year. This is best determined by finding out how many weeks a woman worked during the year, and for how many hours per week during different seasons. Ideally, such data should be obtained by interviewing the same woman several times during the year. If this is not feasible, recall data may be relied upon, since work is a salient aspect of people's lives and is probably reasonably well remembered.

Women often contribute to family earnings in a number of ways, making it important that all *income-earning activities* be reported. For example, a woman may help on the family farm or in a family enterprise. During the off-season she may take in laundry, produce handicrafts, brew beer for sale, or work on some-one else's farm. Especially if she is poor, she may scrape together a living by engaging in several such activities. Unless there is an inquiry into time use or a sequence of questions on multiple jobs, secondary occupations may well be omitted. In some countries, censuses and other surveys have intentionally dis-regarded unpaid family work, whereas in others, these instruments cover such work. Unpaid family labor on farms and in small nonfarm enterprises is an important part of women's work in developing countries and should be consid-ered employment. A special effort is often necessary to make certain that it will not be overlooked.

There is only a very small amount of data now available for developing countries that permits analysis of *wage rates and earnings* simultaneously by age, sex, and occupation. Needless to say, wage rates and earnings data should include income in kind. Full information about all work activities undertaken by a woman will help in estimating her total earnings. When women work for others, a question about their wage rates should be asked; when they are self-employed, their annual earnings from the businesses should be estimated. For women who are doing unpaid family work, individual earnings rates are difficult to identify; they can be estimated statistically only if the work time of each participant and the total earnings from the joint work during the same period are available. As a crude—but perhaps more feasible—alternative to such statistical estimation, women may be asked how much they would have had to pay to hire someone to do their unpaid family work.

Data on women's wage rates and earnings by age are crucial for a number of analytical purposes. First, it is important to distinguish among women who earn little because they are not engaged in full-time work, those who earn little because of low wage rates, and those who earn little because of both limited working hours and a low rate of pay. Second, economists view the wage rate as an important input into decisions regarding amount of time worked. In addition, wage rates obtainable by young girls determine the opportunity cost of time spent in school. Finally, wage rates paid to more mature women represent an opportunity cost of time spent on housework and child care, and therefore they are highly useful for studies of the economic aspect of fertility decisions.

The productivity of work is a function of the capital and technology associated with that work. Women's work often is less productive (and hence less remunerative) than the work of men because women are assigned tasks that require a minimum of capital and employ a traditional, labor-intensive technology. The importance of collecting some data on the kinds of *capital and technology* women have at their disposal for their work (including housework and unpaid family labor) and the constraints they face in gaining access to some forms of these production resources cannot be sufficiently emphasized. Women may have much more difficulty than men in obtaining the *credit* that would enable them to buy the tools and materials with which to increase their earnings, so it is also important to ask men and women about their experiences with, and their perceptions about, local credit agencies (if any exist).

For many women, employment opportunities are constrained by their responsibility for housework and child care. Thus, information on the *time rquired for housework and child care* in families of different sizes and with children of different ages should help to explain the time available for income-earning activities. If some norms could be computed regarding minimal time required for child care and domestic chores in households varying in size and composition, one could begin to identify, on the one hand, women whose income-earning activities are so extensive that such activities may have a detrimental effect on the health of both the children and the women, and, on the other hand, women who are not fully occupied. Housework, of course, may be shared by a number of household members. This pattern of sharing should be investigated, both for the light it throws on the work burden that women carry and for the insights it provides into male, female, and child roles in the household.

The ideal way to collect data on the distribution of time among housework, child care, and income-earning activities is by *time-allocation studies,* which account for all time spent during a particular day. One important advantage of time-use studies is that, unlike conventional employment surveys, they make it feasible for the researcher to separate out activities that are on the borderline between domestic work and income-earning activities. Examples are processing food (which may be partly for domestic consumption and partly for sale), producing clothing or utensils for the household or others, tending a vegetable garden near the house, and collecting food or fuel. In industrial countries, these activities are often shifted to the marketplace; hence they are counted as income-earning activities. Another advantage of time-use studies is that they permit the recording of concurrent activities. Child care, in particular, often takes place simultaneously with housework and leisure and sometimes, in developing countries, with market work.

Since no single day or week can be representative of time use, such studies should be based on several interviews with each respondent, preferably during different seasons of the year. If we want to analyze and understand the division of labor by age and sex, time-allocation studies should cover all members of the household (Kossoudji and Mueller, forthcoming; Cain, Khanam, and Nahar 1979). If income data are collected from the same individuals whose time use has been measured, the relationship of family composition and time use to income can be studied (see for instance, Chaps. 3 and 4 in this volume.) Conducting such studies in developing countries, where respondents cannot be asked to keep written diaries, however, is time-consuming and expensive, and the methodology is still in an experimental stage.[1]

Information on *the setting in which women work* is valuable. Of particular interest, especially for the analysis of fertility decisions, is the question of whether the woman works at home or away from home. Work at home is much more compatible with child rearing than work away from home, but it also exposes the woman less to outside modernizing influences. If she is an employee, the size of the establishment for which she works must be determined. Larger establishments tend to be more modern and to expose women to a larger number of people than smaller ones. More important, larger establishments usually employ more capital and a more advanced technology, potentially enabling them to offer better wages and working conditions. On the other hand, the larger the establishment, the less likely it is that a woman can bring a baby to work or take time off to nurse a baby. Because of their domestic duties and lack of training, and sometimes because of outright discrimination, women in many developing countries have very limited access to jobs in the large-scale, or organized, sector.[2]

Finally, inquiry should be made about *child care arrangements* available to mothers who work away from home and their satisfaction with these arrangements. Some mothers may be able to take children with them to work; others may have relatives who take good care of the children; but many have arrangements that may be inadequate, such as leaving babies or small children in the care of older children. Women who are not doing work outside the home should be asked whether someone would be available to take care of their children if they did wish to work outside the home.

Support Systems

As noted earlier, in most developing societies women typically receive at least part of their subsistence from a familial support system. This is most true of married women, although in the lowest income groups husbands may not earn enough to support their families, so that the wives' labor force participation is a necessity. Table 13.1 shows, for selected developing countries, the proportion of women who are without a husband when they reach their late thirties and the still

TABLE 13.1   MARITAL STATUS OF FEMALES IN SELECTED COUNTRIES
IN TWO AGE-GROUPS (IN PERCENTAGES)

	Age 35–39			Age 50–54		
Country	Married	Single	Widowed, Divorced, Separated	Married	Single	Widowed, Divorced, Separated
India (1971)	91.7	.5	7.7	62.5	.4	37.0
Indonesia (1971)	84.0	1.4	14.6	53.6	1.0	45.4
Colombia (1973)	74.9[a]	16.7[a]	7.7	62.3[a]	15.7[a]	21.2
Peru (1972)	82.2[a]	11.1[a]	6.2	69.2[a]	10.8[a]	19.2
Kenya (1969)	86.2	3.2	10.0	66.4[b]	3.0[b]	30.0[b]
Uganda (1969)	81.7	5.3	12.9	59.3	6.5	34.3

SOURCE: United Nations *Demographic Yearbook, 1976.*
NOTE: Years in parentheses are census years.
[a]"Married" category includes those in consensual unions; "single" category includes women with children but without a stable male partner.
[b]The age-group is 50–59.

larger proportion who are without husbands when they reach their early fifties (see Chaps. 11 and 12 in this volume). Single, widowed, divorced, separated, and abandoned women, and those living in consensual unions, have different degrees of access to nonwork sources of support and they are a substantial proportion of the population. Not only do kinship obligations to women differ among cultures and among economic groups within the same culture, but migration, death, familial conflict, or the lack of close relatives may deprive some women of a reliable source of support in societies where kinship obligations are normally strong. Growing poverty and unemployment as well as urbanization and modernization may erode traditional familial support systems. The pervasiveness of this trend has not been studied, but most observers agree that it is serious and that it adds a new element of uncertainty to the economic welfare of women (Kossoudji and Mueller, forthcoming; Cain, Khanam, and Nahar 1979).

Support systems allow for transfers between and within families.[3] Transfers are flows of goods and services that do not represent compensation for work performed but are given because of kinship ties or social obligations. A family may give and/or receive transfers. Transfers can also occur within a family and between families. In this discussion only interhousehold transfers are analyzed.

The majority of the small number of existing studies on interhousehold transfers in developing countries are concerned with the economic impact of remittances from migrants (see Stark 1976; Johnson and Whitelaw 1974; Knowles and Anker 1977). A review of the literature reveals no studies that focus specifically on the incidence and amount of interhousehold transfers to various categories of women in developing countries.

The dimensions of the support system that are of greatest interest are: (1) the *likelihood* that a woman in a given situation will receive transfer payments; (2) the *amounts* of money, goods, and services transferred; (3) the *characteristics* of givers and receivers of transfers; (4) the *circumstances* under which transfers occur; and (5) the *dependability* of the transfer system. It is quite feasible in a survey to ask people to report all transfers they received and all support they gave to others (excluding transfers within the household) in the course of a year. If some approximate value can be assigned to these transfers, estimated receipts by households can be added to, and estimated disbursements subtracted from, income.[4] In studies of women, inquiries are also needed about the roles of relatives, employers (as in the traditional Indian caste system), and well-to-do individuals in the community. In addition to being asked about who actually provided transfers to whom in the past year, people can be questioned about their expectations. On whom does a particular female respondent think she can rely for economic assistance in times of distress? How certain is she that support would be forthcoming? Under what circumstances might she obtain help?

If some elements of a public support system are available in the study area, questions should also be asked about who in the community has benefited from public transfers—who has received free school lunches, health care in a government clinic, instruction by the extension service, welfare payments, or shelter in subsidized housing. It would be interesting to compare the extent to which men and women benefit from such programs in a particular country.

An investigation into the transfer system could deal most readily with interhousehold and government-to-household transfers; but it must be kept in mind that women may be absorbed into extended families instead of being supported in a separate household. For example, rather than sending funds to a widowed sister's household, a man may move the sister and her children into his own household. She may or may not add to family income by engaging in market work. Likewise, female heads of household may take in relatives who may be secondary earners (see Chap. 12 in this volume), help with child care while the mother goes out to work, or merely share in household consumption. Very few studies have investigated the economic factors influencing household composition in developing countries.

Social Attitudes

A number of studies have dealt with the social attitudes of women in developing countries, but often conceptualization and measurement have been quite haphazard. Such studies should operationally define and measure social attitudes that are related to specific cultural variables and economic circumstances. These attitudes, in turn, can influence behavior such as employment and household decisions.

Many of the studies that have been concerned with women's attitudes have attempted to measure a rather vague concept called "modernization" (see Seti 1976). An exemplary attempt of this kind has been made by David Goldberg (1974) who, in a brief monograph, distinguishes among three aspects of modern-ization: "power" (who makes household decisions), "segregation" (attitudes about sex roles), and "containment" (restriction of wife's activities outside the home). Each of these he relates to background considerations, which are viewed as causes, and fertility decisions, which are viewed as consequences.

Psychologists have developed scales that measure people's sense of *personal efficacy;* that is, their perception of the extent to which they control their environ-ment and their own lives rather than being controlled by fate, other people, or their life circumstances (Gurin and Gurin 1976). These scales, after having been adapted to fit a particular culture, could contribute to our understanding of the psychological implications of poverty. For example, planning for the future and being concerned about the long-run consequences of particular decisions require, and are part of, a sense of personal efficacy.

There are other social attitudes, which may be less deep-seated and lasting, that arise directly out of the economic situation with which women have to deal. Most relevant to this discussion are *attitudes toward work.* Why does the woman work? How does she perceive the advantages and disadvantages of working? What does she like and dislike about her present work? How does she perceive her husband's attitudes toward working women? How adequate in her opinion is the amount of time she can devote to housework, child care, her husband, rest, and leisure? (These questions are discussed in Ranade and Ramachandran 1970; and Freedman and Mueller 1974.) The degree of risk women are willing to take is another attitude that may influence economic decisions. Thus, the relationship between poverty and women's social attitudes must be carefully conceptualized, and poverty-related social attitudes must be studied along with the strictly eco-nomic aspects of poverty, since they may influence household decisions.

COLLECTION OF BACKGROUND DATA

Background data on a woman's own socioeconomic and demographic charac-teristics and those of the household to which she belongs are essential for an analysis of the causes of poverty.[5] To start with, all household members should be enumerated and individual data obtained on their ages, marital status, work status, occupation, education, place of residence while growing up, and recent migration. Questions should also be asked about absent members of the house-hold—that is, people who migrate or have migrated for short or long periods. Such people may be part of the support system on which a woman's economic situation depends.

The demographic data for each woman should include type of marital arrangement, age at which she first entered this arrangement, age of oldest child, number of children born to her, number of surviving children, number of children who died, and the number and ages of children presently in the household. Such data give some clues about the extent to which child-raising responsibilities have competed in the past, and are currently competing, with market work.

Education, like other forms of human capital, is less accessible to women than to men, not only in the form of formal schooling but also in the form of on-the-job training and vocational education. In rural areas, it is especially important to find out whether there are extension or other training programs in which women can participate, whether the women in the household have received any such training, and, if they have, whether the skills taught pertain to income-earning activities or exclusively to their roles as mothers and housewives. Parallel educational data for male members of the household would, of course, be valuable.

Education and training may enhance the productivity of women, not only in market work but also in housework and child care. For example, it is possible that meaningful instruction of young women in nutrition could contribute more to families' nutritional status than a work pattern that allows women to spend long hours on meal preparation. Similarly, it has been argued that in the United States the quality of child care is enhanced by the mother's education (Leibowitz 1974a). Patricia Engle, in Chapter 10, suggests that contact with the more educated women on a project staff may have benefited the mental development of a group of Guatemalan girls. Use of contraceptives has also been shown to increase with female education (Cochrane 1978).

Data on household economic background and on household income and the major sources from which it is derived should be obtained. It is also worth knowing how much is contributed to household income by various categories of household members, although individual contributions cannot be reported separately when several members work on a family farm or in a family business.

Since family income is difficult to measure in some situations in developing countries, data on major household assets may have to be collected as a complement to, or a substitute for, household income. The characteristics of the house in which the family lives and ownership of major durable goods (watches, bicycles, sewing machines—the specific list depending on the society being studied), land, and large animals, are approximate indicators of the family's economic status.

Community-level Variables

Female poverty may be caused by individual circumstances (such as insufficient education), demographic and ethnic characteristics, or lack of land and other kinds of capital that enhance productivity. Other important causes of poverty, however, operate at the community level; examples are climatic conditions, economic and geographic features of the community, and prevailing family structures and values. Such community-level variables can be incorporated into the analysis of women's poverty through comparative studies of communities with different characteristics. Comparative studies of several countries have become quite popular. Yet it is difficult, on the basis of comparative studies, to determine how each of the numerous cultural and economic differences between localities affects the dependent variable, which is, in this instance, observed differences in the economic status of women. Comparative studies do not readily reveal how numerous community, household, and individual characteristics interact to affect the lives of women.

In many developing countries there are great variations in characteristics among the communities that fall into a representative national sample (see, e.g., Indian Council of Social Science Research 1975; Smock 1977). If the most relevant community-level variables are measured with a special questionnaire, they can be incorporated into the statistical analysis to throw light on the reasons for differences in the economic role of women. Inquiry about community characteristics can be made of a few knowledgeable local people, such as the mayor or village headman, other government officials, the head of a cooperative or extension service, schoolteachers, and doctors. Since only one community-level questionnaire needs to be completed for each community, such an inquiry is a rather inexpensive supplement to a household survey.

Obviously a community-level questionnaire must be sensitive to the cultural and economic variations existing in the study area. Examples of data that should be useful for studies of female poverty include availability of local employment opportunities for men and women; whether there is a factory or other large employer in the community; whether people commute to jobs in nearby cities or towns; availability of means of transportation; accessibility to main roads; availability of electricity; prevailing wage rates for men, women, and children; in- and out-migration patterns; location of the most widely used markets; role of women in marketing; type of crops grown; agricultural equipment used by the men, women, and children; agricultural techniques used; major public and private community facilities (health, education, cooperatives, extension, credit) and programs for women that are available in the area and the extent of their relevance to women; mass media penetration; prevailing family structures; attribution of responsibility for economic support of female relatives without husbands and degree of such responsibility; and class structure in the community (see Freedman 1974; Caldwell n.d.).[6]

CONCLUDING REMARKS

Some of the information for which this essay has called could probably be obtained by making modest additions to ongoing censuses and government surveys. The value of such official statistics for analyzing the economic problems of women might thereby be appreciably enhanced. Additions to the traditional employment questions would be particularly desirable.

Much more could be learned, however, if an entire survey could be devoted to the study of female poverty, and still more could be learned if two or three such surveys could be conducted in different parts of the developing world. Since the several elements of female poverty interact with each other and should be studied jointly, and since female poverty should be related statistically to its causes and effects, it would be desirable to obtain for each woman in a representative sample (of women, not households), information on many or most of the categories listed in Figure 13.1.

To be sure, the data needs described in this chapter are very extensive. Thus, the researcher will have to be selective in data collection, using a theoretical framework, his or her knowledge of the country in question, and relevance to local policy issues as the criterion for selection.

Notes

1. An interesting experiment was conducted in rural Nepal, where time-use data were collected from women by a random sampling of periods; see Acharya (1981).

2. One study found that in India prior to 1975, only 6 percent of working women were employed in the organized sector (including government employment and employment in medium-sized or larger private establishments). See Indian Council of Social Science Research (1975), p. 63; see also Chapter 12 in this volume.

3. The importance of intrafamily and intergenerational transfers has been argued forcefully by John C. Caldwell (1976).

4. The value of some important kinds of assistance cannot be quantified—for example, helping someone to find a job or secure a loan, lending work animals or equipment, and exerting political influence on someone's behalf.

5. Guidance in obtaining background information is available in Deborah Freedman and Eva Mueller (1977).

6. For a comprehensive survey instrument, see Anker (1980).

14. Measures of Women's Work in the Third World: Problems and Suggestions

Elise Boulding

How useful are currently available statistics for estimating women's status and for providing a guide to the integration of women into the development process? What information about women do governments collect and why? Statistics serve planning purposes, and those on women gathered by the United Nations reflect the concerns of national governments and their need to know their present and projected labor force capacity and reserve.[1]

Currently, two key measures of development are (1) the growth of the market economy, and (2) population growth in relation to growth of the gross national product (GNP). Thus, the only information about women that governments now require concerns their production and reproduction rates, the size of the economically inactive female reserve labor force, and the educational level of the current and future female labor force. Some attempt has been made to modify the mechanistic orientation of development planners by emphasizing education, life expectancy, and labor force participation as variables that indicate the "quality of life" of women. This attempt, however, has yet to be reflected in statistics used for planning purposes.

This essay begins with a discussion of present practices in the collection of statistics on women for development planning purposes and shows how these practices lead to serious undercounting of women's work. Next, the basic needs approach to development measures is described and indicators of the status of women (and children) that are based on an expanded version of the basic needs framework are suggested. By using the basic needs framework and by emphasizing the importance of the household[2] in meeting basic needs, indicators could be used to shift the focus of development from an exclusive emphasis on economic growth to an emphasis on the less apparent aspects of economic and social life. The basic needs strategy makes possible a more humanly grounded approach to development and a more humane set of social purposes. This proposal to use basic needs–related indicators stresses their potential as a tool for social change, particularly for breaking down rigid sex-role differentiation—since modern social systems tend to value only that which is counted.

It would be naive to believe that social justice could be achieved through the use of indicators alone. Indicators offer a mirror for those societies that are ready to look and see how they are doing, and therefore, some of the indicators suggested here may not be accepted as a legitimate focus of attention for quite some time. Other political processes may bring about social change before the official indicators themselves change, but the creation of indicators is also a political act, which will find a place in the larger political process.

PRESENT PRACTICES: THE COUNTING OF WOMEN

Women are counted by governments in six ways: (1) as a total population of females, usually by age categories; (2) as economically active (by sector, occupation, and status) or as economically inactive; (3) by education received; (4) as migrants; (5) by marital status; and (6) by life expectancy, death, and reproduction rates. For planning purposes, figures on present labor force participation by sector suggest in which directions the present female labor force could be shifted, if desired. Figures on economically inactive homemakers indicate the reserve labor force. Figures on female migration tell where that labor force is; figures on education show what its modernizing potential is; and figures on marital status, life expectancy, and fertility and child-to-woman ratios indicate the capacity for production of the future labor force.

Governments, however, systematically undercount the number of women workers for one or more of the following reasons: the definition of economic activity excludes homemakers and working children and undercounts unpaid family labor; statistical systems simply fail to count large numbers of women workers; and enumeration systems are inaccurate and out of date.

Accurate enumeration of persons of any social category depends on the quality of the enumeration system of a given country, and the enumeration infrastructure is not well developed in many Third World countries. Numbers reported may be based on official guesses or sample surveys rather than on complete enumeration. Relatively few reporting countries have up-to-date and complete census information on their women workers. The target date used in compiling all available United Nations data for the *Handbook of International Data on Women* (Boulding et al. 1976) was 1968; the expectation was that the dates would range from 1966 to 1970—the years for which country data were given in the (1972) yearbooks available at the beginning of the project (in 1974). Because European and North American countries were slow in processing decennial census data, however, many of these countries, as well as many Third World countries, had only pre-1966 data available. Eighty-six of the 124 countries reporting female labor force participation, or 70 percent, provided pre-1966 census data for the 1972 United Nations yearbooks. Twenty-one countries provided "official estimates" (educated guesses), and 24 provided data from sample surveys.

To the general deficiency of reporting infrastructures add the inexperience in counting women at all as separate persons, and the social invisibility of woman's activities, and the most likely outcome is that there will be undercounting of women's work in all societies, and particularly in the Third World.

Definitional Biases

Enumeration of women in the labor force is often undertaken according to rules laid down by the United Nations. They can be summarized as follows: "[The] total economically active female population is the sum of those females above a specified age, generally fourteen or fifteen, who furnish labor for the production of economic goods and services—for market or exchange in contrast to those for individual or family use, subsistence, or consumption. Unless otherwise noted, it must be assumed to include members of the armed forces" (Boulding et al. 1976, p. 296). The economically active female population consists of "the total of *employed* persons (including employers, persons working on their own account, salaried employees and wage earners, and so far as data are available, unpaid family workers) and of *unemployed* persons at the time of the census or survey" (United Nations, *1972 Yearbook of Labour Statistics*, p. 3). Unpaid family workers can be included if they contribute at least one-third of normal working hours to an economic enterprise operated by another household member, and unemployed women are to include those seeking work for the first time. Specifically excluded are students, women who are solely homemakers, retired persons, persons living on their own means, and those "totally dependent on others," as well as all institutionalized persons.

It can be seen immediately that it is easier to leave unpaid family members in the "free labor" category of "economically inactive homemaker" than to count them as economically active. Cultural attitudes toward women affect the degree of bias; some countries report large numbers of women in the "unpaid family worker" category and others report almost none (Youssef, Nieves, and Sebstad 1980).

Whether a woman's products find their way into the market is considered a critical test of economic activity, but in fact there is probably only a small proportion of women in any Third World country who do not produce some food, craft, or service for exchange in their own community. Many sell for cash from their own courtyards without ever entering a market.

Particularly troublesome is the exclusion from the definition of the economically active population of the productive labor of those under age 15 and, frequently, of those over age 65 (Boulding 1979). Children enter the labor force when they are as young as 5 years of age, are regularly active by the age of 10 in many countries, and continue in the labor force until they die. Even with present enumeration standards working against the counting of the work of those under age 15, some countries do report children's work. Tanzania reports 6.6 percent of its females under age 15 in the labor force and Thailand reports 11.7 percent

(United Nations, *1975 Yearbook of Labour Statistics,* table 1). Given that in most rural areas girls carry water and fuel for the household, work in the fields, tend younger children, and frequently work as hired labor in neighbors' fields or as domestic servants, their work should be counted.

Even more disturbing is the use of the concept of "economically inactive homemaker." As has been amply documented in other studies on women's economic roles in developing countries (Boserup 1970; Tinker and Bo Bramsen 1976; Elliott 1977; Boulding 1977), it is the productive work of women both in the home and in the market in the least capitalized traditional sectors of the economy that makes it possible for the agricultural cash crop and industrial sectors of Third World countries to make any showing at all in the world markets. The value in the subsistence sector of the food "economically inactive homemakers" produce and process for family consumption; of the water and fuel they haul long distances for family use; of the craft and construction work they do in producing home equipment and the homes themselves; and of the services they render to men, children, and the elderly in the home is not included in the national accounting system. Even when valued at the miniscule rate of the alternative wages these women could command as paid laborers, the 15-hour (or more) workday of the "economically inactive homemaker" would probably contribute up to one-quarter of the GNP, even in the least industrialized countries. Furthermore, the issue of placing such a low alternative wage value on the work women do for domestic maintenance, even allowing for the lack of efficiency fostered by time spent in hauling water and wood, ought to be reconsidered, since the values assigned are often an artifact of the type of economic analysis made. In the basic needs approach discussed later in this chapter, we see that a large proportion of basic human needs are met by precisely these home-based activities and that they should be appropriately and highly valued.

Women "Unaccounted For"

Perhaps the most serious deficiency in the statistics regarding women's labor is that a large number of women workers simply are not accounted for at all. Table 14.1 shows the mean rates for female crude labor force participation and economically inactive homemakers, and the residual between these figures and 100 percent, by region, for the 32 countries that report both figures. The magnitude of the difference between the total of accounted-for women and 100 percent reflected in this residual category suggests that there is a significant number of unaccounted-for women, which includes women in the formally excluded categories of students, retired persons, those totally dependent, and those institutionalized. Europe and North America, which have the best enumeration procedures, also have the smallest differential. It is not possible that up to 49 percent of the women in the four African and Middle Eastern countries belong, as Table 14.1 indicates, in these formally excluded categories. In general, a good rule to

TABLE 14.1   REGIONAL MEANS FOR FEMALE CRUDE LABOR FORCE PARTICIPATION
RATES AND ECONOMICALLY INACTIVE HOMEMAKERS, AND RESIDUAL

Labor Force Category	Europe/ North America (n = 8)	Latin America (n = 9)	Africa/ Middle East (n = 4)	Asia (n = 11)
Crude labor force participation rate	.24	.15	.11	.19
Economically inactive homemakers	.52	.45	.40	.51
Residual	(.25)	(.38)	(.49)	(.31)

SOURCE: Boulding et al. 1976, pp. 29, 33.
NOTE: Residual = crude labor force participation rates + economically inactive homemakers − 100.

follow in estimating de facto, as contrasted with de jure, employment in subsistence economies is to assume that in low-income groups, all persons aged 10
years and over, both male and female, are "at work," in the sense that they are
regularly engaged in some activity that helps keep them alive. It is recognized
that only the middle classes can "afford" unemployment, because only in the
middle class is there a support system that allows people to choose leisure in the
absence of the type of work they prefer.

What planners need to know—but do not know—is what types of activities the
estimated 67 percent seriously poor and the 39 percent destitute in the Third
World (Boulding et al. 1976) are engaging in to keep themselves alive. (Table
14.2 breaks down these estimates by region.) The majority of those estimated to
be seriously poor and destitute in the Third World are women and children,
precisely those elements of the population we know the least about in terms of
actual productive activities. Not only are all subsistence-sector women at work,
whether counted or not, but they usually work longer hours than men because
they have domestic duties (child care and food preparation) in addition to their
work in the field and their transporting of fuel, water, and market goods. What
information we have about their activities comes from recent time-budget studies
(see Chaps. 3, 4, and 6 in this volume). From an official point of view, this labor
does not exist.

These data pose even more problems for the international planner and the
researcher interested in comparative studies than they do for the national planner,
because enumeration practices vary from country to country. Table 14.3 indicates the officially reported population categories excluded in enumeration procedures; we can be sure that many exclusions are not officially reported. Of the
124 countries reporting female labor force participation rates, 46 officially acknowledge that their data have not been gathered in accordance with practices
recommended by the United Nations because they exclude one or more of the
following categories: unpaid family workers, the unemployed, first-job seekers,

TABLE 14.2   ESTIMATED NUMBERS OF PEOPLE IN DEVELOPING MARKET
ECONOMIES LIVING IN POVERTY, 1972

Region	Total Population (millions)	Seriously Poor (millions)	Destitute (millions)	Seriously Poor (percent)	Destitute (percent)
Asia	1,196	853	499	71	42
Africa	345	239	134	69	39
Latin America	274	118	73	43	27
Total[a]	1,815	1,210	706	67	39

SOURCE: United Nations International Labour Office, *Employment, Growth, and Basic
Needs: A One-World Problem,* p. 22.
[a]Excluding developing countries in Europe and Oceania, with a total population of about
25 million.

women in the armed forces, nomads (who may constitute from 10 to 60 percent
of the population), aborigines, and "others." The two most serious exclusions
are unpaid family workers and nomads, since evidence shows that women in
these categories are fully engaged in work that qualifies them as being "economically active" (see Boulding 1977, chap. 2).

The list of excluded categories in Table 14.3 throws light on what may be the
activities of some of the women in the "residual" category in Table 14.1, and it
highlights even more dramatically the failure of national income accounts to
consider significant sources of national productivity. It is not only the unpaid
family workers and the nomadic women who are important to the GNP, but also

TABLE 14.3   POPULATIONS EXCLUDED FROM THE ENUMERATION
OF CRUDE LABOR FORCE PARTICIPATION OF WOMEN,
AS OFFICIALLY REPORTED BY NATIONAL GOVERNMENTS

Population Categories (Excluded)	Number of Governments Reporting Exclusion, by Region				
	Europe/ North America	Latin America	Africa	North Africa/ Middle East	Asia
Unpaid family helpers in agriculture	1	—	—	3	—
Unemployed or seeking first job	6	3	2	—	3
Women in armed forces	3	1	1	2	3
Nomads, aborigines, "other uncounted"	2	6	2	4	4
Total exclusions	12	10	5	9	10

SOURCE: Boulding et al. 1976, pp. 300–302.

the women who are unemployed and the first-job seekers who are active in household production while seeking work. Social role expectations may permit male job seekers to be idle, but the same does not hold for women.

As time-budget studies for most countries show, unemployed women's housework expands to fill available time (Szalai 1972; Rianday 1976; Robinson 1977). We simply do not know what the productivity is of this kind of work.

TABLE 14.4   INDICATORS OF WOMEN'S LABOR FORCE PARTICIPATION, BASED ON ENUMERATIONS BY A TOTAL OF 159 COUNTRIES AND TERRITORIES

Category	Number of Countries Reporting
Labor Force Participation	
Crude labor force participation	124
Participation by industry	
Agriculture	107
Mining	96
Manufacturing	98
Electrical and other	93
Construction	101
Commerce	106
Transport, storage, and communication	125
Service	108
Participation by occupation	
Professional and technical work	98
Administrative and managerial work	87
Clerical work	87
Sales work	98
Participation by status	
Self-employed	95
Employee	100
Unpaid family worker	94
Economically inactive homemaker	34
Education	
Literacy	94
Student enrollment, first level	137
Student enrollment, second level	132
Student enrollment, third level	86
Marital Status, Life Expectancy, and Reproduction	
Marital status	94
Life expectancy	141
Fertility rate	115
Child-to-woman ratio	120

SOURCE: Boulding et al. 1976, appendix A.

National Data on Women

What are national governments most likely to enumerate about women in their societies, if they enumerate anything at all? Table 14.4 shows that out of a total of 159 countries and territories used as the data base for the *Handbook of International Data on Women,* only 124 did even the most basic counting of women's labor force participation rates. The most frequently counted labor force categories were, in order of frequency: (1) transport, storage, and communication; (2) service (employment as a domestic and other); (3) agriculture; (4) commerce; and (5) construction. (All of these activities are traditional for women in the Third World, and women have continued to engage in them even as the activities have become modernized.) Enumeration of other occupations and statuses is reported by between 87 and 100 countries, indicating a general acceptance of the value of having the data available. The exception is the category "economically inactive homemaker." Only 34 countries reported this category—evidence that it is not considered important information. Judging by the number of countries that collect it, the most important information about women is how long they will live. School enrollment of women and child-to-woman ratios are the next most widely collected categories of data. It appears that planners place a great deal of importance on keeping track of the adult childbearing population and of the education of future childbearers.

The cumulative distortion of data on women's economic participation as a result of undercounting means that the figures cannot be taken at face value; they must be used in each country with careful attention given to their stated limitations and adjustments in the light of other knowledge about a given society (nation and culture) and the activities of women in it. As a basis for policy planning by national governments, these figures are seriously misleading. When they use their own national statistics, policymakers are, in fact, laboring under an illusion as to the size of the actual market-oriented labor force.

THE BASIC NEEDS FRAMEWORK AND SUGGESTED CENSUS CATEGORIES

The basic needs approach to development measures progress by the extent to which the life conditions of the poorest 40 percent of a society are improved, even at the cost of slowing growth as conventionally measured by GNP. The International Labour Office defines basic needs as

the minimum standard of living which a society should set for the poorest groups of its people. The satisfaction of basic needs means meeting the minimum requirements of a family for personal consumption: food, shelter, clothing; it implies access to essential services, such as safe drinking water, sanitation, transport, health and education; it implies that each person available for and willing to work should have an adequately remunerated job. It should further imply the satisfaction of needs of a more qualitative nature: a healthy, humane and satisfying environment, and popular participation in the making of decisions that affect the lives and livelihood of the people and individual freedoms (International Labour Office 1977, p. 7).

It should be noted that many basic needs do not enter into the calculation of the GNP of Third World countries, because the activities that satisfy them are not part of the market sector and are performed by women. Such activities include the provision of food, shelter, clothing, water, fuel, transportation of goods and children, health care,[3] and education in agriculture and handicraft skills; the creation of domestic space in which each person is, to some degree, an individual and individual desires are taken into account;[4] the provision of nurturance and leisure opportunities; and the preparation of feasts and celebrations.

Since these are the activities that satisfy the basic human needs, it is necessary to begin collecting data on them so that they can take their place in national income accounts along with market-based activities. The reasons for collecting such data are threefold:

1. Such data render visible, and assign public value to, basic dimensions of human welfare that are now largely hidden by market-based development measures, and thus give more status to the activities that women traditionally engage in. They include the activities of women in the poorest sectors, both women living with male heads of household and women who head households; they include unpaid family labor and the work of the economically inactive as well as that of the employed.

2. The attention focused on such activities will make visible the imbalances between women's and men's work loads, facilitating a social dialogue on the redistribution of work, on alternative roles for women and men, and on the provision of better tools at the domestic level for meeting family needs.

3. Enumerating valued human activities may encourage an increase in the quality of certain kinds of participation in a society as it becomes known through the enumeration process that these activities are indeed valued. The process of enumeration is in itself a value statement and, therefore, a potential tool for social change.

In the following paragraphs, categories of information that will yield improved indicators of economic and social well-being are identified. The new categories pertain to enumeration of upaid work and access to productive resources; enumeration of health care specialists and community extension workers; and indicators of civic participation, family violence, and individual well-being.

The Unpaid Family Worker

In order to avoid excluding unpaid female workers from the data, an initial assumption must be that all household members over 10 years old are "working." The problem is how to categorize their activity. The census taker should be instructed to enter each household member over 10 years of age in the "home production worker" category, if no other category applies. The category "economically inactive homemaker" then disappears. If a family member is an unpaid worker for a household cash-producing enterprise, then the existing category "unpaid worker" should be used. Many women in near-subsistence economies will be listed as having two occupations: unpaid family worker and home production worker. Whenever a man is categorized as an agricultural worker, in agricultural areas, then the women members of that household are probably also agricultural workers, whether listed as such or not.[5] (This does not necessarily apply in areas where men are landless agricultural laborers, or in some strict purdah societies of North Africa.) In both rural and urban areas, women spend a considerable amount of time in domestic craft production and in trade—for cash, barter, or both. Women who trade for cash should be listed as traders as well as home production workers. To cover the full range of activities of the homemaker, the following occupational subcategories should be added to existing census categories:

> Home Production Worker (check which subcategories apply):
>   Home craft production (producing articles for family use)
>   Home agriculture (raising food for family consumption)
>   Home services (cooking, child care, health care, home maintenance)
>   Home-based barter (exchanging articles with others outside the household, not for cash)

A home production worker can be categorized as being engaged in home production either full time or part time, depending on whether there is other market employment. The worker can be of any age, can be of either sex, and can belong to any social class. In middle-class urban settings, homemakers may be described as producing only home services in their role of home production workers. In the impoverished urban sector, homemakers may well be included in all four categories, particularly if they have been able to find a small piece of unused land in the city (not uncommon but also sometimes illegal, so reporting these data may be a problem). In the rural subsistence sector, women will certainly be included in all four categories. By aggregating national statistics on these four subcategories of the home production worker and seeing how many women have additional employment in the market economy, a different image of the role of women may develop. As more men begin reporting home production work, a different image of sex roles may also develop. It is very important that women who act as de facto heads of household, whether or not a husband is occasionally present (as with migrant workers), be reported as such in connection with home production. A woman head of household who is a full-time home producer with no cash income usually lives in serious poverty (see Chaps. 11 and 12 in this volume).

Land Ownership and/or Use Rights and Membership in Cooperatives or Credit Associations

Because lack of access to land and capital compounds rural women's dependent situation in many Third World countries, reporting rights to land and access to capital by enumerating memberships in cooperatives and credit associations by sex would help legitimize the need for women, as well as for men, to have such access in the subsistence sector. A considerable amount of evidence now available shows that women will use innovative agricultural methods, and will take some risks in doing so, if they have the necessary resources (Skjönsberg 1977; Staudt 1979). Access to land and credit are among the major resources they need.

Health Care Specialists

Health is one of the most discussed issues in Third World development planning, yet health programs are the least effectively implemented. Health is a prime determinant of the quality of life, but city-based planners tend to see (incorrectly, more often than not) most local health care practices as dangerous. Planners are beginning to acknowledge and to work with traditional folk medicine practitioners and traditional midwives in Third World countries, but the process is slow. The training of nurses to function autonomously in rural areas in cooperation with traditional practitioners, as well as the training of paramedic "barefoot doctors," is also growing—again, slowly. These developments would be encouraged if the total number of nonphysician health care specialists, both traditional and modern, were enumerated and reported in United Nations yearbooks (just as the number of teachers at the first, second, and third educational levels is now reported), since the position of women and men already in this field or attracted to it would thus be enhanced, and the information flow between traditional and modern practices would be reinforced.

There is sufficient reason for beginning to list nurses and modern and traditional paramedical personnel in the general statistical yearbooks. (Presumably some of this information is to be found in World Health Organization yearbooks but is not seen by general users of United Nations statistics.) The high cost of hospital-based care and its irrelevance to the health of a total population is now producing new role definitions for nurses in the West (Musallem 1969). Community health practitioner–nurses are beginning to replace the general practitioner, who then tends to become a hospital-based specialist. This movement is reinforced by reports that the presence of nurses in a community is positively correlated with the health of that community, but the presence of doctors is not.

In the future, the nurse may come to play an even more important role than the schoolteacher in community development. The nurse, like the traditional folk practitioner, interacts with individuals in family settings and can assist with a variety of problems at each level—individual, family, and community. Wherever interaction takes place between folk and modern health practitioners, it apparently upgrades the skills of both. For instance, the difficult problem of changing traditional food taboos that prevent pregnant and lactating women from ingesting necessary protein can probably best be handled by an alliance of folk practitioners and nurses. Plans to upgrade the nutritional level of families in the poverty sector through food distribution programs, even if they include special-purpose and specially labeled foods for women and children, cannot, in the long run, be as effective or as economical as changes in the attitudes toward and practices of family food sharing that could be brought about by the respected traditional healing figures in a community. Such a change would require the active participation of nurses trained to work with folk practitioners.

Enumerating and publishing, as frequently as possible, the number of nurses and folk practitioners available in a country will both legitimate a viable, if somewhat new, approach to public health and attract more women and men into the field of nursing.

Community Extension Workers

It would also be valuable to have a separate tabulation of community extension workers. At the moment most of them are men, but the social mirroring that the reporting process would trigger would make it easier to increase the number of women extension workers. Presently, men are agriculture specialists and women are nutrition specialists. A shift to giving combined agricultural and nutritional training to all extension agents (men and women) would break down the unrealistic program differentiation that denies men the nutritional information they need and women the agricultural information they require. Women extension workers with broad agriculture-nutrition training would provide needed help to women with their farming problems. At the same time, male extension workers could help break down traditional food taboos by including discussions about nutrition in their interactions with male farmers.

Postharvest food loss, a major cause of food shortages, is another area that can best be dealt with by educating both men and women farmers, since both are responsible for certain key aspects of the food storage process. In most Third World countries, men's and women's meetings with extension agents are presently held at separate times and places; only by giving broad training to workers of both sexes can a holistic approach to agriculture, food processing, and nutrition be made a reality.

Civic Participation

One way to encourage the participation of women, men, and children in civic activities outside the home would be to collect census data on the number of organizations—civic, religious, political, cultural, and economic—that each person belongs to. Collection of such data compromises privacy, however, and in totalitarian societies information on civic participation could be used against individuals. Thus, this suggestion is made to encourage long-range thinking about developing norms of civic participation rather than to advocate immediate action.

Family Violence

No country at present collects statistics on family violence—wife, husband, and child abuse. There is, however, growing awareness of the seriousness of this problem in all countries, at all levels of industrialization. Women and children are the chief, although not the only, victims. Unfortunately, the beating of a woman because a meal is not served when wanted, or the beating of a child for less than instantaneous compliance with a command, is a problem associated with long-standing practices of age and sex discrimination that cut across cultures and economic systems. Although it is not practical at this time for the United Nations to try to collect statistics on the subject (they simply would not be reported), it is worth thinking about acceptable indicators of trends in the practice of physical violence in the home, particularly since the acceptance of violence at home increases the probability of violence taking place outside the home.

Measuring Individual Well-Being

The indicators that have been suggested were chosen on the assumption that the data could be collected from individual households in census enumerations, and that the categories would lend themselves well to cross-national comparisons as well as to socially useful national reporting. Furthermore, each indicator was chosen on the ground that it would reveal more about the economic and social well-being of women and men than is revealed by current market and demographic indicators. Even if these indicators were used, however, the problem of assessing the situation of women living in poverty by analyzing national aggregate data would remain. To answer questions about the situation of women living in poverty, data on well-being would still need to be disaggregated by income groups, and the reporting infrastructure of most countries is inadequate to undertake this task. An alternative measure of well-being is people's time allocation, the best method presently available for discovering the reality of experienced welfare levels behind aggregate statistics. It has been remarked that time may be the most attractive social indicator "when we have no obvious direct measurement for a social concern" (Tunstall quoted in Robinson 1977, p. 24). Everyone has the same 24 hours in a day, and how those 24 hours are distributed between work and leisure tells us very quickly how one group or class of people is doing compared with another. It has been noted in all time-budget studies that sex is associated with greater differences in time use than almost any other variable, and that women work longer hours and have less leisure (particularly if they are also employed outside the home) than men. Time-budget studies would therefore be an excellent way to monitor the work load imbalance that reduces the quality of life for so many of the world's women. Such studies would also provide feedback on the choices that different groups in a society make with regard to discretionary time and would thus provide the basis for a society's self-evaluation.

CONCLUDING REMARKS

As noted earlier, statistics serve planning purposes and these planning purposes may disregard human well-being. Integrating women into a mechanistically conceived development process continues the manipulation and exploitation that women have experienced for so long. Increased women's labor force participation, given current universal expectations that women will continue to carry out domestic functions in addition to working outside the home, will only increase the existing work load imbalance between women and men. More efficient collection of information within existing data categories will only render women more vulnerable to further exploitation. "Quality of life" indicators, such as life expectancy and literacy, are meaningless when a human being's value is measured primarily in terms of availability to participate in the labor force. Thus, in order to ensure that women are not only integrated into the development process, but also benefit from such integration, the focus, as well as the measures, of development must change.

Notes

1. See Oakley and Oakley (1978) for a discussion of the broader issue of sexism in statistics, which is not discussed here.

2. The emphasis on the household in this essay is not meant to exclude the single woman, but rather to focus on that majority of women, with or without partners, who have household responsibilities in the Third World.

3. The failure to estimate the amount of health and nursing care provided by women to their families is one major source of bias in estimating gross national product.

4. With all the emphasis on participatory roles in developing societies, it is rarely noticed that the family is the primary setting in which participatory roles are possible. Even when family relations are relatively authoritarian, some shaping of the environment is possible for each person in the household.

5. A study of farm women in the southwestern United States suggests that middle-class farm housewives put a substantial number of hours daily into farm work all year long, including work in the fields. In peak work seasons they put in very long hours indeed. Yet these women are classified by the census as housewives only (Boulding 1980).

References

Abreu, Alice de Paiva. 1977. "Mão de Obra Feminina e Mercado de Trabalho no Brasil." Servico Nacional de Aprendizagem Comercial, *Boletím Técnico* 3:5–19.

Acharya, Meena. 1981. "Time-Use Data from Nepalese Villages: Policy Implications." Paper presented at the Anniversary Meeting of the Population Association of America, Washington, D.C., March 28.

Ahmad, Zubeida M., and Martha F. Loutfi. 1981. *Programme on Rural Women*. Geneva: International Labour Organisation.

Alauddin, Talat. 1980. "Contribution of Housewives to GNP: A Case Study of Pakistan." M.S. thesis, Vanderbilt University.

Allen, R. G. D. 1959. *Mathematical Economics*. New York: St. Martin's Press.

———. 1938. *Mathematical Analysis for Economists*. New York: St. Martin's Press.

Anker, Richard. 1980. *Research on Women's Roles and Demographic Change: Survey Questionnaire for Households, Women, Men, and Communities with Background Explanations*. Geneva: International Labour Organisation.

Anker, Richard; Mayra Buvinić; and Nadia H. Youssef, eds. 1982. *Women's Roles and Population Trends in the Third World*. Geneva: International Labour Organisation.

Ashenfelter, Orley, and James Heckman. 1974. "The Estimation of Income and Substitution Effects in a Model of Family Labor Supply." *Econometrica* 42:73–85.

Baker, S. W., and A. A. Ehrhardt. 1974. "Prenatal Androgen, Intelligence, and Cognitive Sex Differences." In R. C. Friedman, R. M. Richart, and R. C. Van de Wiele, eds., *Sex Differences in Behavior*. New York: Wiley.

BAM [Brothers to All Men] Zambia. 1981. "Some Observations on Households Run By Women Alone." Luwingu, Zambia. Mimeographed.

Barnes, Richard H. 1976. "Dual Role of Environmental Deprivation and Malnutrition in Retarding Intellectual Development." *American Journal of Clinical Nutrition* 29:912–17.

Barroso, Carmen. 1978. "Sozinhas ou Mal Acompanhadas—A Situacão da Mulher Chefe de Familia." *Anais: Primeiro Encontro Nacional de Estudos Populacianais*. Rio de Janeiro: Associação Brasiliera de Estudos Populacianais.

Barrera, Manuel. 1978. "Diferencias Salariales entre Hombres y Mujeres en América Latina." Paper presented at the Instituto Universitário de Pesquisas do Rio de Janeiro Seminar on Women in the Labor Force in Latin America, Rio de Janeiro, November.

Becker, Gary S. 1976. "A Theory of Social Interactions." *Journal of Political Economy* 82:1063–93.

———. 1974. "On the Relevance of the New Economics of the Family." *American Economic Review* 64:317–19.

———. 1965. "A Theory of the Allocation of Time." *Economic Journal* 75:493–517.

———. 1962. "Investment in Human Capital: A Theoretical Analysis." *Journal of Political Economy* 70:9–49.

Bender, Donald. 1967. "A Refinement of the Concept of Household: Families, Co-Residence, and Domestic Functions." *American Anthropologist* 69:493–507.

Birdsall, Nancy. 1980. "Measuring Time Use and Nonmarket Exchange." In William Paul McGreevey, ed., *Third World Poverty: New Strategies for Measuring Development Progress*, pp. 157–74. Lexington, Mass.: Lexington Books.

———. 1976. "Women and Population Studies." *Signs* 1:699–712.

Birks, J. S., and C. A. Sinclair. 1977. "Movements of Migrant Labor from Part of the North of the Sultanate of Oman." Paper based on data gathered by International Migration Project. Durham, N.C.: University of Durham, Department of Economics.

Bishop, Y. M.; S. E. Feinberg; and P. W. Holland. 1975. *Discrete Multivariate Analysis*. Cambridge, Mass.: MIT Press.

Bittencourt, Sonia. 1979. *Child Care Needs of Low-Income Women: Urban Brazil*. Washington, D.C.: Overseas Education Fund.

Blumberg, Rae Lesser. 1978. *Stratification: Socioeconomic and Sexual Inequality*. Dubuque, Iowa: William C. Brown.

Blumberg, Rae Lesser, and María Pilar García. 1977. "The Political Economy of the Mother-Child Family: A Cross-Societal View." In Luis Leñero Otero, ed., *Beyond the Nuclear Family Model*. London: Sage Publications.

Boserup, Ester. 1975. "Employment of Women in Developing Countries." In Leon Tabah, ed., *Population Growth and Economic Development in the Third World*. Liège, Belgium: International Union for the Scientific Study of Population.

———. 1970. *Women's Role in Economic Development*. London: George Allen and Unwin.

Boulding, Elise. 1980. "The Labor of U.S. Farm Women: A Knowledge Gap." *Sociology of Work and Occupations* 7:261–90.

———. 1979. *Children's Rights and the Wheel of Life*. New Brunswick, N.J.: Transaction Press.

———. 1977. *Women in the Twentieth Century World*. New York: Halsted Press.

Boulding, Elise; Shirley Nuss; Dorothy Carson; and Michael Greenstein. 1976. *Handbook of International Data on Women*. New York: Halsted Press.

Boulier, Bryan L. 1977. "An Evaluation of Time Budget Issues as Complements to Conventional Labor Force Surveys." Paper presented at the meeting of the Population Association of America, Saint Louis, April.

———. 1976. "The Influence of Children on Household Economic Activity in Rural Philippines." Paper presented at the Agricultural Development Council Seminar on Household Studies, Singapore, August.

Box, G., and D. Cox. 1964. "An Analysis of Transformation." *Journal of the Royal Statistical Society*, Series B, 26:211–43.

Bratton-Kearns, D. 1979. "Feeding Behavior: Observations within Families in a Rural Guatemalan Village." M.S. thesis, University of California at Los Angeles.

Briscoe, John. 1978. "The Role of Water Supply in Improving Health in Poor Countries." *American Journal of Clinical Nutrition* 31:2100–2113.

Brockman, L., and H. Ricciuti. 1971. "Severe Protein-Calorie Malnutrition and Cognitive Development in Infancy and Early Childhood." *Developmental Psychology* 4:312–19.

Bronfenbrenner, Urie. 1976. "Research on the Effects of Day Care on Child Development." In *Toward a National Policy for Children and Families*. Washington, D.C.: National Academy of Sciences Advisory Committee on Child Development.

Brown, Judith. 1970. "A Note on the Division of Labor by Sex." *American Anthropologist* 72:1073–78.

Bruschini, Maria Christina A. 1978. "Sexualizacão das Ocupações: O Caso Brasileiro." Paper presented at the Instituto Universitário de Pequisas do Rio de Janeiro Seminar on Women in the Labor Force in Latin America, Rio de Janeiro, November.

Bunster B., Ximena. 1977. "Talking Pictures: Field Method and Visual Mode." In Wellesley Editorial Committee, ed., *Women and National Development: The Complexities of Change*. Chicago: University of Chicago Press.

Buvinić, Mayra. 1980. "CBIRD [Community-based Integrated Rural Development] Revisited." Report to the Office of Private and Voluntary Cooperation, Agency for International Development. Washington, D.C.: International Center for Research on Women.

Buvinić, Mayra, and Nadia H. Youssef with Barbara Von Elm. 1978. "Women-Headed Households: The Ignored Factor in Development Planning." Report submitted to the Office of Women in Development, Agency for International Development. Washington, D.C.: International Center for Research on Women.

Cabañero, Teresa A. 1977. "The 'Shadow Price' of Children in Laguna Households." Paper presented at the Symposium on Household Economics, Manila, May 27–28.

Cain, Mead. 1977. "The Economic Activities of Children in A Village in Bangladesh." *Population and Development Review* 3:201–27.

Cain, Mead; S. R. Khanam; and S. Nahar. 1979a. *Class, Patriarchy, and the Structure of Women's Work in Rural Bangladesh*. Center for Policy Studies, Working Paper no. 43. New York: Population Council.

———. 1979b. "Class, Patriarchy, and Women's Work in Bangladesh." *Population and Development Review* 5:405–38.

Caldwell, John C. 1976. "Toward a Restatement of Demographic Transition Theory." *Population and Development Review* 2:321–66.

———. n.d. "Community Information Sheet." Document 6(1). Canberra: Australian National University, Department of Demography.

Campos, Maria Machado Malta. 1977. "As Creches no Brasil." Deposition to the Mixed Parliamentary Inquiry Commission on the Situation of Women, Brazilia, April 28.

Central Bureau of Statistics. 1975. *1970 Population Census of Ghana*. Vol. 3, *Demographic Characteristics*. Accra: Central Bureau of Statistics.

Centro Venezolano de Estudios de Población y Familia. 1972. "El Status Ocupacional de los Jefes Hogares de Bajos Ingresos en Caracas." Caracas: Cordiplan.

Chávez, A., and C. Martínez. 1979. "Consequences of Insufficient Nutrition on Child Character and Behavior." In D. Levitsky, ed., *Malnutrition, Environment, and Behavior: New Perspectives*. Ithaca, N.Y.: Cornell University Press.

———. 1975. "Nutrition and Development of Children from Poor Rural Areas, pt. 5: Nutrition and Behavioral Development." *Nutrition Reports International* 11:477–89.

Cleaves, Peter S. 1980. "Implementation amidst Scarcity and Apathy: Political Power and Policy Design." In Merilee S. Grindle, ed., *Politics and Policy Implementation in the Third World*. Princeton: Princeton University Press.

Cochrane, Susan Hill. 1978. *Fertility and Education: What Do We Really Know?* Baltimore: Johns Hopkins University Press.

Comisión Económica para América Latina. 1973. "El Estrato Popular Urbano: Informe de Investigación sobre Santiago." Cited in M. Wolfe, "Participation of Women in Development in Latin America." Paper presented at the Regional Seminar for Latin America on the Integration of Women in Development with Special Reference to Population Factors, Caracas, April.

Corrèze, Anne-Marie. 1977. "Rapport de Mission en Haute-Volta." Paris: Institut de Recherches et d'Applications de Méthodes de Développement.

Dauber, Rosalyn, and Melinda L. Cain, eds. 1981. *Women and Technological Change in Developing Countries*. Boulder, Colo.: Westview Press.

DaVanzo, Julie, and Donald L. P. Lee. 1978. "The Compatibility of Work and Child Care: Preliminary Evidence from Malaysian Data." Paper presented at the Conference on "Women in Poverty: What Do We Know?" Belmont Conference Center, Md., April 30–May 2.

David, Cristina C., and Richard D. Meyer. 1979. "Measuring the Farm-Level Impact of Agricultural Loans in Low-Income Countries: A Review Article." Prepared for the Workshop on Rural Financial Markets and Institutions, Wye College, Wye, England.

Davidson, Nicol, and Margaret Croke, eds. 1978. *The United States and Decision-Making: The Role of Women*. Vol. 2: *Papers Presented to a UNITAR Colloquium at Schloss Hernstein, Austria, 13–16 July 1977*. New York: United Nations Institute for Training and Research.

Deere, Carmen Diana. 1978a. "The Development of Capitalism in Agriculture and the Division of Labor by Sex: A Study of the Northern Peruvian Sierra." Ph.D. dissertation, University of California at Berkeley, chap. 5.

———. 1978b. "Intra-Familial Labor Deployment and the Formation of Peasant Household Income." Paper presented at the Conference on "Women in Poverty: What Do We Know?" Belmont Conference Center, Md., April 30–May 2.

———. 1977. "The Agricultural Division of Labor by Sex: Myths, Facts, and Contradictions in the Northern Peruvian Sierra." Paper presented to the panel on the subject, "Women: The New Marginals in the Development Process?" at the joint meetings of the Latin American Studies Association and the African Studies Association, Houston, November. Forthcoming in *Economic Development and Cultural Change*.

Deere, Carmen Diana, and Alain de Janvry. n.d. "A Conceptual Framework for the Empirical Analysis of Peasants." *American Journal of Agricultural Economics* 62:601–11.

DeLicardie, E. R., and J. Cravioto. 1974. "Behavioral Responsiveness of Survivors of Clinically Severe Malnutrition to Cognitive Demands." In J. Cravioto, L. Hambreus, and B. Valliquist, eds., *Early Malnutrition and Mental Development*. Uppsala, Sweden: Almquist and Wiksel.

de Piza, Eugenia López. 1977. "La Familia Matrifocal como Mecanismo de Adaptación de la Mujer a su Marginalidad." Mimeographed. Available at International Center for Research on Women, Washington, D.C.

Ehrhardt, A. A., and S. W. Baker. 1974. "Fetal Androgens, Human Central Nervous System Differentiation, and Behavior Sex Differences." In R. C. Friedman, R. M. Richart, and R. C. Van de Wiele, eds., *Sex Differences in Behavior*. New York: Wiley.

Elliott, Carolyn M. 1977. "Theories of Development: An Assessment." In Wellesley Editorial Committee, ed., *Women and National Development: The Complexities of Change*. Chicago: University of Chicago Press.

Elmendorf, Mary Lindsay. 1976. *Nine Mayan Women: A Village Faces Change*. New York: Schenkman.

Engle, P. L.; M. Irwin; R. E. Klein; C. K. Yarbrough; and J. W. Townsend. 1979. "Nutrition and Mental Development." In M. Winick, ed., *Nutrition: Pre- and Postnatal Influences*. New York: Plenum.

Engle, P. L.; R. E. Klein; J. Kagan; and C. K. Yarbrough. 1977. "Cognitive Performance during Middle Childhood in Rural Guatemala." *Journal of Genetic Psychology* 4:291–307.

Escola Paulista de Medicina, Instituto de Medicina Preventiva, Universidade de São Paulo. 1975. "Estado Nutricional de Crianças de 6 a 60 Meses no Município de São Paulo." Vol. 2, "Data Analysis."

Evenson, Robert E. 1977. "Notes on Household Economics and Its Relevance to the Developing Countries." Paper prepared for the Australian Agricultural Economics Conference Workshop on Household Economics, Canberra, February.

————. 1976. "On the New Household Economics." *Journal of Agricultural Economics and Development* 6:172–183.

Evenson, R. E.; B. M. Popkin; and Elizabeth Quizon [King]. 1979. "Nutrition, Work, and Demographic Behavior in Rural Philippine Households: A Synopsis of Several Laguna Household Studies." New Haven: Yale University, Economic Growth Center.

Fagley, R. M. 1976. "Easing the Burden of Women: A 16-hour Workday." *Assignment Children* 36:9–28.

Farouk, A., and M. Ali. 1975. *The Hardworking Poor*. Dacca: University of Dacca, Bureau of Economic Research.

Ferraro, Gary. 1980. "Swazi Marital Patterns and Conjugal Roles: An Analysis and Policy Implications." University of Swaziland. Mimeographed.

Ford, C. S. 1970. "Some Primitive Societies." In G. H. Seward and R. C. Williamson, eds., *Sex Roles in Changing Society*. New York: Random House.

Fraiberg, Selma. 1977. *Every Child's Birthright: In Defense of Mothering*. New York: Basic Books.

Freedman, Deborah, and Eva Mueller. 1977. *A Multi-Purpose Household Questionnaire: Basic Economic and Demographic Modules*. Washington, D.C.: World Bank.

————. 1974. *Economic Models for Use in Fertility Surveys in Less Developed Countries*. Occasional Paper no. 12. Voorburg, Netherlands: International Statistical Institute, World Fertility Study.

Freedman, Ronald. 1974. *Community-Level Data in Fertility Surveys*. Occasional Paper no. 8. Voorburg, Netherlands: International Statistical Institute, World Fertility Study.

Friedl, Ernestine. 1978. "Society and Sex Roles." *Human Nature* 1:68–75.

Friedman, R. C.; R. M. Richart; and R. C. Van de Wiele, eds. 1974. *Sex Differences in Behavior*. New York: Wiley.

Galbraith, John K. 1973. *Economics and the Public Purpose.* New York: Signet.

Garai, J. E., and A. Scheinfield. 1968. "Sex Differences in Mental and Behavioral Traits." *Genetic Psychology Monographs* 77:69–299.

Germaine, Adrienne. 1977. "Poor Rural Women: A Policy Perspective." *Journal of International Affairs* 30:161–72.

Giele, Janet Z., and Audrey C. Smock. 1977a. *Women and Society: In International and Comparative Perspective.* New York: Wiley-Interscience.

―――. 1977b. *Women: Roles and Status in Eight Countries.* New York: Wiley.

Goldberg, David. 1974. *Modernism: The Extensiveness of Women's Roles and Attitudes.* Occasional Paper no. 14. Voorburg, Netherlands: International Statistical Institute, World Fertility Study.

Gonzalo, Susan Ybanez. 1976. "Major Factors Affecting Rural Household Food Consumption." Discussion Paper 76-13. Manila: University of the Philippines, School of Economics.

Gonzalo, S. Y., and R. E. Evenson. 1977. "A Note on the Production of Nutrients." Paper presented at the Symposium on Household Economics, Manila, May 27–28.

Graves, L. 1976. "Nutrition, Infant Behavior, and Maternal Characteristics: A Pilot Study in West Bengal, India." *American Journal of Clinical Nutrition* 29:305–19.

Griliches, Z. 1970. "Notes on the Role of Education in Production Functions and Growth Accounting." In Lee Hansen, ed., *Education and Income.* Studies in Income and Wealth, vol. 35. New York: National Bureau of Economic Research.

Grindle, Merilee S. 1980. "Policy Content and Context in Implementation." In Merilee S. Grindle, ed., *Politics and Policy Implementation in the Third World.* Princeton: Princeton University Press.

Gronau, Reuben. 1976a. "Leisure, Home Production and Work—the Theory of the Allocation of Time Revisited." National Bureau of Economic Research Working Paper no. 137. New York: National Bureau of Economic Research.

―――. 1976b. "Who Is the Family's Main Breadwinner? The Wife's Contribution to Full Income." National Bureau of Economic Research Working Paper no. 148. New York: National Bureau of Economic Research.

―――. 1973. "The Effect of Children on the Housewife's Value of Time." *Journal of Political Economy* 81:8168–99.

Grootaert, Christiaan. 1980. "Selected Problems in the Implementation of Household Surveys." In Christopher Saunders and Christiaan Grootaert, eds., *Reflections on the LSMS Group Meeting,* pp. 23–43. Living Standards Measurement Study Working Paper no. 10. Washington, D.C.: World Bank.

Gross, Daniel R., and Barbara A. Underwood. 1971. "Technological Change and Caloric Costs: Sisal Agriculture in Northeastern Brazil." *American Anthropologist* 73:725–40.

Gurin, Gerald, and Patricia Gurin. 1976. "Personal Efficacy and the Ideology of Individual Responsibility." In Burkhard Strumpel, ed., *Economic Means for Human Needs.* Ann Arbor: University of Michigan, Institute for Social Research.

Handwerker, W. Penn. 1974. "Changing Household Organization in the Origins of Market Places in Liberia." *Economic Development and Cultural Change* 22:229–48.

Harrington, Judith A. 1978. "Education, Female Status, and Fertility in Nigeria." Paper presented to the meetings of the Population Association of America, Atlanta, November.

————. 1971. "A Comparative Study of Infant and Childhood Mortality in West Africa: Ghana, Niger, and Upper Volta." Ph.D. dissertation, Cornell University.

Hause, J. C. 1972. "Earnings Profile: Ability and Schooling." *Journal of Political Economy* 80:8108–38.

————. 1971. "Ability and Schooling as Determinants of Earnings or If You Are So Smart Why Aren't You Rich?" *American Economic Review* 61:289–98.

Hawrylyshin, O. 1976. "Value of Household Services: A Survey of Empirical Estimates." *Review of Income and Wealth* 22:101–31.

Heckman, J., and S. Polachek. 1974. "Empirical Evidence on the Functional Form of the Earnings-Schooling Relationship." *Journal of the American Statistical Association* 69:350–54.

Herrin, Alejandro. 1979. "Rural Electrification and Fertility Change in the Southern Philippines." *Population and Development Review* 5:61–86.

Hertzig, M. E.; H. G. Birch; S. A. Richardson; and J. Tizard. 1972. "Intellectual Levels of School Children Severely Malnourished during the First Two Years of Life." *Pediatrics* 49:814–24.

Ho, Teresa J. 1979. "Time Costs of Child Rearing in the Rural Philippines." *Population and Development Review* 5:643–62.

Horowitz, G. 1979. "Review of the Data on Intra-family Distribution of Food in Less-Developed Countries." Mimeographed. Available at International Center for Research on Women, Washington, D.C.

Howells, K. F.; J. M. L. Holme; and T. C. Jordan. 1979. "Sex-related Differences in the Response of Fast and Slow Muscle Fibers to Early Undernutrition." *Research in Experimental Medicine* 176:137–41.

Husen, T. 1968. "Talent, Opportunity, and Career: A 26-Year Follow-up." *School Review* 76:190–209.

Indian Council of Social Science Research. 1975. *Status of Women in India*. New Delhi: Indian Council of Social Science Research.

Inkeles, A., and D. H. Smith. 1974. *Becoming Modern: Individual Change in Six Developing Countries*. Cambridge, Mass.: Harvard University Press.

International Center for Research on Women. 1980a. "The Productivity of Women in Developing Countries: Measurement Issues and Recommendations." Report prepared for the Office of Women in Development, Agency for International Development. Washington, D.C.: International Center for Research on Women.

————. 1980b. "Limits to Productivity: Improving Women's Access to Technology and Credit." Report prepared for the Office of Women in Development, Agency for International Development. Washington, D.C.: International Center for Research on Women.

Irwin, M.; P. L. Engle; C. K. Yarbrough; R. E. Klein; and J. Townsend. 1978. "The Relationship of Prior Ability and Family Characteristics to School Attendance and School Achievement in Rural Guatemala." *Child Development* 49:415–27.

Jaffe, A. J., and K. Azumi. 1969. "The Birth Rate and Cottage Industries in Underdeveloped Countries." *Economic Development and Cultural Change* 9:52–63.

Jain, Arrudh K.; Ronald Freedman; T. C. Howard; and M. C. Chong. "Demographic Aspects of Lactation and Amenorrhea." Taiwan Population Studies I. Ann Arbor: University of Michigan, Population Studies Center.

Jayme-Ho, Teresa. 1976. "Time Budgets of Married Women in Rural Households:

Laguna.'' Discussion Paper 76-26. Manila: University of the Philippines, School of Economics.

Jeliffe, Derrick B. 1966. *The Assessment of Nutritional Status of the Community*. WHO Monograph Series no. 53. Geneva: World Health Organization.

Jeliffe, Derrick B., and E. F. Jeliffe. 1977. *Human Milk in the Modern World*. New York: Oxford University Press.

Jelin, Elisabeth. 1977. ''Labor Migration and Female Labor Force Participation in Latin America: The Case of Domestic Service in Cities.'' *Signs* 3:129–41.

Jesus, Carolina Maria de. 1962. *Child of the Dark*. Translated by David St. Clair. New York: Dutton.

Johnson, G. E., and W. E. Whitelaw. 1974. ''Urban-Rural Income Transfers in Kenya: An Estimated Remittance Function.'' *Economic Development and Cultural Change* 22:473–79.

Jordan, T. C., and K. F. Howells. 1978. ''Effects of Early Undernutrition on Individual Cerebellar Lobes in Male and Female Rats.'' *Brain Research* 157:202–5.

Jordan, T. C.; K. F. Howels; and S. M. Piggott. 1979. ''Effects of Early Undernutrition on Motor Coordination in the Adult Rat.'' *Behavioral and Neural Biology* 25:126–32.

Joreskog, K. G., and D. Sorbom. 1976. ''Statistical Models and Methods for Test-Retest Situations.'' In D. N. De Gruijter and Leo J. Van Der Kamp, eds., *Advances in Psychological and Educational Measurement*. New York: Wiley.

Kawata, Kazuyoski. 1978. ''Water and Other Environmental Interventions.'' *American Journal of Clinical Nutrition* 31:2114–23.

Kerven, Carol. 1979. ''National Migration Study: Urban and Rural Female-Headed Households' Dependence on Agriculture.'' Botswana: Central Statistics Office.

King, Elizabeth M. 1977. ''The Economics of Time Allocation in Philippine Rural Households.'' M.A. thesis, University of the Philippines.

Klaus, Marshall H., and John H. Kennell. 1976. *Maternal-Infant Bonding*. Saint Louis: C. V. Mosby.

Klein, R. E.; M. Irwin; P. L. Engle; and C. K. Yarbrough. 1977. ''Malnutrition and Mental Development in Rural Guatemala: An Applied Cross-Cultural Research Study.'' In N. Warren, ed., *Advances in Cross-Cultural Psychology*. New York: Academic Press.

Klein, R. E. 1975. ''Malnutrition, Poverty, and the Development of Mental Abilities in Rural Eastern Guatemala.'' Paper presented at the Conference on Ecological Factors in Human Development, Cambridge, England, May.

Kmenta, Jan. 1971. *Elements of Econometrics*. New York: Macmillan.

Knight, Peter T., ed. 1980. *Implementing Programs of Human Development*. World Bank Staff Working Paper no. 403. Washington, D.C.: World Bank.

Knodel, John. Forthcoming. ''Demographic Aspects of Breastfeeding.'' *Science*.

Knowles, James C., and Richard Anker. 1977. *An Analysis of Income Transfers in a Developing Country: The Case of Kenya*. Working Paper no. 59. Geneva: International Labour Organisation.

Konczacki, Zbigniew A. 1972. ''Infant Malnutrition in Sub-Saharan Africa: A Problem in Socioeconomic Development.'' *Canadian Journal of African Studies* 6:439.

Kossoudji, Sherrie, and Eva Mueller. Forthcoming. ''The Economic and Demographic Status of Female-Headed Households in Rural Botswana.'' *Economic Development and Cultural Change*.

———. 1978. "The Economic and Demographic Status of Female-Headed Households in Botswana." Ann Arbor: University of Michigan, Population Studies Center. Mimeographed.

Kudat, Ayse. 1978. "Effects of External Migration on the Turkish Rural Society." METU Working Paper. Ankara: Middle East Technical University.

Kumar, Shubh K. 1978. "Role of the Household Economy in Determining Child Nutrition at Low Income Levels: A Case Study in Kerala." Occasional Paper no. 95. Ithaca, N.Y.: Cornell University, Department of Agricultural Economics.

Kusnic, Michael W., and Julie DaVanzo. 1980. *Income Inequality and the Definition of Income: The Case of Malaysia*. Publication Series R-2416-AID. Santa Monica, Calif.: Rand Corporation.

Kuznets, Simon. 1976. "Demographic Aspects of the Size Distribution of Income: An Exploratory Essay." *Economic Development and Cultural Change* 25:1–94.

———. 1974. "Demographic Aspects of the Distribution of Income among Females: Recent Trends in the United States." In W. Sellekaerts, ed., *Econometrics and Economic Theory*. White Plains, N.Y.: International Arts and Sciences Press.

Lancaster, K. J. 1966. "A New Approach to Consumer Theory." *Journal of Political Economy* 74:132–57.

Lasky, R. E. 1975. "Birthweight and Psychomotor Performances in Rural Guatemala." *American Journal of Diseases of Children* 129:566–69.

Latham, Michael C. 1964. "Maternal Nutrition in East Africa." *Journal of Tropical Medicine and Hygiene* 67:90–91.

Leibenstein, Harvey. 1981. "Economic Decision Theory and Human Fertility Behavior: A Speculative Essay." *Population and Development Review* 7:381–400.

Leibowitz, Arleen. 1974*a*. "Education and Home Production." *American Economic Review* 64:243–50.

———. 1974*b*. "Home Investments in Children." *Journal of Political Economy* 82:111–31.

León de Leal, Magdalena. 1980. *Mujer y Capitalismo Agrario: Estudio de Cuatro Regiones Colombianas*. Bogotá: Asociación Colombiana para el Estudio de la Población.

Levinson, F. J. 1974. *Morinda: An Economic Analysis of Malnutrition among Young Children in Rural Punjab*. Cornell/M.I.T. International Nutrition Policy Series. Cambridge, Mass.: MIT Press.

Lewin, Helena; Jaqueline Pitanguy; and Carlos Manuel Romani. 1977. *Mão-de-obra no Brasil*. Petrópolis, Brazil: Editor Vozes.

Lewis, H. Gregg. 1975. "Economics of Time and Labor Supply." *American Economic Review* 45:29–34.

———. 1957. "Hours of Work and Hours of Leisure." In L. Reed Tripp, ed., *Proceedings of the Ninth Annual Meeting of the Industrial Relations Research Association*. Reprinted in John F. Burton, Lee K. Benham, William W. Vaughn, and Robert J. Flanagan, eds., *Readings in Labor Market Analysis*. 1971. New York: Holt, Rinehart, and Winston.

Lindert, Peter H. 1977. "Sibling Position and Achievement." *Journal of Human Resources* 12:198–209.

Lloyd-Still, J. D.; I. Hurwitz; P. H. Wolff; and H. Shwachman. 1974. "Intellectual Development after Severe Malnutrition in Infancy." *Pediatrics* 54:306–11.

López de Piza, Eugenia. 1977. "La Familia Matrifocal como Mecanismo de Adaptación de la Mujer a su Marginalidad." Paper presented at the Primer Simposio Mexicano Centro-Americano de Investigación sobre la Mujer [First Mexican Central American Symposium on the Study of Women], Mexico City, April.

Lubell, Harold. 1974. *Calcutta: Its Urban Development and Employment Prospects.* Geneva: International Labour Office.

Maccoby, E. E., and C. N. Jacklin. 1974. *The Psychology of Sex Differences.* Stanford, Calif.: Stanford University Press.

Machado Neto, Zahide. 1978. "As Meninas—Sobre o Trabalho da Criança e da Adolescente na Familia Proletaria." Presented at the Instituto Universitário de Pesquisas do Rio de Janeiro Seminar on Women in the Labor Force in Latin America, Rio de Janeiro, November.

Madeira, Felicia, and Paul A. Singer. 1973. *Estrutura do Emprego e Trabalho Feminino no Brasil: 1920–1970.* São Paulo: Centro Brasiliero de Pesquisas, Caderno [Exercise book] 13.

Martorell, R., and R. E. Klein. 1980. "Food Supplementation and Growth Rates in Preschool Children." *Nutrition Reports International* 21:447–54.

Martorell, R.; R. E. Klein; and H. Delgado. 1980. "Improved Nutrition and Its Effects on Anthropometric Indicators of Nutritional Status." *Nutrition Reports International* 21:219–30.

Mata, Leonardo. 1978. "Breast-feeding: Main Promoter of Infant Health." *American Journal of Clinical Nutrition* 31:2058–65.

Mazumdar, Vina. 1979. "From Research to Policy: Rural Women in India." *Studies in Family Planning* 10:353–60.

McAlpin, Michelle, and Wellesley Editorial Committee, eds. 1977. "Women and National Development: The Complexities of Change." *Signs* 3:1–338.

McGreevey, William P. 1977. "Issues in Measuring Development Performance." Excerpts from *Socioeconomic Performance Criteria for Development,* Annex D. Washington, D.C.: Agency for International Development.

McKay, H.; L. Sinisterra; A. McKay; H. Gomez; and P. Lloreda. 1978. "Improving Cognitive Ability in Chronically Deprived Children." *Science* 200:270–78.

McSweeney, B. G. 1979. "Collection and Analysis of Data on Rural Women's Time Use." *Studies in Family Planning* 10:379–83.

———. 1977. "An Approach to Collecting and Examining Data on Rural Women's Time Use and Some Tentative Findings: The Case of Upper Volta." Working paper prepared for the Seminar on Rural Women and the Sexual Division of Labor. New York: Population Council.

Merrick, Thomas W. 1977. "Household Structure and Poverty in Families Headed by Women: The Case of Belo Horizonte." Paper presented at the joint meetings of the Latin American Studies Association and the African Studies Association, Houston, November.

———. 1976. "Employment and Earnings in the Informal Sector in Brazil: The Case of Belo Horizonte." Paper presented at the joint meetings of the Latin American Studies Association and the African Studies Association, Houston, November.

Merrick, Thomas W., and Douglas H. Graham. 1979. *Population and Economic Development in Brazil.* Baltimore: Johns Hopkins University Press.

Michael, Robert T. 1974a. "Education and the Derived Demand for Children." In T. W. Schultz, ed., *Economics of the Family.* Chicago: University of Chicago Press.

———. 1974*b*. "The Effect of Education on Efficiency in Consumption." In T. W. Schultz, ed., *Economics of the Family*. Chicago: University of Chicago Press.

Mincer, J. 1974. "Schooling Experience and Earnings." New York: National Bureau of Economic Research.

Miranda, Glaura Vasques de. 1977. "Women's Labor Force Participation in a Developing Society: The Case of Brazil." *Signs* 3:261–74.

Momeni, Djamchid A. 1976. "Husband-Wife Age Differentials in Shiraz, Iran." *Social Biology* (Winter), pp. 341–48.

Monckeberg, Fernando. 1977. "Recovery of Severely Malnourished Infants: Effects of Early Senso-effective Stimulation." Paper presented at the International Conference on Behavioral Effects of Energy and Protein Deficits, Washington, D.C., December.

———. 1968. "Effect of Early Marasmic Malnutrition on Subsequent Physical and Psychological Development." In N. S. Scrimshaw and J. Gordon, eds., *Malnutrition, Learning, and Behavior*. Cambridge, Mass.: MIT Press.

Mora, J. O.; L. de Navarro; J. Clement; M. Wagner; and B. de Paredes. 1978. "The Effect of Nutritional Supplementation on Calorie and Protein Intake of Pregnant Women." *Nutrition Reports International* 17:217–27.

Mora, J. O.; B. de Paredes; M. Wagner; L. de Navarro; J. Suescun; N. Christiansen; and G. M. Herrera. 1979. "Nutritional Supplementation and the Outcome of Pregnancy, pt. 1: Birthweight." *American Journal of Clinical Nutrition* 32:455–62.

Moses, Yolanda. 1977. "Female Status, the Family, and Male Dominance in a West Indian Community." California State Polytechnic University, Pomona. Mimeographed.

Mueller, Eva. 1982. "The Allocation of Women's Time and Its Relationship to Fertility." In Richard Anker, Mayra Buvinić, and Nadia H. Youssef, eds., *Women's Roles and Population Trends in the Third World*. Geneva: International Labour Organisation.

———. 1979. *Time Use in Rural Botswana*. Ann Arbor: University of Michigan, Population Studies Center.

Murphy, Martin. 1981. *Comparative Estimates of the Value of Household Work in the United States for 1976*. Washington, D.C.: Department of Commerce, Bureau of Economic Analysis.

Musallem, Helen K. 1969. "The Changing Role of the Nurse." *American Journal of Nursing* 69:514–17.

Muth, Richard F. 1966. "Household Production and Consumer Demand Functions." *Econometrica* 34:699–708.

Nag, M.; B. N. F. White; and R. C. Peet. 1978. "An Anthropological Approach to the Study of the Economic Value of Children in Java and Nepal." *Current Anthropology* 19:293–306.

Nash, June. 1976. "A Critique of Social Science Roles in Latin America." In June Nash and Helen Safa, eds. *Sex and Class in Latin America*. New York: Praeger.

Navera, E. R. 1978. "The Allocation of Household Time Associated with Children in Rural Households in Laguna, Philippines." *Philippine Economic Journal* 36:47–59.

Nerlove, Marc. 1974*a*. "Household and Economy: Toward a New Theory of Population and Economic Growth." *Journal of Political Economy* 82:200–218.

Nerlove, Sara B. 1974*b*. "Women's Workload and Infant Feeding Practices: A Relationship with Demographic Implications." *Ethnology* 13:207–14.

Nerlove, Sara B.; J. M. Roberts; R. E. Klein; C. Yarbrough; and J. P. Habicht. 1974.

"Natural Indicators of Cognitive Development: An Observational Study of Rural Guatemalan Children." *Ethos* 2:265–95.

Newland, Kathleen. 1975. "Women in Politics: A Global Review." *Worldwatch Paper 3.* Washington, D.C.: Worldwatch Institute.

Nibhon, Debavalya. 1976. "A Study of Female Labor Force Participation and Fertility in Thailand." Paper presented at the Council on Asian Manpower Studies-Overseas Demographic Association Seminar on Labor Supply, Makati, Philippines, June.

Nieves, Isabel. 1979. "Household Arrangements and Multiple Jobs in San Salvador." *Signs* 5:134–41.

Oakley, Ann, and Robin Oakley. 1978. *Demystifying Social Statistics.* London: Pluto Press.

Oballe de Espada, Aída. 1971. "Estudio de la Comercialización Minorista Tradicional en Lima Metropolitana." Lima: Dirección de Asistencia Técnica de la Dirección General de Comercialización de Agricultura.

Oliveira, Maria Coleta F. A. 1978. "A Individualizacão da Força de Trabalho e o Trabalho Feminino em Pederneiras—SP." Paper presented at the Instituto Universitário de Pesquisas do Rio de Janeiro Seminar on Women in the Labor Force in Latin America, Rio de Janeiro, November.

Palmer, Ingrid. 1976. "The Basic Needs Approach to the Integration of Rural Women in Development: Conditions for Success." Paper presented at the Conference on Women and Development, Wellesley College, Wellesley, Mass.

Pananek, Hanna. 1979. "Research on Women by Women: Interviewer Selection and Training in Indonesia." *Studies in Family Planning* 10:412–15.

———. 1978. "Development Planning for Women." In Wellesley Editorial Committee, ed., *Women and National Development: The Complexities of Change.* Chicago: University of Chicago Press.

Papola, T. S. 1982. "Sex Discrimination in the Urban Labor Market: Some Propositions Based on Evidence from India." In Richard Anker, Mayra Buvinić, and Nadia H. Youssef, eds. *Women's Roles and Population Trends in the Third World.* Geneva: International Labour Organisation.

Patch, Richard W. 1973. *La Parada, Estudio de un Mundo Alucinante.* Lima: Mosco Azul Editores.

Pearce, D., and H. McAdoo. 1981. *Women and Children: Alone and in Poverty.* Washington, D.C.: National Advisory Council on Economic Opportunity.

Pebley, A. R.; H. Delgado; and E. Brineman. 1978. "Family Sex Composition Preference among Guatemalan Men and Women." Mimographed. Available at International Center for Research on Women, Washington, D.C.

Piho, Verve. 1975. "Life and Labor of the Woman Textile Worker in Mexico City." In Ruby Rohrlich-Leavitt, ed., *Women Cross-Culturally: Change and Challenge.* The Hague: Mouton.

Piñera, S., and M. Selowsky. 1976. *The Economic Cost of the Internal Brain Drain: Its Magnitude in Developing Countries.* World Bank Staff Working Paper no. 243. Washington, D.C.: World Bank.

Pivaral, V. Mejía. 1972. "Características Económicas y Socio-Culturales de Cuatro Aldeas Ladinas de Guatemala." *Guatemala Indígena* 8:21–37.

Pollak, R. A., and M. L. Wachter. 1975. "The Relevance of the Household Production

Function and Its Implications for the Allocation of Time." *Journal of Political Economy* 83:255–78.

Pollitt, E. 1980. *Poverty and Malnutrition in Latin America: Early Childhood Intervention Programs*. New York: Praeger.

Poole, Janet A. 1972. "A Cross-Comparative Study of Aspects of Conjugal Behavior among Women of Three West African Countries." *Canadian Journal of African Studies* 6:223–59.

Popkin, Barry M. 1978. "Economic Determinants of Breast-feeding Behavior: The Case of Rural Households in Laguna, Philippines." In W. H. Mosley, ed., *Nutrition and Reproduction*, pp. 461–97. New York: Plenum.

———. 1976. "The Role of the Rural Filipino Mother in the Determination of Child Care and Breast-feeding Behavior." Discussion Paper 76-12. Manila: University of the Philippines, School of Economics.

Popkin, Barry M., and Florentino S. Solon. 1976. "Income, Time, the Working Mother, and Child Nutrition." *Journal of Tropical Pediatrics and Environmental Child Health* (August), pp. 156–66.

Psacharopoulos, G. 1973. *Returns to Education*. San Francisco: Jossey-Bass.

Quinn, Naomi. 1977. "Anthropological Studies on Women's Status." *Annual Review of Anthropology* 6:181–225.

Ranade, S. N., and P. Ramachandran. 1970. *Women and Employment: Reports of Pilot Studies Conducted in Delhi and Bombay*. Bombay: Tata Institute of Social Sciences.

Rawlings, Steve. 1980. "Families Maintained by Female Householders, 1970–1979." Report prepared for the Bureau of the Census. Washington, D.C.: Department of Commerce.

Recchini de Lattes, Z., and C. H. Wainerman. 1979. "Información de Censos y Encuestas de Hogares para el Análisis de la Mano de Obra Femenina en América Latina y el Caribe: Evaluación de Deficiencias y Recomendaciones para Superarlas." E/CEPAL/L.206. United Nations Economic and Social Council, Economic Commission for Latin America.

Reid, Margaret. 1934. *Economics of Household Production*. New York: Wiley.

Remy, Dorothy. 1975. "Underdevelopment and the Experience of Women: A Zaria Case Study." In Rayna Reiter, ed., *Towards an Anthropology of Women*. New York: Monthly Review Press.

Reynolds, H. T. 1977. *The Analysis of Cross-Classifications*. New York: Free Press.

Rianday, Benoit. 1976. "Besoins et Aspirations des Familles et des Jeunes." *Analyses Complementaires, Tome III: Le Budget-Temps des Mères de Famille*. Paris: Caisse Nationale des Allocations Familiales.

Richardson, S. A. 1976. "The Relation of Severe Malnutrition in Infancy to the Intelligence of School Children with Differing Life Histories." *Pediatric Research* 10:57–61.

Robinson, John P. 1977. *How Americans Use Time: A Social-Psychological Analysis of Everyday Behavior*. New York: Praeger.

Rogers, Barbara. 1979. *The Domestication of Women: Discrimination in Developing Societies*. New York: St. Martin's Press.

Romney, A. K. 1965. "Variations in Household Structure as Determinants of Sex-Typed Behavior." In F. A. Beach, ed., *Sex and Behavior*. New York: Wiley.

Rosenzweig, M. 1977. "The Demand for Farm Children." Economic Growth Center Discussion Paper. New Haven: Yale University.

————. 1976. "Female Work Experience, Employment Status, and Birth Expectations: Sequential Decision-Making in the Philippines." *Demography* 13:339–56.

Rosenzweig, M., and R. E. Evenson. 1977. "Fertility, Schooling, and the Economic Contribution of Children in Rural India: An Econometric Analysis." *Econometrica* 45:1065–80.

Ross, Heather L., and Isabel V. Sawhill. 1975. *Time of Transition: The Growth of Families Headed by Women.* Washington, D.C.: Urban Institute.

Ross, Lee Ann. 1977. "Yemen Migration—Blessing and Dilemma." Paper prepared for the Agency for International Development Seminar on Near East Flows. Mimeographed.

Rubin, J. Z.; F. J. Provenzano; and Z. Luria. 1974. "The Eye of the Beholder: Parents' Views on Sex of Newborns." *American Journal of Orthopsychiatry* 44:512–19.

Safa, Helen. 1975. "Class Consciousness among Working-Class Women in Latin America: Puerto Rico." In June Nash and Helen Safa, eds., *Sex and Class in Latin America.* New York: Praeger.

Saffioti, Heleieth I. B. 1978. *Emprego Doméstico e Capitalismo.* Petrópolis, Brazil: Editor Vozes.

————. 1969. *A Mulher na Sociedade de Classes, Mito e Realidade.* São Paulo: Quatro Artes.

Safilios-Rothschild, Constantina. 1980. "The Role of the Family: A Neglected Aspect of Poverty." In Peter T. Knight, ed., *Implementing Programs of Human Development.* World Bank Staff Working Paper no. 403. Washington, D.C.: World Bank.

Sant'Anna, Anna M.; Thomas W. Merrick; and Dipak Mazumdar. 1976. *Income Distribution and the Economy of the Urban Household: The Case of Belo Horizonte.* World Bank Staff Working Paper no. 236. Washington, D.C.: World Bank.

Satyanarayana, K.; A. N. Naidu; and B. S. Narasinga Rao. 1979. "Nutritional Deprivation in Childhood and the Body Size, Activity, and Physical Work Capacity of Young Boys." *American Journal of Clinical Nutrition* 32:1769–75.

Sawhill, Isabel, and Heather Ross. 1976. *Families in Transition: The Growth of Households Headed by Women.* Washington, D.C.: Urban Institute.

————, eds. 1974. *Economics of the Family: Marriage, Children, and Human Capital.* Chicago: University of Chicago Press.

Schmink, Marianne. 1980. "The Plight of Poor Women in the Latin American Metropolis: An Exploratory Analysis of Policy Issues." New York: Population Council.

————. 1979. "Community in Ascendence: Urban Industrial Growth and Households' Income Strategies in Belo Horizonte, Brazil." Ph.D. dissertation, University of Texas, Austin.

Schultz, Theodore W. 1980. "Effects of the International Donor Community on Farm People." *American Journal of Agricultural Economics* 62:873–78.

Schumacher, Ilsa; Jennefer Sebstad; and Mayra Buvinić. 1980. "Limits to Productivity: Improving Women's Access to Technology and Credit." Prepared for Office of Women in Development/Agency for International Development, Grant no. AID/OTR-C-1801. Washington, D.C.: International Center for Research on Women.

Secretaria do Trabalho e Administracão, São Paulo. 1970. "Mão-de-Obra Feminina—

Levantamento Socio-Económico em Industrias da Capital.'' São Paulo: Governo do Estado de São Paulo.

Seti, Ray Mohini. 1976. *Modernization of Working Women in Developing Societies*. New Delhi: National Publishing House.

Shah, A. M. 1976. *The Household Dimension of the Family in India*. Berkeley and Los Angeles: University of California Press.

Sharman, Anne. 1970. ''Nutrition and Social Planning.'' *Journal of Development Studies* 6:77–91.

Singh, Andrea Menefee. 1977. ''Women and the Family: Coping with Poverty in the Bastis of Delhi.'' *Social Action* 27:242–65.

Skjönsberg, Else. 1977. ''Women and Food and the Social Sciences: Perspectives on African Food Production and Food Handling.'' Oslo. Mimeographed. Available at International Center for Research on Women, Washington, D.C.

Smock, Audrey Chapman. 1977. ''Ghana: From Autonomy to Subordination.'' In Janet Z. Giele and Audrey C. Smock, eds., *Women and Society: In International and Comparative Perspective*. New York: Wiley-Interscience.

Soldo, M. E. 1977. ''The Determinants of Temporal Variation in Living Arrangements among the Elderly: 1960–1970.'' Ph.D. dissertation, Duke University.

Solon, Florentino S.; Barry M. Popkin; Tomas Fernandez; and Michael C. Latham. 1978. ''Vitamin A Deficiency in the Philippines: A Study of Xerophthalmia in Cebu.'' *American Journal of Clinical Nutrition* 31:360–68.

Standing, Guy, and G. Sheehan. 1978. *Labour Force Participation in Low-Income Countries*. Geneva: International Labour Office.

Stark, Oded. 1976. *Rural-to-Urban Migration and Some Economic Issues: A Review. Utilizing Findings of Surveys and Empirical Studies Covering the 1965–75 Period*. Working Paper no. 38. Geneva: International Labour Organisation.

Staudt, Kathleen. 1979. ''Tracing Sex Differentiation in Donor Agricultural Programs.'' Paper presented at the annual meeting of the American Political Science Association, Washington, D.C., August 31, 1979.

———. 1978. ''Agricultural Productivity Gaps: A Case Study of Male Preference in Government Policy Implementation.'' *Development and Change* 9(July):439–58.

———. 1976. ''Women Farmers and Inequities in Agricultural Services.'' *Rural Africana* 29:81–94.

Stoler, Ann. 1978. ''Class Structure and Female Autonomy in Rural Java.'' *Signs* 3:74–89.

Stycos, J. Mayone, and Robert H. Weller. 1967. ''Female Working Roles and Fertility.'' *Demography* 4:210–17.

Szalai, Alexander, ed. 1972. *The Use of Time: Daily Activities of Urban and Suburban Populations in Twelve Countries*. The Hague: Mouton.

Tienda, Marta. 1978. ''Dependency, Extension, and the 'Family Life Cycle Squeeze' in Peru.'' Revised version of a paper presented at the annual meeting of the American Sociological Association, San Francisco, July.

Tienda, Marta, and Sylvia Ortega Salazar. 1980. *Female-Headed Households and Extended Family Formation in Rural and Urban Peru*. Center for Demography and Ecology Working Paper. University of Wisconsin, Madison.

Tinker, Irene, and Michele Bo Bramsen. 1976. *Women and World Development*. Washington, D.C.: Overseas Development Council.

Torun, B.; Y. Schultz; R. Bradfield; and R. E. Viteri. 1975. "Effects of Physical Activity upon Growth of Children: Recovery from PCM [Protein-Calorie Malnutrition]." In *Proceedings of Tenth International Congress of Nutrition*, Kyoto, Japan, pp. 247–49.

United Nations. Department of International Economic and Social Affairs, Population Division. 1981a. *Estimates and Projections of the Number of Households by Country, 1975–2000*. ESA/P/WP. 73. New York: United Nations.

United Nations. Department of Technical Co-operation for Development and Statistical Office. 1981b. *Handbook of Household Surveys*. New York: United Nations. Unpublished draft.

United Nations. 1977a. *Demographic Yearbook 1976*. New York: United Nations.

United Nations. International Labour Office. 1977b. *Employment, Growth, and Basic Needs: A One-World Problem*. New York: Praeger.

————. 1975. *1975 Yearbook of Labour Statistics*. Geneva: International Labour Organisation.

United Nations. 1974a. *Report on the World Social Situation*. New York: United Nations.

United Nations. Economic Commission for Africa. 1974b. *The Data Base of Discussion of the Interrelations between the Integration of Women in Development, Their Situation, and Population Factors in Africa*. Addis Ababa, Ethiopia: United Nations Economic Commission for Africa.

United Nations. Department of Economic and Social Affairs. 1973a. *Manuals on Methods of Estimating Population*. Manual VII: *Methods of Projecting Households and Families*. Population Studies no. 54. New York: United Nations.

United Nations. Food and Agriculture Organization Ad Hoc Committee. 1973b. *Nutritional Requirements of Pregnancy*. Rome: United Nations Food and Agriculture Organization.

United Nations. Food and Agriculture Organization/World Health Organization Expert Group. 1973c. *Energy and Protein Requirements*. Rome: Food and Agriculture Organization.

United Nations. 1972. *1972 Yearbook of Labour Statistics*. Geneva: International Labour Organisation.

————. 1969. *Principles and Recommendations for the 1970 Population Census*. Statistical Papers, Series M., no. 44. New York: United Nations.

United States. Bureau of the Census, International Demographic Data Center. 1980. Unpublished data from The Women in Development Data Base.

Uphoff, Norman. 1980. "Political Considerations in Human Development." In Peter T. Knight, ed., *Implementing Programs of Human Development*. World Bank Staff Working Paper no. 403. Washington, D.C.: World Bank.

Villalta, Maria Teresa García. 1971. "El Problema Social de la Madre Soltera: Estudio de 100 Casos Attendidos en la Maternidad del Hospital Roosevelt." Guatemala: University of San Carlos.

Vis, Henri; Michael Bossuyt; Philippe Hennart; and Michel Carael. 1975. "The Health of the Mother and Child in Rural Central Africa." *Studies in Family Planning* 6:437–41.

Visaria, Pravin. 1980a. "Poverty and Living Standards in Asia." *Population and Development Review* 6:189–224.

————. 1980b. *Poverty and Living Standards in Asia: An Overview of the Main Results and Lessons of Selected Household Surveys.* Living Standards Measurement Study Working Paper no. 2. Washington, D.C.: World Bank.

———. 1979. "Demographic Factors and the Distribution of Income: Some Issues." In *Economic and Demographic Change: Issues for the 1980s. Proceedings of the [February] Conference.* Liège, Belgium: International Union for the Scientific Study of Population.

Vuori, L.; L. de Navarro; N. Christiansen; J. O. Mora; and M. G. Herrara. 1980. "Food Supplementation of Pregnant Women at Risk of Malnutrition and their Newborns' Responsiveness to Stimulation." *Developmental Medicine and Child Neurology* 22:61–71.

Wagley, Charles. 1971. *An Introduction to Brazil.* Rev. ed. New York: Columbia University Press.

Watts, Harold W., and Felicity Skidmore. 1978. "Household Structure: Necessary Changes in Categorization and Data Collection." Report prepared for the Census Bureau Conference on Issues in Federal Statistical Needs Relating to Women, Bethesda, Md., April 27–28.

Weekes-Vagliani, Winifred. 1976. "Family Life and Structure in Southern Cameroon." Paris: Development Centre of the Organisation for Economic Cooperation and Development.

Wellesley Editorial Committee, ed. 1977. *Women and National Development: The Complexities of Change.* Chicago: University of Chicago Press.

White, Benjamin. 1976. "Problems in Estimating the Value of Work in Peasant Household Economies: An Example from Rural Java." Paper presented at the Agricultural Development Council Workshop on Family Labor Force Use in Agricultural Production, Hyderabad, Pakistan, April.

Whiteford, Michael F. 1978. "Women, Migration, and Social Change: A Colombian Case Study." *International Migration Review* 12:236–47.

Whiting, Beatrice B. 1977. "Changing Life Types in Kenya." *Daedalus* 106:211–25.

Whiting, B., and C. P. Edwards. 1973. "A Cross-Cultural Analysis of Sex Differences in the Behavior of Children Aged 3 through 11." *Journal of Social Psychology* 91:171–88.

Wiest, Raymond E. 1973. "Wage Labour Migration and the Household in a Mexican Town." *Journal of Anthropological Research* 29:180–209.

Winick, Myron. 1976. *Malnutrition and Brain Development.* New York: Oxford University Press.

———. 1975. "Malnutrition and Environmental Enrichment by Early Adoption." *Science* 190:1173–75.

Woolsey, Suzanne H. 1977. "Pied Piper Politics and the Child-care Debate." *Daedalus* 106:127–45.

World Bank. 1980. *World Development Report, 1980.* Washington, D.C.: World Bank.

Yang, R. K., and H. A. Moss. 1978. "Neonatal Precursors of Infant Behavior." *Development Psychologist* 14:607–13.

Yarbrough, C. K.; J. P. Habicht; R. M. Molina; A. Lechtig; and R. E. Klein. 1975. "Length and Weight in Rural Guatemalan Latino Children: Birth to Seven Years of Age." *American Journal of Physical Anthrolopology* 42:439–48.

Youssef, Nadia H. 1974. *Women and Work in Developing Societies.* Population Monograph Series no. 15. Berkeley: University of California, Institute of International Studies.

———. 1973. *Women and Work in Developing Societies.* Westport, Conn.: Greenwood Press.

Yousseff, Nadia H., and Carol Hetler. Forthcoming. *Rural Households Headed by Women: A Priority Issue for Policy Concern.* Geneva: International Labour Organisation.

Youssef, Nadia H.; Isabel Nieves; and Jennefer Sebstad. 1980. "Keeping Women Out: A Structural Analysis of Women's Employment in Developing Countries." Report prepared for the Office of Women in Development, Agency for International Development. Washington, D.C.: International Center for Research on Women.

A Note on the Editors and Authors

Nancy Birdsall is currently a staff economist in the development economics department at the World Bank. She received her Ph.D. in economics from Yale University. Her work has focused on the various human resources aspects of development and their relation to demographic issues including female employment and fertility.

Elise Boulding, chair of the sociology department at Dartmouth College, also serves as the vice-president of the governing council of the United Nations University. She earned her doctorate in sociology from the University of Michigan. Her research has covered the relations of conflict and peace, development, family life, and women in society.

Ximena Bunster B. is currently an associate professor at the University of Maryland, Baltimore County. She holds a Ph.D. in anthropology from Columbia University. Her field research and professional writing have focused on women's economic, political, and family roles among the rural and urban poor in Latin America.

Mayra Buvinić is director of the International Center for Research on Women, located in Washington, D.C. She received her doctorate in social psychology from the University of Wisconsin, Madison. Her current work focuses on the economic roles of women in Latin America.

Julie DaVanzo is a staff member of the economics department of the RAND Corporation and is currently associate director of RAND's Center for Population Studies. She received a Ph.D. in economics from the University of California. Her research has involved the economic determinants of demographic phenomena, such as fertility, marriage, and female labor force particpation and migration.

Carmen Diana Deere is assistant professor of economics at the University of Masschusetts, Amherst. She received her Ph.D. in agricultural economics from the University of California, Berkeley. Her field work has included research both on rural women and agrarian change in Colombia and Peru and on peasant women's role in Andean agriculture.

Patricia L. Engle is an associate professor in child development at California Polytechnic Institute. Her research and publications have been in the areas of nutrition, the consequences of adolescent motherhood for children's physical and mental development, sex differences in mental abilities, and bilingual education.

Robert E. Evenson is director of the international and development economics program at Yale University and professor of economics. He received his Ph.D. in economics at the University of Chicago. He has focused his research on agricultural development problems, including the study of the economics of rural household behavior in the Philippines and agricultural technology transfer.

Judith A. Harrington is a demographic analyst with Statistics Canada. She received her Ph.D. in sociology and demography from Cornell University. Her research has covered nuptiality trends, female role change and fertility, and the relationship of infant and child mortality to breast-feeding.

Carol B. Hetler is a staff associate at the International Center for Research on Women. She holds master's degrees in anthropology from George Washington University and in demography from Georgetown University. She is currently engaged in research on woman-headed households in rural areas.

Elizabeth King is a staff member of the RAND Corporation. She received a doctorate in economics from Yale University. Her research has focused on the various dimensions of rural household economics including time allocation and the demand for education.

Robert E. Klein is chief of the human development division of the Institute of Nutrition of Central America and Panama (INCAP) in Guatemala City.

Margaret A. Lycette is the staff economist of the International Center for Research on Women. She is a Ph.D. candidate in the Department of Political Economy at the Johns Hopkins University. Her current work focuses on mechanisms for assisting small-scale enterprises and providing credit to low-income women.

Donald Lye Poh Lee is a member of the faculty of economics, University of Malaya. He is currently a Ph.D. candidate at the University of London.

William Paul McGreevey is a senior economist at the World Bank. He has worked on human resource and development issues since receiving his Ph.D. in 1965 from MIT. He is the author of *An Economic History of Colombia, 1845–1930* and editor of *Third World Poverty*.

Thomas W. Merrick is director of the Center for Population Research of the Kennedy Institute for Bio-Ethics at Georgetown University. He earned his doctorate in economics at the University of Pennsylvania. His professional work focuses on population and economic development, market structure, and the role of women, particularly in Latin America.

Eva Mueller is professor of economics and research associate at the Population Studies Center, University of Michigan. She holds a Ph.D. in economics from Harvard University. Her recent work has explored the economic and motivational determinants of household behavior in the United States and demographic and economic household decisions in developing countries.

Barry M. Popkin is an associate professor of nutrition at the University of North Carolina and is a fellow of the Carolina Population Center. He earned his Ph.D. in agricultural economics at Cornell University. His professional work has focused on applied micro-economic nutrition and human resource issues, including examination of the role of women as it affects child health and nutrition.

Marianne Schmink is executive director of the Amazon research and training program at the Center for Latin American Studies at the University of Florida, and a consultant to the Population Council. She earned her Ph.D. in anthropology at the University of Texas. Her professional work has focused on urbanization and development in Latin America and its impact on women.

Marcelo Selowsky is the research advisor to the operations policy staff of the World Bank. He received his Ph.D. in economics from the University of Chicago. His research has centered on the effects of investment in human resources on the productivity of labor, income distribution, and economic growth, including the economic impact of education and child nutrition, and the effectiveness of food programs.

Charles Yarbrough is currently owner of Base 2, a computer marketing company in San Francisco.

Nadia H. Youssef is research director at the International Center for Research on Women. She holds a doctorate in sociology from the University of California at Berkeley. Her professional work has focused on the economics of women-headed households and the relationship between fertility and women's employment. She is now investigating differences in life cycle stages between developed and developing countries.

Index

THE JOHNS HOPKINS UNIVERSITY PRESS

Women and Poverty in the Third World

This book was composed in Times Roman text
and Helvetica display type by The Composing
Room of Michigan, Inc., from a design by
Lisa S. Mirski. It was printed on S. D.
Warren's 50-lb. Sebago Eggshell paper and
bound in Holliston Roxite A by the Maple
Press Company.